WILLIAM WYLER

William Wyler

THE AUTHORIZED BIOGRAPHY BY

Axel Madsen

THOMAS Y. CROWELL COMPANY
New York   Established 1834

Designed by Ingrid Beckman

Manufactured in the United States of America

ISBN 0-690-00083-9

1   2   3   4   5   6   7   8   9   10

Library of Congress Cataloging in Publication Data

Madsen, Axel.
　　William Wyler: the authorized biography.

　　Bibliography: p.
　　1. Wyler, William, 1902–
PN1998.A3W92　　　791.43'0233'0924 [B]　　　73-10450
ISBN 0-690-00083-9

CONTENTS

PART ONE

The Early Years

1

When Melanie and Leopold Wyler's second son was born July 1, 1902, Mulhouse was called Mülhausen. It had no Common Market aspirations then. It was simply a provincial town on the western marches of the good Kaiser Wilhelm's empire.

Berlin was far away.

Stuttgart, Zurich, Baden, Frankfurt, Ulm, and Freiburg were much closer and the whole family had to know right away. As soon as Melanie could sit up in bed, she wrote about Willy to the Wylers in Endingen and to her own family, the Auerbachs. When Leopold wasn't minding the store down on Wildemannstrasse, he was running to the post office. Writing to the family was always Melanie's passion and all through childhood, Willy would remember vacations with Mama sending off postcards. Hundreds of them, it seemed, to relatives all over southern Germany and parts of Switzerland.

After Robert, Melanie had wanted a girl. On grand occasions, she had fun dressing Willy like one. They looked pretty together in photographs—Robert, two years older, in his new sailor's uniform and Willy with a little bow in his brown locks, a chiffon collar, and little lacquered shoes, all from Papa's show window. "Sit still," she admonished, while the photographer ducked under his black cover. It was always something to make Willy stay quiet.

Although she wasn't a native, Melanie liked Mülhausen. She never had trouble making friends and she could practice her French. They had always called her *Franzosenkopf* at home because she adored things French. There were older families in town, even older Jewish families, who spoke French. Leopold met them, the Engel-Dollfus brothers, the Brisachs, at the synagogue. Fleetingly. He didn't go that often. As newcomers to Elsass—or Alsace as the French called the province—the Wylers had little nostalgia for the French past fading with the old century. Leopold was Swiss, from the Argau canton—Endingen was the old ghetto of Baden. Melanie was from Stuttgart. Her famous novelist uncle, Bertold Auerbach, was from Nordstetten. The Lämmles on her mother's side were from Laupheim and were all over also. Cousin Carl had gone to America, but he might possibly return one day, as her father Ferdinand had done.

Mülhausen was not that little. The 1900 census had disclosed a population of nearly ninety thousand. Textile printing was the main industry and after 1871, cautious men of commerce had managed to transplant the city's business into the German economy without major disruption. The new prosperity, circumspect and hard-earned, also helped them forget the French past. Prussians spoke a little funny but they knew how to get things done. Besides, a lot of new ideas were in the air. The twentieth century looked more than promising even if the city elders thought caution was the only civic virtue.

The city fathers had always governed prudently, as men do who live between powerful neighbors. Nothing had foreordained the confluence of the Dollar and Ill rivers as a hub of human activity, the spot was neither geographically inviting nor strategically important, which may explain why the town didn't appear until long after Gauls, Romans, Franks, Teutons, Visigoths, and Attila's hordes had trampled the marshy left bank of the upper Rhine. Mülhausen first appeared in 803 and was next mentioned in the twelfth century when the territory was divided between the bishop of Strasbourg and the Hohenstauffen family. Between crusades, Frederick Barbarossa founded a village for artisans and merchants next to the bishop's hamlet and, in 1224, the new town received its imperial privileges and the right to fortify itself.

Charles the Foolhardy of Burgundy tried to bullwhip the good burghers into a league against King Louis of France, but the city of Mülhausen signed a treaty with neighboring Basel and, in 1515, joined the thirteen cantons in their confederacy as an "associate locality." [1] For the next two and a half centuries, Mülhausen chose to tie its destiny to that of the Swiss.

In 1523, the burghers of Mülhausen voted in favor of the Reformed Church and the city stayed neutral in the religious wars, escaping the pain and destruction that ravaged both shores of the Rhine.

When the Treaty of Westphalia put an end to the Thirty Years War, the city's political independence was respected and Mülhausen did not become a French province along with the rest of Alsace.

In the middle of Voltaire's century of Enlightenment, the first shop for "indiennage"—textile prints in the East Indian manner—appeared. By 1769, the city had fifteen factories. A stock exchange sprang up along with an opera house, and Johann Heinrich Lambert wrote his treatises on mathematics and cosmology. Lambert was the city's only illustrious son. Mülhausen was also the birthplace of a famous—some said infamous—French army officer—Alfred Dreyfus.

Economics, not ideology, were behind the city's decision to join the French Revolution. As Napoleon was about to seize power and embark on empire building and endless wars, Mülhausen voted to abandon its independence and to join the French Republic. After Napoleon's downfall, the decision did make sense. Bigger markets and bigger horizons spurred the *Mulhousiens*, made them build Alsace's first railway, Europe's first "workers' city," and from textile printing branch into lithography and photography.* The Franco-Prussian War of 1870-71 was an exercise in brinkmanship that went too far, proved disastrous for France, and achieved unification for Germany. The gains came all too easily, proved to be an embarrassment for Germany, gave aristocratic statesmen the first taste of national hatreds, and lighted the long fuse that exploded in 1914. Otto von Bismarck did not usually sympathize with popular emotions and not even his principle of sorting people out into their linguistic "tribes" seemed to justify laying claims to German-speaking Alsace. Not in the beginning at

* Friedrich Engel-Dollfus (1818–1883) was the Mulhouse industrialist who proclaimed "factory owners owed more than wages to their workers," a slogan that found its application in the *cités ouvrières* and the creation, in 1867, of workmen's compensation insurance.

5

least. At the end, Bismarck was trapped by his own impetuosity, became the prisoner of German public opinion, and of a military high command that wanted to crown its victory with tangible gains. When a humiliated France capitulated and sued for peace in 1871, Alsace-Lorraine became part of the Reich.

Recent history was taught a little differently in the schools Willy went to—and was thrown out of. Behind Professor Dr. Schmeltzle's pince-nez and the Gothic lettering on the textbooks was the might of Germanismus. By becoming Elsass-Lothringen, Alsace-Lorraine had found its natural destiny and obvious place in the modern world. And why not? as so many said. The reign of Wilhelm II was cautious, liberal, and—as Leopold said—there was not a streak of anti-Semitism in the emperor. Melanie would sometimes laugh and tell them it was a well-known fact that if you spat in the face of a German Jew, he would say it was raining. But wasn't her own brother an officer? Since when had you heard of Jews making careers in the army? The French might have *their* Dreyfus affair; here at home, thank God, all that was the past. This wasn't Kiev or Warsaw. This was Imperial Germany. Nineteen hundred and ten! Besides, what mattered was that business was good.

Leopold Wyler couldn't complain. When it got a little too hectic around the house, when Melanie insisted the boys take both French and violin lessons on Thursdays or she organized theatrical *soirées* with the Cahen children, the Jacob boys, and who knows who else, he could trot down to the store and go over the figures again. They had a nice home—even a maid now; the Badenweiler *succursale,* as Melanie called the branch store, was coming along. She and the boys spent the summers over there— tending the little branch wasn't much work—when they didn't go on real holidays, last year clear across France to Deauville—well, Trouville—on the Channel coast. Of course sea resorts were the *dernier cri.* For a boy from Endingen who had started as a traveling salesman, he could be worse off.

If Leopold was what he was—a thrifty salesman who, with his wife's modest dowry, had set himself up in the haberdashery business and made things prosper—Melanie was her own center of dynamics. Frau Wyler, they said, was the kind of person people fell in love with after five minutes. Complete strangers came away smiling. She was full of imagination and ideas, energy and endless curiosity. Of course, she was an Auerbach, as she would say.

Melanie loved her boys and the only black cloud in her life was that little Gaston, the third son, seemed definitely retarded. They had tried everything, but there was nothing doctors could do. Or so they said. Luckily, there were Robert and Willy, even if Willy was a *garnement*.

Was it necessary to dare and doubledare every boy from Riedesheim to Brunstadt? If somebody dared Willy to drink the ink out of the school-bench inkwell, he would do it. "I bet you don't dare . . ." was all anybody had to say.

The earliest memory Edmond Cahen had of the younger of the Wyler brothers was seeing Willy eating a goldfish on a dare. "I bet you're too scared to swim the Ill," and Willy was already wading in. Paul Jacob, who like Cahen was to become a lawyer, remembered Willy crossing the ice on the Tivoligarten pond on the way to school one winter's morning and *not* making it. Cahen was never to forget Willy's going swimming in the Ill. When Melanie learned where her ten-year-old had gone, she became more than upset. Several boys had drowned in the river that summer. When he didn't return by nightfall, her anger turned into fright. Other boys were questioned, Papa was called from his card game. By ten o'clock, the neighborhood was marshaled. She was beside herself, asking the same question to the same boys again and again, imploring and praying when suddenly Willy came slinking around the corner. In a second, her tears turned to radiance and in another second to the fury of a mother who has been at her wits' end for no reason. To Leopold she suddenly cried out, *"Schlag ihn tot!"*—"Beat him to death!"

Elsasserdeutsch wasn't the purest of German, but it was unmistakable. Few could believe what they were hearing in November, 1944, when a U.S. Air Force major climbed out of his jeep in the middle of Rue du Sauvage and began to speak Alsatian. The American just grinned and said his name was Willy.

Luckily, Robert was a bit more sensible. He didn't get himself thrown out of every Realschule and Gymnasium he was sent to. He was interested in math and Melanie wanted to send him to college in Lausanne. And Willy? He'd just have to learn haberdashery and take over the business one day. In the meantime,

---

7

Professor Schmeltzle had to give him private lessons in mathematics.

When Robert had the measles, Willy was sent to Stuttgart to stay with his grandparents. Grandpa Ferdinand Auerbach told marvelous stories. As a young man, he had gone to America and once there, he had never stopped traveling. A civil war had broken out and he had become a wandering salesman as the Americans called it, going from town to town with a cartful of wares. Willy sat fascinated and listened when he wasn't asking about skyscrapers forty stories high. Grandpa had been to Baltimore and even way west to Chicago. He had liked it and had come back to Stuttgart to marry Grandma. But she had doublecrossed him, he laughed. Once they had gotten married, she had refused to go to America with him. Stuttgart was all right; he had prospered in real estate and America was just a gleam in his eyes now. Except on the 4th of July. On that day, he flew an American flag in memory of his youth and opportunities across the sea.

Others had gone to America. The Lämmle brothers, Joseph and little Carl. Joseph lived in New York. Carl had first settled out in Indian country—in Oshkosh, Wisconsin, Grandpa said. Then he had moved again, to Chicago, where he was now in this new "moving pictures" business.

Melanie loved the new fad. There were three movie theaters in Mülhausen. One of them had a black doorman—the only Negro Willy and his friends had ever seen. Children made detours on the way home from school, just to pass by the Kino and watch the black man in his uniform.

In the afternoons, Melanie sometimes treated the boys. She loved Asta Nielsen in pictures like *Der Abgrund*. No wonder they called the Danish actress "la Duse du Nord." For Willy, she sat through the Otto Ripert serials—action, chases, a man standing on a railway track with a train bearing down on him. Or the Fantomas, two-reelers with the masked detective chasing villains over the rooftops of Paris and always disappearing just before the end so you would come back next week. Once there was a Tonfilm, but the sound turned out to be nothing more than a scratchy record.

Melanie also took the boys to serious things: concerts, theater, and, when good companies visited, the opera. Willy was fascinated. He even promised he would study the violin. Imagine, to stand in the pit and conduct the orchestra—a hundred musicians maybe! And up behind the *feu de la rampe,* the stage, the singers. And the sets! Deep mysterious forests for Siegfried to swear eternal love or for Boris Godunov to rally his men. Or the exotic garden where the American officer abandoned Madame Butterfly. Melanie cried each time.

On winter evenings, she organized theatrical events in the parlor. Paul Jacob and the other boys came over and everybody had to help. Melanie let them hang new sheets to serve as curtains and had everybody singe bottlecorks to make black mustaches. Then they had to write plays, or at least sketches, and learn lines. She had to arbitrate disputes over who should play Ivanhoe. Outdoor recreations included primitive skiing in the Tannenwald.

In the summer, they were in Badenweiler, on the Black Forest side of the Rhine. It was beautiful in August and September. The shop was tiny and next door was the best *konditorei* in all of Schwartzwald. They had strawberry tarts so good nobody could eat dinner. And there was baker Greter's daughter, the same age as Willy. Everybody teased him about her. As if a ten-year-old were interested in dumb girls.

Leopold came every Saturday night from Mülhausen and sat reading his newspapers on the veranda. Sometimes Herr Greter came around after dinner and they argued about war, admitting that it was unthinkable in this century. Leopold thought wars were like motorcar accidents. Every accident was caused, in the last resort, by the invention of the internal combustion engine and by people's desire to get fast from one place to another. The "cure" for road accidents was to forbid automobiles.

They could never agree on whether wars had profound causes or grew out of specific events. But Herr Greter insisted Germany was right to make herself strong since she was squeezed on all sides. Leopold wasn't so sure, but then again, as Herr Greter insinuated once or twice, he was Swiss.

When he was alone, Leopold Wyler wondered. It was all Wilhelm the Second's Reich, but the feelings were different on this side of the Rhine. In Schwartzwald, they clamored for a strong Germany and in Elsass, twenty kilometers away, people thought it was wise not to vindicate, not to condemn. To Leopold, what was important was to understand. The purpose of politics was prosperity and peaceful intercourse among nations. Germany and

9

France and everybody else had been in peace for over forty years now. Statesmen knew that. History, he was sure, was without heroes and perhaps even without villains.

Sometimes Melanie had to laugh. How Swiss could anyone be? That made him less sure. Dr. Jacob and some of the others were so cynically clever. They said Mülhausen lived in "splendid isolation" and that even if the bourgeoisie controlled the city's economy, all real power was concentrated in Berlin.

Even after the murder of Austria's Archduke Franz Ferdinand in Sarajevo, he believed. Like everybody else. That had been in June and it was now July. They had just celebrated Willy's twelfth birthday. He sat on the veranda and watched his blue cigar smoke disappear into the night. In September, Robert would be fourteen. The boy was already in Lausanne and Switzerland was certainly not interested in war. Besides, who had ever heard of fourteen-year-olds going to war. He had nothing to fear himself. After all, he *was* Swiss.

To Willy, the war rumors were terribly exciting. When mobilization notices were plastered on street corners and people gathered, Willy and another kid bored into the crowd. Most people were worried. When others tried to sound a reassuring note— after all, war might still be avoided—Willy's face fell.

Together with the Catholic family from the third floor and the Protestant family from the ground floor, the Wylers spent August 6 and 7 in the cellar listening to the shells fly overhead. The women prayed together and everybody cringed at each terrifying detonation. The men took turns running up to empty slop buckets and were able to retrieve a loaf of pumpernickel bread Melanie suddenly remembered was on the back shelf. They all shook their heads with disbelief. On July 28, Austria-Hungary had declared war on Serbia over the murder of Archduke Franz Ferdinand. On August 1, the Russian mobilization in support of Serbia provoked Germany to declare war on Russia and two days later on France, Russia's ally. On August 4, Berlin's refusal to respect the neutrality of Belgium provoked Great Britian to declare war on Germany.

Willy and one of the other boys climbed on top of the crates stacked by the window to peer up into the street. All they could see were feet, soldiers going back and forth. And they could all hear shooting, sometimes distant and sometimes frighteningly near.

When Melanie saw the boys looking out the window, she quickly made them get down. They were soon back up on the crates. They didn't want to miss any of the excitement. A dead soldier had fallen in front of the grating, grotesquely blocking the view. The boys got a broomstick, shoved it through the grating and rolled the dead man over so that they could see again.

On August 8, the bombardment stopped and again they heard marching soldiers. Willy was back up on the crates, while the adults consulted each other and the men decided to venture upstairs.

"Get down," Melanie pleaded. All Willy could see was marching feet.

"Sssssssh!"

". . . . de la patrie, le jour de gloire est arrivé."

The war was over. Singing soldiers kept marching by. Within an hour, the women of Mülhausen had five-liter coffeepots steaming and *tartines* ready. Willy and the other youngsters, who all thought this was much more fun than going to school, handed coffee and sandwiches to the marching French soldiers. Melanie lost some of her best china before she told Willy that when he handed a soldier a cup of coffee, he should run alongside until the man had finished it and then get back the empty cup. Down on the Rathausplatz—hastily renamed Place de la Réunion— everybody was going crazy. They hauled down the German flag and ran up the tricolor. *Vive l'Alsace française!* Old men wept, girls smiled at soldiers, and one youth got onto the shoulders of another boy and, reaching to the clock above the city hall steps, while everyone cheered, he sat the clock back one hour to *l'heure française*. The military band played *La Marseillaise* and *Sambre et Meuse* and somebody read the telegram from President Poincaré. August 8 was written in the hearts of all Frenchmen.

Three days later, everybody was back in the cellars. When the bombardment ended, the Wylers—like everybody else—came out to see whether they were French or German.

The women made *butterbrot* and coffee and again the children ran alongside marching men until they had emptied their cups. It was like waking up sober, some said. Others cursed and still oth-

---

11

ers thanked God. On the Rathausplatz, they hauled down the tricolor and, to the tune of *Die Wacht am Rhein,* ran up the imperial colors. They got out the big ladder and someone moved the clock forward to regulation time.

During August Mülhausen changed hands four times, with the same people cheering both armies. The ceremony down on Rathausplatz/Place de la Réunion didn't change and Willy and the other kids soon caught on. They hadn't understood all the grownups' "reasons." Now they knew. War was to decide what time it was.

2

In September, the front stabilized west of the city and Mülhausen remained German to the end. Metz and Verdun were over a hundred miles to the north. On this southern flank, the trenches didn't move for four years. Except for Hartmannswillerkopf. All through the war, this first big knoll of the Vosges mountains stretching toward France was taken, lost, recaptured, and lost again by both sides. They said so many men died there that their bones could make a second Hartmannswillerkopf.

Because Leopold was a Swiss national, he received an exit visa for himself and his family and they all went to Endinger to stay with the Wyler relatives. It was decided that Robert should study in Switzerland and Melanie went with him to Lausanne, where she had him pass the entry exam to the *Collège scientifique.* She also found room and board for him in the nice Jewish Pensionat Bloch. But Leopold worried about the business left in caretaker hands and after two months on neutral territory, the Wylers, with the exception of Robert, were back in Mülhausen.

There were no longer flowers on the Rathausplatz. Around the clock they heard the guns. At night, Willy could see the flares over the front from the bedroom window. Since Alsatians were patriots suffering under the heel of the Hun, the French never shelled Mülhausen. Perhaps for the same psychological reason, the Germans treated its residents as frontline defenders of the fatherland. But Alsatians were a people with allegiances to rival cultures and the city was ringed with the newest in technology—

an electrically charged fence. Nobody could get in or out except through checkpoints. That was the theory, at least. Spies remained a problem and in 1915, it became unlawful to speak French.

Willy watched it all with the other kids. When the French had marched in that first time, he had noticed they didn't all carry their rifles on the same shoulders and that they had poppies in their rifle muzzles. "I found this sloppy and undignified," Wyler recalled later. "I was impressed with German efficiency. I saw them go to war all marching in step. Their rifles were all on the same shoulders and every piece of equipment was brand new. Obviously, they had prepared themselves. Then came the French. They were not efficient and didn't sing in unison. They had not planned for war, but to a kid who in school had been taught discipline and respect for armies and uniforms this was a sign of decadence. It took a while to *realize* it was really the other way around—a sign of freedom and not putting the military first."

The French had put up posters saying that if any German soldiers were seen, they should be reported immediately to the commandant. German posters now warned that if any Frenchman was found in a house, every male living there would be shot. The French had requisitioned public buildings; the German army quartered its officers and men in private homes and Mülhausen settled into the war as army headquarters, railway nerve center, garrison, troop staging area, and evacuation base for casualties. The lines of wounded men never ended.

Like everyone else, the Wylers kept a low profile. But Robert in French-speaking Switzerland would get them into trouble. As the years of war grew longer, Melanie's tears at never seeing her eldest son (although he was only a hundred miles away) became mixed with secret smiles of gratitude. At least he was safe. They were calling up eighteen-year-olds now and Alsatian boys died for the fatherland as far away as the Russian front. They also fought each other across the Marne. The newspapers didn't mention it, of course, but twenty-three thousand had enlisted on the French side.

On Robert's seventeenth birthday, German armies conquered Rumania. The Bolsheviks overthrew the tsar. Russia seemed to be on her knees and ready to sue for separate peace, but then, in April, America entered the war on the Allied side.

If Melanie couldn't see Robert, she could at least write. And one of the reasons she had chosen the Pensionat Bloch, Avenue des Alpes, Lausanne, was the house rule that all boys should write home once a week. It was Robert's weekly letters that got the Wylers into trouble.

After over three years in Lausanne, Robert was totally francophile and wrote letters home calling the Germans the *sales boches* and telling his family what the world situation looked like from a neutral point of view. Since all mail was censored, Leopold and Melanie were called down to the Kommandantur and asked to explain. Then Melanie would write to Robert, in German so the censors could see it, asking him please not to discuss the war in his letters. But the Reich censors blacked out any reference to the war and the message was lost. Until the end, Robert continued to send his anti-German epistles.

With rations being tightened, Melanie began to raise vegetables in the flower beds. Risking trouble with the army, she tried to help starving Rumanian prisoners-of-war on the station platform by dropping food to them from the Altkirch railway bridge.

With Willy, the problem was keeping him out of mischief and in school. Instead of studying, he sat on the roof watching aerial dogfights and formations of Allied planes heading east to bomb Freiburg. Once, a plane was shot down so close that Willy could see where it crashed into a field. He ran as fast as he could to be the first person to reach the wreck. It was a French plane. The pilot still sat in the cockpit, dead, which didn't prevent Willy from getting out his pocketknife and cutting a piece of canvas from the wing. No other boy this side of Tannenwald had such a trophy.

Despite paternal threats and Melanie's tears, Willy kept getting into trouble.

"I didn't rebel against anything," he recalled years later. "I wasn't consciously rebelling. I was just having fun doing a lot of mischief and showing off to other kids. The others would laugh and say, 'Look at that Wyler. He's a terrific cutup.' It would make me feel important. It was just showing off."

With the others, he hung around the railway depot. There were only military trains now—trains pulling in with fresh troops and leaving again with the wounded. From the Altkirch bridge, they watched the crippled lift each other into cars and legless men limp after departing trains. The trains never stayed long. The end was as pathetic as the beginning had been dramatic.

The German army was beaten and in retreat when Berlin gave in and agreed to the Allied armistice offer. But on November 11, Mülhausen was still German. The first French soldiers marched in three days later. They had walked all the way.

Vive l'Alsace française! the shouts were a little subdued on Place de la Réunion. There were gaping holes in every family's ranks—France and Germany alone had lost over three million men. But it had been *la der' des ders,* the war to end all wars. A little fearful, Alsace joined the new order. An American company came to Mülhausen and all the children were out in the streets inviting soldiers home to meager dinners. Willy found a black soldier—that was the second Negro he had seen—and what turned out to be a Jewish soldier from Brooklyn who spoke a little Yiddish. Yiddish–German, they got the points across, slowly, over potato soup and meatloaf.

A new order it was. Georges Clemenceau, Lloyd George, and the newest of statesmen, President Woodrow Wilson, with his idealistic principles and generosity toward the fallen enemy, were sitting down in Versailles to chart a just peace and a noble future.

Melanie sat on her kitchen stool and looked at the new *cartes d'identité.* The *Franzosenkopf* had become a Frenchwoman, although under Swiss law they were, of course, Swiss nationals. If it was a little late to make Leopold speak anything but his *Schwitzerdytsch* and shopkeeper's basic French, her boys would not be pariah under the new order. They would have no heavy accents to set them apart and provoke anti-Semitic jokes as she had experienced in college at Stuttgart. Robert was entirely Gallicized after his four years in Lausanne. Willy would have to go to a French school also. For little Gaston, it didn't matter so much. He would always have to stay with her, she was sure.

Paris was a little too far away and—to Melanie's mind—perhaps a little too turbulent for a boy like Willy. The obvious choice was Lausanne, where he could board with Robert at the Pensionat Bloch. With Willy in tow, she took the train to Lausanne. Robert was ordered to give his kid brother cram courses in arithmetic—despite Professor Schmeltzle's private tutoring, Willy was still weak in mathematics. Incredibly, Willy passed the entrance exams to the *Ecole supérieure de commerce.* With new admonishings to Willy to behave and to Robert to look after him, Melanie returned home.

To take over his father's store—Badenweiler was now in Germany and the *succursale* written off as a mercifully light war casualty for the Wylers—didn't particularly appeal to Willy. But if anyone pressed him and asked what he did want to do, he didn't know. *L'Ecole supérieure de commerce* was Melanie's strategy, to keep her husband passably happy and Willy in school. Leopold couldn't see why the boy had to go to a business school to learn to count francs and centimes or to tell the difference between terry cloth and pile fabric. What the boy needed was practical experience, tending the *Geschäft* or becoming an apprentice to some colleague of his.

Melanie waited nervously for a couple of weeks for a telegram or a letter telling her that Willy had been dismissed, then consoled herself. No news was good news.

If Willy was a poor correspondent—sneaking one-page scrawls into Robert's letters despite the Pensionat Bloch house rules—Melanie kept the letters flying. Once a week, she wrote to her sons, nicknamed Schatz and P'tit Schatz, after her habit of addressing her oldest son Lieber Schatz * on open postcards that made the rounds of the whole boarding house before reaching Robert. Her letters were witty epistles and lengthy recommendations, sprinkled with news from home and family.

And she wrote everybody, slowly untangling the fate of scores of relatives. Nearly everybody had survived, but some were worse off than others. The Wylers in Switzerland had not suffered. It was now the Auerbachs and the Lämmles around Germany who were the poor ones. Leopold's trips to the post office for his wife now were with little parcels for across the border. Relatives in Ulm and Frankfurt wrote that a pair of shoes which had cost twelve marks before the war now cost three thousand! Politicians said it was the war reparations the victors extorted from Germany that caused the inflation. From cousin Siegfried, who dealt in antiques in Munich, Melanie heard they had *revanchards* who suggested Germans tear up the Versailles treaty.

Not all news was bad. There was the amazing success story that Melanie's correspondence helped spread around. Cousin Sieg-

* Literally: *dear treasure;* cf. *tesoro* in Italian, *trésor* in French.

fried's brother Carl had become fabulously rich in America and, best of all, he had not forgotten his own.

In 1904, Cousin Carl and his wife, Recha, had made a first trip home—a belated honeymoon, they called it, with their one-year-old Rosabelle. They had visited again in 1912 and, as Melanie heard it, motion pictures had become big during the war. German countries had been cut off from all that and it was only now that the three cinemas in Mulhouse—no longer Mülhausen—began showing "Allied pictures." Cousin Carl had built a studio on a three-hundred-acre tract of land in California and called it Universal City. In Chicago, he had opened the first of the huge picture palaces and in New York, he owned a skyscraper on Broadway, they said.

Impish Carl Lämmle—whose name was written Laemmle in America—an impulsive, unpredictable and cheerful man of five feet, two inches, had followed his brother, Joseph, to New York when he was seventeen years old. He was going on forty when he settled a second time in Chicago, looking for a business opportunity to invest what he had earned in the clothing business. Robert Cochrane, a younger advertising man also looking for an enterprise to multiply his modest savings, suggested they go into the new five-and-dime-store business. To everybody's surprise, the little Laemmle announced he was getting into nickelodeons.

In 1906, Laemmle rented a vacant building on Milwaukee Avenue and converted it into one of the new playhouses devoted to the showing of "moving pictures" at a nickel (soon, a dime) per customer. To give the impression of cleanliness and respectability, the facade was painted white and the little theater named Whitefront. The enterprise was so successful that two months later Laemmle opened a second house on Halsted Street. When local exchanges gave him poor service and scratched prints, he set up the Laemmle Film Service, in which Cochrane bought a tenth interest for $2,500. By 1908, when his son, Carl Jr., was born, the Laemmle Film Service had established exchanges in Minneapolis, Portland, Salt Lake City, Montreal, and Winnipeg.

Laemmle got into the film business just in time. The primitive flickers had been confined to vaudeville theaters, carelessly offered as novelty items on straight variety bills. By 1907, when Louis B. Mayer also bought his first nickelodeon in Haverhill, Massachusetts, the new entertainment phenomenon was sweeping the

United States. Two years later, Adolph Zukor, William Fox, and Marcus Loew were running chains of nickelodeons. Three years later, the movies were an international industry concentrated in forever fewer hands. Five years later, came the Motion Picture Patent Company. A trust in the full Theodore Rooseveltian sense, it was composed of the largest producers and distributors and, through its pooling of patents, controlled licensing of both cameras and projectors—the cameras solely to its own members, the projectors to those theatermen who would agree to purchase only movies produced by the member companies. Eight years later Laemmle was himself a movie mogul.

Like Fox and Zukor, Laemmle defied the Motion Picture Patent Company. The Patent Company had decided that no audience would sit through a movie running longer than eleven minutes and had established a single reel as the length for all its films.* While Zukor imported the four-reel *Queen Elizabeth*, starring Sarah Bernhardt, and charged the shattering sum of one dollar a ticket, Laemmle founded the Independent Moving Picture Company of America—soon shortened to IMP, and began making films in a studio on New York's 11th Avenue and 53rd Street.

Since his haberdashery days, Laemmle had a way with publicity. His success in movies was phenomenal and much of it was due to his ability to ballyhoo the box office. "You can bet it is classy or I wouldn't make it my first release," he said without blushing of his initial offering, an eleven-minute version of Longfellow's poem *Hiawatha*. IMP made a dozen little pictures in 1909 and more than one hundred the following year. In battling the patent trust, Laemmle managed to create the star system.

Up to 1910, leading players were known by the characters they played or the company they worked for. Florence Lawrence was one of the most popular performers, known as the Biograph Girl. With promises of publicity and a weekly salary of twenty-five dollars, Laemmle lured her away from Biograph. When newspapers reported that Miss Lawrence had been killed in a streetcar accident in St. Louis—a story IMP's cutthroat competitors or perhaps Carl himself had invented—the resourceful Laemmle sent the actress and her leading man, King Baggot, to St. Louis to

---

*At correct silent speed, one reel equaled 11.1 minutes. Hence, a two-reeler ran just over 22 minutes and—later—a five-reeler, just under an hour.

---

prove she was still alive. Newspapers picked up the pace of the drama so that when the two actors arrived at the St. Louis railway station, they were greeted by an emotional crowd larger than the one that had welcomed President Taft a week earlier. By 1912, Mary Pickford and Thomas Ince were making IMP pictures.

As operations expanded, the IMP imprint gave way to another corporate entity. Legend had it that when Laemmle was asked at a director's meeting to come up with a new name, he glanced out of the window and caught sight of a passing truck which heralded Universal Pipe Fittings.

On March 15, 1915, Universal Film Manufacturing Company opened its new studio in San Fernando Valley, just over the Cahuenga Pass from Hollywood. The spot was historic—there, in 1847, Mexican General Andres Pico and U.S. Army Colonel John Frémont had signed the treaty that ceded Upper California to the United States.

Uncle Carl, as he was increasingly called, was a hard-nosed picturemaker, and a steady stream of formula movies kept Universal City busy and on an even keel. Through the gates on Lankershim Boulevard passed an endless parade of colorful characters. The little Laemmle was able to get good people to work for him, but didn't always pay top salaries. Over the years, he lost his best creative talents to his rivals. Metro-Goldwyn-Mayer, Paramount, and, somewhat later, Warner Brothers and Columbia all harbored top executives who had started at Universal. Even when Universal became a power in the film industry, he continued to run his enterprise in chaotic, slapdash fashion. Always flitting between 1600 Broadway and the West Coast, his comings and goings were unscheduled and left turmoil in their wake.

Everywhere, he collected people. Erich von Stroheim was a penniless immigrant the day he accosted Laemmle at the studio gate, hoping to interest the movie mogul in a scenario he had written. Laemmle was on his way home, but invited the Austrian along. At midnight, the two men were still talking, switching from English to German and back. The result was a typical Laemmle gamble. On condition that the film—Stroheim's first—wouldn't cost more than $25,000, he assigned the Austrian to direct, design, and star in *Blind Husbands*. The film was brought in for $85,000, but it was a box-office hit and Universal's prestige success of 1918.

20

While on a brief vacation on Long Island with his family the year before, Laemmle had set up a projector on the front porch and showed his latest movies on a bed sheet. He invited all the neighbors to attend and listened carefully to their comments and reactions. Among them was Irving Thalberg, a slender and cold-eyed youth with heart disease who was to become corporate Hollywood's *wunderkind* and die young enough to become a legend. Thalberg was soon Laemmle's private secretary. On his next trip west, the unpredictable movie tycoon took Thalberg along, left him in the scenario department and left for Europe. Whether on board oceanliners or resting at Czech spas, Laemmle received a cablegram every night from the studio giving a day-to-day report of operations. When something went wrong, Laemmle cabled back firing the general manager and putting Irving Thalberg in charge. At the studio nobody knew who Thalberg was, but finally found this kid in the scenario department. Frantic wires went east, but Laemmle duly confirmed that Thalberg was indeed the new general manager. For a while the new studio boss couldn't sign checks. He wasn't twenty-one yet.

Laemmle not only brought over everyone in his family who was ambitious and wanted to see America, but strangers he met in his travels. When the United States closed itself to mass immigration, he sponsored scores of refugees, some very distantly related, others not at all. His generosity extended to Jewish, Catholic, and Protestant institutions. In later life, he frequently visited his home town and made bequests for public baths, a gymnasium, and a little park. Laupheim rewarded him with a Carl Lämmle Strasse.

When his wife died in 1919, he kept her picture in a locket which he wore next to his heart. He never remarried, but began to haunt casinos. He played at Tijuana, on the Mexican-California border, for up to forty-eight hours nonstop, losing and winning sizable fortunes. Always health conscious, he went to hot springs and baths all his life and his legend later took full account of his eccentricities. An early pet project he was proud of was a species of white chicken. He made the eggs available to employees —at a reasonable price. As a form of advertising, he ran a regular letter column in *The Saturday Evening Post*. Robert Cochrane, who since their Chicago days had moved right along and was vice-president, wrote the column, but Laemmle signed it and read the correspondence it invited. Here, too, he picked up employees.

If the stories of Cousin Carl reached Melanie through tortuous family channels and in bits and pieces, Willy's dismissal from the Pensionat Bloch came in one terse letter. Again, she traveled to Lausanne and found room and board for Petit Schatz with the Pasteur Curchot, a Protestant clergyman with a big family who took in five or six students as boarders.

The pranks were not over. If anything, the troubling proximity of a very proper *pensionat* for young girls egged on the pastor's boarders. It was an alluring yet inaccessible bastion. The girls were so protected that if one of them wanted to mail a letter, she was chaperoned to the corner mailbox.

The pastor's boarders were freer, free enough to discover *Charlot*, as Charles Chaplin was called in French. The boys were so crazy about Chaplin movies that they constantly watched the Lumen Theater playbill. When a new program included a new Charlot, they trooped to the moviehouse *en masse* and were all seated half an hour before showtime.

"We sat there in anticipation looking at a blank screen and pretty soon we would begin to imagine what might come," Willy recalled years later. "Somebody would begin to chuckle and to laugh and long before the house went dark, we were howling with laughter—completely in stitches and nothing had been shown yet. What other artist or actor could make kids' imagination reel with what they're going to see."

One of the upstairs windows of the pastor's house afforded a partial view of the girl's dormitory next door. At night, Willy and the others sneaked up there, turned out the light and peered into the darkness, hoping to catch a glimpse of an undressing girl. They never saw anything and in frustration, one of the boys, who was a wizard with things electric, rigged together a chain of light bulbs. On the assigned night, they sneaked upstairs and delicately lowered the chain of bulbs outside the window. At the count of three, they turned it on. The no-man's land between the two big houses was ablaze and, sure enough, the girls came running to the windows. But everyone of them was in a nightshirt.

It was less the lure of as yet unattainable feminine flesh than a wish for real freedom that made Willy begin a persuasion campaign at home to be allowed to go to Paris. He stuck out the year at the *Ecole supérieure du commerce* and, despite floodlight attempts to discover girlish nudity, managed not to have himself dismissed from Pasteur Curchot's home. In fact, even Robert left the Pensionat Bloch, for a similar room-and-board arrangement in the Chaillot section near his university.

The stratagem worked. Melanie was for having her son at the *Ecole des hautes études commerciales* in Paris. Leopold had his own plan and had Willy sell ties in the store for a while. Wyler *père* went to Paris twice a year to see the wholesalers and business connections and on his next trip took Willy along. If nothing else, the boy could speak French now. Even his mother was impressed after the year in Lausanne.

"I want you to meet my son, Willy, who is going to take over my business one day. He wants to go to the *Ecole des hautes études commerciales*. What do you think about that?"

At the words "graduate studies," the wholesalers and retail colleagues invariably smiled and said that what the boy needed was practical experience.

"That's exactly what I thought," Leopold would chime in. Years later, Willy still suspected that his father had told them in advance what to say.

In due course, a job was found and room and board arranged with the Louveau family near the Gare du Nord. Willy would share a room with another young man, a student. Leopold paid the *pension* and Willy would keep his apprentice's salary of two hundred francs, or eight dollars, a month as pocket money. Willy helped his father aboard the train at Gare de l'Est.

Freedom! At eighteen, Willy's encounter with the realities of life at society's lower rungs was, if nothing else, sobering. The store was in grimy Charenton. It was open from eight A.M. to seven P.M.—until nine on Saturdays—and to get there in time, Willy was up at dawn. Half a century later, the road to work was still burned into his mind: on foot to Gare du Nord, the *métro* to Place de la Bastille (changing first at Place de la République), a bus to Vincennes, a streetcar to Charenton, and a walk to the store itself. *Faire de la manutention,* as the job was called, consisted of sweeping and cleaning, taking cases and mannequins out for sidewalk display in the morning and in again at closing time, pulling down boxes, folding men's shirts, and wrapping socks and suspenders. Willy's already moderate enthusiasm for haberdashery sank to a new low and the inevitable happened. One day he snapped back at the boss and was fired.

This time, however, Willy didn't repair to Mulhouse. He stayed in Paris and managed to forget to write home for a while. It could have been worse. He still had room and board with the Louveaus and he had his freedom. He started to look for a job with the big department stores.

Since he already had experience, he was soon doing *manutention* at the Les Halles branch of the big 100,000 Chemises men's clothing chain. The fact that he was working in the middle of Paris and that the department head took a vague liking to him somehow made sweeping, wrapping, and rearranging displays a little less boring. In fact, he was soon *chef du rayon de faux cols, cravattes et boutons de manchette.* To be department head of collars, ties, and cuff links sounded impressive even if it translated into nothing more than a tiny counter.

Haberdashery didn't seem to send his imagination soaring. On Sundays, he roamed the city and soaked up his new nationality. He liked the Left Bank and sat in literary cafés listening to heady conversations or watching flamboyant artists with their lady-friends on Montparnasse. Not that anybody paid attention to the curly-haired eighteen-year-old who sat with his *demi* and tried to hide his youth in a screen of Gauloise smoke.

There was also another Paris that fascinated him—*les grands Boulevards* with their gaudy honky-tonk, their electric brashness, and their whores. He began his nightly meanderings at Sebastopol-St. Denis and worked his way clear over to the Boulevard des Italiens, ducking in and out of the stores, surging with the crowds. In one of those new record stores, they had a *comptoir d'audition.* For fifty centimes, you could hear a whole record over earphones. He sat for hours at the counter, plugged into 78 rpm Beethoven. He had gone to concerts, but this was cheaper. He had gone to the theater also. He had seen Sarah Bernhardt in what was to be one of her last performances, playing *Athalie,* that biblical legend Racine had turned into his most powerful tragedy.

He let the prostitutes proposition him. He had neither the money nor the courage to go with any of them, but he let them tell him all the things they would do to him. *Je vais te faire des choses.* On the next block, he feigned interest and another girl would tell him more.

But he was lonely and the hours seemed endless. He had had a lot of friends in Lausanne, but here he didn't really know any-body. One day, he impulsively quit the 100,000 Chemises. With the severance pay, he bought a railway ticket home and an hour with the prettiest of the girls on the *grands Boulevards*. She al-most threw him out when he told her he had never been with a woman before.

This time, Melanie saved her tears and instead ordered Willy to dress his best and come with her to Zurich. On the train, she explained. Cousin Carl was in Europe. He had been to Czechoslo-vakia, to the baths at Karlovy Vary, as the Czechs insisted on call-ing Carlsbad, and to Laupheim. He was now in Zurich. What she didn't tell him was that, in desperation, she had written to Cousin Carl saying there was nothing she could do anymore, that her son was a healthy youth, even intelligent. Perhaps America could straighten him out.

Willy never knew they had that many relatives. Everybody was there, slipping in and out of the inner sanctum of Cousin Carl's hotel suite. Willy was duly impressed when he was introduced to Harry Zehner, Laemmle's secretary. Willy could see by his clothes that Zehner was an American and thought that if this tall gentle-man was a secretary, what would Carl Laemmle be like.

Finally, Cousin Carl appeared, a very little man with an owlish face and blue eyes behind steel-rimmed glasses.

"So you're your mother's sorrow, eh?" he asked Willy when he had been introduced. Willy smiled wanly, feeling his mother's eyes in his back.

"Want to go to America?"

The smile remained.

"I can give you a job, twenty dollars a week." Cousin Carl smiled, peering over his glasses. "After that, everything depends on *you!*"

America! Willy wondered if he would ever see his parents or Mulhouse again. With endless recommendations and deep tears, Melanie and Leopold sent him off to Southampton to join Cousin Carl and his entourage. They sailed aboard the *Aquitania,* Willy in first class like the rest of the Laemmle party. He soon was to find out that his salary was twenty-five dollars but that Laemmle would have the price of the ticket deducted from the pay enve-lope at the rate of five dollars a week to make him feel he was paying his own way.

3

Willy arrived with his violin and something few New Yorkers had seen in 1920—a pair of skis. The new world started with *manutention* at the Universal home office on New York's Times Square; it all looked suspiciously like a rerun of the Paris debut, for the bilingual albeit not English-speaking second cousin of the boss was set to work as an office boy.

During the first week, Cousin Carl's man in charge of relatives put Willy up with another Universal employee in Flatbush. Instead of *métro,* the underground train was called subway, but it took as long to get from the far end of Brooklyn to Times Square as it did from Gare du Nord to Charenton.

Carrying interoffice memos and cans of film around the 1600 Broadway building wasn't so bad, but, he decided, the Flatbush commuting had to end. After less than two weeks, Willy managed to arrange accommodations at a rooming house on Manhattan's 91st Street, soon to be followed by more permanent quarters in Yorkville. This was a rooming house on 86th Street and Park Avenue, where Paul Kohner, another young man Laemmle had brought over, had a room. Then and there, the two became lifetime friends.

Willy and Paul had a lot in common besides identical steamer trunks and rooms so tiny they had to pull the trunks into the hallway to open them. They were both eighteen, they both spoke German, both worked in Universal's shipping department at twenty-five dollars a week (although the payroll department was taking five dollars out of Willy's pay envelope for the first class transatlantic fare). At the Yorkville, both had to come up with eight dollars every Sunday morning for the rent.

Together, they explored New York and the pitfalls of what henceforth was to be their native language. Kohner was a little craftier than Willy and had some experiences in the baffling world of motion pictures. He was the son of the publisher of *Internationale Filmschau,* a Prague trade paper, and owed his presence in New York to his press credentials.

As a representative of *Internationale Filmschau,* Paul had traveled to Carlsbad to interview, if possible, the American film magnate. When he arrived, after the three-hour journey from Prague, he was told Laemmle had no time. Kohner left a card saying he had taken three hours to get there and that surely Mr. Laemmle could find three minutes to see him. His persistence earned him an invitation to come for breakfast at seven the next morning.

Kohner was ushered in while Uncle Carl was having his pedicure. The sound of Strauss waltzes filled the Bohemian mountain air and Kohner had to join Laemmle and drink half a dozen glasses of hot mineral water before walking through dewy gardens to a breakfast table where members of the Laemmle family joined them.

The meeting concluded with Laemmle putting the eighteen-year-old journalist into his temporary employ and, a month later, offering him a job in America.

Carrying memos and film cans around the Universal building was not what Kohner had had in mind when he accepted the offer to come to the United States. He had bought a gimmicky little piggy bank for nickels, dimes, and quarters. It had a calibrated glass front, telling exactly how much money was in it, but it couldn't be opened until twenty dollars was saved up. Paul already had sixteen dollars in it. He was determined to become rich quick.

The chance came when they had been in America a couple of weeks. One Saturday night, Laemmle invited them to have dinner with him at the Progress Club, a West Side establishment known less for its culinary art than for its back-room gambling. As soon as they had eaten, Uncle Carl disappeared. Both Paul and Willy had their week's salaries in their pockets. Manfully, they nudged each other toward the gambling area.

"We soon separated," Kohner recalled. "I remember Chuck-a-Luck. After an hour, we ran into each other. We both had a fistful of money and exchanged experiences. Well, I thought this was the beginning of the road to fame and fortune.

"Except when about an hour later I looked around for Willy to borrow a dollar. He also had lost everything."

They left the club mortified, unable even to tip the hat-check girl when they got their overcoats. The raw November wind cleared their heads as they walked home across Central Park. Clear air, however, didn't solve the problem of the two times eight dollars rent their landlady, Mrs. Stiefel, would demand in a few hours.

Back in their rooms, they both realized Paul's see-through bank was the only solution. Since Willy was the one who had to borrow, he proposed to solve the dilemma. Shortly after seven o'clock, he walked into the corner drugstore with Paul's kitty and explained to the owner that if he gave him four dollars in change, he would feed the money into the savings bank which would then spring open. The man would get his four dollars back and Willy would buy something.

Whether his story was too fishy or his accent too thick, the drugstore owner refused. When two other early Sunday morning coffee shops also turned him down, Willy went into a restaurant, ordered and ate a full breakfast and with the bill in hand crossed to the cashier, put the piggy bank on the counter and said, "If you want to get paid, the money is in there!"

Mrs. Stiefel was paid in nickels, dimes and quarters and the change left from Willy's breakfast was spent on Nabisco crackers and cans of tomatoes which they stirred into a gruel and ate morning, noon, and night until the following Saturday.

Penniless evenings, however, brought about the real breakthrough. To improve his English, Paul translated stories from *Universal Weekly,* a magazine distributed to exhibitors across the United States. Besides publicity stories from Universal City, the weekly contained the famous "Carl Laemmle, Straight from the Shoulder Talk" column, where a few years earlier the feisty Laemmle had told theatermen *his* version of the Biograph Girl caper and warned about other dastardly deeds planned by the Motion Picture Patent Company.

Once he had translated *Universal Weekly* into German, it occurred to Kohner to send the stories to his father. Next, he made carbon copies and sent them to various magazines he knew.

"It was shortly after the war and they were hungry for news from America," Kohner recalled. "They printed page after page of the stuff. They asked for pictures and I sent them mats from the publicity department. I even received a few money orders— twenty kronen from Prague, fifty marks from Berlin, one hundred schillings from Vienna, perhaps."

When he had an impressive pile of clippings, Kohner went downstairs to the Laemmle office. He knew both Manny Goldstein, the boss's "hatchet man" who was sent to the Coast when the payroll had to be cut, and Harry Zehner, the secretary who had once taken Willy and him to visit his mother at Rockaway Beach. Within a few hours, Zehner called the enterprising Kohner in the shipping department, ordering him downstairs with a warning: "Boy, are you in trouble."

Kohner's English hadn't progressed enough fully to understand Zehner's explanation, but one glance at Uncle Carl once he was in his office made him realize he had committed a major crime.

"How dare you," Laemmle began.

"What, Mr. Laemmle?"

"How can you commit this company to spend this kind of money on all this publicity?"

"But, Mr. Laemmle, this costs nothing."

The boss looked at him.

"You mean to say we're not paying for any of this?"

"No, Mr. Laemmle. They are very happy. I can get anything in print you want over there."

Within hours, Kohner was the head of a new foreign publicity department, had been given a five-dollar raise, moved to another floor and, when Willy came to see him in his new splendor, had a painter stenciling his name on a glass partition.

"Willy was crestfallen," Kohner recalled. "It didn't let him sleep for days. Then suddenly lightning struck him and he came and said, 'Since I speak French, why can't I translate and send the stories to magazines in France, Belgium, and Switzerland?'

"So Willy got busy translating my German articles into French and sending them out. Sure enough, same result. Everybody, it seemed, was hungry for American news. They printed the stuff and pretty soon clippings came in. I don't know if I went down or Willy, or we both did. Laemmle was presented with the French stuff and we asked whether Willy could join the foreign publicity department. Yes, he could, Laemmle said.

"After a couple of nights of buttering me up, Willy said, 'Couldn't I also get my name on the door?' I said, 'I see no reason why not.'"

The two-man foreign department turned out reams of German- and French-language ready-to-print stories datelined Hollywood and Universal City. When they didn't translate, they invented "fillers" and column items about Lon Chaney and Harold Lloyd, the "new faces" Rudolph Valentino and Zasu Pitts, or *Foolish Wives,* continuing Erich von Stroheim's Universal formula of sophisticated sex, seduction, and intrigue in the Continental setting.

The twosome explored the world beyond the Yorkville and 1600 Broadway as much as their means permitted. Lack of money and smooth English set a natural limit to the interest girls could find in the two eighteen-year-old immigrants. Despite the *dépucelage* by the pretty Parisian streetwalker, Willy was still shy and, besides, New York femininity seemed so obviously beyond his reach.

Kohner's ingenuity helped them flesh out the long winter Sundays in a way that rapidly expanded their knowledge of both movies and English. On *Internationale Filmschau* letterhead, Paul wrote that he was the New York correspondent for eastern Europe's most influential trade paper. Soon, the Rialto, Rivoli, and Capitol theaters issued working-press passes—"valid for you and one guest." It sometimes seemed they spent their entire lives in the movies.

But coming out of the Capitol at midnight *was* impressive. The Great White Way was a fabulous streak of never-never land. It was hard to explain in writing and Willy discovered photography. Pictures were great; you could explain the scene in one line on the back and send them to Mulhouse without adding a long letter. With his Kodak box camera, he snapped pictures around Manhattan and when he had bought a tripod and had mastered open-shutter exposure, he tried night shots and finally got the Great White Way on film. Staying after hours until everybody was gone, he got up on the roof of 1600 Broadway and crawled between electric signs to the edge to set up his tripod and camera.

Melanie knew better than to write back and ask how he had managed such aerial snapshots of the Manhattan canyon.

Friday nights were the loneliest since Willy and Paul invariably were broke and had to forego dinner at Stuckitz's, their Hungarian *stammcafé* on 84th Street. Instead, they usually took a walk around the block, mentally spending Saturday night's pay in advance. One Friday night, they stopped across from the 86th Street Synagogue and stood watching people go in.

"Let's go in," Paul said, reminding Willy that they had never been to a temple in America. They were both thinking that they had nothing better to do anyway.

They were almost inside when Paul whispered he would run home and get a prayerbook his grandmother had tearfully thrust into his hands the day he left for America.

"I'll wait for you," Willy said.

When Paul came back with the *sidur*, they joined the congregation. They both knew little of Jewish liturgy but dutifully imitated the men around them. When everybody got up and opened their *sidur*, Paul did the same. Something fluttered out of the prayerbook. A thousand Czech kronen! Willy looked heavenward.

They didn't wait to the end of the services, but sneaked out and over to Stuckitz's. Stuckitz recognized the bill and told them to sit down while he changed it. Fifty dollars!

By spring, Willy got a little tired of perpetual moviegoing at the Capitol—even the action thrillers, with their spectacular spills and dangerous stunts. Despite recurring and sometimes acute attacks of homesickness, Willy was convinced that he was in America to stay. He worked hard on his English and his fine-tuned bilingual ear soon had him talk with only the slightest accent—the r's were the hardest linguistic obstacle. He was impressed with the "new country," which rolled in riches, hummed to the tunes of a contagious "jazz age," and cared little about the rest of the world. If he wasn't smitten by the disillusioned yet nationalistic mood, he felt the sharp antiforeign sentiment and hurried to conform. Perhaps because he had seen too many stretchers and invalid soldiers on the Mulhouse *Bahnhof*, what impressed him most was the fact that there was no military draft in America. He noticed that the army formed no privileged caste and that people actually looked down on soldiers and considered them kind of unimaginative for not knowing how to seize the opportunities the robust land proverbially offered everyone.

When someone told him he could shave two years from the five-year residence requirement for citizenship by volunteering for National Guard service, Willy was off to the nearest armory. He became a member of the 104th Field Artillery, was given uniform and gun, and did his soldiering one night a week at the armory. In the summer of '21, the company did two weeks' training at Montauk Point on Long Island.

Willy was given a horse which was, during maneuvers, loaded with field glasses for artillery spotting. Playing war was strenuous and when the company returned to camp after a day in the field, Willy, like other privates, had to clean his horse's hoofs, wash, brush, and feed the animal before he was free to go eat in his tent.

"One day, I had just finished with my horse, dead tired, when an officer approached the stables leading his horse. I was the first man he spotted and he handed me his horse, saying, 'Here, take care of him.'

"Very much annoyed, I took the horse, grabbed his hind leg to clean the hoof. I was careless. The horse didn't know me and kicked me right in the face. I passed out."

When Willy woke up, he was in the field hospital. No broken bones or teeth, but a badly swollen face. While he was still half-unconscious, the officer who had given him the horse came to see him. A couple of days later, when the swelling had gone, Willy was released and punished with guard and latrine duties. "It seemed that when the officer had come to see me, even though I wasn't conscious I had called him every dirty name in French. He had been in France during the war and understood."

Earlier, a sergeant had found Willy and another private in a fight. The sergeant separated them and immediately booked them as preliminary fighters for the regimental boxing night. With gloves, they did three two-minute rounds in the ring. Willy won the decision, but didn't continue his career as a prizefighter. He did pursue the violin. Coming back to the Yorkville one sizzling August evening, Kohner saw across the street a group of gawking and laughing people. Following the direction of their collective gaze, he saw Willy in his open window playing his violin stark naked!

If Willy had had no strong urges to make haberdashery his profession, he somehow felt publicity was not his calling either. To himself, he was truthful enough to admit that if Cousin Carl had been in the pipe-fitting business, he would still have come to the States, but if anyone asked him what he wanted, he still had to admit that he didn't know.

Yet, as he translated the reams of West Coast publicity, he couldn't help wondering what it was really like out there.

To tycoons and financiers, Manhattan might be the corporate heartthrob of American film, which since the war had come to dominate the world market. To Willy, New York was increasingly a transmission point of excitement that took place three thousand miles away.

The roistering, carefree ways of the first two decades were coming to an end. The studios were no longer back-lot shirt-sleeve operations, but increasingly sophisticated factories. If Hollywood was still Victorian in content and form, the glitter was more than ever part of the "sell": the *kitsch*, "glamour," synthetic romanticism, heavy-handed artiness and theatricality that, to a modern mind, tend to make 1920s screenfare seem more remote than nineteenth-century fiction.

Publicity stories described the acres of Universal City villages, city streets, wharves, and railroad stations that only awaited the designer's touch to become locales for new adventure. Spanish bungalows were really facades of service buildings and the architecture was deliberately hodgepodge—English colonial giving way to log cabins, Japanese teahouses, and classic antiquity. Two restaurants served a thousand customers a day—a melange of crusaders, pirates, dance-hall girls, circus performers, and Indians in war paint mingling with directors in jodhpurs and puttees and writers in loud sports jackets. The studio had its own police and fire departments, a bus system, a school for child stars, a zoo, and a slaughterhouse.

Other stories told of the world of westerns—cowboys and studio ranches kept permanently stocked with horses, cattle, and covered wagons. Although there were few of them, the publicity stories that really fascinated the former daredevil from Mulhouse were writeups about stuntmen. Willy read how Harold Lloyd's "thrill pictures" were shot just as high above the Los Angeles streets as they appeared on the screen. Sometimes a false section was constructed on the roof of a tall building. At other times, Lloyd worked above a wooden platform. Once, a unit decided to see what would happen if Lloyd slipped. They dropped a dummy onto the platform and saw it bounce to the street below.

And there were men falling off motorcycles, jumping from bridges onto moving trains, leaping out of airplanes. Isadore Bernstein, who before Thalberg had been the Univeral general manager and now was the overseer of western and action pictures, hired men who took to stunting out of desperation. Everybody wanted to get into the movies.

Publicity stories about stars told of the glamour of their lives and the king's ransoms they were paid weekly. No angle was too improbable if it captured headlines or space in the increasingly important fan magazines. Through Willy's French-keyboard Remington flowed the successive chapters of publicity man Harry Reichenbach's irrepressible attempts at putting Valentino back in public favor. Reichenbach persuaded the Latin lover to grow a beard and kept his name on the front pages by reporting the protests of women and barbers. He capped it all with a great "de-bearding," performed by representatives of the Master Barbers of America.

If the publicity flow wasn't enough to make Willy restless, Melanie one day forwarded a letter that had arrived in Mulhouse for him. It was from Alex Manuel, a boy who had gone to school with Robert in Lausanne. Alex was the son of a wealthy Swiss family. He was now a Hollywood stuntman.

The next time Cousin Carl was in New York, Willy asked to see him. When Zehner pushed him into the boss's office, Willy explained he had been a year in New York and asked if there was a chance that he might be sent out to the Coast.

"Maybe, but do you have any money?" Laemmle asked, looking up at him.

"Not much," Willy confessed.

Before he dismissed Willy, Laemmle was on the phone giving instructions to the payroll department to make additional weekly deductions of five dollars from Willy Wyler's salary until the $160 New York–Los Angeles train fare had been paid back.

All he still had to do was report to the 104th Field Artillery and explain his transfer. He was given an honorable discharge. As Leopold might say, the boy was growing up, finally.

34

4

"But, *mon vieux,* I was thinking that with you working at Universal, I mean permanently, *you* could get *me* stunt jobs."

Alex Manuel helped Willy carry the suitcase into the blinding sunlight outside Union Station. Willy laughed. To be called *p'tit Schatz* six thousand miles away from Lausanne was more incongruous than palm trees. It was great to see Alex and maybe he could get Alex work now and then once he got settled. On the way up to Hollywood on the Sunset Boulevard streetcar, Alex told him all about it. There were a couple of other Swiss guys, Athur Hurni and René Traveletti. Maybe Willy wanted to share an apartment with them. Traveletti was studying architecture. Sure, they all hung around casting offices—what else was there to do. Hollywood was positively crawling with small-town belles and beauty-contest winners convinced that they were the next Mabel Normand. With Willy working at Universal, wow!

The first glimpse of moviemaking was hypnotic—five strong men each holding a section of a live boa constrictor stretched out so it couldn't coil up and strike while a little makeup man named Jack Pierce painted the snake's natural lines over white tape around its jaws. "The frightened face of little Jack Pierce and the big eyes of the boa looking at each other is something I haven't forgotten in fifty years," Wyler remembered.

But it was back to *manutention.* Or almost. Willy's first job was as office boy to the casting director. When he wasn't carrying memos and cans of film, he was sent out to buy cigars. He was also told to check in extras, which was exactly what Manuel, Hurni, and Traveletti had hoped for.

Sprawling Universal City was an exciting place. The superspectacle currently shooting was *The Hunchback of Notre Dame*. The Notre Dame décor was so big that for Wallace Worsley's night scenes with two thousand extras, Universal was borrowing every competitor's sun arcs. At sundown, an army of trucks fanned out to Republic, Paramount, Warner's, William Fox, and Metro and at dawn the same trucks brought the arc lights back to their respective owners.

"Light your torches!" Worsley commanded through a megaphone almost as large as himself.

The crowd, which included Manuel, Hurni, and Traveletti, surged forward and hissed at Lon Chaney, hideously swinging between the towers of the Paris cathedral.

Once Willy was sent to the actor's dressing room with a message. They said Chaney always came two hours early and always made himself up. They also said young Thalberg had ordered Worsley to shoot additional crowd scenes so the Victor Hugo classic would be given top treatment by the sales department. Laemmle was in Europe and wouldn't know about the added scenes until he returned.

To get closer to the excitement, Willy managed to help with research in the art department. If the portals and *parvis* formed a full-sized replica, the upper towers and roof of the nave were a miniature. Willy soon spotted an historical error—when Hugo's story took place in the Middle Ages, the cathedral had no steeple on the nave. The spire was dutifully lifted off the model and *The Hunchback of Notre Dame* filmed in the historically correct setting. Once in release, however, hundreds of scornful letters arrived at Universal. "The letters said, 'You idiots, haven't you ever looked at the church in Paris? It's there for everyone to see—a spire in the middle," Wyler recalled. "Not one letter arrived saying how clever we were. It's kind of a lesson: Sometimes you shouldn't tell it like it is, but tell it like they *think* it is!"

Before *The Hunchback of Notre Dame* was finished, Willy managed to get still closer to the action, by becoming an assistant to the assistants of Worsley—Jack Sullivan and Jimmy Dugan, who among other things taught him to shoot craps. Being their assistant meant sometimes being an errand boy again, but he didn't mind. When they were shooting, he was there. Sometimes, Sullivan and Dugan were too busy to remember him and he could stand and watch or get lost in the crowds. With their outsized megaphones and authority, directors seemed glamorous fellows.

Kohner also managed to get himself shipped west. When von Stroheim had come to New York to find a composer for *Foolish Wives,* Paul had arranged meetings and appointments for him. He had also found the composer Sigmund Romberg and had introduced the filmmaker to the Austrian Metropolitan Opera crowd at the Blue Ribbon on 44th Street. In turn, von Stroheim had spoken enthusiastically about the gifted young man in publicity and Laemmle had agreed to let Kohner go west.

The night Kohner arrived in Los Angeles, Worsley was still shooting crowd scenes.

"I was overwhelmed," Kohner recalled. "Hundreds of extras milling around under the arc lights. I had never seen anything like it. I made my way toward the Notre Dame and just stood there and watched. Slowly, I discovered that people kept popping in and out of the huge central door. I went closer and saw a black curtain.

"Since people kept going in and out, I went in, too. On the other side of the curtain was a tremendous hall and two immense tables, stretching perhaps thirty feet each. On each side, hundreds of extras were shooting craps. All the extras who were not in a scene were shooting their five-dollar or seven-fifty checks. I made my way through them and there was Willy with a handful of checks, shooting craps."

Willy had moved into a room on Mariposa Avenue with Hurni and Traveletti, and for a while Paul lived there also. The hours at the studio were long, the week even longer, and Willy was practically never home. Since he paid the rent most of the time, he had one of the two beds and Hurni and Traveletti alternated sleeping on fold-out couches. Manuel had his own place. Small checks from Lausanne supplemented his stuntman's earnings.

To get Sundays off, crews often worked far into Saturday nights. But, however late the "wrap," a crap game immediately started up behind the sets.

"I'd come home at four or five in the morning—busted, having lost my twenty-five dollars," Willy recalled. "Then, I'd borrow five bucks from an assistant and somehow the three of us would get through the week on that. It was the biggest gambling I ever did because I gambled not only my own food but two other guys' groceries. Later on, when I gambled much bigger sums in Las Vegas or in Tijuana the breakfast would be there just the same."

Once he won. Hurni and Traveletti howled into the Sunday morning light and had neighbors cursing a block away when Willy staggered in and began to empty his pockets.

"I couldn't tell you what we did the whole week—one continuous party. We had the greatest food, we had girls, we had automobiles that we rented. We couldn't spend the hundred dollars. At the end of the week there was still money left."

Since Alex and Willy had money—or Alex had money and Willy could, in theory, pay back a loan—the two of them bought a pair of sleek, four-cylinder Henderson motorcycles and roared off to the beach at Santa Monica or over to Glendale, Burbank, or Culver City. Only hoodlums and policemen rode motorcycles, and the Manuel–Wyler easy riders scared motorists. They raced up along flivvers and grinned to the flappers in the back seat if a driver began to pull over. The machines heated up so much underneath they had to put their feet on the handlebars sometimes.

The Henderson finally got Willy into trouble. He was pinched once too often speeding over the Cahuenga Pass on the motorcycle and was sentenced to spend three days planting tomatoes on an honor farm in San Fernando Valley. When he came back, Thalberg made fun of the incident and called him "the jailbird." Driving too fast was to remain a Wylerian trait and ten years later, he was to be sentenced to one weekend in jail.

Willy spent his twenty-first birthday on his Henderson. There wasn't much else to do. Los Angeles was an overgrown railway depot three thousand miles away from everything. It was no good even thinking about home. The fastest train took three and a half days to get to New York and the fastest liner another five days to Cherbourg—that is, if you had the money in the first place: in day coach across America and third class across the Atlantic over $300, one way.

When the movies had fled west to escape the patent trust strongmen, Los Angeles boardinghouses had advertised "Rooms for Rent—no dogs or actors allowed." As late as 1919, the exclusive Garden Court apartments were still holding out against "picture people." By 1923, however, the attitude was mollified by the $20 million the studios spent annually in salaries and the $12 million in services. By now, eighty percent of the world's motion pictures were made in Southern California, yet the *New York World* could write that "Hollywood has no art galleries, no institutions of learning aside from primary schools and kindergartens—nothing that makes the slightest pretense to culture, civic or otherwise." [1] As late as 1927, the sarcastic H. L. Mencken could write that the wildest nightlife he encountered in Hollywood was at Aimee Semple McPherson's tabernacle.[2]

With hundreds of thousands of dollars riding on each production, the studios sought to protect their investment. A top-ranking star provided an almost foolproof insurance because the public responded to determined starmaking. Not only the success but even the approximate box-office "take" could be confidently foretold when films featured such players as John Barrymore, Pola Negri, Gloria Swanson, Valentino, or Chaplin. Dozens of lesser stars—Clara Bow, Madge Bellamy, Bebe Daniels, Jackie Coogan—made any picture they appeared in a reasonably safe investment. Selling their films on the strength of star names, the studios zealously built up their roster of box-office performers until, late in the 1920s, MGM was proud to be identified as "the home of the stars." [3]

Despite invincible public enthusiasm—toward the end of the decade over fifty million Americans went to the movies every week *—silent screenfare was generally obvious, naïve, and mechanical in story line and plot. Born on the lower rungs of dime-store literature and baggy-pants vaudeville, the movies grew up in healthy middlebrow and only mutated under stress. It didn't help when stars began to believe their own publicity and behave as kings and queens who could do no wrong. After a series of scandals outraged the public and the protest assumed the form of a threatened national censorship, the industry ran for cover. It appointed Will H. Hays, a Presbyterian elder and postmaster general in the Harding administration, as overseer and "czar." By creating ground rules and enforcing them, Hays averted national censorship, but the "Hays Office" code further standardized plots

---

* After a 1946 peak of upward of 80 million, U.S. weekly admissions slumped for 25 years to stabilize at about 20 million weekly patrons in the early 1970s.

and stories. Virtue was *always* rewarded, sin *always* punished, even if studios soon realized they could present six reels of ticket-selling sin, provided, in the last reel, all sinners came to a bad end. By cloaking his stories in biblical righteousness, Cecil B. De-Mille trumpeted his moral lessons so sententiously that his films had more sensational sinning than anybody else's. While Moses received the Law on the mountain in *The Ten Commandments,* DeMille made the most of the bacchanalian revels around the golden calf below.

Willy and his friends belonged to the lower order of extras, cowboys, stagehands, and "people working for Universal." In the hierarchy of studios, Laemmle's film farm was near the bottom. Half the great names of Hollywood stopped in at Universal on their way up the ladder, but the studio remained a maker of formula fare. In his most active years, Uncle Carl was closer to exhibitors and distributors and geared Universal productions to their demands. *The Hunchback of Notre Dame* and the two-year tenure of Thalberg were exceptions, although both paid off handsomely. The film was Universal's biggest moneymaker to that date and boosted the company's prestige.

As witnessed by Jack and Harry Cohn, who had left him to form Columbia Pictures, Uncle Carl did not know how to hang on to talent. He was never happy to see too much power concentrated in one employee and his displeasure increased when Thalberg began courting his daughter Rosabelle. Over a question of a raise in his $450-a-week salary, Laemmle let Thalberg go, although the youthful general manager had already shown a talent for developing stars and doctoring scripts. After listening to offers from DeMille and Hal Roach, Thalberg was hired by Metro's Louis B. Mayer. For a momentous decade, the two of them were to form Hollywood's most successful partnership.

Laemmle's bread-and-butter grind had an advantage for Universal workers—steady employment. For Willy, it meant a unique apprenticeship and a lot of wonderful excitement. Directors like Clifford S. Smith and Bob Hill were megaphone wielders on action pictures often featuring airplanes. The studio stunt pilot was Art Gobel and one day Willy made his maiden flight with him. Once aloft, Gobel tried to make the baptism exciting with aerial stunts that included "looping the loop" and he had Willy hanging upside down five minutes after they had left the field. Next, they were off to Griffith Park, Willy in the front seat with a girl's wig on.

"The scene was supposed to be in France with a girl intervening in a duel. We circled above and at a certain signal from the ground—there was no radio in those days—Gobel started diving. I saw what they were shooting—two men drawing their pistols and our plane coming down to break up the duel in the nick of time. Gobel went toward the clearing, pulled out of the dive a few feet from the ground. I was supposed to turn back and wave before we cleared the treetops. I felt we were lucky to be alive when we were signaled to do it again."

Westerns were the archetype of action pictures and Willy started at the bottom rung of moviemaking—assistant to assistants on two-reelers.

Without an equivalent abroad, westerns were the only American film form with enough vitality to impose itself and to remain unique in the annals of the cinema. Westerns were first declared passé in 1914, but audiences would tolerate no final fadeout to stories of crooked sheriffs and dapper gamblers, of improbably pure dance-hall girls and lean strangers, of adventure and wide-open spaces where promises of riches, freedom, and happiness for all were just over the next ridge.

The genre had plots that were formula and stars that made serialization a natural. Inexpensive to make, westerns were the staple of the industry, with every studio producing endless numbers of two-reelers and five-reelers. Too humble to play big theaters in big cities, the westerns escaped the influence of Hollywood's continued wooing of European directors with artistic reputations. Together with slapstick comedy, the westerns were uninhibited and characteristic of what was best in American movies—speed, tightness, timing of action and editing, plus clean, bright photography.

Universal made over two hundred two-reelers a year. They were made very quickly and efficiently. One week per segment. Monday, Tuesday, and Wednesday: shooting; Thursday and Friday: editing; Saturday: casting next week's story. A young cowboy was the star. He didn't have to be a good actor but he had to ride superbly. The picture had to open in slambang fashion with a chase or the heroine on a runaway horse or stagecoach. The story would have the hero come along and rescue her, followed by a little romance, the appearance of villains, a posse, action, and a big finish. Big chase, big action, happy ending was the formula. The hero never smoked and never kissed the girl until the last shot. Characterization was kept to a minimum: the man who came out of a saloon and kicked a dog before swinging into his saddle was the villain; the one who came out and patted the dog was the hero.

Worsley, Clarence Brown, and Tod Browning were Universal's towering directors and John Ford had just left to direct Tom Mix for William Fox after a five-year stretch on two- and five-reel westerns for Uncle Carl. The studio's directors were Jack Conway, Stuart Payton, Hobart Henley, Art Rosson, and Bill Craft, all hardy fellows who could ride as well as any of them and get an action-filled two-reeler in the can in three days. Willy started sweeping the saloon on the set of King Baggot, who had been Uncle Carl's first leading man back in 1911 and was now directing Universal's newest male star, William Haines.

To become assistant director on two-reel westerns was not very difficult and soon Willy was in Idaho on a serial directed by and starring William Duncan, a dashing daredevil who had started in movies two years earlier. Twelve episodes, twenty-four reels—fours hours of finished film in six weeks.

If a director agreed to do two segments of a series back to back, he could take his cast and crew out of town—all the way up to Lone Pine in the High Sierra, on the back side of Sequoia National Park. Otherwise, exteriors were shot on the sprawling back lot or along Mulholland Drive and Laurel Canyon in the Hollywood Hills or Frenchie's Ranch in Newhall, thirty miles out in San Fernando Valley.

During the summer of 1924, Willy got terribly homesick and made his first trip home. "I don't know how I managed it, I saved money and went on the *Savoie*, a little ship that took nine days," he recalled. "I had gone to Laemmle and tried to borrow a couple of hundred dollars. He said, 'What for?' I told him and he answered that if I ever wanted to make a trip home, it would have to be on my own money." That was how he began to save, which was the purpose of Laemmle's refusal.

Willy was barely inside the door on Rue de Ferrette before he wanted to leave again. Mulhouse was such a tiny place all of a sudden. Everybody was delighted to see him, Melanie most of all.

To old friends, he posed as an American with a copy of the Paris *Herald-Tribune* sticking out of his pocket.

To do something with himself once the initial flush of excitement had passed, he visited Salzburg, where forty years later he was to scout locations for *The Sound of Music*. He also talked to his brother a lot. Robert was not too keen on emigrating. He was finishing his engineering at the Technische Hochschule in Zurich, but he had to admit that his new passion was the theater. He was active in the academic drama society in Zurich and had produced two Ibsen plays and acted in several student plays. In less than a year, Robert would also be in California.

Willy was back in the States within two months. He was given his old job back and was suddenly sure he knew what he wanted.

"I never felt I could act or write," he said half a century later. "Directing seemed glamorous and it was something I felt I could do. I had a certain eye for the camera. I'd watch the director, see where he put the camera, and figure out why. Occasionally, I'd come up with a suggestion and be told to get lost."

For a second cousin of a movie mogul with aspirations toward directing, the future looked more than promising. Yet, in a flash, he was suddenly out of it all.

Pool was his undoing. Along with other assistants, he was hanging out in the pool hall across Lankershim Boulevard one day when he suddenly was needed. Something had gone wrong on the set and everybody turned to where the assistant should have been with the script. When Willy turned up half an hour later, he was fired.

He sat a couple of days on the couch on Mariposa Avenue. The motorcycle had been sold after Alex had taken a spill on Vermont Avenue that left him near death with an open skull and, once he had recovered, he quit stunting for medicine. Willy wondered what to do next, when the news went out that all unemployed assistants should report immediately to Metro for crowd-control work on the *Ben-Hur* chariot race sequence.

Ben-Hur had been an impressive undertaking from the beginning. General Lew Wallace's book—the first work of fiction to be blessed by a pope—had been turned into an awesome stage version in 1899, including a chariot race with two horses pounding a treadmill while a painted panorama of Antioch's Circus Maximus revolved behind them. Ben-Hur was played by Ernest Morgan and Messala by the future western star William S. Hart. In 1907, two years after Wallace's death, a film version was made. "Sixteen magnificent scenes with illustrated titles, positively the most superb motion picture spectacle ever made," read the Kalem Co. advertising of Sidney Olcott's film. Publisher and stage producers promptly sued for breach of copyright. Kalem, filled with righteous indignation, stoutly defended its film as being a good advertisement for book and stage play. Film rights had never been disputed before and the test case dragged on until 1911. Conceding defeat, Kalem paid $25,000 in damages.

After D. W. Griffith's three-hour *The Birth of a Nation* had shattered all records ("like writing history in lightning," Woodrow Wilson described it) and proved that the sky was indeed the limit, *Ben-Hur* again attracted producers' attention. But Henry Wallace, son and now owner of the rights to the volume that, apart from the Bible, had sold more copies than any book in history, loathed the movies. By 1919, however, he relented and let it be known he might sell the screenrights for $400,000. Zukor, Griffith, and Loew expressed interest, but *Ben-Hur's* theatrical co-producer, Abraham Erlanger, formed a partnership with Charles Dillingham and Florenz Ziegfeld, bought the rights for $600,000, and, in 1921, offered them for sale for a million dollars.

Erlanger and his partners, as it turned out, were too greedy. Griffith's daring *Intolerance* (1916) was the most expensive picture ever made and it had not cost a million dollars *finished!* In 1922, Frank Godsol persuaded Erlanger to entrust the Goldwyn Company with *Ben-Hur*. No money down, but Erlinger and his partners would receive one-half of every dollar the picture earned. Convicted on embezzlement charges in Paris during the war for selling its own mules to the French government, Godsol was a tall, handsome ladies' man, who, by marriage, was a relative of Broadway's producer Al Woods. He had convinced people like the Du Pont de Nemours, the theatrical Shuberts, and Woods that he knew more about movies than Samuel Goldwyn and had managed to have Goldwyn resign from his own company. In one of his last reckless gambles for the Goldwyn Co., Godsol also gave von Stroheim the go-ahead on *Greed*.

By the time Willy and all other available assistants were told to report to work in Culver City, the failing Goldwyn Co. had merged with Metro to become the middle-name of Metro-Goldwyn-Mayer and Godsol had disappeared. *Ben-Hur* had been in production in Italy for nearly two years and was rapidly becoming the most expensive movie ever made. The immensity of the historical drama and the problems of staging numerous spectacle scenes had made for delays and misadventures. Loew had finally appealed to his management team on the Coast and Mayer and Thalberg had fired the original director, Charles Brabin, and thrown out most of the footage. They had picked Fred Niblo as director and young Ramon Novarro as Ben-Hur, while retaining Francis X. Bushman as Messala. After yet another year's disastrous shooting in Italy—marked by armed clashes between Fascist and anti-Mussolini extras, hushed-up drownings of poor fishermen who had lied themselves into extra jobs for the sea battles—Mayer had sounded the retreat in January 1925.

Cedric Gibbons, MGM's chief art director and later designer of the Academy Awards Oscar statuette, had conceived a new plaster Circus Maximus that in four months four hundred workmen had erected on a five-acre lot off Venice Boulevard.

Willy and other unemployed assistants were called in for the opening day's shooting of the chariot race for which some three thousand extras were on call. Forty-two cameramen were hired for the sequence and *le tout-Hollywood* crammed the Circus Maximus. Directors turned up en masse for the event—Reginald Barker, George Fitzmaurice, Henry King, and, from Universal, Clarence Brown. The cameras were concealed in high statues, buried in pits, hidden behind soldiers' shields. The cameramen shot fifty-three thousand feet of film. There were twelve chariots and forty-eight horses. Stuntmen drove ten of them, and Bushman and Novarro drove their own for this special day. To insure a real hell-for-leather epic race, a special bonus was offered to the stunt drivers—mostly cowboys. The fact that the race was fixed for Ben-Hur didn't matter; that day was being devoted to establishing shots with massed crowds. Ben-Hur would win some other day. Bets were placed in the crowd and the stuntmen put on an astonishing display. One race was enlivened by a spectacular pileup.

"I was paid ten dollars for that day—a lot of money," Willy recalled. "I was given a toga and a set of signals. The signals were a sort of semaphore, and I got my section of the crowd to stand up and cheer and to sit down again, or whatever Niblo called for. Each assistant had a couple of hundred of extras in his section."

45

Niblo directed from a podium with the help of a megaphone as big as himself. He had a list of the assistants in charge of the different sections. Behind him were the star visitors and executives from all studios in a specially constructed gallery.

"Over this outsized megaphone, I suddenly heard my name," Willy remembered. "I came running to Mr. Niblo standing on his podium and he told me what he wanted from my section. I looked up behind him and there was the man who had just fired me at Universal. He was very impressed. It looked as if I were Fred Niblo's right-hand man. The next day, I was hired back at Universal."

Thirty-three years later when Willy stood on the podium in Rome's Cinecitta directing the opening sequence of the chariot race of his own *Ben-Hur,* he had Charlton Heston and Stephen Boyd, the charioteers and the thousand extras wait five expensive minutes while he told the story of Fred Niblo and his assistants and asked the thirty-odd assistants disguised in the crowd, "Which one of you is going to be the director of the next *Ben-Hur?"*

5

Willy beat Fred Niblo to the screen. By the time *Ben-Hur* opened at the George M. Cohan Theater in New York on December 30, 1925, *Crook Buster* had been in release for four days. That both could be projected on screens was about all the two pictures had in common. The completed *Ben-Hur,* which had finally cost just under four million dollars, was an epic, and, on the whole, a world success although banned in Italy and China. Mussolini had imagined the magnificent Roman and not the Jewish charioteer to be the hero, while in China the picture was called "Christian propaganda decoying the people to superstition." The film grossed more than $9 million, but the distribution costs and Godsol's original deal giving fifty percent of all earnings to Erlanger and his partners left MGM with a net deficit of a million dollars. *Ben-Hur* was reissued with music and sound effects in an abridged version in 1931, but was found old-fashioned by talkie-struck audiences and passed into legend.

Willy Wyler's first film was a two-reel western. After his star performance under Niblo's podium at the Circus Maximus, he was determined to make the grade as a director. His chance came one day up on Mulholland Drive when old Bill Craft yawned and said he had a dentist's appointment. Craft had directed bigger things in his day and wasn't exactly burning with enthusiasm over a two-bit western.

"You know what happens here," Craft grumbled to his assistant. "You can shoot the scene, can't you?"

"Yes, yes!"

"Okay, you shoot."

Craft got in a saddle and majestically rode down the hill toward the production cars. He never looked back. The next day, Craft was back behind the megaphone and no roar was heard from Isadore Bernstein, Universal's "supervisor" of westerns. What Willy had shot that afternoon was neither too superior nor too inferior not to look like Craft's footage.

Next, Willy was assigned to Arthur Rosson, a more ambitious filmmaker doing time on westerns while waiting word from Paramount on a full-length feature that he and Ben Hecht had written about a Chicago gunman. Rosson and Hecht were both newcomers and *Underworld* was an eighteen page idea of Hecht's, a newspaperman lured west by his former colleague, Herman Mankiewicz, and now gainfully employed in the Paramount writers' pool. Mankiewicz, who was to write *Citizen Kane,* had taught Hecht all there was to know about writing movies. "I want to point out to you that in a novel, a hero can lay ten girls and marry a virgin for a finish," Mankiewicz had explained. "In a movie, this is not allowed. The hero, as well as the heroine, has to be a virgin. The villain can lay anybody he wants, have as much fun as he wants cheating and stealing, getting rich and whipping the servants. But you have to shoot him in the end. When he falls with a bullet in his forehead, it is advisable that he clutch at the Gobelin tapestry on the library wall and bring it down over his head like a symbolic shroud. Also, covered by such a tapestry, the actor does not have to hold his breath while he is being photographed as a dead man." [1]

Underworld derived logically from Mankiewicz's lesson. It contained no heroes or heroines, only villains and their molls, a formula Hecht was to remember when Howard Hughes hired him to write *Scarface.* Hecht underestimated the powers of rectitude, however, and *Underworld* was censored into a moralizing tale.[2]

Hecht and Rosson expanded the writer's original eighteen pages and when the word came that Rosson had been chosen to direct the film, he quit Universal and the western he was directing on the spot.

"Why don't you let him finish it," Rosson told Bernstein, pointing toward Willy.

Uncle Carl was, by chance, on the Coast and Willy was too impatient to miss the opportunity. He immediately requested a meeting with Laemmle. When he was ushered in, he told Uncle Carl he wanted to be a director.

"You think you know how?" Laemmle asked, at the same time pressing his intercom and asking his secretary to have Bernstein come in.

"Yes, I do," Willy lied.

When Bernstein arrived, Laemmle was laughing.

"This boy here says he can direct. Let's see if he can," Laemmle told the western supervisor.

"But it's too soon," Bernstein protested. "He's not ready."

"Let's see if he's telling the truth." Laemmle said. "Give him a two-reeler."

Rosson never finished *Underworld*. He was replaced by Josef von Sternberg. But Willy got to finish the Universal two-reeler.* Behind closed doors, Laemmle and Bernstein screened the picture and the next day, Willy was called into Bernstein's office. "Look, Willy, I'm gonna give you a *whole* two-reeler," Bernstein grunted. "Let's see what you can do."

The climb to full director called for one change. Even if his legal name was Willy, people kept telling him that in English, it sounded like a diminutive. Willy was what you'd call a boy. William *sounded* adult.

Although twenty-three, Willy still looked like a teen-ager. For years to come, he was to lie about his age but take offense when Mervyn Le Roy, two years his senior, called himself the youngest director in Hollywood.

Crook Buster was one of the 135 Mustang two-reelers Universal made between 1925 and 1927. The Mustang serial starred such cowboys as Edmond Cobb, Fred Gilman, Jack Mower, the Ben Corbett–Gilbert "Peewee" Holmes duo, and Ted Wells. The eleven credited directors on the series were (in alphabetical order): John O'Brien, Lew Collins, William Crinley, Hoot Gibson, George Hunter, Edward Kull, Ernest Laemmle, Vin Moore, Victor Nordlinger, Ray Taylor, and William Wyler.

Gibson was himself a cowboy star, a leftover from John Ford's Universal days. Laemmle and Nordlinger were two other young

---

* Rosson (1889–1960) did stay with Paramount and became DeMille's second-unit director—a profession he practically invented while an assistant to Allan Dwan in 1918. For sixteen years, Rosson was DeMille's "associate director."

men Uncle Carl had brought over.* Besides Wyler, the only other Mustang directors to attain simple lexicographical notoriety were Moore and Taylor. Vin Moore (1878–1949) started directing in 1917 and remained a B-picture maker until 1940. Ray Taylor (1888–1949) started as an assistant to Ford and directed action pictures until his death.

Wyler made twenty-one Mustangs, beginning with *Crook Buster,* starring Jack Mower, and ending with *Daze in the West,* a comical little fantasy about the making of a two-reel western.

"It was all routine, but it taught you the business of movement," Wyler recalled. "It was all action. We didn't have real actors, but cowboys who could ride. I made a test of cowboys one day. The test consisted of riding down the western street, making a flying dismount, running up to the camera, counting to ten and making a Pony Express mount, which was getting on a horse already running. That was the test. Years later, Gary Cooper told me he had been one of the hopefuls in my test. He wasn't fast enough, I guess, because he wasn't hired.

"The two-reelers were a training school for everybody, even girls. Any young fellow who showed he was eager, ambitious, and wanted to get to direct a western could get it. It wasn't hard. The whole picture cost two thousand dollars and wasn't any great risk for the studio. Also, if a pretty girl came on the lot, they'd put her in a western. That was her test. If she looked good on the screen, they'd sign her up.

"I got sixty dollars a week. The cameraman got seventy-five. I did try to make the pictures a little different, to invent a little something that would make them interesting. The studio didn't care what you did. You had great leeway. If you wanted to change the script, fine. You didn't have to ask anybody. The stories were elementary. They were all formula, but they had to have action."

After *Crook Buster,* Wyler made five more Mustangs starring Jack Mower—*The Gunless Bad Man, Ridin' For Love, Fire Barrier, Don't Shoot,* and *The Pinnacle Rider. Fire Barrier* contained excellent stuntwork by Mower and had a grand forest fire

---

* Besides Ern(e)st, there was also Edward Laemmle as Universal's western director. Ernst, born in Munich in 1900, directed such items as *Broncho Buster* and *One Man's Game* and became a foreign dialogue supervisor during the changeover to talkies in 1930. Edward, born in Chicago (1887–1936), directed *Cheating Cheaters, 13th Juror,* and *Held by the Law.*

finale, apparently footage from another, more ambitious Universal western. *Don't Shoot* had Fay Wray as the leading lady. This Canadian beauty queen had entered the movies under Hal Roach after a short career in the theater and soon graduated to more dramatic roles. *Don't Shoot* was one of her last two-reelers before being discovered by Erich von Stroheim and cast as his leading lady in *The Wedding March.* Another girl who passed through a Wyler two-reeler was Janet Gaynor, later in Frank Borzage's *Seventh Heaven* and F. W. Murnau's heroine in *Sunrise.*

Leading ladies and bit actresses all offered possibilities but precious few actual affairs. Wyler got himself a little black book and collected names and phone numbers. The field was increased further when he got his first car—a secondhand 1925 Chevrolet coupe—but even for an up-and-coming film director, the girls "willing to go all the way" were few and far between. "You might have a date with a girl for a soda, but there was damn little sex," he recalled. "Sometimes, you'd work on a girl for a week, for two weeks and maybe make it. Or maybe not."

One thing that made him switch on the engine again when he was sitting in the Chevrolet smooching with a girl under the stars on Mulholland Drive was the slightest hint of marriage.

"I was determined never to get married, or at least not until I was forty." Evelyn Pierson, the first real romance, was still months away.

Following the Jack Mower quintet of two-reelers, Wyler made a trio with Edmond Cobb as his star—*Martin of the Mounted, Two Fister,* and *Kelcy Gets His Man.* After *Tenderfoot Courage,* starring Fred Gilman, he made *The Silent Partner,* a title used twice before, followed by *Galloping Justice.* Also with Gilman, he did *The Lone Star* and *The Ore Riders,* the latter containing enough action to fill an entire feature.

Doing two of them back to back, Wyler went to Lone Pine on location. Bad weather set him a day behind schedule and the company was ordered back whether or not the second of the two two-reelers was finished.

"I had photographed the exterior of a shack with Mount Whitney in the background and could of course shoot the ending at a cabin set at the studio. We had only a couple of hours left that afternoon before wrapping up and we had to have entrances and exits even if I didn't know how to end the picture.

"I thought I had better get all the characters inside the shack, then on the way home figure out the ending and shoot that the next day at the studio. So we didn't just film everybody going in and coming out of the shack, but everybody going in and coming out in every conceivable way—the boy and the girl together, the boy and the girl separately, the villain alone, the villain coming out shot, the characters riding up fast, riding up slow, coming in on foot, crawling in, coming in through the door, breaking through the window, coming out wounded, carrying the girl out."

Since the beginning of Universal City, Uncle Carl had charged twenty-five cents to people wanting to watch filmmakers at work. When shooting on the back lot, Wyler & Co. had a regular act to get rid of these spectators. It started with Wyler calling the leading man.

"Hey, come here! We're making a picture here, what's the idea of keeping me waiting!"

"Listen, I'm the star of this show. Be careful how you talk to me!" the cowboy would answer.

"I'm the *director* of this picture."

They would get into a big argument. With the visitors holding their breath, Wyler would suddenly grab a breakaway bottle and hit his star over the head. The cowboy would get a breakaway chair and hit back. The spectators usually fled at this point although there were instances when burly men wanted to join in the fun.

Another way of getting rid of crowds was to end the argument with faking the death of one of the antagonists. Suddenly, Wyler would pull a sixshooter and pump the cowboy full of bullets—catsup running from stomach wounds. As director, Willy now had assistants and once his crew pulled a fast one on Edgar Ulmer, a Viennese assistant to Max Reinhardt whom Uncle Carl had brought over and who later also became a director. The stunt was done on a stage and was very elaborate, involving an argument, a shooting, and the lights going out. "When the lights came on again," Willy remembered, "one of the fellows was lying sprawled in his blood and Edgar stood over him, dumbfounded, with a gun in his hand. He didn't know how he had gotten the gun. As he stood there watching his 'victim' in horror, a studio sheriff, who was in on it, put a hand on his shoulder, telling him he was under arrest for murder."

Ulmer fainted. When they brought him to and told him it was all a joke, he fainted again.

Wyler made five more with Gilman—*The Home Trail, Gun Justice, The Phantom Outlaw* (another popular title of silent westerns), *Square Shooter,* and *The Horse Trader,* the latter apparently shelved for slightly over a year after its completion. *The Phantom Outlaw* gave Willy his first newspaper review. "This Mustang western has the usual ingredients of thrilling riding and hard hitting, in addition to a mystery angle which will provide the thrill hunters with a very desirable fare," [3] the New York *Daily Review* wrote.

Two months later, the *Daily Review* mentioned Wyler by name in its two-paragraph review of *The Home Trail.* "The action starts right off at a merry clip, introducing some corking riding," the paper said. "A snappy story, capably handled by William Wyler, keeps the interest well sustained." [4]

The last two-reeler Willy made was the one he remembered with the greatest affection. *Daze in the West* was the story of a movie company going on location on a ranch to shoot a western. The star of the film within the film was a pansy who dressed up for the part with silver spurs but couldn't ride very well or do any stunts. The plot had the director look among the ranch hands for someone to double for the star, which was where the real star came in. Billy Engle, a pint-sized scenarist who had been a Keystone Kop for Mack Sennett, wrote the movie-within-the-movie plot. Running into Vin Moore on the lot, Wyler asked him if he would play his director.

"Okay," grinned Moore, "if you play my assistant."

A couple of dozen two-reelers back when Wyler had been Vin's assistant, Moore had had his company in stitches by luring his apprentice into the cage of an old, toothless lion, slipping out himself and, for half an hour, telling the frightened Wyler just to stand still while somebody supposedly was fetching the key.

If Wyler thought *Daze in the West* was going to be his revenge, he was mistaken. The picture almost never got in the can so convulsive was Wyler's laughter when it came to shoot the scenes with the director and his assistant. Moore showed up in puttees and with an outsized megaphone and hammed it up as Cecil B. DeMille.

"When we were both in front of the camera, he'd strut around and in mime make me understand that as an assistant all I had to do was always to be behind him with his canvas chair. He'd get up and walk to a new position and sit down without looking back. I'd better be behind him with the chair. Everytime he did something, he broke me up laughing."

Wyler had to yell "Cut!" and start over again only to be confronted with new gags. It was only when he invented a saving twist that he could get behind the real camera and finish *Daze in the West:* he had Moore fire him as his on-camera assistant.

In the fall of 1926, Wyler made the next big step up, directing his first full-length feature. Bernstein assigned him to the new five-reel Blue Streak series.

Fifty-three Blue Streak westerns were produced by Universal between 1925 and 1927. The series' directors included Albert Rogell, Clifford S. Smith, and G. Dell Henderson. Rogell was to settle into a career in B pictures for Columbia with an occasional A thrown in, such as *Song of India* (1949), the original Sabu picture. Smith, who had directed the Griffith Park duel sequence which had allowed Willy to make his maiden flight, went on to make Tom Mix and William S. Hart westerns at Fox while Henderson became a character actor in the 1930s. Wyler directed seven Blue Streaks.

Five-reelers were a big advance. Each of these formula westerns cost $20,000. The actors were cowboys, but considered stars and although the pictures had to have a lot of action, there was room for character development and for plot. Nothing elaborate was attempted—lights were never used outdoors, only reflectors which also served as the leading lady's folding screens when she changed costume. A simple mirror was usually used to highlight her hair, and when there were no reflectors, she changed behind a bush. Production manager Martin Murphy was there to keep the lid on expenses, always trying to cut down the posse from eight cowboys ($7.50 each per day) to six or from six to four. Going on location meant living two or three to a room in claptrap hotels, but going out of town added "production values" to the film. "Stealing the train" was one "value" not possible on the back lot. No budget included provisions for rental of rolling railway stock and "stealing" a train meant setting everything up in advance and having the 4:40 roll into camera range. In Lone Pine, Willy staged a whole sequence complete with stagecoach and badmen riding up during the ten minutes the Union Pacific was at the station.

Wyler's first Blue Streak, filmed while he was in the midst of his romance with Evelyn Pierson, was *Lazy Lightning,* a tale of dark conniving to get a crippled boy's inheritance. It was written by Harrison Jacobs, a prolific scenarist who dreamed up Hopalong Cassidy plots during the early talkie wave of "singing cowboy" westerns.

"It was a corny little story," Wyler recalled. "In the first shot, this cowboy was so lazy, he fell asleep on his horse. He never moved fast unless somebody needed rescuing."

Lazy Lightning starred Art Acord.

"He was not a great actor, but he had a kind of sincerity," Wyler remembered. "He wasn't handsome but he looked good on a horse. Also, he was a nice fellow and we got along fine."

Acord had started under Art Rosson in the *Bison* serial and was to commit suicide in 1931, another victim of sound. Fay Wray was the heroine and, surprising or not, considering their hilarious differences on *Daze in the West,* Vin Moore played the sheriff. Bobby Gordon, who later became a director, was the boy in the wheelchair.

Stolen Ranch, released December 26, 1926, also told a story of an inheritance. With Fred Humes playing a war veteran returning to find his dead uncle's ranch claimed by usurpers, *Stolen Ranch* had William Norton Bailey playing the villain and Louise Lorraine (in actual life, Mrs. Art Acord), the neighboring rancher's daughter who never loses faith.

Next came *Blazing Days,* written by Florence Ryerson, a newspaperman's daughter who was later to become the screenwriter of *Wizard of Oz.* Universal released *Blazing Days* with Humes in the lead on February 27, 1927, and two months later *Hard Fists,* starring Acord and Miss Lorraine, a story of a ranchhand with a shady past who is blackmailed into continuing his evil ways until he rescues a woman, becomes enamored with her daughter, and is reformed by her love.

Again with Humes high in the saddle, with Joyce Compton as the honest rancher's daughter, and with Willy's girlfriend, Evelyn Pierson, a "featured player," Wyler made *The Border Cavalier,* a comedy-drama where the comedy quartet of Gilbert "Peewee" Holmes, "Smilin'" Benny Corbett, Dick L'Estrange, and Scott

Mattraw ran away with the show. It earned Wyler his first *Variety* review, a back-handed compliment to the directing. The trade-paper critique (which failed to mention Miss Pierson) called the film an instance of "spirited filming of the oldest of old stuff. Whole formula is here: land shark, cow country, divekeeper, hard-riding hero, honest rancher and beautiful daughter, not to speak of the dancehall girl." [5]

Next, Wyler made *Straight Shootin'*, another western with both comic and romantic moments. It starred a new Universal cowboy from Texas who was to have his career clipped by sound—Ted Wells. The leading lady was Lillian Gilmore, a Gish-like girl who was also a newcomer to westerns. The story of the gold mine, the menace, and happy ending for hero and heroine was close to formula. The fact that the old and injured father was allowed to live in the fadeout to make the hero guardian of his daughter was a novel twist.

Straight Shootin' was also reviewed by *Variety* and called "one of the usual westerns . . . with enough riding, shooting and fist fights to meet the needs of the market it was created for." [6] The *Chicago Herald* was more charitable, calling Ted Wells "a two-fisted, hard-riding young fellow who rather looks and acts like Jack Dempsey and who has not yet become so used to production activities that he hasn't still some natural modesty." [7] The picture was scripted by William Lester, who wrote a total of eleven of Wyler's two- and five-reel westerns. *Shooting Straight* had been the title of the western that had made John Ford into a feature director in 1917. Ford was supposed to have made a Harry Carey two-reeler, but he stretched his story about homesteaders and cattle barons reconciling over a newborn baby to five reels. When Uncle Carl happened to sit in on the screening with Bernstein, the superviser told the boss the picture was going to be cut down to two reels. Laemmle wondered why.

"Well," Bernstein replied, "it was only supposed to be a two-reeler."

To which Laemmle observed that if he ordered a suit of clothes and the tailor gave him an extra pair of trousers free, he wasn't going to throw the pants back in the man's face.[8]

Wyler's last Blue Streak western was *Desert Dust*, starring Ted Wells. This time it was a tale about a young rancher paroled into the custody of a wealthy senator's daughter. With Lotus Thompson playing the heroine, *Desert Dust* was a contemporary western which featured no desert and not a speck of dust, but a last-reel chase with the hero riding faster than a speeding automobile to rescue the senator's daughter and retrieve his money from the fleeing crooks.

Robert had succumbed to Willy's tantalizing letters from America in 1925. Uncle Carl didn't mind a second and well-educated Wyler at Universal and let Robert start in the scenario department. With both Willy and Robert in America, Leopold and Melanie also made a trip over, spending the winter of 1925–26 in California before returning to Mulhouse. For the occasion, Willy rented a little house on Curson Avenue between Hollywood and Sunset boulevards. Melanie energetically set about learning English and nudged her sons to begin looking for wives.

Willy's interest in Evelyn Pierson had been brief but passionate. Even while on location in Long Pine, he had driven to Los Angeles to see her which meant leaving location after calling it a wrap at six P.M., driving six hours to L.A., spending two hours with Evelyn, and then driving the six hours back to Lone Pine to start the next day's directing.

Robert, who was a suave ladies' man—everybody at Universal called him "the Frenchman"—had his leg pulled while making the grade as a western assistant director. "There was a girl on the ranch where they were on location. My brother must have boasted that he had got some place with her, so to teach him a lesson, the cowboys and the crew told him the girl's brother had heard about it and was after him to kill him, challenging him to a duel on a fast draw. When they saw my brother believed them, they said the only thing to do was to ride to Mexico. They had it all arranged and said they had all chipped in and got him a little money and a horse. Robert had never been on a horse before. They carried on right up to the moment when they put him in the saddle before he found out it was all a joke."

Still in 1927, Willy directed *Thunder Riders*, a five-reeler again starring Wells in a script by Basil Dickey, the pioneer and forefather of all series. Dickey had started writing Pearl White *Perils of Pauline* cliffhangers and was still hacking out *Flash Gordon, Green Hornet,* and *Flying G-Men* scripts in the 1940s. In *Thunder Riders,* an eastern heiress (Charlotte Stevens) arrives on the ranch to take over her father's estate. Her guardians and a gang of cowhands stage a phony western atmosphere of primitive barbarism to make her sell, but she sees through their deceit. During the masquerade, the hero is locked up while the girl's eastern fiancé runs off with her to force her into a quick marriage. Much to everybody's surprise, it appears that the blue-blooded Bostonian is an ex-convict who is unmasked in the final reel by the hero. "Lots of wasted footage, but a few well-staged fist fights," was *Variety*'s comment.

Thunder Riders was the eighteenth picture Universal copyrighted in 1927 with William Wyler as the director, making this his most prolific year, with fifty-four reels—or over ten hours of final screentime—to his credit.

Yet it suddenly didn't mean anything. Ten days before *Straight Shootin'* went into release October 16, Warner Brothers had Al Jolson's shadow sing from the silver screen in *The Jazz Singer*. Within a single year, every important picture would "talk" and the public would forget that the silent film ever existed.

6

Lights! Camera! *Interlock!*

The talkies not only crippled careers of stars whose voices recorded as a high-pitched squeak, they dislocated the whole industry. The casualties were enormous. Scriptwriters who had trained themselves to think in terms of pictures gave way to playwrights who thought dialogue. Established filmmakers were either replaced by New York stage directors hauled west with few questions asked or humiliated by special dialogue directors.

Sound *was* a whole new world. Sets became silent as tombs. When the new tyrant, the soundman, turned on his red light, everybody froze in his position—a cough or a belch would wreck the scene. "To the nervous snit of the non-stage silent actors— over having to memorize lines for the first time—the funereal hush added the willies. They shook with stage fright," Frank Capra recalled.[1] Metro-Goldwyn-Mayer hoisted a "silence" balloon to warn aircraft that they were shooting sound.

Wyler first met the new mandarin called the sound engineer after he had made *Anybody Here Seen Kelly?*, a comedy about an American soldier returning home to New York after World War I and his French sweetheart coming to look for him. Starring Tom Moore and Bessie Love, the film was shot as a silent picture during the summer of '28.

For Wyler, this was again a big step. This Irish program comedy was his first nonwestern. It had a commanding budget of $60,000 and director, cast, and crew were allowed to go to New

York for exteriors. *Anybody Here Seen Kelly?* had Jeanette Lavelle (Bessie Love) in love with swaggering Pat Kelly (Tom Moore), a member of the American Expeditionary Force who, with Irish generosity, invites every French gal to come to America and be his wife. Pat tells everybody he is a bigshot back in New York, someone who just has to lift a hand for everything to come to a stop. Jeanette takes the suave Irishman at his word. Before leaving France, Pat gives her a postcard of New York's Metropolitan Museum and tells her that this is his residence. Getting herself a job as a stewardess on an ocean liner, Jeanette follows her Pat. Arriving in New York, she is met by Buck Jones (Tom O'Brien), once a rival for her hand and now a U.S. Immigration official. Jeanette rejects him, finds her Pat, and proceeds to settle down with him with the confidence of a girl who believes she is loved. Johnson, however, attempts to have her deported while her jealous Pat is held in jail for assaulting him. Assisted by an Irish sergeant, Pat manages to claim Jeanette before the ship sails and marries her, thereby thwarting Johnson's sinister intentions of having her deported.

Wyler shot Miss Love's search for Pat as a documentary. He concealed his camera in a closed laundry pushcart to film her disappointment when she reached the Metropolitan Museum. Her search through the streets of New York was also shot *cinéma direct*-style, including her finally spotting him—a policeman directing traffic on the 42nd Street–Broadway intersection, standing with outstretched arms in the middle of the flow of traffic. Jeanette ran out to him also stretching her arms. At the emotional impact, she managed to turn him enough to make his outstretched arms command the side traffic to pour forward. "I told you, I just have to lift my hand and everything stops," was the payoff line in the ensuing traffic jam which took an hour to untangle.

"I almost went to jail for that," Wyler chuckled later. "I had cameras everywhere, in cars, in taxis, up in windows. We couldn't rehearse. I just sent Bessie out in the middle of the street to kiss him."

Anybody Here Seen Kelly? was a pleasant program picture. "Frequently the simplest screen stories are the most interesting," the *Los Angeles Express* wrote, adding that the film introduced "among other things, a new young director, Willie [sic] Wyler,

who gets a lot of charm, both Irish and French, in his work." [2]
The film even pleased in France and earned Wyler his first foreign reviews. In London, *Today's Cinema* agreed the story might be simple, "but few popular patrons will be able to resist the compelling appeal of its treatment." [3] The Paris *Hebdo* wrote a funny, argot-filled synopsis of *Un Coeur à la traine*. "After having won the war—all by themselves as everybody knows—the American soldiers recrossed the pond, leaving dragging behind the hearts of our cousins, aunts, wives, mistresses and mothers-in-law," the review began. [4]

Meanwhile, Wyler was handed *The Shakedown,* a boxing movie involving fixed fights. For the part of Dave Roberts, a young man sent ahead to towns to become known for his boxing prowess, Wyler got Universal to hire James Murray, an actor he had seen in King Vidor's silent masterpiece *The Crowd* two years earlier. Willy's leading lady was a Universal contract player, Barbara Kent, who had just been in Reginald Denny's *That's My Daddy.* To play the villain, Battling Roff, Wyler found a Greek boxer, George Kotsonaros.

When the New York sales people saw *The Shakedown,* they liked it enough to send it back to Hollywood with instructions to put on twenty-five percent sound.

Wyler was called into a conference where Roy Hunter, the new sound department chief, asked him if he knew how to say "Good morning." Others had looked puzzled or admitted they didn't know. Willy didn't blink, but said, "Sure, I know. I say it every morning."

Flippant or not, it worked.

"Most directors thought talking pictures were a big mystery," Wyler recalled. "I decided then and there that people should talk naturally. I had always been concerned with what people said in front of a camera. In silent pictures, people talked, of course. It didn't matter what they said—except to deaf-mute lip-readers—as long as their expression was right. If a fellow came in to argue with someone, he had to *look* argumentative. A lot of times actors said all kinds of nonsense or they counted to ten. It always bothered me. They said, 'What the hell does it matter as long as I have the right attitude!' I said, 'Yes, but it *bothers* me.'"

Wyler welcomed sound and immediately realized its storytelling potential. He also found talkies more honest. "We used to be able to change the story in the cutting room with a title. With a title you could add to the plot, clarify, and even alter the story. The moment an actor opened his mouth to say yes, we could put in a title saying 'no.' With sound, this was no longer possible."

The first encounter with the awesome soundman and his ear-phones plugged into black magic boxes with dials and knobs was intimidating. "He was up under the rafters of Universal's only sound stage, like God. After a scene, everybody looked up to hear His verdict. If He had heard the words properly, it was okay. If not, you had to repeat."

Soundmen ran Hollywood for a nervous couple of months. They concealed microphones in flowerpots, dictated where actors could stand in order to record, yelled "Cut!" if an actor turned his head away from the mike. Since sound film ran at twenty-four frames per second instead of sixteen, it meant twice as much light was needed to expose the same strip of film and actors already nervous were soaked to the skin under the heat of added candle-power.

Like other directors momentarily knocked out, Wyler began to reclaim the lost territory. As Ford did on *Napoleon's Barber*, Capra on *It Is to Laugh* and Vidor on *Hallelujah*, Wyler chose to make his stand on the now verboten moving of the camera. He was shooting sound versions of scenes already filmed silent and re-membered how he had moved the camera in on James Murray or little Jack Hanlon the first time around.

"You can't do that," the sound engineer protested.

"Why not?" Wyler shouted back toward the rafters.

"It'll make noise."

"I'll move it *without* making noise."

With the help of fourteen hefty stagehands, the shack-sized blimp—Michael Curtiz called it an "ice house"—with camera and cameraman inside was moved. The taming of sound was far from over, however, only postponed to *Hell's Heroes*.

As with *Anybody Here Seen Kelly?*, *The Shakedown* had been discovered by Robert. At Universal, Willy's elder brother had now spent two years learning. His field, it seemed, was to be producing—or "supervising" as it was called. He had found the Leigh Jason story that, with the help of six scenario writers, had become *Anybody Here Seen Kelly?* [5] and, together with Charles

Logue, had a hand in writing *The Shakedown*. A supervisor was something new, but 1929 was a year of upheaval.

Uncle Carl was now sixty-two and relinquishing his powers to his only son. The elder Laemmle was very devoted to Carl, Jr., whom everyone called simply Junior. After he had married Rosabelle to Stanley Bergerman, who was briefly to become studio boss when the old man and Junior had a falling out in 1935, Uncle Carl put his son in charge of the studio on his twenty-first birthday, April 28, 1929.

Junior's beginnings looked auspicious.

Universal was not—like MGM, Paramount and, now with sound, Warner Brothers—a major studio. It had made money producing inoffensive little comedies and low-budget westerns in the *Blue Streak* vein. The list of its stars under contract was substantial if not overly impressive. It included Lon Chaney, Margaret Sullavan (who was soon to become Mrs. William Wyler), Laura La Plante, William Powell, Edmund Lowe, Sally Eilers, Chester Morris, Paul Lukas, Russ Columbo, Boris Karloff, Buck Jones, Binnie Barnes, Slim Summerville, Zasu Pitts, Henry Hull, Victor Moore, and June Knight.

While Robert Cochrane and other executives groaned, Uncle Carl stood behind his son when Junior decided a major switch away from routine screenfare to big-budget features with challenging themes was necessary. Except for Vidor's 1926 *The Big Parade* for MGM, everyone knew that war pictures were box-office poison and every executive except the old man himself voted against Junior's first decision—to adapt Erich Maria Remarque's *All Quiet on the Western Front*.

Junior hired Lewis Milestone to direct (at $5,000 a week) and got playwright Maxwell Anderson to do the script. Director and screenwriter spent expensive weeks on Catalina Island writing, tearing up, and rewriting. Talkies were so new, Milestone wrote scenes as if they were silent and Anderson later added dialogue. The film was shot with an unknown in the lead, although Lew Ayres was to come out a star. The remarkable and angry film became a worldwide hit, hailed for its direct attack on the senseless human waste of war. *All Quiet* won the 1930 Academy Awards for best picture and best director and, in 1936, became the only movie ever proposed for a Nobel Peace Prize. Milestone was hailed as the American Sergei Eisenstein and Junior as the new boy wonder.

The Shakedown garnered Willy his first *New York Times* notice, a critique that was far from flattering. Calling the picture "a combination of romance, maudlin sentiment and pugilistic encounters," the review said it was "fairly well acted, but far better results could have been obtained from the players had the director, William Wyler, not been so keen to win sympathy." [6]

As the title implied, the picture was about the activities of a band of swindlers putting up fake fights. As written by Charles Logue, Clarence J. Marks, and Robert Wyler, the story had Dave sent ahead to a town to show off his boxing abilities, followed by his racketeer friends setting up fights with Battling Roff. The townsfolk, who have seen Dave's bravery in an emergency, eagerly wager on him. Since the fight is fixed, Dave is defeated by Roff. Love for Marjorie (Barbara Kent) and a little boy's blind admiration cause Dave to give up the racket and set things straight by engaging in a fair fight with Roff. The urchin, played by nine-year-old Jack Hanlon, nearly stole the show from James Murray and Barbara Kent.

Whatever the *New York Times* thought, the powers that be at Universal were sufficiently impressed by *Anybody Here Seen Kelly?* and *The Shakedown* not to veto Laura La Plante's choice of Wyler as her director in *The Love Trap*.

Miss La Plante was a comedienne married to William A. Seiter, a mundane director who loved golf as much as pictures and who was to make Shirley Temple and Abbott–Costello movies during the 1930s. Seiter had directed his wife in *Smiling Irish* and Frank Lloyd, who was about to start *Mutiny on the Bounty* with Charles Laughton, had had Miss La Plante as his leading lady in *Weary River*.

Before the Seiters would give their okay on Wyler, they decided to run *The Shakedown* at the studio one evening.

"I heard about that and I got into the booth with the projectionist for the screening," Wyler recalled. "Whenever there was anything remotely humorous on the screen, I laughed loud so as to make them think, 'If the projectionist thinks it's funny. . . .' Of course, I sneaked out just before the picture was over.

"They must have thought *The Shakedown* was all right because the next day, Laura La Plante said I could direct her. *The*

Love Trap was again a promotion. The cost here was maybe seventy-five thousand dollars, which meant better photography, better sets, better cast, more time—I had Neil Hamilton, who was very much in demand, as my leading man."

The story, written by Clymer (*Anybody Here Seen Kelly?*) and Marks (*The Shakedown*), is a comedy-drama with a backstage setting. The heroine, Evelyn Todd, appears in a series of quick establishing scenes—the stage of a theater from which she is ingloriously dismissed, a wild bachelor party at which she is a guest because of her good looks and from which she makes a dramatic escape when her host becomes too ardent. She returns home to find herself evicted because her rent is in arrears. A sudden storm finds her drenched and disconsolate in the midst of her furniture on the sidewalk, but a gallant young man (Neil Hamilton) comes to the rescue and invites her to seek shelter in his taxicab. "But what about my furniture?" she asks him. "I wouldn't be so heartless as to let helpless furniture suffer," he answers and three more taxis are chartered to convey the furniture, the fleet proceeding through the night into the country where demands for payment of the large sums registered on the meters lead to the ejection of passengers and furniture. At dawn, they set up the furniture in the woods and play husband and wife. *The Love Trap* was made "twenty-five percent sound." Wyler's first all-talkie was to be a raw western, *Hell's Heroes,* a picture that was to get him his first real attention.

7

The daylight raid on the Wickenburg National Bank that December morning had been well planned, boldly and cleverly executed, and the four bandits had gathered a fortune in paper money and gold. Nevertheless, the holdup was not a success. The assistant cashier's shouts had aroused all Wickenburg, Arizona, and an elderly citizen had shot one of the fleeing horsemen clear off his saddle and wounded another.

Tom Gibbons, Bill Kearny, and young Bob Sangster made it to the Colorado River that night, rode their jaded horses into the floor until the waters lapped their bellies, then shot them and shoved the carcasses off into the current. On the California side, they reckoned they were safe, even if Gibbons' shoulder wound didn't look too good. After resting, they struck out across the desert to the north toward the Santa Fe Railway tracks. There were lonely stations out there in the sands, like the new mining camp called New Jerusalem. After drinking deeply, bathing, and filling their canteens, they struck out for Terrapin Tanks, a little-known waterhole where they could rest for a few days before trying the last desperate leg to the railroad. Gibbons' shoulder was swollen and inflamed and it was a relief to him when the bandages were kept wet.

At Terrapin Tanks, they found the waterhole dry and, in a wagon without horses, a whimpering woman about to give birth. Her story was that instead of digging, her inexperienced husband had tried to dynamite water from the hole. He had cracked the granite floor, making the water run out in the sand. As the three men cursed and wished he had dynamited himself instead, the young woman told them he was now braving the desert, looking for help. Gibbons gave the woman a generous drink of water, young Sangster got a clean towel out of the tailbox. where he also found three tins of condensed milk. A boy was born at nightfall, but it was evident the mother would not live. She realized that herself. After asking each his name and naming her infant Robert William Thomas after them, she asked them to save her baby. With the rashness and generosity of youth, Sangster was the first to say yes. In turn, Gibbons and Kearny said they would help.

After they had made a coffin from the wagon boards and buried her, they set out on the forty-mile trek toward New Jerusalem. Kearny carried the last two canteens of water, Gibbons let go of his sixshooter and belt and carried the baby. Sangster carried nothing. His two companions both knew they would never make it and wanted to save young Sangster's strength until the end. Every six hours, they halted and Sangster fed the baby a mixture of tinned milk and water. Gibbons was the first to die, of his wounds and of thirst. Kearny died two days later, of thirst and madness, but after first pointing toward Cathedral Peaks on the horizon and telling Sangster how to reach New Jerusalem in one scorching day's march. On Christmas morning, Sangster reeled the last hundred yards into New Jerusalem, a bleeding, raving wreck of a man hugging a bundle to his breast. From a saloon, he heard organ music. As he stumbled inside, he held Robert William Thomas toward a woman and collapsed. Perhaps at that moment the woman, too, like the three bad men, beheld the King!

The Three Godfathers fascinated moviemakers more than once. The Victorian frontier retelling of the Gospel According to St. Matthew was written by Peter B. Kyne, a prolific writer whose short stories appeared in *Collier's, The Saturday Evening Post,* and *Sunset.* Kyne's most famous character was Cappy Ricks, a man whose favorite pastime through two novels was beating his son-in-law in big deals, but he also wrote such offbeat yarns as *They Also Serve,* World War I told from a horse's point of view. *The Three Godfathers,* published as a novel in 1913,[1] was an old Universal standby. A first version was made in 1916 starring Harry Carey and directed by Edward J. Le Saint, that oldest of silent pioneers who, in his eighties, was to become a talkie character actor. Again with Carey playing Sangster, John Ford remade it in 1917 as a five-reeler called *Marked Men.*

Following Wyler's 1929 version, *Hell's Heroes,* Richard Boleslawski made a new *The Three Godfathers* for MGM in 1936, this time with Chester Morris, Walter Brennan, and Lewis Stone atoning for their sins in the desert. The Polish-born director, who had just guided Greta Garbo through *The Painted Veil* and Charles Laughton through the remake of Victor Hugo's *Les Misérables,* lent his own touches to the story. He had Walter Brennan read Schopenhauer between violence and retribution and focused most of the interest on Sangster's regeneration.

A year after Carey's death in 1947, Ford returned to the old story and had *The Big Parade* scripter, Laurence Stalling, and ex-*New York Times* man Frank Nugent do a rewrite that changed the name of New Jerusalem to Welcome, made Gibbons into a Mexican, and in general sentimentalized it. Ford shot the 1948 *Three Godfathers* (sans article) in the Mojave Desert in thirty-one days with John Wayne playing Sangster and Pedro Armendariz and Harry Carey, Jr., as the sidekicks. The Technicolor version (camera: Winton C. Hoch) contained some of Ford's most beautiful photography of the American West, but after a promising start, characters and atmosphere bogged down in mawkish excess.

In later years, Ford's standing joke when running into Wyler was that it was now Willy's turn to remake *The Three Godfathers.*

Hell's Heroes was shot in the Mojave Desert and the Panamint Valley on the edge of Death Valley.

"It was the first all-sound, outdoor picture Universal made," Wyler remembered. "It was made under tremendous difficulties because the camera had to be muffled in the padded booth with a soundproof window in front and a padded door in the back. Of course, George Robinson, the cameraman, was stuffed into the booth *with* the camera. Since the story had the men fleeing or trying to reach salvation, I couldn't very well have them stop all the time to declaim. They *were* fugitives and had to move even when they spoke. So, we had to devise *moving* shots with dialogue. That meant putting the padded box on rails. Just imagine a dozen guys pushing this padded shack on rails in Death Valley in August in absolute silence. Microphones were concealed in cactus and sagebrush every ten feet or so.

"One time when we opened the door, the cameraman had fainted. He had passed out with the camera running. Outside, it was a hundred degrees, perhaps. *Inside* the Black Maria, it was a hundred and twenty degrees!"

Tom Reed's screenplay included a few ingenious twists on Kyne's original. There is no Wickenburg, only New Jerusalem, the town they both rob and have to return to. Once they become godfathers, they have to head *back* to New Jerusalem, knowing the fate awaiting them, even if they do make it, is hanging. Kearny and Gibbons die of thirst while Sangster deliberately drinks from a poisoned waterhole to make the last mile. Kyne leaves us with the impression that young Sangster's sacrifice and heroism have redeemed him, that he will live and, as he raved about in the desert, bring up Robert William Thomas. Finally, Sangster doesn't collapse in a saloon handing the baby to a Mary Magdalene but at a church step.

Hell's Heroes was Wyler's first adult work. It was the first film where he imposed his concept and where he showed he had broken with formula westerns. Despite the cameraman's objections that skies without clouds looked flat and unending and pancake landscapes were horrible, he forced Robinson not to prettify the photography.

"I want it to look horrible," he shot back at the cameraman, squinting into furnace vistas. He moved the company to ever more hellish locations and near Mojave, California, found pancake desert.

To send temperatures soaring further, Wyler had as a leading man an actor who was more than opinionated. Charles Bickford had been brought out by Cecil B. DeMille to star in *Dynamite*, after a meteoric career as a New York stage actor. Bickford's attitude toward Hollywood and Hollywood directors was, to put it politely, condescending. When it came to dialogue, he *knew* where they fumbled in the dark. The crunch came during the filming of Sangster's final day in the desert with the baby.

"He's dying of thirst, staggering forward and, in the next scenes, has to begin to shed things—first the rifle, then the gunnysack, then the gold, and finally, for a wild moment, the baby," Wyler recalled. "So, we discuss this and I suggest he should let the rifle drag in the sand for awhile and then just let it go."

"That's lousy," Bickford said.

"What's your idea?"

Bickford showed him, staggering along with the baby, finally looking at the rifle and, in a mad moment, throwing it.

"No matter how far you throw it in the desert, it's gonna look like nothing," Wyler said. "I don't think it's so good."

"Well, that's the way I'm going to do it."

"Why don't we try it both ways?"

Bickford would not budge and refused to shoot it Wyler's way.

"Well, on a day when he wasn't working, I got someone to wear his boots and I shot it *my* way," Wyler remembered. "I didn't shoot the boots, just the tracks they made. It was easier on Robinson, also, since it didn't have to have any sound. I shot the footprints. First, they went straight, then weaving, then you saw a place where he had fallen and picked himself up, then suddenly a crease appeared along the footprints. You didn't know what it was—just this crease and, after a while, you saw the rifle lying there.

"I said, 'I'll fool this guy.' Then I said to myself, 'Why stop here?' I made a longer track and shot slightly erratic boot prints, then the gunnysack. Then more boot prints, then the gold, spread out in the sand, then the hat or something, and finally, the baby lying there. I did the whole thing without him even knowing it."

Hell's Heroes had its measure of sentimentality, but it succeeded in catching the spirit of westerns of two decades earlier— and four decades later, when badmen could be heroes. The picture disregarded the 1930 imperative of a happy ending and Charles Bickford's Sangster was played in the best tradition of William S. Hart. Fred Kohler played Kearny, Raymond Hatton was Gibbons, and Fritzi Ridgeway the woman dying in labor. *Hell's Heroes* was edited to a spare sixty-five minutes during the fall and released January 5, 1930.

"It was uncompromising, completely bleak and it received a great deal of attention," Wyler recalled. "I was completely unknown and [Darryl] Zanuck, who was running Warner Brothers, sent out a memo to all his directors telling them to catch this picture by this new director and to pay particular attention to an inventive sequence where the camera tracks along boot prints in the desert."

Universal was happy enough with *Hell's Heroes* to give Wyler a new contract and to nurse the picture carefully into release.

The *New York Times* said, without mentioning Wyler's name, that "despite its title, which means little to the story, *Hell's Heroes* happened to be an interesting and realistic bit of characterization about three men who suffer retribution in the desert and undergo privations in their wish to atone for a crime." [2]

The New York edition of *Variety* called the picture, "gripping, real and convincingly out of the ordinary." [3]

In The *New York Post,* a young writer with whom Willy was one day to work called *Hell's Heroes* a "daring new direction in talkies." "Vidor's *Hallelujah,*" Robert E. Sherwood wrote, "was a first attempt at new things and recently, we have seen three even more daring attempts—*Hell's Heroes,* directed by William Wyler, *Seven Days Leave,* the infinitely touching realization of J. M. Barrie's best play and now, [Ford's] *Men Without Women.*" The future playwright said it was "heartening to observe that the impulse to experiment, to run worthy risks in the effort to create something new, is not entirely dead in Hollywood." [4]

Hell's Heroes grossed $18,000 during its first week in New York and was soon tagged "Universal's best dialog picture" by *Variety.* In San Francisco, it broke the Casino Theatre's house record and the pattern continued in Chicago and Philadelphia. The reason was obvious—the public was getting a little tired of the backstage stories, revues, and stage adaptations of the first flush of talkies. *Hell's Heroes* was realism with a bang and the picture became a holdover in all major cities. In February, it appeared on newspapers' best-of-the-month lists (along with Greta Garbo in Clarence Brown's *Anna Christie.*)

The success continued overseas. *Les Héros de l'enfer* was "unforgettable" *Cinémonde* said [5] and in Berlin, *Höllen Helden* was a sensation, with Will (sic) Wyler singled out as "a director to remember."

But a new contract, more money, critical and box-office attention didn't mean escape from the grind and before Wyler could imagine himself the Griffith of the talkies, he was handed a triangle drama of two men and a girl in the snowbound wilderness of arctic Canada. Again, it was a talkie remake of a silent Universal picture. By Willy's own admission, *The Storm* was to remain his worst film.

Langdon McCormick's play, *Men without Skirts,* had been filmed in 1916 by Paramount. Reginald Barker, who had been

Thomas Ince's right hand and Universal's great outdoor director (but wasn't making it across the sound barrier), had made a second version in 1922.

Written by Wells Root and Charles Logue, *The Storm* starred vivacious Mexican actress Lupe Velez as Manette, the Québecois lass stranded in a cabin with two men for a whole winter. William Boyd and Paul Cavanaugh played Burr and Dave, two men who were the closest of friends, one having risked his life during the war to save his comrade, the other saving his friend's mine by arriving in the nick of time with needed capital. But when Manette, the daughter of a smuggler shot by the Mounties, arrives in the log cabin, everything is forgotten.

If nothing else, shooting *The Storm* was fun. Wyler filmed the picture near Truckee, seven thousand feet up in the California Rockies along the old emigrant trail northeast of San Francisco. He had a whole choo-choo train to play with.

"We all lived in railroad cars—cast and crew," he recalled. "My train was three cars long—a sleeping car with berths, a diner with a chef, and a flatcar where we put the gear and filmed from. We also had a four-to-five-mile stretch of track that was not being used. I could tell the engineer to go forward and backward, to go slow or fast."

The train was so much fun, doubledaring Willy had to nearly kill himself showing off on skis. "When we got through work, I used to get on a pair of skis and get behind the train and have it pull me. The whole crew sat on the flatcar watching. One day, I was being pulled outside the track where there was more snow and in a curve, I couldn't see ahead.

"Suddenly from under me comes a trestle. I jumped in between the tracks. There was enough snow on the railway ties and practically on one ski, I got across. On the other side, I dropped the rope and sank into the snow."

Lupe Velez had her boyfriend, Gary Cooper, visiting, and on Saturday nights, when wives of crewmembers joined them, the sleeping car shook with sporty ardor. On Sundays, Cooper did his bodypainting on Lupe. Sometimes, she bared enough skin to show his artistry with a lipstick.

The Storm—the title was used by Universal again in 1938 for a he-man thriller with Charles Bickford, directed by Harold Young —"rates a fairly good programmer," *Variety* said in its review, adding that if the storm scenes were "not so hot" (Wyler's wind machines sounded like a bandsaw); the fight between the two men was "one of the most exciting filmed." [6] The picture opened in New York during the same week as D. W. Griffith's first talkie, *Abraham Lincoln* (with Walter Huston in the title role). The *New York Times's* Morduant Hall found *The Storm* had "particular merit in the natural performances of all three players," while conceding the climax was "rather obvious" and noticing the noise made by the wind machines in the storm sequence.[7]

With *Hell's Heroes* giving him some attention, with *The Storm* in the can, and nearly $3,000 in a savings and loan association account on Ivar Avenue, Wyler decided he had had enough of both desert and mountain. He took all his money out, went to Europe, and lived it up. He didn't return until he was broke three months later. The trip proved an instance where extravagance, not thrift, was rewarded. When he returned, the savings-and-loan on Ivar Avenue had gone bankrupt, another victim of the deepening Depression, and all deposits were lost.

Wyler had become an American citizen in 1928—not three but eight years after his arrival, despite the fling with the 104th Field Artillery. In October 1923, he had presented himself to the immigration office in downtown Los Angeles, saying he was ready for citizenship. When asked if he had taken out "first papers," he said he had done better than that. He had joined the National Guard and sworn allegiance, which, he said, was more than filling out a Declaration of Intention. However patriotic the martial gesture, the immigration office had him start over again—first papers, followed by the compulsory five-year waiting period before citizenship. The three-year rule, he was told, had applied only during World War I.

Wyler first went to Mulhouse, then to Lausanne to visit relatives and old friends. He rented a car and drove to Salzburg, where he stayed for the length of the Mozart and Reinhardt festival. The big excitement of the trip, however, was Berlin, where *Hell's Heroes* was still playing at the Mozart Saal, and he was to have his first press conference.

Berlin in 1930 was everything to everybody—a charming city with avenues and cafés, a grotesque city of vice and intrigue with its fauna of millionaires and mobs, a city with a sheen of horror and brilliance unmatched elsewhere. It was a city where money, morals, and art were lost together in inflationary fantasies.

Wyler was introduced to everything and everybody from frenzied hedonists in dark environments and brown-shirted bully-boys to Bertolt Brecht and the proletarian poet-heroes. A frequent guide to smut, kinky nightclubs and *Wandervögel* hippies was *Variety*'s man in Berlin, Max Magnus. Wyler stayed at the Eden Hotel, famous for its glass-roofed penthouse garden, where a *thé dansant* was held every afternoon.

"It was a whirlwind of people," Wyler recalled. "With nothing to lose but the paper money the Social Democrats printed, it was tango and rain falling on the glass roof and every night a different girl."

Erich Pommer, Germany's celebrated movie mogul and founder of *UFA*, personally took Wyler on a tour of the Babelsberg studios, where Fritz Lang was about to start *M*. Wyler didn't meet the monocled director until Lang came to Hollywood in 1935. By that time, everybody who was anybody in Berlin would be in Ernst Lubitsch's garden in Beverly Hills on Sunday afternoons.

Magnus dutifully reported the goings-on: how *Hell's Heroes* was shown in a private screening to Berlin's literary and artistic élite as well as to members of the film industry. "It was agreed that the director, William Wyler, was gifted and had been able to make this work of art of a dozen wild west films," Magnus wrote. "It will readily be admitted that, at times, the film is too long-winded and boring . . . [but] the consensus of opinion was that the direction is of a high standard." [8]

Wyler's press conference was held at the Eden Hotel. "It was arranged by Universal," he recalled. "And it seemed the whole German press was present. Of course, I was impressed. I was twenty-eight."

Wyler left Berlin in a somber mood. He realized the significant experience was not cultural but moral. The next time he was in Berlin, it was a moonscape and a heap of rubble teaming with people who hadn't learned anything from the most devastating war in recorded history.

He returned to California with a split personality, both shaken and exhilarated by what he had seen. Nobody in America cared. The mood of the United States was isolationist if not downright xenophobic, and anti-European. The war propaganda had backfired, they said. The Allies had been human after all, and it had become popular to claim Uncle Sam had been tricked into the war by slick British propaganda, bankers, and munitions makers. Public opinion was against foreign entanglements and couldn't care less about Europe sinking into Fascism.

But Wyler also returned full of ideas. Still others came as a result of his meeting with Sergei Eisenstein, whose *Potemkin* he had admired. As Willy returned, the Soviet cinéaste, who was on his way to Mexico to shoot *Que Viva Mexico,* was being lionized by young Hollywood.

Before Wyler got to make socio-political statements, there were three programmers to get through—routine screenfare for the twice-a-week playbill change that the vast majority of exhibitors (and the public) demanded. The first was *A House Divided,* where he directed Walter Huston, met his son, John, and put him on the payroll as a dialogue writer, and had Paul Kohner as his supervisor.

If Willy had spent ten impatient years climbing the directorial ladder, Paul had had a more flamboyant decade, mainly as Uncle Carl's man in Europe, dashing between capitals, scouting for new Greta Garbos, suggesting projects, meeting the unpredictable boss, and, of all things, negotiating with the Vatican.

From the crap game behind Notre Dame, Paul had come to be assistant casting director, supervisor, and someone generally considered to be Uncle Carl's nephew—a mistake Kohner rarely tried to dispel. Like the old man, Paul had a knack for publicity and, by 1929, was the boss's roving ambassador. Uncle Carl loved personal publicity and Kohner was always on the lookout. One of his ideas was a biography. Laemmle loved it and John Drinkwater, the biographer of Abraham Lincoln and Lord Byron, was commissioned to write the movie mogul's life story. Drinkwater earned his substantial fee with such statements as "Laemmle, a man without whom modern civilization would have been a different story . . ." and "In the early organization of the medium, Laemmle must always be remembered as the ablest, wisest and the most intrepid of pioneers." [9]

Paul's Vatican caper started on a platform at Vienna's railway station. A friend of his had pointed to a cleric in purple also boarding the Berlin express and told him that the cleric was the papal nuncio to Berlin. On the train, Cardinal Pacelli—who was to become Catholicism's spiritual leader from 1939 to 1958 as Pope Pius XII—and Kohner began talking. The cardinal was an admirer of the current pope, Pius XI, and of his progressive politics, which included his Lateran agreement with Benito Mussolini giving back to the Holy See its territorial independence in Rome.

Kohner had an inspiration and asked the cardinal if his excellency was aware of the new invention called talking pictures. To Pacelli's affirmative answer, Kohner asked if the cardinal thought it possible to induce the Pope to speak to the world through the new invention. "He can give any message he wants to convey, whatever is most meaningful to him. We could show the Vatican and its glories, and this could be a very splendid film indeed."

By the time the train pulled into Berlin, the cardinal and Paul had a tentative agreement. Further discussions were held. Paul wired Uncle Carl that he had the scoop of the century—the Pope before Universal newsreel cameras.

Laemmle urged negotiations to continue in utmost secrecy lest other studios get the same idea—Louis B. Mayer was a friend of New York's Cardinal Spellman (and Cardinal Pacelli was indeed to tour the MGM studios in 1936). Paul was about to leave for Rome and the final round of talks when Pacelli's secretary called, saying there was one little matter they had not yet discussed.

What the Holy See had in mind, it turned out, was a donation, a token recognizing the papal gesture—$100,000. Kohner wired Laemmle, suggesting that the publicity might be worth it. But the return telegram was an unusual model of brevity: FORGET POPE. LAEMMLE, it read.

After *All Quiet on the Western Front,* Junior had followed with another hit. He had lured John Murray Anderson from Broadway to direct Paul Whiteman in the superproduction *The King of Jazz.* His policies of prestige output pitted Universal directly against MGM, Paramount, and Warners, but it wasn't easy.

The retooling to sound had been costly. Most studios needed vast sums of new working capital and both equipment and financing led ultimately to the same sources—Western Electric, Radio Corporation of America (RCA), and their affiliated companies and banks. Their representatives now sat on film company boards, making policy with—and sometimes in place of—veteran showmen who had brought their enterprises from obscurity to world prominence. Standard Electric was eventually to own a hefty share of Universal.

What didn't help was that Uncle Carl never really understood sound. He was now in his mid-sixties and mentally, he hadn't made the quantum jump to talkies. He had applauded the opposition to the talkies in 1929 and couldn't help agreeing when his son bought George S. Kaufman's *Once in a Lifetime,* a play satirizing Hollywood's tragicomic attempts to come to terms with sound.

If Junior missed out on the newspaper movies—he let Milestone go to United Artists to make the first and fastest of them all, *The Front Page*—he started a whole new trend—horror films. The gothic fashion began with Tod Browning directing *Dracula,* with Bela Lugosi in the title role. (Browning wanted Lon Chaney but the actor died in 1930.) It continued with an adaptation of Mary Shelley's century-old *Frankenstein.* Directed by James Whale, an Englishman who, like Chaplin, had come to America as a member of a theatrical troupe, *Frankenstein* catapulted his fellow-Britisher, Boris Karloff, to eerie fame. After *The Old Dark House,* in which Charles Laughton made his American debut, and two other pictures, Whale made *The Invisible Man,* another genre classic, and then, in 1935, the gem of horror movies, *The Bride of Frankenstein.* Yet another Universal adaptation of a fantasy classic was *Murders in the Rue Morgue,* directed by the Frenchman Robert Florey, with Lugosi playing Doctor Mirakle.

But Junior's excursion into ghost, horror, and science-fiction films could not save the studio. In New York, sales chief Phil Reisner had trouble selling big-budget features mainly because Universal's biggest were not *better* than other studios' top output. A series of angry wires flew across the continent—Reisner insisting on a return to oldtime programmers, and Laemmle refusing to admit his son was wrong. The clash ended with Reisner's dismissal. While Laemmle took to the baths, Reisner was snapped up by RKO as sales manager. Uncle Carl hired Sol Lesser, the founder of the Fox West Coast Theatres, paid him $1,000 a week, but gave him no precise directives or duties. Lesser was also to join RKO. Laemmle and Junior were no longer on speaking terms, although Kohner once managed to reconcile them during a marathon gambling session in Tijuana.

8

As the country hit the bottom of the Depression in early 1932, Wyler made a bleak father-and-son-in-love-with-the-same-woman picture, a boys' town patriotic cheer, and a comedy about a would-be sailor and his nagging wife. The public liked the comedy best.

If *Hell's Heroes* had indicated Wyler's touch with male stars, Walter Huston's performance in *A House Divided* confirmed that talent. Almost twenty years older than Wyler, the Toronto-born actor had started in the movies in 1929. He had just played D. W. Griffith's Abraham Lincoln and, opposite new bombshell Jean Harlow, the hero of Charles Brabin's *Beast of the City.* In *A House Divided,* he gave his first memorable screen performance.

The story is a grim, Calvinistic plot patterned after Eugene O'Neill's *Desire Under the Elms,* in which Huston had starred in a 1928 Broadway revival.* Adapted from Olive Eden's magazine story "Heart and Hand," the film was screenplayed by *Anybody Here Seen Kelly?* and *Love Trap* scripter John Clymer and by Dale Van Every, with young John Huston getting dialogue credits. *A House Divided* opens with a graveside ceremony as Seth Law (Walter Huston) buries his wife. Seth Law is a fisherman who likes his liquor straight, his women strong, and his somewhat delicate son (Kent Douglass) not at all.

From a matrimonial agency, Ruth Evans (Helen Chandler)

---

* O'Neill's 1924 play reached the screen in 1958, directed by Delbert Mann and with Burl Ives, Anthony Perkins, and Sophia Loren acting the father-son-young wife triangle.

comes into the home of widower and son as the father's potential wife. What the elder Law wants is a hardy woman who can not only look after the house, but help with the fishing. What he gets is a young girl. He nevertheless marries her. The cowed son has already fallen for his stepmother and, in a scrap over her, the father falls downstairs and is paralyzed. With love between his wife and his son transpiring under his eyes, Seth is ready to kill his own kin. Son and stepmother decide to leave, but the night of their prepared departure a storm blows up, providing a big finish in the raging surf. With the girl adrift in the fishing vessel, the elder Law ties himself to a smaller boat and rushes to her rescue. To prove he is no weakling, the son swims out to save the girl while the father's boat capsizes and he is drowned.

"Kent Douglass and Helen Chandler, each of whom is currently in New York legit," *Variety* wrote, "give capable support to Huston. No one else matters." [1]

Walter Huston's characterization was a small sensation. The role of Seth Law was astutely developed, alive throughout, and never overdone, from his drinking himself silly after his wife's funeral, to his humiliating loss of the use of his legs and his stubborn death, tied to the rowboat. From a directorial standpoint, *A House Divided* was an exercise in moods—achieving a credible grandeur and making the sea the protagonist. The film was a box-office success where reviewers underlined the direction, its honesty, and, as the London *Times* said, Wyler's "control over the material." The *Boston Herald* even felt he had directed with the "strong suggestiveness of the imaginative qualities of the late Frank [sic] Murnau." [2] In France, where Constant Remy "doubled" Walter Huston for the French-language soundtrack, *Orages* had an exceptionally long career, running a year in Paris, Toulouse, and Marseilles.

A House Divided gave Wyler his first scrap with the peculiar Golden Era phenomenon called the preview, which, if Irving Thalberg didn't invent, he brought to a ritualistic and ruthless perfection. During Hollywood's imperial days when all creative talent was under contract to the almighty studios, all films were dry-run at previews to paying customers, returned for doctoring, and previewed again until audiences in outlying Los Angeles and San Francisco areas laughed or cried at the right places, or at least didn't walk out in the middle.

One of Thalberg's more celebrated instances of preview doctoring concerned *The Big House* (1930), a tough prison film with a message in favor of penal reform directed by George Hill. When the Wallace Beery-Robert Montgomery-Chester Morris starrer received a cold preview reception, Thalberg analyzed the failure: "I think I found out what's wrong," he told his staff. "When Morris gets out of prison, he goes to see Montgomery's wife and gets into a romance with her. Women flinch at that; they don't like it. Now, supposing we make the girl Montgomery's sister instead." [3]

In *Tugboat Annie,* Thalberg had Mervyn Le Roy reshoot a scene to get Wallace Berry's shoes to squeak because it made the sequence funnier. Another famous instance of doctoring a disaster to a hit on preview indications was Frank Capra's own decision to throw out the first two reels of *Lost Horizon* (1938) after the Santa Barbara preview audience had seemed too hushed for the first twenty minutes.

When Universal previewed *A House Divided* in a Glendale neighborhood house (with Kohner, Wyler, and John Huston spread around the audience), women walked out in droves during the first ten minutes.

"I had sort of played New Wave with the graveyard scene," Wyler chuckled years later. "I had made it absolutely grim, with father and son broken up and the coffin scraping along the side as it is lowered into the grave. I showed everything, really wanting to prove myself. I had a microphone put inside the coffin and the mourners threw little pebbles instead of earth on the coffin so it would *sound* dramatic."

After the preview, most of Wyler's macabre handiwork came out.

Wyler and John Huston hit it off well enough to try another joint effort. Young Huston, who had wanted to be a painter, had been drawn to the dramatic arts after meeting Eugene O'Neill during his father's Broadway starring in *Desire Under the Elms.* "I think I learned more about films from O'Neill than anyone; what a scene consisted of and so forth," John Huston was to say later. "By the time I came to Hollywood as a writer, I was conscious that I wanted to direct, and working with such greats as Wyler and Howard Hawks only served to reinforce it." Indeed, young Huston had been so impressed by Willy's directing on the sound stage that he had managed to get himself a second writing credit—on the adaptation of Edgar Allen Poe's *Murders in the Rue Morgue.*

Wyler and Huston wanted to do something contemporary and meaningful. Seventeen million Americans were jobless. Men in tattered clothes, newspapers stuffed into broken shoes, waited outside locked factory gates. President Hoover still insisted the nation's economy was basically sound, but shanties springing up on the edge of cities were called Hoovervilles. Franklin D. Roosevelt had just won the Democratic nomination in Chicago and, to unseat Herbert Hoover, asked for "bold, persistent experimentation." Huston, who had traveled the lower rungs of society, including poorest Mexico, was up on the latest trends in fiction and theater. The new thing, he said, was to use symbolism in the service of naturalism.

To get into the proper framework, Willy and John spent twenty-four hours on Los Angeles' skid row. "To know what it was to be a bum, we both took ten cents with us, went downtown in old clothes and said, 'That's it till tomorrow morning,'" Wyler remembered. "We got a lousy free dinner in a mission after we had listened to a spiel and signed statements to the effect that we had come to Christ. Then we spent the night in a flophouse. Ten cents it cost."

Everybody wanted to make socially significant movies and several of Willy's older colleagues got away with it. At Warner's, Mervyn Le Roy made *I Am a Fugitive from a Chain Gang* and, at Universal, John Stahl made *Back Street.* King Vidor did *Street Scene* and was rumored to be preparing a real proletarian statement—*Our Daily Bread.* For Frank Capra, Walter Huston had just starred in *American Madness,* a picture grappling directly and openly with the Depression.

Almost by mistake, Universal had bought the rights to Oliver LaFarge's 1929 Pulitzer Prize winner, *Laughing Boy.* LaFarge was an aristocratic New Yorker who specialized in anthropology, a Harvard man who made archaeological expeditions to Arizona, Mexico, and Guatemala in search of the first Americans. His understanding of Indian culture was complete and *Laughing Boy*—the title was in itself a sarcastic swipe—was a piercing look at Indians and whites rubbing together in the dehumanizing squalor

81

that white men had brought with them. The theme was enough to make any studio nervous. And the plotline! It dealt with prostitution and sexual mixing of the races! *

"Let me have a crack at it," Wyler asked Junior.

Wyler had John Huston hired for a first draft screenplay and together they took off for Navajo country to write and to scout locations. In Flagstaff, Arizona, they met LaFarge and spent days conferring with him.

Next, Wyler and Huston went to Monument Valley, Arizona, and lived two weeks with the Navajos.

"We visualized it like another *Nanook of the North,* another Robert Flaherty semidocumentary," Wyler recalled. "But we couldn't cast it. For Slim Girl, we made tests with Zita Johann, who later became John's girl friend. We worked on it for months, but we couldn't get it off the ground."

Laughing Boy was the first of many films that Wyler was *not* to make. Not only was Huston's laundered first draft still too hot, the casting difficulties were an excuse for Junior to sell the property to MGM, which was looking for a story for Ramon Novarro. *Laughing Boy* became a movie in 1934, running into immediate censorship flak over miscegenation. Directed by the prolific W. S. van Dyke and costarring Lupe Velez as Slim Girl, the film was a disaster. Novarro was laughed off the screen for trying an Indian accent ("he sometimes sounds like Maurice Chevalier," *Variety* said), and the New York Board of Censors scissored gaping holes in the plot. A sequence showing Slim Girl and Laughing Boy spending the night on a mountain top disappeared altogether and heavy cuts were made in the sequences involving her playing a white lover against her husband, Laughing Boy.

To Wyler and Huston, the stillborn project was to remain a private joke for decades. "All right, so when are we going to do *Laughing Boy?*" one of them would say when they met after years and continents apart.

Undaunted by the *Laughing Boy* failure, director and screenwriter threw themselves on another Universal property, Daniel

* La Farge's novel was banned from public school libraries in Amarillo, Texas, and in a rural Georgia county as late as 1960. In the Santa Fe, New Mexico *New Mexican,* where LaFarge wrote a weekly column from 1950 until his death in 1963, he defended his book once by likening its heroine to Melina Mercouri in Jules Dassin's *Never on Sunday.* Oliver LaFarge, *The Man with the Calabash Pipe,* Houghton-Mifflin, Boston, 1966.

82

Ahearn's story *The Wild Boys of the Road*. This was the Depression at its rawest, the tale of small-town boys leaving home to avoid being an added burden to harassed families and, on a freight car, meeting a young girl beating her way to an aunt in Chicago. Again, Willy and John were out of luck. The property was sold to First National from under their noses and ended up being directed by William Wellman, who married the picture's only girl, Dorothy Coonan. *The Wild Boys of the Road* was to play a curious role at the dawn of the anti-Communist hysteria. Footage from the film was used in a fake newsreel, manufactured at MGM by staunch Republican Irving Thalberg to help defeat ex-Socialist Upton Sinclair running for governor of California on a Democratic ticket that promised heavier taxes on higher incomes and special taxes on movie studios. The bogus newsreel, using one of the sequences pulled from *The Wild Boys of the Road,* had extras dressed as an anarchist and other riffraff crossing the border to assume control of Hollywood if Sinclair was elected. Sinclair was defeated.

A second no-go was enough for Huston. With his last paycheck, he took off for Europe, tried to write for British Gaumont, drifted to Paris only to resurface in Hollywood in 1937 when Willy managed to get him a writing assignment on *Jezebel.* Alone, Wyler looked around and, in the writer's building, stumbled over John Wexley, a playwright brought out after his first play, *The Last Mile,* had proved an off-Broadway success.

Five years younger than Wyler, Wexley was unhappy with his highly paid inactivity. Junior had put him under contract because what Universal needed now was not scenarists conditioned by silent routine but writers skilled in dramatic construction. But, like so many others, Wexley was told to just look around and get acquainted.

Wyler's enthusiasm soared when he read *The Last Mile* and saw a road company production of what was an open plea for prison reform. Without asking anybody, he made a screen test of the actor playing the convicted murderer in the road company version—Clark Gable.

"He came out to the studio and I made a test for him," Willy remembered. "He was very good as the killer—unshaved and looking mean and nasty. After the test I thanked him and he took me aside and, in a low voice said, 'Oh Mr. Wyler, I brought a tuxedo.' I said, 'Yes, what for?' He said, 'I can shave in a minute; maybe you'd like to see what I look like in a tuxedo.' I said, 'No thanks. This was fine. We'll let you know.' "

Wyler thought Gable should play the part, but Wexley was all sold on the actor playing the murderer on the stage in New York.

"Who is it?" Willy asked.

"A guy named Spencer Tracy."

"Never heard of him."

Which of the two unknowns they chose was to remain an idle question because they couldn't sell Universal on *The Last Mile*.

"We took the old man, Laemmle, to the Los Angeles production of the play. By this time, he was hard of hearing. We sat him in the first row. I think Paul Kohner was with us. When someone was shot on the stage, Laemmle said, very loud, 'Why did he shoot him?' People around us tried to hush him. 'Why did he shoot him?' Laemmle would ask again."

Laemmle and Junior decided *The Last Mile* was too grim and Wyler had to abandon it, too. Wexley sold his play to an independent production company and it reached the screen in a diluted adaptation directed by Sam Bischoff and with Howard Phillips playing the killer. Howard Koch did a remake, also a watered-down version, in 1959 with Mickey Rooney in the lead.

Wyler was handed *Tom Brown of Culver*. A breezy "juveniles' picture," it starred a bunch of kids, the Culver Military Academy, and in a minor adult role, Universal's chief comedian, Slim Summerville.

With the exception of incidental parts such as nurses in a hospital, *Tom Brown of Culver* was an all-boys film in which, The *New York Times* said, "the boys act like boys instead of like road company Hamlets." [4]

The young actors included Tom Brown in the lead named after him; Richard Cromwell, catapulted into fame in the sound version of *Tol-able David* and to be cast again by Wyler in *Jezebel;* Ben Alexander; and Tyrone Power.

Wyler went twice to Indiana, first with screenwriter Tom Buckingham and later to shoot the picture. During the exploratory trip, Wyler heard about terrorizing of freshmen by older boys. From a background far removed from this Anglo-American tradition, Wyler wouldn't believe the extent to which older boys would carry their tyranny and had two of them hide him in a closet to observe the ritual.

"There, I watched through the curtain how the older boys called the 'plebes' together and had them come running instantly. Some of the younger boys came running stark naked, dripping from showers. Then, their tormentors asked them questions, slapping them around for no reason. I copied this scene in the picture."

The story traced Tom Brown's conversion from a moody, rebellious youngster to a little stalwart of life in uniform. Because Tom's father is believed to have been killed in action in the World War, the American Legion puts him through Culver, and when the father (H. B. Warner) appears on the scene with a story of shell shock and desertion, Tom has to face the first crisis of his life.

Universal remade the picture in 1939, calling it *Spirit of Culver*. Thomas Hughes' juvenile classic, *Tom Brown's School Days* was filmed twice, in 1940 and 1952, and in 1973 was rumored as a possible television series.

Next, Willy was handed *Her First Mate*, the third and best of a series of wacky comedies Slim Summerville and Zasu Pitts made as a man-and-wife duo. Adapted from the Dan Jarrett-John Golden Broadway hit *Salt Water (a Fresh Play)*, the picture was full of inventive and unexpected gags, even if the story was a bit long.

The scenarists Clarence Marks (already a writer or dialogue polisher on *The Shakedown, The Love Trap,* and *Tom Brown of Culver*), Earl Snell, and H. M. Walker fashioned the story of the sea-loving candyman into a solid skeleton for the particular talents of fluttery Zasu Pitts and the would-be heroic Slim Summerville.

"There were little pieces of business that were sort of advanced for the time," Willy recalled. "The wife claims she's pregnant, then her husband discovers she is not but still uses the stratagem. We had a showy finale shot in San Francisco harbor. A big farewell on the ferryboat dock. She is crying, the whistle is blowing and he is saying, 'Don't worry, darling. I'll be back in eight minutes.'"

Her First Mate included such tired routines as Slim breaking a set of dishes in a fit of anger, but, unlike the earlier Zasu–Slim comedies—*They Just Had to Get Married* and *Out All Night*—it had, as reviewers noted, a plausible story line, a congenial atmosphere, and plenty of inventive ingenuity.

With *Her First Mate,* Wyler's apprenticeship, as it were, came to an end. The comedy was released August 1, 1933, a month after his thirty-first birthday, thirteen years after his arrival in America, and eight years after that first two-reeler, *Crook Buster.* He had showed glimpses of talent over an astonishing steeplechase of twenty-one primary two-reelers, ten westerns, a juvenile programmer, three dramas, and two comedies. With *Counsellor at Law,* the John Barrymore vehicle that was to be his first important work, he started the stride of his career. The moment was propitious. The "novelty" of sound had passed and ahead was a period which was to become the classic age of the American cinema.

PART TWO

The Stride

9

John Barrymore was not the first choice for the glib Jewish lawyer in Elmer Rice's story-with-a-heartbreak, *Counsellor at Law*.
Yet this first cinematic sniff at melting-pot politics and anti-Semitic snobbery was to be one of the few screen appearances that revealed his measure as an actor, his fabulous "presence," and the
fireworks of the Barrymore tradition. For Wyler, *Counsellor at
Law* was a first exploration of the inner maze of that movie staple,
the adaptation. Almost instinctively, he realized that "opening
up" a play didn't mean sending characters on walks or car rides,
that direct speech didn't have the same volume between quota-
tion marks as in the mouth of a screen idol seen in closeup, that
to transpose usually meant to simplify, although *not* adding anything could be betrayal by omission, that to show what a writer
tells could mean transforming prose into dialogue and even rewriting dialogue.

Counsellor at Law was Junior's big gamble of 1933. It was a
hot property, the 1931 Broadway hit. Barrymore was paid $25,000
a week—Wyler was supposed to finish with him in a fortnight.
Rice, who had studied law at night school before setting out on a
writing career that had included a stint with Samuel Goldwyn,
was hired to do his own screen adaptation. In a twist on the usual
writer vs. director attitude toward a text, Rice cut his own play
freely and Wyler restored the cuts.

As his play, Rice's script was energetic, naïve, melodramatic,
and touchingly generous. A concession to the movies was a slight

softening of the vigorous supporting characters and types, and a corresponding buildup of the romantic element. But it remained *Counsellor at Law,* the story of George Simon, a shrewd Jewish lawyer and a self-made man, who finds he is in danger of being disbarred for unprofessional conduct committed some years earlier. It is the story of his private life, showing how he unburdens himself to his selfish gentile wife and gets no sympathy, how he saves himself by his own shrewdness but contemplates suicide when he finds his wife has left him, and how he is saved from himself by, and finds happiness with, his secretary, who has always loved him secretly.

"You can't have a Jew playing a Jew, it wouldn't work on the screen." The Goldwynism was exemplary of both the fear of an industry largely in Jewish hands that Jewish faces on the screen might be going "one step too far," and of Hollywood's splendid and insolent insularity in its imperial days. Goldwyn used his aphorism to give to Frank Sinatra the part in *Guys and Dolls* that Sam Levene had interpreted on Broadway. As for isolation, it never occurred to Wyler, John Huston, Universal, or anyone else that instead of abandoning *Laughing Boy* as "uncastable," they might have looked outside Hollywood and found a real Indian.

In *Counsellor at Law,* it *did* occur to everyone to have the actor playing George Simon on the stage repeat the role for the cameras. In this instance, however, the actor didn't want the movie part. Thanks largely to *Counsellor at Law,* Muni Weisenfreund had escaped the Yiddish theater and become Paul Muni. He had carried the play for the length of the Broadway run but didn't want to become identified in films as a Jewish actor and when he did make his screen debut, it was as a fictionalized Al Capone—in Howard Hawks' *Scarface.* Universal had bought *Counsellor at Law* (together with Rice's other play, *The Left Bank*) with the hope that Muni would repeat for the cameras.

It had been a very good year for Rice. In addition to the Universal deal, he had sold *Street Scene* to Goldwyn, written the script himself, and seen King Vidor direct a sharp screen version of this drama of slum life, murder, and love without solution. He was in Mexico City with his family when he received a telegram from Junior asking him to come to Hollywood and assist in the casting of *Counsellor at Law.* Muni had refused to live up to the

Willy, 3, and Robert, 5

ABOVE, 13 rue de Zurich, in Mulhouse as it looks today
OPPOSITE PAGE, TOP LEFT, a carnival in Basel in 1919. Willy, seated at left, has changed clothes with cousin Dorely (top left, with friend Oskar Brenner). At right, cousin Recha Wyler.
BOTTOM LEFT, Willy with Uncle Carl
FAR RIGHT, foreign publicity department—Paul Kohner (top) and Willy Wyler

LEFT, on the roof of 1600 Broadway

ABOVE, astride the four-cylinder Henderson

BELOW, Francis X. Bushman and Ramon Novarro in Fred Niblo's 1925 *Ben-Hur*

ABOVE, Edmond Cobb as *Martin of the Mounted*

BELOW, directing Fred Gilman in a two-reeler

ABOVE, Willy being "fired" by Vin Moore in *Daze in the West*

BELOW, "stealing" a train in Lone Pine. Willy is in riding boots next to locomotive.

ABOVE, with Edna Gregory and Fred Humes on *Blazing Days* set—on Frenchie's Ranch in Newhall

BELOW, Bobby Gordon and Art Acord in *Lazy Lightning*

ABOVE, *cinéma vérité* 1928—Bessie Love and Tom Moore on New York's 42nd Street and Broadway in *Anybody Here Seen Kelly?*

BELOW, rollerskating in on Laura La Plante in *The Love Trap*

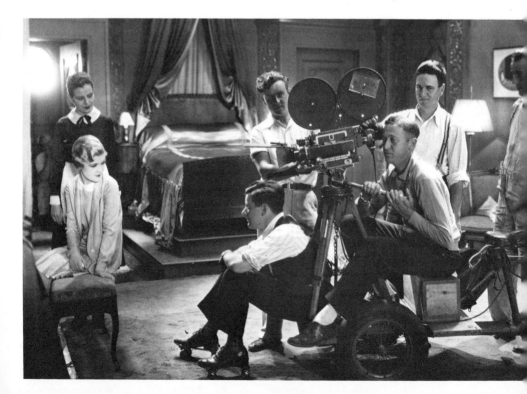

"understanding" and had signed up with Le Roy to star in *The World Changes*. Rice didn't want to interrupt his Mexican sojourn, which included fascinating evenings with the painters Diego Rivera and David Siqueiros. Instead, Wyler went to Mexico City.

It was a frustrating experience in early air travel. Once in El Paso, Texas, Wyler heard that the train took three days to reach Mexico City, a fact that made him decide to fly. As the only passenger, he boarded a Mexican plane at Ciudad Juarez, the border town opposite El Paso, only to see the pilot set down in León, halfway to Mexico City, because of bad weather over the capital. Three days later, they were still in León. Hanging around the airfield shack, Wyler spotted a Mexican worker with both eyes bandaged and learned that the man's only hope of keeping his eyesight was an urgent operation in Mexico City. Claiming that the poor man's blindness would forever be on the pilot's conscience, Wyler shamed the pilot into taking to the skies again. For hours, it seemed, they climbed and climbed, but when there was a hole in the clouds, Wyler saw they were just over the treetops. Only when they landed did he get the explanation. Mexico City is situated on an eight-thousand-foot plateau.

But Rice didn't want to see Universal's young director of *Counsellor at Law* during his vacation. "Very nice meeting you, see you back in Los Angeles," he told his visitor. Rice had just met René d'Harnoncourt, an authority on Aztec culture who was later to become the director of New York's Museum of Modern Art, and was too interested in pre-Columbian art to be bothered with rewrites. Wyler didn't really mind. He saw Mexico City on company time.

Once back at Universal City, director and writer began to work together. After much turmoil, Barrymore was engaged. "I admired him as an actor, but had doubts about his rightness for the part," Rice was to write in his memoirs. "Moreover, he was definitely on the decline. But, in view of his great talents and great name, I could hardly have objected to him even if I had had the veto power." [1]

Wyler didn't object, either. To direct an actor of Barrymore's magnitude (a man twenty years his senior) was not a chance every formula-picturemaker was given. When they were introduced in the office of Henry Henigson, the studio manager, who was one day to be Willy's production manager in Rome, he was visibly nervous.

To put him at ease, Barrymore took his director into a corner and put his arm around him. "You and I are going to get along fine, you know. Don't worry about all the temperamental stuff you've heard about the Barrymores. It all comes from my sister and she's full of shit!"

Barrymore's antisocial habits were, nonetheless, a well-known fact. He lived all his brilliant, violent, and much-married life in glass houses. A steady drinker at fifteen, he kept drinking until his death in 1942. In his first ten years in Hollywood—*Counsellor at Law* was made in his eighth year there—he earned $2.6 million and squandered almost every cent of it. It was not only for the cameras that he created characters. Dozens of different Barrymores appeared in his life, from the strut and oratory to the bankrupt, disheveled, and forlorn Jack (as his friends called him) who kept dying slowly. In comparison, his sister, Ethel, brother, Lionel, and daughter, Diana, were pale eccentrics.

Jack had just whipped through *Topaze,* a Ben Hecht script, directed by Harry d'Arrast, and after a summer of hard work and marital unhappiness, began *Counsellor at Law.* The year, 1932, had brought him $375,000 for five pictures made at a fast clip. His health was not the best, but he was his own good self, witty, learned, and magnetic, an actor who had, in Hecht's felicitous phrase, "a talent for painting on the air the soul of what he was playing, for writing it on the moment as if every part of him were a pencil." [2]

Wyler assembled the rest of his performers from the New York and Chicago stage productions of *Counsellor at Law.* Bebe Daniels was cast as Regina, the secretary in love with her boss, Doris Kenyon as the wife, and Onslow Stevens as the partner-in-law. Others included Isabel Jewell, Melvyn Douglas, Thelma Todd, and John Qualen. Three future directors were in the cast—Vincent Sherman played an old-fashioned anarchist, Bobby Gordon was the office boy, and thirteen-year-old Richard Quine was Barrymore's bratty stepson.

Shortly before shooting, Barrymore told Wyler he was delighted to have him direct the picture. Willy was pleased—Barrymore had been directed by the likes of Ernst Lubitsch—and puzzled. Why would this great actor enjoy being directed by a young unknown? When he asked, Barrymore said, "Because you're Jewish you'll be able to help me a great deal with the character."

Willy wasn't sure how he should take this and the first day of shooting, as it turned out, wasn't quite what Barrymore had expected either. In the first scene, lawyer George Simon was at his desk talking on the telephone and before rolling the first take, Barrymore asked his director if he had any ideas or suggestions.

"No," said Willy, "pick up the phone and talk."

Barrymore played the scene letter-perfect but with an odd little gesture when picking up the receiver. Wyler asked what this mannerism meant.

"Did you like that?" Barrymore smiled.

"Frankly, I don't know what it was supposed to mean."

Barrymore explained the gesture was Jewish. Wyler said he thought Jews would pick up a phone like everybody else and that, in any case, George Simon was a brilliant, modern attorney who wouldn't *act* his origins. "Only one time in the picture, when his mother comes to see him can he maybe betray a Bronx Jewish gesture," Wyler added. The expression on Barrymore's face obviously said, 'This kid is not going to be much help.'

The scene was repeated and Barrymore again had a gesture which he felt was appropriately Jewish. Again Wyler corrected, saying he was sure George Simon wouldn't have such mannerisms.

Wyler felt they were getting off to a bad start. Because of talk that he was miscast, Barrymore wanted to give an interpretation that made him believable as a Jew—even if it was wrong for the character. It was not the last time Wyler had to face actor ego over interpretation.

Ethnic mannerisms were not Wyler's only concern. George Simon was a difficult part, with a lot of legal verbiage and an extremely fast delivery of dialogue. "It was his character to talk fast. It was fashionable then to talk very fast on the screen, to rattle it off."

Because of the steep weekly compensation for Barrymore's services, Wyler was under strong front-office pressure. When he couldn't finish Barrymore's part in two weeks, Junior allowed an extra week, which was also overrun, although only by a few days. "It was mad. In every scene, I shot only Barrymore, skipping closeups of anybody talking to him for later. It's a terrible way to make pictures."

Counsellor at Law was not Wyler's first adaptation of stage material—both *The Storm* and *Her First Mate* had theatrical origins—but it was the first play for which he solved the transition from stage to screen with any degree of inventiveness.

Wyler, who was to score better than most in this ungrateful game of re-creating other people's creations, realized almost instinctively that the transition from stage to screen was first of all a matter of physics, of dramatic space. Instead of "opening up" *Counsellor at Law* by sending his characters all over New York, he added to the stage décor in the wings, so to speak. To George Simon's attorney's office, he added back room, front office, inner office, secretary's area, etc., and by staging the action in and out of these rooms, created pace and fluidity. He was to repeat this with deft effectiveness in *The Little Foxes* and *Detective Story* and make it part of the "styleless style" with which he was to treat compact and intense drama.

But, on *Counsellor at Law*, he was not yet one of the top American directors and the pressure was intense from Junior and Henigson to open up. Admirably, he did not give in.

"The front office told me, 'Jeez, you gotta get out of this office, you must open it up!' I said, 'No, I don't see why.' I wanted to retain the construction of the play and at the same time, have movement. It was only an illusion; we never left the lawyer's offices." Also, it was a picture without a score. Front and end titles only had music, a novelty in the days when big music departments were being organized in all the studios and theme songs were the rage. "I stood firm, 'No music,' but when the picture was released they published a sheet music with Barrymore's picture on the cover entitled, *Counsellor at Law, I Love You.*"

Despite the breakneck speed of filming, he restored some of the unessential elements that made essential scenes essential, feeling that a character did not have the same dimension on a proscenium and in closeup. "I remember that when I did a scene where Rice had cut what he thought was unnecessary, it had lost its 'build.' The buildup was in a sense as important as the punch line, or the punch line was not as effective without the build. All during the picture, I worked with the script in one hand and the play in the other—both by Elmer Rice—restoring things he had cut out."

Opening up led to other discoveries. In a scene where George Simon tries to get urgent information from someone who can never get to the point, Wyler realized that the camera allowed a delightful shift in emphasis, that the interest was in the man listening, not in the man talking.

"Barrymore was very good. His kind of aristocracy made the lawyer's climb from the ghetto even more spectacular and he allowed us to make an extra little point about this emancipated Jew in the scene with his old mother. I think it was the first time in a picture that anti-Semitism was broached, with his snobbish gentile wife and the children. But it was done very gently. You wouldn't dare say a word, just touch upon it."

After finishing *Counsellor at Law,* Barrymore completed *Long Lost Father* for RKO studios. He was then called back by Wyler for the reshooting of one scene with John Qualen. The date was October 30.

Qualen was letter-perfect—he had played Breitstein on the stage with Muni. After Barrymore finished one of his long speeches and Qualen made the proper rejoiner, Jack stumbled over his next brief line. He made a comic face and everybody laughed. On the next take, Barrymore blew up in his lines at almost the same place. A third take was rolled and he failed again. After two more, Barrymore became angry. He continued to falter during the next six trials and the effect spilled over on Qualen, who also blew. Wyler ordered a recess and Barrymore was given an opportunity to consult the script.

When the actors resumed their places in front of Norbert Brodine's camera, Barrymore stumbled again. Wyler and Brodine exchanged glances while Tom Hotchener, Barrymore's manager, stood in sad amazement on the sidelines. Henigson arrived on the set, watched a take, and said to Hotchener, "Is he *that* drunk?"

"He's a little tired, not drunk."

"Nobody ever got *that* tired," the studio manager replied.[3]

Barrymore still was fighting to conquer the scene. He persisted and flunked time and again.

"He'll have it in a few minutes," Hotchener said. But Jack was perspiring, his face drawn, his jaw set. "Why not put it over to tomorrow night," Hotchener finally pleaded.

According to Barrymore's friend and biographer Gene Fowler, they went through fifty-six takes before giving up that night. Wyler would only remember a score, or perhaps twenty-five, but the next day, the story was running through the Hollywood grapevine. "Fifty takes would be insane," Wyler said years later. But part of his reputation as a punctilious perfectionist and scourge of stars was made that night.

Two weeks before Christmas, *Counsellor at Law* followed George Cukor's *Little Women* into New York's Radio City Music Hall, grossing $96,000 during the first week and Rice sent wires to Junior and Wyler:

> I HAVE JUST SEEN A SCREENING OF *Counsellor at Law*
> AND WANT TO EXPRESS TO YOU MY CONGRATULATIONS AND
> THANKS STOP THE PICTURE IS EXCELLENT IN ALL ITS
> DETAILS AND YOU HAVE EVERY REASON TO BE PROUD OF THE
> FINE JOB YOU HAVE DONE STOP I AM SURE THAT YOUR
> WORK WILL RECEIVE GENERAL RECOGNITION BEST REGARDS

The press hailed Barrymore's clear-eyed performance and the film's sense of pace and action despite the confinement of a lawyer's office. "Seldom has a play been transferred to the screen with such fidelity," *The New Yorker* wrote,[4] while the *Herald Tribune* called it "a striking, intelligent and invariably interesting motion picture."[5] The *New York Times* said Barrymore was giving to George Simon "the vigor, imagination and authority one might expect." Wyler was given a curious nod: "Parts of the stage work have perforce been omitted, but where this occurs, Mr. Rice and the director, William Wyler, leave nothing in doubt."[6]

Posterity has been kind to *Counsellor at Law*. Twenty years later, *Cue* could write that "despite a definitely dated quality in play construction, dialogue and the frenetic quality of its overacting, and jumping editing, the film, for the most part, stands up against the ravages of time and celluloid."[7]

In 1967, *Cinema* would call it "an extremely creative, smooth-flowing adaptation [in which] Barrymore gives what is perhaps his best performance in a talking picture."[8] A year later, Pauline Kael would say that "the 1933 production has by now the patina of a period piece, and what a good movie period it was, full of gold-diggers, social climbers, dedicated radicals, etc. William Wyler directed, and despite his later reputation for such 'polished' works as *The Little Foxes, The Best Years of Our Lives, Roman Holiday, The Desperate Hours,* etc., I prefer this earlier Wyler, fresh from more than fifty two-reel westerns, willing to tell his story simply."[9]

10

Before *The Good Fairy* and Margaret Sullavan, with whom he quarreled so much during the shooting that they married before it was over, Wyler still had to do what he later called "a kind of screwy picture that wasn't very good."

Although he was never to meet Edna Ferber, Wyler did one and one-half pictures based on her work—*Glamour* and *Come and Get It,* the latter a Samuel Goldwyn presentation that Howard Hawks walked off from and Wyler was forced to finish. The author of *Show Boat, Cimarron* and, later, *Saratoga Trunk, Ice Palace,* and *Giant* had often been in Hollywood, wooed by Goldwyn for his writers' seraglio, but she had never stayed more than a few weeks. *Glamour* was an old short story of hers, a fluffy little exercise in writing that tried to catch nothing more than mood and episode—one day in the life of Linda Fayne, Broadway star.[1]

Wyler tried to resist the project. He didn't like the script, written by Doris Anderson and Gladys Unger, which stretched the Ferber story and its inherent plot to tear-jerking conclusions and made the unerotic day in Linda Fayne's life into a triangular, albeit Hays Office-passable, sob story.

Tempers were growing shorter at the studio as everybody sensed the power struggle shaping up over Carl Laemmle's succession. There were new fights between Uncle Carl and his son, supposedly over Junior's plans to marry Constance Cummings, a marriage opposed by the conservative, if nondisciplinarian, father. When Junior and Henigson insisted on Willy's directing

Glamour—starring, of all actresses, Miss Cummings—he had no choice but to make the picture. For the first time, however, Wyler realized that he might have to leave Universal.

It was something he didn't discuss openly, but something he had to face squarely. His entire professional life had been spent at Universal. It had been home for thirteen years and the source of his opportunity, but it became evident that being Uncle Carl's second cousin was not necessarily a recommendation. The lot contained a veritable riot of relatives, known as Laemmle's Foreign Legion. Producers were careful to say "sir" to janitors because they might be grandnephews to Laemmle's wife's brother-in-law. There were little reflections, condescending half-smiles that hurt. Also, it seemed all the exciting pictures were made elsewhere.

Paul Kohner was Universal's titular head of European production. When he made dashes west to confer with Uncle Carl, he was full of intrigue and worldly knowledge, right from Berlin. Since Adolf Hitler had come to power in January, Berlin was different, no doubt about it. But, Hitler didn't make precise demands, he just announced that Germany had been wronged in 1918 and waited for other countries to make concessions or to suggest compensations. Everybody knew he didn't know any foreign countries at first hand, that he rarely read the reports of his ambassadors, and that he judged world leaders by intuition. He spent most of his time at Berchtesgaden and people in Berlin weren't sure the National Socialist would last another year. In the meantime, the catchword was to muddle through.

Kohner administered Universal's considerable assets in Germany with a slightly lowered profile but a firm hand. Other U.S. majors, wishing they had a man in Berlin with Kohner's savvy, did likewise. Corporate Hollywood's relations with Berlin were correct up to the brink of World War II. As late as 1938, Louis B. Mayer screened *Three Comrades* for the German consul in Los Angeles to be sure that there was nothing in the Frank Borzage adaptation of Erich Maria Remarque's antiwar novel that could possibly offend the Third Reich. In 1940, when German bombs were raining on London, Mayer asked Wyler to go easy on anti-German sentiments in *Mrs. Miniver*.

While Willy made *Glamour,* Paul was in Greenland producing *S.O.S. Eisberg* for Universal. The picture, starring Leni Riefensthal and Ernst Udet, was directed by outdoorsman Arnold Fanck and supervised by Arctic explorer Knud Rasmussen. It was to be Riefensthal's last as an actress. Her next (and first as a director) was to be, at Hitler's insistent request, *Triumph des Willens,* the hypnotic Nazi superspectacle which Frank Capra was to study frame for frame during World War II. Paul's next, as a producer, was to be a Margaret Sullavan starrer, *Next Time We Love.*

Paul got Willy an invitation to the Lubitsch Sundays. Anyone who was anybody in the German-speaking colony was at Leni and Ernst Lubitsch's stately southern mansion on Beverly Drive, a few houses down from Pola Negri's, on Sunday afternoons.

If Erich von Stroheim had put Uncle Carl's shirt-sleeve operation on the cinematic map with the mordantly sophisticated *Foolish Wives* in 1921, Ernst Lubitsch had put the little studio of the brothers Harry, Albert, Sam, and Jack Warner on the road to fame three years later. After wandering years between Warner Bros., Paramount, and MGM during the 1920s, Lubitsch settled at Paramount. By 1934, the most elegant of screen magicians had many imitators, but no one had his wit, charm, and raffish versatility. He was the spirit of Paramount and the "touches" just peeled off the screen and off his personality.

"In appearance, he looked like a combination of Napoleon and Punchinello," Wyler recalled. "The Sundays at his house were marvelous. Just being there was a tremendous thing."

The short, thickset man with his perpetual cigar, his ponderous shoulders and huge twinkling eyes was what Germans called an *intrigant,* a stream of impish frolickings, anecdotes, *bons mots,* gossip, tall yarns, and interjections. He commanded a natural obedience with a sensual guile and sharp psychological perception.

"Those people were all older than I," Wyler recalled. "I was not a friend, I was invited as a young fellow."

Wyler was particularly fascinated by Lubitsch's stories about directing, both tall yarns about "tag lines," the meaning of a quick or even a slow fadeout, the innuendo that essentially was the "Lubitsch touch": an officers' revolt against the tsarina put down in three quick shots—the general's hand moving to his sword, the chamberlain's hand pulling out a checkbook, the general's hand loosening from his sword—or his handling of actors.

"He was the kind of director I could never be, I'm sorry to say. I remember the story he told me about directing Emil Jannings as the mad tsar in *The Patriot* [1928]. Jannings played Paul I,

99

the idiot son of Catherine the Great, a pathetic monster, cruel and childish, a boorish clown and yet a pitiful, moving human being."

To introduce the tsar, Lubitsch had devised a huge scene, a palace hall filled with courtiers and a grand entrance with trumpets announcing the arrival of the monarch. Lubitsch was known for his "simple" directing of actors, for not tiring them and never losing patience or courtesy. For the first take, Lubitsch let Jannings play the scene as the actor thought it should be played. After the trumpets blared, the mad tsar came in crouching like Quasimodo in *The Hunchback of Notre Dame.*

"Very effective," Lubitsch said. "But, I've got an idea. Let's try it once more and maybe this time you shouldn't crouch so much."

"You think so?" Jannings asked.

They tried the scene again—the courtiers, the trumpets, the grand entrance, Jannings stooping a little less.

"How did you like it, Ernst?" the actor asked.

"You know, I think it's better."

"You think so?"

"Let's try it again; we don't have to use it, but this time, come in more majestically."

Wyler was to remember Lubitsch on his back lawn with most of the guests gasping for air in convulsive laughter as the master of the house acted out the scene, successively playing Jannings and himself. At the end, Jannings made an imperial entrance ramrod straight, as Lubitsch had wanted all along.

"What Lubitsch went through to get Jannings to stand straight I'd never have the patience to do," Wyler recalled years later. "I would have said, 'Look, I think this is crazy; you have to stand up straight.' I would have hurt the actor's feelings, a fight would have ensued over 'interpretation,' and half a day's work would have been ruined."

The German colony that Lubitsch held in stitches on his terrace was, in S. N. Behrman's words, "like a crowd in Renaissance Florence." The full list read like the Almanach de Gotha; it grew forever longer as Nazism chased Germany's best minds into exile, and most of them, even Bertolt Brecht, ended up in greater Los Angeles. The "intellectuals" included Thomas and Heinrich Mann, Lion and Martha Feuchtwanger, Otto Klemperer, Bruno Walter, the Franz Werfels. Actors included occasionally Greta

Garbo, who said *Ninotchka* was "the only time I had a great director in Hollywood," Pola Negri, Conrad Veidt, Paul Leni, Paul Stein, Vilma Banky and her husband, Rod La Rocque, Victor Varconi, and Marlene Dietrich. Others were Lubitsch's personal screenwriter Hans Kräly, and a couple of up-and-coming scripters from Paramount's overstocked writers' building—Walter Reisch and Billy Wilder, who, together with Charles Brackett, were to write *Ninotchka*. Designers included Hans Dreier and Ernst Fegté, movie mogul Ernst Pommer (who once brought Albert Einstein along). Sometimes, the French crowd was there also —Maurice Chevalier and his friends. Chevalier had starred in three Lubitsch comedies and they were just about to begin their fourth together—*The Merry Widow*—for Irving Thalberg. Robert Florey, who was as great an admirer of Lubitsch as was Wyler, was often there and, a few years later, Julien Duvivier. Chevalier and Thalberg had clashed over the choice of the actress to play the widow. "But Irving has imposed a hundred-and-twenty-five-pound weight limit on all actresses," Lubitsch grinned, adding that Chevalier's choice, Grace Moore, refused to stand on the scales in Thalberg's office. "Now, we're looking at Jeanette MacDonald, much to the disappointment of our Frenchman."

Wyler drove home or over to see Sheila with Lubitsch's mocking leer and elfin smile in his mind and Lubitsch's stings ringing in his ears—"We, in Hollywood, acquire the finest novels in order to smell their leather bindings" was one of them. Wyler wondered whether he himself could learn to tilt the studio windmills as daringly as the little Berliner did, whether he could come to terms with box-office demands with as few concessions as Lubitsch managed.

The romance with Sheila was "adult," and adequate. He had known her for two years and spent lovely Sundays in Palm Springs, La Jolla, and other Southern California resorts with her. She had come into his life after the affair with Evelyn Pierson had ebbed for lack of privacy. Although her mother also lived in Los Angeles, Sheila had her own house and their relation was comfortable and civilized. She was an actress, playing bits. She had a talent for making life for herself and others cozy and to spread physical ease and well-being around her, but she was, somehow, not the girl Willy could fall deeply in love with.

His mother kept telling him he should get married. With Gaston quietly in tow, Melanie and Leopold spent their winters in California. Willy usually rented a house for them on Crescent Heights Boulevard within walking distance of his own rented home on Fairfax Boulevard, above Hollywood Boulevard. Melanie wanted to spend at least half the year near Robert and Willy. The trouble was that Robert was as often in France and England as he was in California, embarked on a separate directing career away from his brother's overwhelming shadow. Leopold wanted to return to the business in Mulhouse, and every spring they sailed back to France.

Robert had great success in France in 1932 with *Papa sans le savoir,* a Gallic version of *The Little Accident,* which launched the career of a new comedian, Noël Noël, and featured Françoise Rosay as his mother. Another was *Une Etoile disparait,* directed under the name Robert Villers and starring Constant Remy, Suzy Vernon, and Robert's fiancée, Sandra Ravel. Produced by Paramount, it was a whodunnit, where the real criminal acted so outrageously suspicious that audiences began suspecting everybody else.

Melanie liked California. She had learned English quickly and, as in Mulhouse, made many friends. She had acquaintances everywhere and traveled around Los Angeles in a large automobile that Willy had bought her. Also, she continued her voluminous correspondence. When she saw the clouds gather over Germany, she tried to persuade relatives still there to flee. After Robert's death in 1971, Willy found bundles of their mother's correspondence that had been in Robert's possession, including letters to Albert Einstein and, in a frame, a thank-you note from President Franklin Roosevelt for a Mulhousian heirloom she had sent to the White House.

"She was a wonderful woman, Mother Earth, really," Kohner recalled. "Mother hen, also, defending her sons against all comers. If she thought something was done that wasn't right, she'd go directly to Carl Laemmle or she'd write endless letters. She traveled around in her big car and she had places where she stopped, places where she knew a policeman on the beat, a newspaper vendor. She had nuns coming to visit her. She met students, blacks, had friends everywhere."

When she invested a modest sum in the stock market, Willy gave her broker instructions to the effect that if her stock fell, he would make up the difference and that his mother was not to know about this. At afternoon teas in Beverly Hills, ladies would complain about atrocious losses on the skittish stock market, to which Mrs. Wyler would innocently say she couldn't understand; she was winning all the time. Among her secret but sound investments was the purchase, together with a Mrs. Chambers, of a small apartment house on Hollywood Boulevard. Bought in the mid-1930s for a couple of thousand dollars, the property still belonged to Melanie and Mrs. Chambers a quarter of a century later.

The filming of *Glamour* was without incident. If nothing else, the cast was delightful. Wyler paid little attention to his leading lady's after-hours romance with the boss. On the set, Constance Cummings was a delight, an actress who knew how to walk, talk, and wear sartorial creations. She had just appeared, with Walter Huston, in Frank Capra's "gee-whiz" Depression comedy, *American Madness*. As Linda Fayne—democratically scaled down to a chorus girl from the Broadway star of Edna Ferber's short story—she divorces one man, weds another, only to see her second husband play her false. After her child with her first husband dies, she returns to him. The poignant moment in the film shows the parents reunite at the child's funeral. Paul Lukas, discovered by Rouben Mamoulian for *City Streets,* played the first husband, a composer. Philip Reed was the smooth-talking younger costar and second husband while Joseph Cawthorne played Ibsen, an unconvincingly written Broadway producer.

The cameraman was, again, George Robinson, with whom Willy had fought in the Mojave Desert over clouds on *Hell's Heroes* and who had also photographed *Her First Mate*. Although reviews gave an approving nod to the acting and directing, *Glamour* was generally dismissed as a woman's picture "with a story that's pretty much along usual and unoriginal lines," as *Variety* said.[2] After a Hollywood preview, some fifteen minutes were cut from the film.

Next, Wyler was handed *The Good Fairy,* one of Ferenc Molnar's lesser comedies, a project which, in its tow, brought a friendship that was to have a great influence on him and lead to a flamingly disastrous marriage. *The Good Fairy* was a brilliant miss, almost a metaphor, as it were, of the incandescent union of Margaret Sullavan and William Wyler.

11

Preston Sturges was the first of Wyler's contemporaries to influence him profoundly. Four years older than Wyler, Preston Sturges was not to direct until 1940, when he bribed Paramount into letting him direct a script he sold them for ten dollars, but the tall, curly-haired Chicagoan with his collection of eccentric hats and careers had done a lot of other things in his colorful and chaotic life when the two of them met and became friends over the screenplay of *The Good Fairy*.

"He was a genius," was Wyler's way of summing him up. "He was also a tremendous egomaniac. I mean this in the most friendly sense because I loved Preston. We always spoke French together, funny enough. He wrote everything, directed everything, played everything out for actors. He later had a table at luncheon at Paramount where he held forth. As long as you didn't open your mouth but let him do the talking, everything was fine. He was a marvelous friend and a great companion."

Sturges was an impressionistic Cinderella story himself. He was the inventor of kissproof lipstick and of movable restaurant-booth tables. He had built and owned a diesel engine factory and, at one time, ran two restaurants in Hollywood. His other talents included painting, sculpture, and conversational wit in English and French. He had begun writing in 1927 after a ruptured appendix immobilized him for several weeks in a hospital bed.

Sturges had spent most of his childhood in Paris, where his mother was the founder of various perfumery and cosmetics ventures and, for a quarter century, the closest friend of Isadora Duncan (she lent her the scarf which, wound too casually, got caught in a car wheel and broke the dancer's neck). His mother's maiden name was Mary Dempsey, but, in addition to changing her name six times by marriage, she styled herself Mary Desti. Her first salon in Paris was named after Leonardo da Vinci's model, Beatricci d'Este, a name Preston's mother arrived at through genealogical research, which led her to believe the Renaissance family of d'Este had founded an Irish branch and that Dempsey was a mere corruption of d'Este. When the Italian family complained, she compromised by calling herself Mary Desti.

When the first Desti shop opened on New York's 9th Street, Preston was in charge. He studied the chemistry of makeup and became skilled in the manufacturing end of the business. His first customers were few but select and included Lillian Russell, Mae Marsh, and the first black millionairess, the famous Madame Walker, who invented the process for straightening kinky hair. By 1927, however, Preston's first wife had left him and he was regarded as a dreamer and a dabbler, seeking shortcuts to fortune. After *The Guinea Pig,* which he wrote at Chicago's Presbyterian Hospital, he decided to make one more go at the profession of playwright. *Strictly Dishonorable* was a comedy hit that ran on Broadway for nearly two years, brought him $300,000 in royalties, and a new wife. He had met Eleanor Hutton, the stepcousin of Barbara and equally rich, on a train to Florida and had immediately begun to woo the eighteen-year-old. The Huttons were opposed to the marriage because his connection with the cosmetics business raised doubts about his virility. Despite all obstacles, the lovebirds achieved headline-making elopement in the spring of 1930. Still proceeding on the momentum of *Strictly Dishonorable,* he traveled to Hollywood to look for a job, challenging institutions such as story conferences as "log-rolling congressmen meeting on pork-barrel legislation" and claiming that one head was better than twenty.

When Wyler and Sturges met, Preston had divorced the Hutton heiress and was trying to make up his mind how to beat the insane illogic of Hollywood success. He had come to Universal after a couple of years at Paramount, where he had toiled under the ubiquitous Herman Mankiewicz, who, a few years earlier, had instructed Ben Hecht in the art of screenwriting. In 1931, he had adapted *Strictly Dishonorable* and seen John Stahl direct Paul Lukas in the role of his flirtatious opera tenor who marries a southern heroine. He had been so happy with the film version that he had congratulated Carl Laemmle on the film's fidelity to the play. For William K. Howard, he had written *The Power and the Glory,* the story of a tycoon (Spencer Tracy) told in Chinese-box-puzzle form of flashbacks and disturbingly close to the *Citizen Kane* script his boss, Mankiewicz, was to deliver eight years later.

At Universal, Sturges worked, without credit, on the Paul Kohner project *Next Time We Love* and on Stahl's *Imitation of Life. The Good Fairy* was his most prestigious official project. Molnar had written his three-acter during his years of decline, twenty years after *Liliom,* but it still contained its measure of the bubbly romanticism and witty character sketches that had made the Hungarian famous.

The play, which Max Reinhardt had directed in Berlin and Vienna and Gilbert Miller had brought to Broadway in 1931 with Helen Hayes playing Lu, had too much banter about marital infidelity for the Hays Office (although Ben Hecht and Lubitsch had smuggled chunks of Noel Coward's amoral text past the Motion Picture Producers Association censors in the ménage à trois *Design for Living* the year before). But, besides sanitizing Molnar, Sturges made *The Good Fairy* into a filmable script. As rewritten by Sturges, the parable about the dangers of doing good became a whimsical story of a rapturously innocent movie usher, Lu, whose capacity for being naïve is vast enough to disorganize the lives of three men. Released from an orphanage in order to become an usherette—a beginning wholly invented by Preston—Lu proves to be so alarmingly helpless that an eccentric waiter, Detlaff, decides to protect her from the city evils. When she attracts the less than paternal eyes of Konrad, she tells him she is married. When Konrad decides, purely out of a spirit of generosity, to make her husband a rich man, Lu, in desperation, picks a name out of the phonebook—Max Sporum, who turns out to be a stern lawyer, starving of pride. And so on, through madcap situations until a finish similar to Molnar's. The most Sturgean scene has Lu in her movie house watching on the screen a cast-from-home-and-hearth sequence where a remorseless husband points toward the door with one word:

"Go!" to great comic effect. Sturges was to develop other movie-within-the-movie routines for *Sullivan's Travels* and *The Miracle of Morgan's Creek* when he became a director.

Willy and Preston saw each other constantly both during the writing and the filming, with Sturges taking a keen interest in directing.

"Preston was a night owl and we sat up half the night in his restaurant drinking wine and inventing things," Wyler recalled. "He had started a restaurant on Sunset Boulevard which was later to become Imperial Gardens. It was a bungalow home on top of a little hill and he decided that instead of tearing down the hill and constructing the restaurant, he would take away the hill *under* the bungalow and gradually build from the top down—second floor, first floor and finally the ground floor. He did it although it cost a fortune. He later got involved with Howard Hughes—it was somehow foreordained that the inventor of kissproof lipstick should meet the inventor of the aerodynamic bra. Then Hughes sat up in the restaurant drinking with Preston.

"They set up a corporation together to make a picture called *The Sin of Harold Diddlebock.** Anyway, we also had another project after *The Good Fairy.*"

Their project was Luigi Pirandello's 1921 *Come prima, meglio di prima* (*As Before, Better Than Before*), a play about a woman's attempt to assume a personality other than her own.

"We didn't really care for the story, but we liked one episode and worked on it for weeks. The scene dealt with a beautiful rich woman who decides on one last gastronomic fling before committing suicide. For this last supper, she decides to invite an old admirer, not a glamorous man, but an old, fat *bon vivant,* who is overjoyed at being asked to take her out.

"We consulted every gourmet magazine and called Robert Florey, who was a member of the Société Gastronomique, to give us advice and we wrote and wrote this most fabulous dinner.

"At one point, a procession would start coming from the kitchen; boys in uniform, one taller than the other, followed by the sommelier. The procession would go down to the cellar and open iron gates, into another cellar and come to a big safe. The

_____

* Actually made in 1947 by Columbia under the title *Mad Wednesday,* with Preston Sturges directing and Harold Lloyd starring.

_____

wine steward would open the safe and take out one brandy bottle and, in procession, carry it up to the kitchen. There, he would decant the bottle, pour it and set it on fire. The chef would then dip a knife in the flaming brandy and peel a peach. We wrote and wrote—the discovery of a piece of fat in the roast, etc."

Come prima, meglio di prima never reached the screen with or without the Sturges-Wyler culinary touches, but *The Good Fairy* went into production in October with the best cast Universal could assemble. Margaret Sullavan was given the role of Lu, Herbert Marshall, with whom Wyler was to make two more pictures, played a rejuvenated Max Sporum. Frank Morgan was Konrad and Reginald Owen was Detlaff, the waiter.

Margaret Sullavan was a girl who brought the best adjectives out in critics, a vivacious, gray-eyed Virginian who had just turned twenty-three and had just divorced fellow newcomer Henry Fonda. She was a girl with two films and two hits—*Only Yesterday* and *Little Man, What Now?* The former was a picture in the tradition of broken-hearted girls loving ardently, a trifle indiscreetly, and dying very young. John Stahl had put together an intelligent picture with a scabrous plot, the story of a woman twice seduced by the same man—twelve years apart and not recognized by him the second time.

"An analysis of why she seems so promising would probably revert to the old truism that the best actors work with their brains and Miss Sullavan seems to possess mentality," *Variety* wrote in reviewing *Only Yesterday*. "Her beauty is not stunning or vivid as others on the screen, but it may be more enduring, for it is founded on character and personality. Her impersonation breathes conviction and, as the story unfolds, she has a chance of displaying a range of emotions from girlish mischief to mature mellowness that is a convincer for those who doubt publicity departments." [1]

Little Man, What Now? was Frank Borzage's cinematization of Hans Fallada's novel with Margaret Sullavan playing Lämmchen Pinneberg and Douglass Montgomery her husband, in the bittersweet tale of little people in Weimar Republican Germany.

She had met Henry Fonda while doing stock on Cape Cod. Other hopefuls in Massachusetts that summer were Joshua Logan and James Stewart. Fonda had started in the theater in 1928 and managed a first Broadway walk-on the following year. After playing his first leading role in S. N. Behrman's *Love Story*, he had signed with theatrical agent Leland Hayward, who was to figure in the lives of Margaret Sullavan, Fonda, and Wyler and in the creation of the vast MCA talent agency.

Margaret Sullavan had come to Universal straight from a Broadway engagement—Edna Ferber and George S. Kaufman's *Dinner at Eight*. With the raves of *Only Yesterday* and *Little Man, What Now?* singing in her ears, she plunged into *The Good Fairy* with enthusiasm and a good measure of self-dramatization. Soon, she was at dagger's edge with her director.

"She was a good actress," Wyler recalled. "She had a marvelous voice, something very peculiar in the voice that was very attractive. We were constantly fighting, over the interpretation of her part, over everything. I remember one instance—and there she was probably right. She was this sweet, innocent girl out of the orphanage coming into this fancy restaurant and saying, 'Oh, isn't this wonderful.' She said, 'I'm not going to say that another time.'

"She had a mind of her own and so did I. The picture was important to me. I was getting into high comedy and I was doing one of Universal's important pictures. The story appealed to me, Preston had written a very good script, and the other actors were marvelous. Frank Morgan was very funny, playing the dirty old man. You felt that while he was after this girl, he wouldn't really harm her or do anything nasty. It was the first time I had Herbert Marshall. He played Sporum with a beard, all uptight and full of ethics, starving with pride. They were an interesting combination."

The fights with Maggie, as friends called her, showed up on the screen in closeups of haggard, nervous expressions. Wyler saw it for the first time in a screening room with his cameraman, Norbert Brodine.

"The girl looks terrible, what's the matter?" Wyler asked Brodine.

"You had a fight."

"What has that to do with it?"

"Each time you have a fight with her and she's tense or unhappy, she looks terrible. I can put all the light on her, she won't look good."

They watched in silence.

"That's terrible," Wyler sighed after a while, "what am I going to do?"

Brodine shrugged his shoulders.

Wyler decided that for the good of the picture, he would have to make his peace with his leading lady. The next day on the set, he was extra careful and in the afternoon, asked her to dinner. She was startled, but she accepted.

That evening at his house they discovered they could get along fabulously. A couple of nights later, he took her over to Sturges' restaurant for a nightcap. A week later, he dropped in, alone, on Sturges.

"What would you say if I got married to Maggie?" Willy asked.

"Well, she's not marrying you for your money, that's for sure."

They both grinned. It was not to be the last time Wyler would hear hints about Maggie earning four or five times as much as he. Preston was for it, in his own blasé way. If it worked, fine; if not, what the hell.

There were still the parents. He brought Maggie over to Crescent Heights Boulevard one Sunday. Melanie burst into tears. She was delighted. Finally, a daughter-in-law! Robert was thirty-four and Willy thirty-two. It was about time. She had to sit down for a moment.

Leopold just watched. His English was more than scratchy, but he got the idea. When he and Willy were alone for a moment, he looked at his son with an inquisitive gaze, and said, hopefully,

"What did you say her name was? Salomon?"

"No, Papa. Sullavan."

Margaret Brooke Sullavan and Willy Wyler were wed November 25, 1934, by the justice of the peace of Yuma, Arizona.

"I had chartered a DC3 and we flew to Arizona—Maggie, my lawyer, Mark Cohen, and myself—because in California, you had to wait three days. Just across the California-Arizona state-line. Terrible place. The justice of the peace was in his slippers and bathrobe and he stood there and married us with the radio blaring behind him. He had to get his wife to witness. She was in the bedroom and couldn't come out, so he handed her the papers to sign under the door. It was terrible."

Back on the airstrip, the pilot made an ominous joke, congratulating the newlyweds by asking if they wanted him to fly them directly to the divorce city of Reno, Nevada.

The marriage was something of a sensation. With the usual glee, gossip columnists had reported the fights going on between director and star on Universal's *The Good Fairy* and here on a

Monday morning, the papers announced they were married. On the same Monday morning, Mr. and Mrs. Wyler were back on the set, finishing the picture in another two nervous weeks.

The Good Fairy opened at New York's Radio City Music Hall to sparkling reviews. "Margaret Sullavan Scores Triumph in Superb Portrayal," read the headline of Leo Mishkin's review in the *New York Telegraph*.[2] "A delightful, heart-warming comedy with an incessant ripple of laughter ruffling the charm of its surface," began the *New York American*[3] while the *Herald Tribune* said the film "spins a lively, if talkative, fable, about the potential perils of benevolence."[4] "Enchanting and whimsical little orphan girls have become the new fad in movie heroines but none has been more appealing and captivating than the latest, Margaret Sullavan," the *Daily Mirror* began.[5] The *Times*'s new critic, André Sennwald, went almost all out: "When it is hitting its stride, the film edition of Molnar's *The Good Fairy* is so priceless that it arouses in one the impertinent regret that it is not the perfect fantastic comedy which it might have been."[6] "Sullavan's 'Good Fairy' One You Mustn't Miss," headlined the *Buffalo Times*[7] and the *Washington News*[8] bannered it, "Margaret Sullavan Annexes More in 'Good Fairy'!"

To be married to a movie star was a baffling experience, both irritating and exhilarating—irritating because he was more in his wife's shadow than she in his limelight and stimulating because it spurred him on. If *Glamour* had made him think of a career away from Universal, the temptation was being reinforced by the ever-lengthening list of films that didn't happen—at least, not for *him*.

The studio constantly announced projects for Wyler. There had been three pictures to star Lew Ayres—*Manhunt,* to be based on Bret Harte's "Outcasts of Poker Flat," *U-Boat,* and a gangster flick, *Babyfaced Killer*—that all fell through. In 1933, he had turned down a three-year contract offered by Universal and to placate the young "ace director," as the studio publicity department called him, there had been reports of loaning him out to Columbia to direct John Barrymore in the screen version of the Ben Hecht–Charles MacArthur stage hit *Twentieth Century.* Then, there had been three other Universal projects—Anthony McGuire's *Then the Time Comes,* L. G. Blochman's *The Golden Fleece,* to feature Paul Lukas, and (after Blaise Cendrars' *L'Or*), *Sutter's Gold,* for which he would like Charles Laughton. On his return from the New York premiere of *Counsellor at Law*, Wyler had told reporters that of the recently bought plays, *She Loves Me Not* would make the best movie and that *The Dark Tower* would make an excellent vehicle for Barrymore. "I enjoyed Miriam Hopkins in *Jezebel*," he had said, "it would make a much better picture than a play." * Now, he marched into the front office and asked to be released from his contract. To his dizzying surprise, he got it.

He was free. And jobless.

But far from poor. During the last year at Universal, his weekly salary had been one thousand dollars, so, instead of looking for work, Mr. and Mrs. Wyler went on a winter honeymoon-vacation in Europe.

During the New York stopover, Maggie wanted to see a play called *The Farmer Takes a Wife*. The Frank B. Elser–Marc Connelly play starred Henry Fonda. After the last curtain, Maggie insisted on going backstage.

"I'm afraid I didn't take it very gracefully," Wyler remembered. "I sort of felt funny and I was all prepared to hate this former husband, but Fonda turned out to be charming, delightful, and attractive. I had never asked her why their marriage hadn't worked." A few years later, when Wyler had Fonda as his leading man on *Jezebel*, they were to kid about this first meeting of two former husbands of Maggie Sullavan.

Two days later, the newlyweds sailed on the *Île de France*. In London, where they rang in the New Year 1935 with Robert and his fiancée, Sandra Ravel, Maggie was adulated.

"One time at Claridge's where we stayed, a crowd wanting to see her and get autographs got us separated. I stood and waited for her to get through. One girl felt sorry for me and finally came over and stuck out her scrapbook and pencil. 'Here, you, too,' she said. I said, 'Thank you, very much' and signed: 'Mr. Sullavan.'"

On the Continent, they rented a car. After Paris and a compulsory stop in Mulhouse to introduce Maggie to Edmond Cahen, Paul Jacob, and other childhood friends, they drove to Switzerland and went skiing. In Vienna, they went on the set of Walter Reisch's *Episode* starring Paula Wessely, who had played Lu in

* Directed by Joseph Newman, *Outcasts of Poker Flats* was filmed in 1952; *Twentieth Century* was directed by Howard Hawks in 1934; *Sutter's Gold* by James Cruze in 1936; and *She Loves Me Not* by Elliot Nugent in 1934.

Max Reinhardt's Viennese production of *The Good Fairy*. They crossed into Germany via Salzburg and checked into the chic Vier Jahreszeiten in Munich. The hotel's celebrity service spread the word of their arrival and the next morning's newspapers announced the visit of Hollywood star Margaret Sullavan and her director husband, William Wyler.

While Maggie had her hair set the next day, Willy went for a walk and ended up at the Odeonsplatz where he was irresistibly drawn toward the new monument commemorating the attempted assassination of the Führer.

"Two stormtroopers guarded the monument under a huge Swastika banner. Everybody went by with a Nazi salute. I went by, stopped, and looked. The guards looked at me as I read the thing and kept my hands in my pockets."

That night, when Maggie and he had dinner at the Vier Jahreszeiten, the waiter came over and said someone wanted to talk to Herr Wyler.

"Well, have him come in," Wyler said.

"He won't come in."

Wyler insisted, saying he was eating, and the waiter disappeared into the entrance hall. The man didn't want to come in. Wyler got up and went into the foyer. Trying to make himself inconspicuous, a man nodded toward him and when they reached each other, Wyler saw a yellow Star of David on the man's overcoat.

"Walter! How are you? Come in."

Despite his distant relative's protest, Willy dragged Walter to his table.

"I made him sit down and order something," Wyler remembered. "Then, I made him and Maggie get up and dance. He was scared to death, but he did it. Then, I danced with Maggie. He was terrified the whole time."

Walter Laemmle was to make it out of Germany a few months later and end up as a prominent Los Angeles antique dealer. He was the last of the Auerbach and Laemmle families to escape the Nazi holocaust.

The honeymoon ended in France when Maggie received a telegram from Paramount offering her the lead in King Vidor's upcoming *So Red the Rose*. They sailed for New York from Cannes aboard an Italian liner.

12

Traveling in style was costly. When Willy totaled the bills, he discovered he was almost broke. But, as Maggie went to work for King Vidor at Paramount, Jesse Lasky offered him a picture at Fox. He quickly accepted.

It was a strange feeling. At $2,500 a week, it was again a big jump up, but it was for ten weeks only. Once the picture was finished, he would be out of work again. He told his agent, Noel Guerney, to keep looking.

The quarrels with Maggie had started again; sometimes they both wondered if they had ever stopped. Married life apparently was an emotional yo-yo with high-low contrasts of an intensity that neither of them had suspected. It all boiled down to two careers in one family, Maggie's fame and Willy's need to assert himself.

So Red the Rose was a sentimentalized adaptation of Stark Young's bestseller—together with Margaret Mitchell's *Gone with the Wind,* the South's 1930s' view of its past. Young's story was a look at the last days of Louisiana aristocracy, with gallant colonels defending honor and tradition against a cruel, vulgar, and vindictive North. The film, which Vidor managed to forget in his first autobiography,[1] was so biased that the *New York Times* felt obliged to caution that "it is difficult in this turbulent day to subscribe to the film's point of view or to share its rage against the uncouth legions of Mr. Lincoln as they dash about the lovely Southern landscape putting crazy notions in the heads of the plantation slaves."² Maggie played "the flower of Southern womanhood" opposite Walter Connolly's venerable planter called to arms after his only son and heir has fallen, and Randolph Scott was her cousin and romantic lead.

Willy's assignment was *The Gay Deception,* his first movie to receive an Academy nomination—for best original story—and lead directly to his long association with Samuel Goldwyn. The writers were a couple of pros: Stephen Avery, who was to pen other Jesse Lasky comedies, and Don Hartman, later the writer of *Road to Zanzibar* and three other of the Bob Hope–Bing Crosby–Dorothy Lamour *Road* pictures. Lasky, who had been one of the founding fathers of Paramount and its vice-president in charge of production until 1932, was an independent producer releasing through Fox (and making such froth as *Berkeley Square, As Husbands Go,* and *Redheads on Parade).*

Willy liked *The Gay Deception* and turned the well-worn Cinderella theme (and most abused romantic situation known to the cinema) into, perhaps, his funniest film. His cast was tops. Francis Lederer dispensed magic and artful whimsy as the prince from a mythical kingdom rushing about the Waldorf-Plaza (sic) as a bellhop while learning the hotel business. Frances Dee was all charm and loveliness as a small-town stenographer with a $5,000 lottery win masquerading as a grand lady. Backing them up were such merry performers as Alan Mowbray, Benita Hume, Paul Hurst, Lennox Pawle, and Luis Alberni. Locale, for most of the action, was a swank New York hotel, gently mocked for its service, institutions, rules on tips, and such dictums as "the-customer-is-always right."

One day halfway through shooting, Wyler couldn't help noticing Frances Dee's expanding waistline. She admitted she was pregnant. When he asked her why she hadn't told him before the film started, she said she had been afraid of not getting the part, which was probably what would have happened. "That's a great way for an actress to get nothing but closeups," Wyler smiled years later after the same thing had happened to him with Jennifer Jones. "I had to shoot her mostly from the chest up!"

When Maggie and Willy weren't fighting, they had some great moments. One day on the Waldorf-Plaza set at Fox, Willy was told an unwieldy package had arrived and was waiting for him outside. When he got the wraps off, it was a sparkling Harley

Davidson—"with love from Maggie." On one of the first rides on the motorcycle, he wheeled over to the newly married Lupita and Paul Kohners. He roared out of their Toluka Lane driveway with Lupita sitting behind him and Paul running after them yelling, "But she's pregnant, she's pregnant. Watch out!"

Such occasions were getting rarer, however. "That was one of the problems," Wyler recalled. "With great pride, I had come home on the first payday at Fox and showed her my check for twenty-five hundred dollars and she showed me hers—for eight thousand, five hundred a week. Well, that's tough. There was nothing I could do for her that she couldn't do herself."

Willy's sense of inadequacy was not only monetary. He tried to stay aloof from her career only to be drawn irresistibly into it in the whirlpool of Hollywood social life. "What's your wife's next picture?" was the ritual question.

Willy had married with rather conventional notions of the roles of husband and wife, and on principle Maggie had no objections. Her goals were no different from his, really. What she wanted was home and kids, perhaps with an occasional movie role or Broadway part. She was not career crazy—in arguments where roles were reversed, Willy would almost accuse her of being a little too relaxed about her professional life. But she loved the intoxication of fame. In the shadow, as it were, Willy couldn't cope.

That they were both spoiled and immature was less important in the end than their shattered expectations. Later in life, Willy felt he was mostly to blame for the breakup, that if it had lasted another year or two or if they had had a child, *he* would have learned to relax, both to assert himself and to tolerate her individuality. When he directed Barbra Streisand in her first film more than thirty years later, he was to recognize in her and her then unknown husband Elliott Gould, his own dilemma as an obscure husband of a star.

"One of the reasons I had left Universal was to become a bigger director, to get my teeth in big, important pictures, and become as big as Maggie. Anyway, we had about a year and a half together—lots of fights, lots of good times. It was fighting, making up, and fighting again."

The ugly scenes grew more numerous than the good times with long cold wars and exhausting reconciliations in between. By the time their pictures opened in New York—*The Gay Deception* at the Radio City Music Hall and, three weeks later, *So Red the Rose* at the Paramount—they were separated. Willy was in New York when Maggie filed for an uncontested Mexican divorce March 13, 1936, at the end of the shooting of Kohner's Universal production, *Next Time We Love,* directed by Edward H. Griffith and starring Maggie and James Stewart. On November 15, she married Leland Hayward and, for a while, abandoned her career. When he returned from the East, Willy rented a little house on Beverly Hills' Bedford Drive and, to show he bore no ill feelings, soon joined the Hayward agency as a client.

For Borzage, Maggie starred in *Three Comrades* in 1938, the year after her husband formed the Hayward-Deverich, Inc. agency. After H. C. Potter's *Shopworn Angel,* she starred with James Stewart in Lubitsch's *The Shop Around the Corner,* followed by another Borzage film, *The Mortal Storm.* The Haywards were considered an ideal couple; their marriage lasted eleven years and produced three children. It ended when she returned to the Broadway stage in *The Voice of the Turtle,* followed by an attempted film comeback in 1950 with *No Sad Songs for Me,* directed by Rudolph Maté. Her fourth marriage, to London businessman Kenneth A. Wagg, lasted until her death in 1960.*

Critics and public loved *The Gay Deception* and Wyler's agent got a call from Samuel Goldwyn, who had also caught the Francis Lederer–Frances Dee comedy.

One of the year's better in-jokes was that Goldwyn had bought an unfilmable play, Lillian Hellman's *The Children's Hour.* Everybody knew the Hays Office frowned upon this tricky play and that Goldwyn had acquired it with the understanding that he couldn't use its title or its plot or even mention the fact that he had bought it. Donating $50,000 for the privilege of carting a dead horse away *was* funny.

When Willy was introduced, with lawyers and agents present, to the most formidable of the independents, Goldwyn wanted to know if Wyler was interested in directing a screen version of Miss Hellman's play. Willy had seen *The Children's Hour* in New York and allowed himself to express mild astonishment. He was

* The Haywards' second daughter, Bridget, committed suicide at the age of twenty-one, ten months after her mother's death.

117

not the first, Goldwyn observed. He, himself, had not believed her play could be transmuted without fatal results, but Miss Hellman had convinced him that the theme was the power, not the nature, of a lie and she had written the screenplay herself. In due course, Miss Hellman was to convince Wyler that her play was not about lesbianism, but the story of a calumny; what this lie did to people was important, not the nature of the lie.

Goldwyn offered Wyler the picture on the condition he sign a five-year contract. Wyler balked at five years and suggested three years instead. The offer was irresistible. Besides the chance to make important pictures for the producer who believed in making important pictures, the contract translated into forty weeks a year at $2,500 a week, freedom to make pictures elsewhere between Goldwyn projects, and a two-year option at $2,750 and $3,000 a week.

Willy said he would give his answer within twenty-four hours. On the way out, he already knew he would say yes.

There was no turning back. It was evident that even if his motives for leaving Uncle Carl had been Universal's inability or unwillingness to produce the kind of movies that would make him as big as Maggie, his leaving had been a wise move.

The way he heard it from Kohner, Universal was going through a grim period. The whole Noah's Ark was adrift. The European facilities were shuttered, the current crop of pictures less than satisfactory, earnings were plummeting, and stockholders ready to revolt. What was needed was imagination, which translated to new blood, fresh initiatives, and, perhaps, a bit of daring. Like *Peter,* for example, the last Universal picture made in Berlin, which had won the grand prize at the 1935 International Exposition of Motion Picture Arts in Moscow as the best comedy. It had been produced by a Hungarian Paul had found, Joseph Pasternak, and directed by a Berliner, Hermann Kosterlitz. The pair had arrived at Universal after the European closedown and had set to work on a routine B script. It was somehow typical. Pasternak and Henry Koster, as Kosterlitz called himself in America, had expected plush assignments, but for their first picture were given the choice of contract players for whom the studio had no plans and few hopes. *Three Smart Girls* was about a mischievous fifteen-year-old who tried to reunite her divorced parents and Pasternak and Koster had cast everybody except the girl.

Uncle Carl, now sixty-nine, was under pressure from his son, his daughter and son-in-law, and some stockholders to sell the studio. But Paul Kohner had been instrumental in yet another conciliation between father and son and the old man had been touched by Paul's generous defense of Junior. Paul was sure he had the old man's confidence and the old man's word that there would be no sellout. A few years earlier, Uncle Carl had been offered—and turned down—$20 million for the whole caboodle: studio, exchanges, and threaters around the world. The Depression had made money scarcer and the price might be somewhat lower today. The old man was now offered $15 million.

The Carl Laemmle regime ended ingloriously early in 1936 when the company was on the verge of bankruptcy. Uncle Carl panicked and sold the entire empire for $5.5 million.

Kohner had had a scheme all worked out to save the studio. He had pleaded with Uncle Carl to hold out while he and three other trusted friends flew around the country raising cash from top exhibitors, advances from large theater owners on next year's product. One night, Kohner was in the Brown Derby on Vine Street. It was a boxing night and the place was nearly empty. Columbia's Harry Cohn recognized him and asked him to come over.

"I hear you're out of a job," Cohn began.

"What do you mean?"

"Well, Laemmle has given Rogers and his New York investors a $150,000 option to buy."

"I don't believe it."

"You better and when you're out of a job, come to me."

Cohn was given to coarse jokes and belonged to the breed of moviemakers in the tough, brassy tradition. The next morning, Paul went straight to Laemmle, repeating that the efforts to raise loans from exhibitors were encouraging, but that he had heard rumors about an option to a group of Wall Streeters. "I think you owe me the truth," Kohner said. "Did you?"

Uncle Carl hedged, then admitted that he had. "But don't worry, Kohner, they'll never take up the option."

"I'm not so sure," said the stunned Kohner. "So, you've sold everything—the real estate, the theaters, the exchanges, the vault?"

"Everything, Kohner."

That had been on the eve of the filming of *Next Time We*

Love. Kohner had still produced this picture, but other projects, including the one Preston Sturges had been working on, were dropped. On April 2, 1936, it was all over. Universal passed under new management.

By the time Wyler began working for Goldwyn, Kohner was a highly paid but unhappy executive at MGM, snatched up by Louis B. Mayer as Irving Thalberg had been fifteen years earlier. With J. Cheever Cowdin as chairman of the board, the new Universal management began struggling back toward solvency and daily turned up facts that it was awfully easy to make fun of. On the payroll they found the names of two men who were dead. Other employees came in only to get their paychecks. All in all, more than a dozen relatives, friends of relatives, and other pensioners of Uncle Carl were uncovered and flushed out.

In December, Universal previewed *Three Smart Girls* and the fifteen-year-old Canadian ingénue Pasternak and Koster had found to play the starring role was an overnight sensation. People stampeded the box office to hear Deanna Durbin sing *Il Bacio* and snatches from two other operas. When the new star reached New York, Mayor Fiorello La Guardia presented her with the keys to the city. By May 1937, there were Deanna Durbin Devotee clubs across America and the millions were pouring in again.

13

Samuel Goldwyn, Lillian Hellman, and *The Children's Hour*—
duly retitled *These Three*—were another crowd. If writers ever
had a chance as cinematic *auteurs,* it was during Goldwyn's autocratic reign on 1041 North Formosa Avenue. Sam loved writers
and was the one studio boss who had more than a measure of respect for creative talent. In many ways, the maddeningly self-cen-
tered producer was the worst of the kind. A believer in his own
publicity puff, he was the ultimate Hollywoodizer. He read Tolstoy and other classics in synopsis form and listened to Liszt as
rearranged by Frank Loesser. He felt writers should write and
directors direct with him as the only organic link between them.

But he *was* independent—as independent as anyone could be
during the big studio era. He wanted his films to be more than
box-office hits. He loved the business and was proud to be called
"a lonely wolf." He produced films that others shied away from—
The Little Foxes was supposed to have too many disagreeable
characters, *Arrowsmith* to be too dull, and *Dodsworth* to be obvious box-office poison since it was about middle-aged people.

His mercurial nature didn't make him easy to work with. "It's
the survival of the fittest," was one of his favorite sayings. Wyler
was to feel the weight of that dictum during the filming of *Dead
End* when Goldwyn had Lewis Milestone stand by to take over.

Goldwyn squeezed minds like oranges. Ben Hecht, who con-
ceded Goldwyn was, with David Selznick and Darryl Zanuck, the
brightest of his Hollywood bosses, compared Goldwyn's treatment
of writers to an agitated man's shaking of a slot machine.

In 1935, Lillian Hellman was the latest of a line of "eminent authors." An early Nobel prize winner to come under the Goldwyn spell was Maurice Maeterlinck, who was forced to cancel an American lecture tour because of his fractured English. Goldwyn pampered the Belgian poet but let him go when the author of *Pelléas et Mélisande* suggested a movie on the life of bees. In 1919, Goldwyn had paid another Nobel prize winner, Anatole France, then nearing eighty, $10,000 for the screen rights to *Thaïs* and had tried to snare George Bernard Shaw. After one of their discussions, a reporter called on Shaw and asked why he had not signed with Goldwyn. "There is only one difference between Mr. Goldwyn and myself," Shaw said. "He's an artist. I'm a businessman."

Born in the Warsaw ghetto in 1882, Sam Goldwyn had been a latecomer to the movies. When he arrived in America alone as a thirteen-year-old, busy immigration officials listened to his mumbled Slavic syllables and wrote him down as Samuel Goldfish. He had been a formidable glove salesman of twenty-nine when his brother-in-law, Jesse Lasky, lured him into a tripartite venture with a less-than-successful Broadway playwright named Cecil B. DeMille. The year was 1912, by no means prehistory but still high antiquity of the movies, and the trio realized their only chance was to be different.

Different but not unique. Adolph Zukor and his Famous Players company were already making features—hour-long pictures instead of one- or two-reelers. With $15,000 in capitalization, the Jesse Lasky Feature Company sent DeMille, a cameraman, and matinée idol Dustin Farnum west to shoot *The Squaw Man.* Lasky had been to Arizona and suggested DeMille shoot the picture in Flagstaff because there were plenty of Indians, but when DeMille saw tall mountains instead of the flatlands his script demanded, he bought supplementary tickets to the end of the line —Los Angeles. Other pioneers were grinding out pictures under the California sun, but DeMille was the first to venture out to the orange groves of Hollywood, where he rented a barn for seventy-five dollars a month as his studio (on the condition the owner's horse could sleep in the barn at night.) With the help of Sam's supersalesmanship, the Lasky company made over $200,000 on that first venture, followed by a comedy, *Brewster's Millions,* and twenty other pictures that first year. Restless Sam handled all the selling, distribution, and exploitation. When the corporation merged with Zukor's company, Lasky decided to back the thoughtfully shrewd Zukor instead of his dynamic if somewhat uncoordinated brother-in-law—a move Sam didn't forgive until both were old men. Not that Zukor and Lasky treated Sam other than generously. They bought him out for $900,000 less than four years after he had gone into partnership with Lasky and DeMille.

In 1917, Sam formed a new company with a playwright, Margaret Mayo, and a theatrical producer, Edgar Selwyn. The new corporation was called Goldwyn—from *gold* in Goldfish and *wyn* in Selwyn and Sam grew so fond of it he had his own name legally changed. Legend has it that Allan Dwan, the first director they hired, somewhat flippantly suggested they reverse the name halves and call their firm the Selfish Company.

The Goldwyn Company signed up whatever names they could —Mabel Normand, Mae Marsh, Maxine Elliott, and the Ziegfeld Follies cowboy Will Rogers. To star in the screen version of Anatole France's *Thaïs*, they signed Mary Garden and paid her the unheard-of sum of $150,000. *Thaïs*, the story of a courtesan, was one of the colossal flops of the silent era. Since Sam knew he couldn't compete on star rosters with the big companies, he hit on the idea of "eminent authors." The first consignment included Gertrude Atherton, an ardent feminist, novelist, and historian, who campaigned with verve against puritanism and whose society novels were considered scandalous when they appeared. Other authors were Rex Beach, Rupert Hughes, and Mary Roberts Rinehart. The company made hits—*Polly of the Circus,* directed by Alfred Santell, who was also to make Goldwyn's biggest silent hit, *The Dark Angel.* It also made flops, like *Thaïs,* and by 1922 was held together only by $7 million invested after the flush war years by the Du Pont dynasty and other families with ubiquitous Frank Godsol of *Ben-Hur* fame brought with him. In 1922, Goldwyn was pushed out by Godsol. Two years later, the failing company merged with Metro to become the middle name of MGM.

Goldwyn retired for a few months to a house on Long Island and dictated his memoirs to a ghostwriter. They were published in *Pictorial Review* and as a book under the title *Behind the Screen,* and supposedly netted Goldwyn nearly $100,000.[1] With this money and a million dollars salvaged from the Goldwyn Company, he went back into moviemaking again. Samuel Goldwyn, Inc., Ltd., was formed in 1924 with no partners, no directors, and no stock; three years later, Goldwyn became owner-member of United Artists, which released his films until 1940.

Goldwyn discovered or greatly furthered the careers of many players. He found Vilma Banky—later of Lubitsch's Sunday crowd—in Budapest, put her on a diet and had her star in *The Dark Angel,* an adaptation of H. B. Trevelyan's World War I melodrama. Vilma Banky's salary went to $5,000 a week in her four years with Goldwyn until the talkies exposed her Hungarian accent. The so-called Goldwyn Girls, a group of chorines who made *The Goldwyn Follies* possible, at one time included Paulette Goddard and Betty Grable. Others discovered by him were Robert Montgomery, David Niven, Teresa Wright, and, later, Danny Kaye, Lucille Ball, Susan Hayward, and Sidney Poitier. Like everybody else, he thought Clark Gable's ears were too big and doubted Greta Garbo's potential, but his most famous miss was Anna Sten, a Rubenesque Ukrainian whom he imported in 1932 after seeing her in Fedor Ozep's early sound version of *The Murder of Dimitri Karamazov.* To do something about her almost impenetrable accent, he hired English coaches; to trim her down, he hired a masseuse, while ordering Lynn Farnol, his press agent, to pull out all the stops. To direct her in *Nana,* the Emile Zola novel of a Parisian courtesan, he hired Dorothy Arzner, Hollywood's only woman director, and at one point scrapped $400,-000 worth of finished footage and had everybody start over again. When the revised *Nana* opened in New York's Radio City Music Hall in 1934, it broke all first-day records, thanks to Farnol's advance publicity. The next day, the reviews killed it.

Fearlessly, Goldwyn gave her a Russian story and a Russian director. *We Live Again* was a rewrite of Tolstoy's *Resurrection,* a drama of sin and regeneration. Rouben Mamoulian, fresh from *Queen Christina* with Garbo, directed the Goldwyn protégée and Fredric March in a lyrical, sensuous exercise in Dovzhenko cinematics.[2] When the picture flopped, Goldwyn got Dorothy Arzner back to direct Anna Sten in *The Wedding Night.* From Paramount, he borrowed Gary Cooper to portray the novelist who becomes involved with a Polish peasant girl while staying on a Connecticut farm. When this drama was laughed off the screen, Goldwyn gave up on Anna Sten. After the termination of her Goldwyn contract, Miss Sten continued to appear in films until 1962. In the early 1970s, she devoted herself to painting.

Other flops included *The Adventures of Marco Polo,* which gave Gary Cooper an opportunity to discover spaghetti in China, and the incredibly named *Woman Chases Man.* Goldwyn usually explained his duds by remarking that he was not around the studio when they were made. In the case of *Woman Chases Man,* directed by John Blystone in 1937, he blamed the writer, Edward Chodorov, who was not there either, but had been called in to see if he could improve the original script. Chodorov gave it one reading and announced the script was so terrible he wouldn't have anything to do with it. Years later, when someone suggested to Goldwyn that he call Chodorov to work on a completely new story, Sam cried, "Chodorov! I won't have anything to do with that fellow. He was connected with one of my worst failures!"

Besides Elmer Rice, Miss Hellman, and Hecht, whom Goldwyn paid $260,000 in 1937 alone, the "eminent authors" toiling on Formosa Avenue during the high thirties included Robert Sherwood, Frances Marion (until Hecht, she was his highest paid writer), Sidney Howard, Sidney Kingsley, S. N. Behrman, Richard Nash, Charles MacArthur, and George Oppenheimer (who won a writers' contest in Goldwynism at a time when the boss forbade the deliberate making of malapropisms with the entry, "It rolls off my back like a duck"). For a few weeks in 1939, Scott Fitzgerald joined the fold, rewriting *Raffles,* a David Niven–Olivia de Havilland film directed by Sam Wood. The deal was agented by Leland Hayward. In his notebook, Scott wrote that he "liked Sam Goldwyn—you always knew where you stood with Goldwyn—nowhere." [3]

Goldwyn's attitude toward directors was ambivalent if not outright hostile. As much as he encouraged writers, he never managed to suppress in himself a feeling of jealousy toward directors. He feared placing too much power in their hands and the notion of the director as a creative force was a concept he could never accept. That, as Hecht put it, would be "a case of two Caesars and one Alp."

"I was constantly trying to get my name in somewhere," Wyler recalled. "But he was very peculiar about directors. He didn't mind publicizing writers and, of course, stars, but he never mentioned directors in publicity.

"About twice a year, I was invited to dinner at his house. With his guests there he was always very generous, telling them I was the best director he ever had. As long as he could keep me from writing, keep me from changing things, as long as I stayed with directing in the strictest sense of moving bodies camera-left to camera-right, I was fine. In intimate circles, he would praise me and my work. Publicly, I was a dark secret."

Wyler had a friend, however. He was Mack Millar, Bob Hope's New York press agent, who on the sly saw to it that Wyler got interviews, at least when he was in Manhattan. At the studio, the publicity department pushed only one name—Goldwyn.

"To give Sam his due, let me say that with all his faults, he was no scrawny little fast buck producer," Wyler said decades later. "He was the first producer to send me back to shoot a scene over again. 'Do it over again,' he'd say as if money didn't matter. 'Who do you want in this part?' he'd also say and I could practically cast any star in any role again regardless of cost. Which doesn't mean we didn't fight, but we fought for what we both thought was right."

The knockdown fights between Goldwyn and Wyler, which sent bystanders scurrying for cover, were to begin with *Dead End* and continue through *The Best Years of Our Lives*.

Frances Howard had been an actress playing a flapper in Gilbert Miller's Broadway production of *The Best People* with Alfred Lunt and Billie Burke, when Goldwyn met her at a housewarming party for *Vogue* publisher Condé Nast in 1925. Three weeks later, he made her his second wife. Sam was forty-three and Frances twenty-one. When he celebrated his ninetieth birthday, they were still together. Their only child was Sam, Jr. Goldwyn never mentioned the daughter of his first marriage during the long and rich summit of his career. Frances ran their stately home high above the Coldwater Canyon in Beverly Hills with exemplary care, supervising small dinners and large soirees with equal poise. An invitation to the Goldwyns' was the film colony equivalent of a summons to Buckingham Palace.

Goldwyn's proprietary attitude toward creative talent didn't sit well with all writers, who were supposed to devote their creative forces, indeed their entire lives, to the making of better Goldwyn pictures. Favorite writers learned to expect calls at all hours. When Robert Sherwood was engaged to write a picture once, he retreated to his Long Island home to begin work. At three in the morning, his phone rang. It was Goldwyn from the Coast, where the time was only midnight. "Do you know what time it is?" Sherwood asked when he was awake. After a moment's silence, he heard Goldwyn speak, "Frances, Bob wants to know what time it is."

The *haute époque* of front-office mania and assembly-line output—"untouched by human hand," as Willy once had it—was also when Glamourland was maligned by writers, from the most famous literati to the most craven trashmasters.

Lillian Hellman belonged to the New York crowd of sophisticates who commuted across the depressed land between mid-Manhattan and Beverly Hills, pulling down $2,000-a-week jobs and finding the whole idea of "working in pictures" flirtatiously immoral. William Faulkner worked for a while for Howard Hawks, and the MGM Thalberg building harbored such luminaries as Anita Loos, F. Scott Fitzgerald, Ring Lardner, Jr., Aldous Huxley, and P. G. Wodehouse, plus Dorothy Parker and her second husband, Alan Campbell. Elsewhere, other founding fathers of the Algonquin set, from Robert Benchley to Donald Ogden Stewart and George Oppenheimer, sat in writers' bungalows, all a little too clever for their own good, telling each other they were going to seed in the California sun, although in the best possible style. In "buzz sessions," as story conferences were called (at Warner's, the conference room was called the "echo chamber"), they "talked" pulp into formula, each trying to add, as one wit had it, "to the compost heap." When they weren't dipping delicate toes into heated swimming pools, sipping margaritas or telling jokes about their obtuse bosses at Mme Berthold Viertel's salon (where the Huxleys, Bertrand Russell, and Igor Stravinsky also foregathered), they recorded their *angst* in novels, talked about Hollywood as a warm Siberia, deplored the Philistinism and the fact, as Dorothy Parker put it, that Hollywood money was like snow; it melted in your hand.

Something changed in the mid-thirties. Mrs. Parker at least came to hate her comic-strip self, and being witty somehow was going out of style. She and the others espoused the causes of what Franklin Roosevelt called the lunatic fringe. They formed the Anti-Nazi League, wrote checks for the Republican Spanish, and signed petitions for the release of Sacco and Vanzetti.

"It is very easy to make fun of that Hollywood group in the light of what we have learned from Mr. Stalin," Donald Ogden Stewart would say later. "I think we all felt a bit guilty about making all that money and not doing anything with it." [4] Or, as Joseph Mankiewicz was to put it, "People are always talking about the 'swimming pool Stalinists' of the thirties—seems they've forgotten about the 'swimming pool Fascists.' "

As the American public sought a better social contract, radical politics seemed to become the only alternative to the extremes of irresponsible hedonism and the Fascist clouds gathering over Europe. So Miss Hellman, Martin Berkeley, and a couple of other Goldwyn writers joined Fredric March, Dorothy Parker, and Ring Lardner in making speeches denouncing Nazism and the supine conduct of the United States in international affairs. Their audiences included those who were compiling lists of names that later would be made available to studio managements and, much later, to the House Un-American Activities Committee.

The Goldwyn writers were incensed by the shelving of Sinclair Lewis' *It Can't Happen Here,* the story of the triumph of an American dictator and the impotence of liberalism, and their indignant wrath was shared by others. As a group, they were all hurt by both the trash they were told to write and by a new turn to the right caused by the Catholic Church. Instead of echoing proletarian plays, poems, and novels that were becoming Broadway plays and bestsellers; instead of exploring the maze of Marxism as all bright students were doing in colleges across the country; instead of writing furious films about silver-shirted Nazis parading in the streets of New York, or about Trotskyites, Townsendites, Socialists, New Dealers, and the toiling masses, they were asked to come up with "screwball comedies" and escapist entertainment, usually set in high society and dealing with millionaires and chambermaids, smart-aleck cab drivers and *nouveaux riches.* Films exposing rackets, corruption, and abuses of power and telling about the inherent strength of democracy and new hopes for a better tomorrow were to come later—*The Life of Emile Zola,* with its *J'accuse* denunciation of anti-Semitism and political intolerance, in 1937. And two years later *The Grapes of Wrath,* John Ford and Darryl Zanuck's exposure of the shocking plight of California migrant workers, and *Meet John Doe,* Frank Capra's daring and angry exposé of American fascism.

There were exceptions. Warner Brothers produced three antilynch films; *Winterset, Fury,* and *They Won't Forget.* But a new caution and constraint had been forced on the movie industry with the formation of the Catholic Legion of Decency in 1934. Many Protestant churches readily supported the Legion in its announced campaign to clean up the movies. The result was a further strengthening of Hollywood's self-censorship institution, the Hays Office. And the tightening up didn't mean only the elimination of the cruder excesses of sex and mayhem, but the disappearance of much of the screen's forthright honesty. The emphasis was more than ever on escapism—big westerns, comedies, costume dramas, historical films, and adaptations of the classics.

Sidney Howard, with whom Wyler was soon to concoct additional *Dodsworth* scenes, was Goldwyn's man on Broadway, a playwright who was to die in a tractor accident at the height of his career in 1939. A native of Oakland, California, Howard had written the screenplay of Sinclair Lewis' *Arrowsmith,* which Goldwyn had had John Ford direct in 1932, and Lewis had liked. At the time, Howard had told the producer that Lewis' new book, *Dodsworth,* would make an excellent film and that Goldwyn could have it for $20,000. But Goldwyn had not been interested and for Broadway producer Gilbert Miller, Howard had written a theatrical *Dodsworth,* which opened in February 1934 at the Shubert, with Walter Huston and Fay Bainter playing Sam and Fran Dodsworth. When Goldwyn bought the screen rights, the price was $165,000.

"Look, I told you I could get it then for twenty thousand!" he told Goldwyn.

"I don't care. This way, I buy a successful play, something already in dramatic form. With this, I have more assurance of success and its worth the extra money I pay."

Which might be sound business reasoning, but somehow couldn't be said to enhance the "eminent authors" theory.

Sinclair Lewis had been impressed both by the situation he had seen that year in Hitler's Gemany and by the proliferation of fanatical politics in the United States. With the examples of the threatening power of Huey Long and the execution of Sacco and Vanzetti, Sinclair Lewis had felt fascism could happen in America. When *It Can't Happen Here* appeared, the book was greeted less as an artistic achievement as a political act, an "angry" novel which sold more than 320,000 copies. "Good old Sidney" had again written a screenplay for MGM and a date had been set for the filming of *It Can't Happen Here.* Now Goldwyn said the film had been halted because of casting difficulties. Howard knew better. He had seen a lengthy memo from Joseph Breen of the Hays Office suggesting drastic revisions and pointing out the "dangerous material" in the screenplay. The controversy over the film helped to keep the novel on top of the bestseller lists, but the Hays Office refused to lift its ban. The film was never made.[5]

Miss Hellman was an intense, unsparing woman of thirty when Wyler met her. Born in New Orleans of German-Jewish parents, she had drifted through New York publishing (working for Horace Liveright and meeting most of his novelists—Ernest Hemingway, Eugene O'Neill, Sherwood Anderson, *et al.*) and one marriage. She had come west when her husband, Arthur Kober (on the strength of her literary connections), got himself a job as a Paramount screenwriter. She now lived with Dashiell Hammett and enjoyed her first success. *The Children's Hour* had been the 1934 Broadway sensation.

She hated Hollywood and later called it a "foggy edge-world of people who had come for reasons they had long ago forgotten." [6] She spent a lot of time with Fredric March, Dorothy Parker, Scott Fitzgerald, and Archibald MacLeish, who suggested that Hemingway, Joris Ivens, and she make a documentary about the Spanish Civil War.

Her influence on Wyler was in lifting his artistic sights and heightening his awareness of himself as a creative person. Her integrity was an example that was to give him the inner security to turn down second-rate projects. Her complete devotion to her work made him demand more of himself and his craft.

Dashiell Hammett was not a great socializer, but he and Willy became friends. In 1950 when Sidney Kingsley declined to adapt his own *Detective Story*, Wyler thought what better writer than Hammett and signed the author of *Red Harvest* and *The Maltese Falcon*.

The significance of the Hellman-Wyler encounter was to be postponed for a couple of years, however. She had already written the screen version of her play and Goldwyn had already cast his stock stars, Joel McCrea and Merle Oberon, when—with her approval—he hired Wyler.

14

In Lillian Hellman's plays, characters regularly discover each other in compromising situations—*The Little Foxes, Watch on the Rhine, The Autumn Garden,* and *The Searching Wind* are made of retrospective confessions and revelations. *The Children's Hour* reaches its crisis through overheard conversation, a device the author was to use as late as *Toys in the Attic* in 1960.

Martha Dobie and Karen Wright are the two teachers at a boarding school for small girls. Between them are evil little Mary and her wealthy grandmother, Mrs. Tilford. The drama is of three adults struggling to cut through the porous fabric of lies— and one grain of truth—told by little Mary, and their defeat in the face of ever-widening circles of *implications* of lies. As Miss Hellman had told Goldwyn, whether the falsehood Mary tells is that Martha has an unnatural affection for Karen, or, as in the amended *These Three,* that Karen's boyfriend has been "carrying on" with Martha is immaterial. The effect is the same—three lives have their courses changed and nothing can be the same again for any of them. What matters is not a verdict, but the consciences of three people faced with a willful and vindictive child's scandalous talk. Unfortunately, the screen version didn't just turn sapphic love into a straight triangle with both teachers in love with the same man, it also invented a happy ending instead of the play's tragic dénouement.

Yet *These Three* was in many ways a brilliant first for Wyler. The film used directing and its composites to the fullest. The performances served a unifying purpose—to keep the consciences of three people the most important factor. Naturalness and hesitancy of speech made the text verbal instead of written. The camera was more fluid than before, used more inventively, and framing, cuts, lights were used to build moods, to give feelings spontaneity and a certain undramatic note. As such, *These Three* was an early defense of form over content which was to become the aesthetic cornerstone of the critical school that led to the *auteur* theory.

Authorship, in film, was always ticklish. On the one hand was the original play, novel, or story and subsequent screen treatment, on the other the various levels of filmic execution. The *politique des auteurs*—which Andrew Sarris translated to the *auteur* theory (leaving the key word in French to avoid the literary connotation of author in English)—was born with an article by François Truffaut in the January 1954 issue of *Cahiers du Cinéma*. Entitled *Une certaine tendance du cinéma français,* the essay was an attack on a segment of French cinema dominated (in Truffaut's view) by a tradition of verbal tyranny. The target of his attack was the well-upholstered, literary, well-acted, carefully motivated films usually scripted (and "dialogued") by the Prévert brothers, Jacques and Pierre, Marcel Audiard, Pierre Bost, Jean Aurenche, and the more illustrous Sacha Guitry. In France, the connection between cinema and intelligentsia had always been close (Jean Cocteau, André Malraux, Marcel Pagnol). Against this "tradition of quality," Truffaut listed Jean Renoir, Max Ophuls, Robert Bresson, Jacques Becker, and Jacques Tati as authentic *auteurs*.

The *auteur* theory was never a manifesto or collective statement but reflected an attitude, mainly toward American films. The theory soon developed into two loose schools—one uniting critics who insisted on revealing a core of meaning, of thematic motifs, and the other grouping those who stressed style and *mise en scène*—that untranslatable Gallicism meaning as much elucidation as, literally, staging, the realm of performance, of transposing into the special complex of filmic codes and channels a preexisting text. Content and form. The *auteur* critic tended to be more obsessed with the wholeness of art and the artist while critics who tended to value the *metteur en scène* above the *auteur* bored deeper into the inner meanings of cinema and "structural approach."

These Three was, in retrospect, a stunning piece of *mise en scène*, stylistic and expressive, all in the form. Wyler was not subordinated to another author (Hellman), his source was only a pretext, and his authorship was there for everybody to see. He was the catalyst, a creator of a radically new work. He made dramatic forces fluid and cinematic and the handling of actors, which was to be his trademark, showed itself with transparent evidence.

These Three also excited contemporary critics. "William Wyler's directing used the distance between us and the characters for the most effective and bloodless Aristotelian purpose, tracking the camera relentlessly up to their faces when we would rather have escaped from the problem, scuttling pitifully away from them when we ached to give them a warm embrace," Alistair Cooke wrote in the British Film Institute's new quarterly, *Sight and Sound*.[1]

Since the script was written and the leading players chosen—Miriam Hopkins had joined Merle Oberon and Joel McCrea—Wyler's only casting coup was twelve-year-old Bonita Granville, the emotional brat whose lies ruin the lives of the three adults.

Wyler plunged into the filming with enthusiasm. Throughout Miriam Hopkins acts as if her desire is for her companion and not the man whom Merle Oberon loves, leading the audience to a conclusion at variance with the script, Goldwyn, and the Hays Office but not with the mood and style of the film. Her confession of love for McCrea, for example, is delivered with her back to the camera. Caustic undercurrents are interjected so as to make the happy ending equivocal. "Not even the film's happy ending can hide the realization that this is a tragedy," Frank S. Nugent wrote in the *New York Times*.[2] Better, the London *Times* found the director's determination to keep the consciences of the three people "the most important factor distinguishing this film from all others of its kind."[3] Wyler, concentrating on acting and camera, had discovered what Goldwyn meant when he said he made "important pictures." Quality suddenly became possible.

"It was a new experience in the sense that until then, I had always worked for producers who wanted things done cheaply," Wyler recalled. "Until then, I had always been told, 'Hurry up' and 'Keep on schedule.' Here all of a sudden was a man who wasn't against sometimes spending more money.

"There were facets of Goldwyn that were irritating, others that

---

were ugly, others that were humorous, but he was trying to do what I wanted—to make better pictures. It was exhilarating!

"The final control was his, of course, but he would often give in to me on things where we differed. Sometimes, he trusted my feelings more than his own."

Wyler used his new freedom to hone performances. The madness of bulldozing John Barrymore through *Counsellor at Law* in a little over twenty days seemed only yesterday, yet here he was creating shades of emotions as he had never been able even to try before. The result was visible. As the London *Times* saw it, "feeling has the right air of spontaneity; loyalty, the right undramatic note; love, the proper emphasis and speech, even at the most intense moments, a naturalness and hesitancy which make it always verbal and never written."

It was all possible thanks to yet another remarkable association for Wyler—Gregg Toland. As the legendary director-cameraman teamings of D. W. Griffith and G. W. "Billy" Bitzer, and of Charles Chaplin and Rolland Totheroh,* the Wyler–Toland association was to produce a series of films that were later to be called "Hollywood classics" and lead to creative innovations that were to influence the critical concept of movies in decades to come.

The aphorism that nothing is new under the sun applies with special evidence to film. Most of the techniques of filmmaking can be said to have been in place by 1910. Color, sound, 3D, double exposure, split screen, animation had all been attempted by Edwin Porter and George Méliès by the end of the century's first decade. By 1915, Griffith and Bitzer had invented closeup, soft focus, fadeout, backlighting, and parallel cutting. In Europe, Abel Gance mounted cameras on bicycles and, in 1926, introduced the triple screen while Alberto Cavalcanti had put gauze over lenses to depersonalize characters, Man Ray saw his characters through mica sheets. By 1920, Karl Freund had been through most trick photography and, in *The Last Laugh* in 1924, strapped a camera to his wrist to get shots of Emil Jannings' drunken point of view.

Although his early death, at forty-four, ended an astonishing ca-

---

* "Rollie" Totheroh was a staff cameraman for Essanay Studios when Chaplin arrived in 1915. Totheroh remained Chaplin's cameraman through *Monsieur Verdoux* in 1947.

reer that had not yet reached its zenith, Gregg Toland is a major figure in American cinematography. Together with James Wong Howe, Lee Garmes, Karl Strauss, William Daniels, Stanley Cortez, and Leon Shamroy, Toland belongs to the great Hollywood cameramen who not only mastered the secrets of light but also pushed the frontiers toward new dimensions. "It was at the end of the thirties, and in the forties, that the most ravishing camerawork Hollywood has given us emerged," Charles Higham has written. "Early color films, now so foolishly discounted, had a delicate beauty seldom captured since: W. Howard Greene's soft landscapes of Ireland in *Wings of the Morning,* the quiet rural textures of James Wong Howe in *The Adventures of Tom Sawyer,* the glowing images of *Ramona;* all these led up to the wonderful first half of *Gone With the Wind,* in which Lee Garmes's soft and subtle color evoked the Georgia of the past and developed beautifully the three-color Kalmus process first seen in *La Cucaracha* and *Becky Sharp* in the early thirties. Black and white, too, became fully developed in that period. Lee Garmes's *Zoo in Budapest* still captivates: shot through delicate traceries of leaves and fronds, its images have a beauty untouched by time. Leon Shamroy's distinctive talent first emerged in *Private Worlds. . . ."* [4]

Toland's work, which was to culminate in *Citizen Kane* and *The Best Years of Our Lives,* developed techniques pioneered by Karl Strauss and Wong Howe. Together with Leon Shamroy, Arthur Miller, and Stanley Cortez, Toland experimented in depth of focus photography, or "forced focus" as Toland called it. By using wide angle lenses and pouring light onto the depth of a scene, these cameramen were able to "carry" the focus—or point where directness and clarity is at its sharpest—from five feet back to thirty or fifty feet. On *Transatlantic,* which Wong Howe photographed for William K. Howard in 1931, he shot eighty percent of the film with a twenty-five millimeter lens and had the art director, Gordon Miles, build full and half ceilings on the ship's engine room set to allow such wide angles.

Toland, in particular, experimented with the so-called Waterhouse stops, which allow a narrowing down of the focus without automatic iris. By shooting with 1,000 footcandles of light and stopping the lens down very hard, he managed to get sharp focus from the foreground to the background forty or fifty feet in the depth of the frame. The technique allowed the staging of scenes in the depth of the field since the background was as sharp as the foreground.

Born in Charleston, Illinois, in 1904, Toland started as a messenger boy at William Fox's Films and through the twenties, worked as an assistant cameraman on innumerable Tom Mix, William Farnum, and Theda Bara movies. "I'll tell you frankly, I was a very good assistant," he told Lester Koenig shortly before he died. "I made sixty dollars a week when others were only making twenty-five or thirty. But I was worth it. I was proud of the camera. I used to stay on nights and polish it." [5]

Together with Georges Barnes, who was to become Alfred Hitchcock's cameraman, he photographed Edmund Goulding's 1929 talkie *The Trespasser,* starring Gloria Swanson. Lee Garmes, who photographed *Nightmare Alley* for Goulding, called the discreet and tasteful Englishman a man of genius who had no idea of photography. "He concentrated on the actors," Garmes told Higham. "He liked the camera to follow the actors all the time. He was the only director I've ever known whose actors never came in out of the sidelines of the frame. They either came in a door or down a flight of stairs or from behind a piece of furniture. He liked their entrances and exits to be photographed. I like that; they didn't just 'disappear somewhere' out of the frameline, as they so often do. But it was 'proscenium-arch' directing." [6]

Barnes and Toland used twelve cameras to film *The Trespasser.* "We didn't know how to cut sound, so we'd shoot the sound in one solid unit and then cut the film from our twelve cameras," Toland recalled in 1947. "Since all our cameras ran continuously, on some days we had thirty thousand feet of rushes."

Toland went to work for Goldwyn in 1929, and his contract with the producer was still in force when he died of a heart attack in 1948. Toland had definite ideas of the camera's creative force. He felt film photography could be judged only in relation to its subservience to the story. Glamorous photography of a plain girl was as silly as *not* changing nature to fit a dramatic concept. His chance came with the Anna Sten pictures Goldwyn made in 1934–35. Since Goldwyn let it be known that nothing should be spared to make his Ukrainian discovery the rival of Garbo and Dietrich, Toland was afforded opportunities in *Nana* and *We*

Live Again to explore both glistening outdoor photography in the heroic Eisenstein-Edouard Tissé style and dreamy, enchanting atmosphere work. The two moods of the Tolstoy adaptation actually dovetail in a seduction scene with subtle shifts and reversals of photographic textures. On loan out to Fox, Toland filmed Richard Boleslawski's *Les Misérables* and had just finished Elliott Nugent's *Splendour* when Goldwyn assigned him to *These Three.*

Wyler and Toland didn't hit it off too well in the beginning.

"I was in the habit of saying, 'Put the camera here and shoot it with a forty millimeter,' or 'Move the camera this way,' or 'Light it this way,' " Willy recalled. "Suddenly, Toland wanted to quit. I didn't understand why and he finally came to me to tell me he wasn't a man to be told every move."

With the exception of Stanley Cortez with whom Wyler had never worked, Universal admittedly had done little to further the art of cinematography. Toland was the first cameraman Wyler met who was not just a competent worker.

"You just didn't tell Gregg what lens to use, you told him what mood you were after. When he photographed something, he wanted to go beyond lights and catch feelings. As we got to know each other, we evolved a smooth and beautiful relationship. We would discuss a picture from beginning to end, its overall 'feel' and then the style of each sequence. Toland was an artist.

"The camera is a marvelous instrument. You have to use it with discipline. Any imaginative director who stages a scene or uses a set gets all kinds of ideas. That's great but you have to discipline yourself. Many cameramen's idea of a good scene is when all the actors hit their cut marks. Soundmen like it when everything is very clear. This is where Toland was different.

"His style of photography would vary, just like my style of directing. In *Dead End,* we had a different style of photography than in *Wuthering Heights* or in *These Three.* Here, we were dealing with little girls' things. What was good was rather simple, attractive photography. In *Dead End,* we had flat, hard lights. We used open sun-arcs from behind the camera. We didn't try to make anybody look pretty. With Toland, I would rehearse and show him a scene. Then, we would decide together how to photograph it. I would have certain ideas and he would contribute to them and together we would determine what was best."

When *These Three* opened in New York March 3, 1936, *The Children's Hour* was in its seventy-first week on Broadway and Wyler was on his way to Europe. A look at the Spanish Civil War and a carefree vacation was what he had in mind before returning for *Dodsworth*. Goldwyn had given him the best possible compliment for *These Three*—picking up the option in their contract and assigning Wyler to the Sinclair Lewis adaptation. Much later, Wyler discovered that Goldwyn had had Gregory La Cava in mind for *Dodsworth*. La Cava had just directed a pair of Claudette Colbert–Charles Boyer and William Powell–Carole Lombard comedies (and was next to do *Stage Door*), when Goldwyn decided to stay with his new director.

These Three—often called a revised *Children's Hour* in Hays Office-stubbing newspaper headlines—was a critical success. "The simple fact first," began the *World-Telegram*, "*These Three*, the screen version of Herman Shumlin's stage production *The Children's Hour*, at the Rivoli Theatre, is an honest, sensitive, beautifully acted film that deserves the admiration and respect of all moviegoers. With this simple fact stated, those of you who may have had several justifiable misgivings as to what the cinema would do with this superlatively good play—most plays suffer when made into film—may now rest easily." [7] In the *Times*, Frank S. Nugent forecast *These Three* would end up on the 1936 Ten Best list.[8] The new *Newsweek*'s critic spent half his column retracing *The Children's Hour* to *These Three* saga before saying that despite the sugar-coating of the ending, "the film has the same quiet distinction [as the play]." The Hays Office's fear of Miss Hellman's original became the banter of columnists. "We did not blame Mr. Will Hays, the cinema's sentinel, for overvigilance in protecting his public from contact with the more insalubrious fact for we knew that to the multitudes, the subject would be disagreeable," Percy Hammond chuckled, "but we did believe that a strong play would be emasculated—to use a word perhaps inappropriate in the circumstances—and that it would be a thoughtless and profitless Hollywood mutilation of a Broadway wonderwork." [9] Leo Mishkin opined that the film was better than the play. "The credit for this achievement can be laid at many doors," he wrote, naming Goldwyn, Miss Hellman, and Wyler ("who directed it with tenderness and sympathy and power rarely matched by anyone in the movies").[10] In Boston, where Mayor

---

Frederick Mansfield had banned *The Children's Hour* as being "indecent and revolting," the *Herald* wrote an absorbing, serious review—"*These Three* has a vitality and an entity all its own" [11] and the *Traveler* came out in the headline saying the film was a screen version of the locally banned play.[12] "Although the producer, Samuel Goldwyn, and the exhibitors have been pledged to keep a dark secret the fact that this film was based on *The Children's Hour*, there are few moviegoers unaware of the picture's origin," Helen Eager wrote, applauding Wyler's direction for making the film into "an exceptionally absorbing and emotionally disturbing masterpiece."

A new critic in London also found *These Three* moving—Graham Greene, who, with the exception of a five-month period in 1938, wrote a movie column every week from 1935 to 1940, most for *The Spectator* but also for the short-lived *Night and Day* magazine. "After ten minutes or so of the usual screen sentiment, quaintness and exaggeration, one began to watch with incredulous pleasure nothing less than life: a genuine situation, a moral realism that allows one of two schoolmistresses, whose lives and careers have been ruined by the malicious lie of a child, a murmur before the rigid self-righteousness of the wealthy grandparent 'It is the very young and the very old who are wicked,' " Greene wrote.[13] The London press agreed. *The New Statesman* called *These Three* "a sultry and admirable film which concerns, pretty intimately, six or seven people," [14] *The Sunday Express* said the basis was pure Ibsen, "the story of three lives made miserable by one haunting thought," [15] while *The Daily Mail*'s Seton Margrave reviewed the film twice. "All my filmgoing friends—who are also my severest critics—have been to see *These Three* and their reactions have been quite remarkable," he wrote the second time. "I can recall only a handful of films having elicited such unanimous praise." [16]

Lillian Hellman's strong political opinions had rubbed off enough on Wyler to have him donate money for an ambulance for Republican Spain and he was more than curious about the documentary *Spanish Earth* which Joris Ivens, Ernest Hemingway, and John Dos Passos were to start shooting in support of the Loyalist cause. Miss Hellman, herself, was to join Hemingway in Valencia a year later. In Paris, Wyler saw the Republican representative for the International Brigades and actually received the *laisser-passer.* When the Franco forces broke through to the Coast, he was told he could still go, via submarine. With most of the Spanish marine in the hands of the Fascists, however, he found it more prudent to cancel the trip.

"And another war was lost," he said. "I went to Juan-les-Pins and learned waterskiing instead."

On the way back, there was still the compulsory stopover in Mulhouse. Everybody was very friendly, overfriendly. It was touching how distant cousins came up and said that although he was divorced now, he was still welcome.

"The divorce was a mark on me. I said to a cousin of mine, 'Nobody has asked me about my wife; last time I came, I had a wife, what's the matter?' And they assured me that it would make no difference, that they liked me and that they were willing to forget and forgive."

PART THREE

The High 1930s

15

Although Wyler was to meet Sinclair Lewis only fleetingly, *Dodsworth* is wholly Lewisian and the film of the Goldwyn years that was to hold up best. Walter Huston had created the role of Sam Dodsworth on the New York stage and was engaged for the film as a matter of course. Ruth Chatterton, all pouts and broken gestures, played Fran Dodsworth against the grain of Wyler's direction, and Mary Astor—the center of the most sensational scandal during the shooting—was "the other woman," the defeated yet passionate and cool Edith Cortright whom Lewis saw as a hope for the evolution of American womanhood.

Dodsworth, which opened at New York's Rivoli Theatre on September 18, 1936, was a curious film. In plot and casting, it made no concessions to the facts of movie life of the period. "In spite of their excellent work, neither Huston nor Mary Astor had ever succeeded in becoming favorites and Miss Chatterton's brief reign as a popular star had already come to an end when Mr. Goldwyn engaged her," Richard Griffith would write twenty years later,[1] adding that the story of a disintegrating marriage of a middle-aged couple was not exactly ideal screen material. One stage over from *Dodsworth,* Howard Hawks was shooting *Come and Get It,* a tale of middle-aged gropings for romance and defeat to youth. As the two pictures completed production, Goldwyn turned fifty-four on August 27. In 1932, he had produced *Cynara,* a story of an unfaithful husband who, by his very determination to do the right thing, makes it harder for everyone concerned. Directed by King Vidor, *Cynara* accorded oddly with accepted movie morality and now *Dodsworth* and *Come and Get It* explored subjects that could be described only as lying near the outer limits of acceptable screenfare.

Sinclair Lewis' novel about a wealthy industrialist who is led through Europe's capital and glitter by his beautiful, spoiled, and deeply loved wife was published in 1929—four years after *Arrowsmith,* two years after *Elmer Gantry,* and one year before he became the first American author to receive the Nobel prize.

In his novels, Lewis offered a sharp and easily assimilated image of the American middle class. Often confused in style and sprawling in structure, his novels liberated new areas of American writers and, as his biographer was to say in a definitive survey, although Lewis was one of the "worst" important writers in modern American literature, "without his writing, one cannot imagine modern American literature." [2] Concentrating on single representative individuals, Lewis was able to define dramatically the best and the worst in American culture and, although he became known primarily as a satirist, the social upheavals of the 1930s made him increasingly ambivalent toward the "middle America" he had railed at a decade earlier.

The theme of *Dodsworth* was not new. Since Henry James, whom Wyler was to tackle in 1949, novels about Americans in Europe had been numerous. In *Dodsworth,* however, Lewis seemed to approve the middle-class, mid-Western virtues he had satirized in *Babbitt* and *Main Street* while, at the same time, representing Europe as a liberating force for his hero.

Bumbling, sentimental, and home-loving Sam Dodsworth *is* his hero. Fran is portrayed as the American female monster, an immature and restless wife full of silvery scorn and tinkling snobbery. Yet, as Wyler saw it, a case could be made for her.

The outcome of *Dodsworth* is by no means a foregone conclusion nor are the protagonists maneuvered into fixed positions by page twenty. The novel, wrote Carl Van Doren when it appeared, is a summing up of "a hundred years of American reflections upon 'Europe' . . . in a crackle of comedy." Ford Madox Ford wrote that "the title might just as well have been 'Europa, An Epic.' For Mr. Lewis presents to you practically all of Europe that counts in our civilization, including New York which isn't America." [3]

Three months after its publication, *Dodsworth* had sold 85,000 copies and Samson Raphaelson expressed an interest in making a dramatic adaptation. Nothing came of it, however, and it was not until 1932 that a deal was worked out with Broadway producer Gilbert Miller and Sidney Howard to write the stage version.

Howard's dramatization was closer to the screen than to the stage. The story was told in no less than fourteen scenes. This structure of "master scenes" was retained in the screenplay with much of what took place off the stage rewritten into action. Much of Sam Dodsworth's interior monologue, his reflections on Europe and the United States, and his confusion were jettisoned to make him a stronger and more confident man. But what carried the stage version, as Brooks Atkinson had emphasized, was first of all the fact that Walter Huston played Dodsworth.[4]

Back from Europe, Wyler caught one of the last performances at the Shubert, went backstage, and talked with Huston. They hadn't seen each other since *A House Divided,* both looked forward to working together again, and Huston invited Willy to spend Christmas at the actor's mountain retreat in California on the way back.

"You get off the train in San Bernardino and drive up the mountain to Running Springs," Huston said. "Call, and I'll pick you up at the local grocery store."

While he found Howard's script excellent, Wyler still wanted to loosen it up and, with Goldwyn's permission, he stayed in New York to work with the writer. Comfortably settled at the Waldorf-Astoria, Willy either went to Howard's 88th Street apartment or the author came to the hotel for their sessions. Together they invented new details of Fran and Sam Dodsworth's grand tour abroad, including things that weren't in the novel. Much of their work, however, never got on the screen, like their tabletop sequence designed to show in cinematic terms Fran's silly snobbery.

In the sequence, the Dodsworths were in Paris and had met a painter. Fran wants the artist to do her portrait because he is famous, but the painter finds her ordinary and pretentious. Although she objects that no chic people sit in sidewalk cafés, Sam enjoys sipping an aperitif on a café terrace and watching life go by. While Fran is shopping, he is having a drink at the Café de la Paix. The painter happens by, Sam invites him to sit down and have a drink with him. While they chat, the painter sketches Sam's portrait on the tabletop. Certain that Fran will enjoy this, Sam buys the table, gets it into a taxi, and takes it to their hotel. Going out again, he misses Fran back from her shopping. She sees the chalked-up table and with an irritated gesture, wipes it clean.

TABLETOP SCENE WILL HAVE TO WAIT FOR OTHER FAMOUS AMERICAN MOVIE, Willy wired Sid Howard once he got into production at Goldwyn's. The scene did appear, as it were, twenty-five years later in a French film. To show two young men's friendship, François Truffaut used a similar vignette in *Jules et Jim* (1961), with Jules making a chalk sketch of a woman's head on a café *guéridon* and Jim wanting to buy the table. The bistro owner, however, will only sell all twelve tables together.

On the way back from New York, Willy got off the Super Chief in San Bernardino, sixty miles east of Los Angeles, looking forward to a chance to ski in the Big Bear Lake area high above the desert. When he got to the phone booth, however, he couldn't remember the name of Walter Huston's tiny resort town.

He tried the telephone operator, "a town near here with something like water in the name, very small town, maybe just a few numbers." The operator hesitated, then suggested White Water. Wyler was sure that was it and asked her to connect him with the grocery in White Water.

"Hello, White Water? Is Walter Huston there?" he began.

"Who?" a man's voice came back.

"Walter Huston."

"You mean the movie actor?"

"Yes, yes."

"No. He ain't here."

"But he lives near you."

"You don't say!"

"Yes, and he's to meet me there in his sleigh and take me to his house."

"A sleigh?"

"Yes."

"Listen, it's ninety-five in the shade here."

White Water, it turned out, was a little town in the desert, fourteen miles from Desert Hot Springs and seventeen miles from Thousand Palms. What Willy wanted was Running Springs.

After Wyler spent a lovely Christmas–New Year's vacation with the Hustons three thousand feet up in the San Bernardino mountains and going skiing with John Huston, *Dodsworth* went into production in early 1936.

It was a 1930s movie and, as such, was not shot all over Europe but at 1041 North Formosa Avenue. "We sent a cameraman to London but otherwise did everything else on the backlot and in rear projection," Willy recalled. "The cameraman also went to Paris, Vienna, Montreux, and Naples for background shots. I gave him detailed instructions, of course, and the sets were built so there would be props in the foreground and back projection of matching locations."

"No one objected, Rudolph Maté or anybody. Going to all those places was out of the question. Maybe if there had been one location, but wandering all over Europe just wasn't done in those days."

Rear projection or process-screen photography enabled characters to sit or stand in front of a screen on a sound stage and appear to be anywhere in the world. Telltale signs of process work —too brightly lit characters in the foreground and a grainy or fuzzy background combined with echo chamber sound—too often made it obvious no one ever stepped out of the studio, but some process photography was remarkable. Only the most meticulous examination of Alfred Hitchcock's *Foreign Correspondent* (1940) would reveal that the key sequence, where seven survivors of a plane crash sit on a detached wing in a stormy sea, was shot in a studio tank with rails on the bottom to make the plane sink on cue. Wyler had known tank work on *A House Divided*.

Filming began in the spring. Walter Huston was in top form, as was Goldwyn's new contract player, David Niven, who incarnated an Englishman of half Fran Dodsworth's age and ten times her experience. The leading ladies were a different story. Wyler and Ruth Chatterton didn't see eye to eye on the interpretation of Fran and *l'affaire* Mary Astor blew sky-high a couple of weeks into production.

The diminutive honey-haired Ruth Chatterton, who had been a Broadway star at twenty-one and a Hollywood leading lady in such vehicles as Dorothy Arzner's *Sarah and Son,* John Cromwell's *Unfaithful,* and Bertold Viertel's *Magnificent Lie,* was a movie star in the most neurotic sense of the word.

"She played Fran like a heavy and we had momentous fights every day," Wyler remembered. "There was no reason why Fran should be a heavy because Sam Dodsworth was sympathetic. You could make a great case for Mrs. Dodsworth, a woman who for twenty-five years had been a good wife, taken care of her husband while he got rich, brought up their children and everything. Now he's retiring, and she wants a fling; she wants to live. As she says, 'You're rushing at old age, I'm not ready for that yet!' She wants to get involved in a romance, go to Europe and, of course, gets involved with an absolute phony."

The trouble with Mary Astor was off camera. Playing Edith Cortright, the "spacious" woman who cannot be possessed and does not want to possess and who could become Sam's alternate solution, she was on loanout from Warner Brothers. She embroiled Goldwyn and soon the entire motion picture industry in a tragicomical scandal that held the nation spellbound for months. The wife of Dr. Franklyn Thorpe, she had had an affair with playwright and columnist George S. Kaufman during the writer's sojourn in Hollywood in 1935, when he had screenplayed Sam Wood's Marx Brothers hit, *A Night at the Opera,* and during a stay in Palm Springs, where he and Moss Hart had written part of their play *Merrily We Roll Along.* Miss Astor, who had literary aspirations, kept a diary of her amorous encounters, but the romance had ended in a civilized manner with Kaufman returning to New York and his wife, Beatrice. The actress had agreed to a divorce, which had awarded her daughter, Marilyn, and $60,000 in securities to Dr. Thorpe. That had been 1935.

A year later, Mary Astor changed her mind and instructed her attorneys to bring suit in court to set aside the divorce, get an annulment, and award her the child, the money, and the real estate. To counter her action, Dr. Thorpe brought a second suit and tried to have his former wife's diary entered as evidence; when this failed, he "leaked" large portions of it to the press.

The parties went into Los Angeles Superior Court, Judge Goodwin J. Knight presiding. Since Mary Astor was working on *Dodsworth,* she was allowed to appear in court at night. From mid-July to mid-August, scandal flowed. It was so juicy, so loaded with names, so intimate, so far beyond anything the media had ever turned up about Hollywood—and right out in court where the press was immune to libel suits—that Hitler's Berlin Olympics and the Spanish Civil War were knocked clear off the front pages. The August 11 *New York Times* had two headlines of equal size: CORN CROP WORST SINCE '81 and WARRANT OUT FOR KAUFMAN. Without quoting directly from the diary, *Time* six days later said Miss Astor's record of sexual events contained references to one "thrilling ecstasy" and described Kaufman's powers as such that his amorous trysts reached twenty a day. Other papers published the actress' Top Ten lists of lovers, with Kaufman leading the field.

The author (with Edna Ferber) of *Dinner at Eight* was working with Moss Hart on *You Can't Take It with you,* and Frank Capra was set to direct when Miss Astor's attorney told the court he wanted to stop the innuendos and have the diary produced and presented as evidence. That night, there was a high-level meeting at Goldwyn Studios with Harry Cohn, Jack Warner, Irving Thalberg, Louis B. Mayer, and Jesse Lasky trying to convince the actress that it would be better for the motion picture business, and incidentally for herself, not to have the diary brought in as evidence. She told the assembled moguls that the diary did not describe sexual acts with every known actor in town with a box score for performances. They didn't believe her.

Judge Knight, however, refused to allow the diary as evidence as there were many pages missing and a "mutilated document" was not admissible. When her lawyer called Kaufman as a witness on her behalf, the writer failed to appear and Judge Knight promptly issued a bench warrant for his arrest. What followed was out of a Marx Brothers script. When sheriff's deputies came looking for him at Hart's house, Kaufman fled through the bushes. MGM had him smuggled to Catalina Island aboard Irving Thalberg's private yacht. When Judge Knight felt the movie industry was making a national fool of him for not being able to find the writer, he sent deputies to Catalina and the chase continued on the high seas.

Reporters kept stakeouts at Goldwyn Studios and, to keep her sanity, Miss Astor plunged into her fictional character. If the reporters could never figure out why they couldn't catch her when she went home, it was because she was living at the studio, in a dressing-room apartment.

"I know this is going to sound a little strange, but the person I clung to as a friend through all this was the character I was playing," Miss Astor wrote in her autobiography. "Edith Cortright was three-dimensional in my mind, and I knew all about her. She was a lot of things I wasn't, she was a lot of things I would like to have been. She had also been a little foolish and human. But she had complete confidence in herself, and I had very little. . . . So when I went into court and faced the bedlam of sightseers, newsmen and women, photographers, attorneys (in the halls, they were hawking ice cream cones and hot dogs for the spectators), when I sat in the witness chair for long hours and answered questions that would have broken me up completely, I kept the little pot boiling that was Edith Cortright." [5]

Her director and fellow workers tried to be helpful.

"She had told me about it before we started, saying this is going to make a big stink," Wyler remembered. "I said, 'No, nobody's going to pay much attention.' So much for my prophecy. Reporters came out from the East by the planeload for the trial."

"Wyler was an inspirational director, tough and exacting but sensitive," Miss Astor wrote, describing his "evil, little grin" and solicitous help during the filming of the fadeout scene, when Dodsworth comes back to her. "There were cuts of Walter Huston. The audience knew, but they wanted to enjoy the reaction of the woman when she *saw* him," she said, explaining how Wyler filmed the reaction shot of her radiance.

Kaufman was still in hiding. After another stay at Hart's house and another early morning police visit that drove him to hysteria, friends had him shipped out of California (and, temporarily at least, out of Judge Knight's reach) on a stretcher carried aboard a train. With the press jeering and cheering the "Public Lover No. 1," Kaufman reached New York. To avoid the reporters' crowd at the platform, he slipped off at a suburban station and went into hiding at his sister Ruth's apartment.[6]

The end of the trial was a dud. After thirty days in court, Judge Knight ruled in favor of divided custody—little Marilyn was to spend nine months of the year with her mother and the remaining three months with her father.

The first screenings produced congratulatory telegrams to Wyler.

I CANNOT REMEMBER HAVING ENJOYED A PICTURE AS MUCH
AS DODSWORTH IN A LONG TIME IT IS REALLY MARVELOUS

STOP MY HEARTIEST CONGRATULATIONS TO YOU, Ernst
Lubitsch wired.

From New York, Sidney Howard cabled:

I HAVE JUST SEEN DODSWORTH FOR FIRST TIME AND USED
UP ALL MY SUPERLATIVES IN WIRES TO SAM AND RUTH STOP
I CAN ONLY THANK YOU FOR SUCH A DISTINGUISHED AND
LIVELY JOB OF DIRECTING AND REGRET WITH YOU THE TIME
I WASTED FOR YOU WRITING SCENES THAT COULD NOT BE
USED STOP WE MIGHT MEET ONE DAY AND TAKE A FRENCH
PAINTER OUT TO DINNER JUST TO MAKE ALL THAT
WORTH WHILE.

The reviews were beautiful and all Huston's. Setting the tone,
The New Yorker said, "It would have been an inexcusable accident had Walter Huston's Dodsworth not been fine, but there
hasn't been any accident and the Huston Dodsworth should
please people who saw the play and people who didn't." [7] Also
without mentioning the director, Archer Winsten wrote, "Walter
Huston, the most dependable of actors, gives a performance that
makes you forget acting," [8] while Frank S. Nugent threw a bone
to Wyler by saying "the director has had the skill to execute it
[Howard's script] in cinematic terms" and calling Mary Astor's
performance "alert and intelligent." [9]

As *Time* noted, audiences often cheered Mary Astor, both at
her first appearance when, in a ship's lounge, she suggests Dodsworth try to steady his nerves with stout, to her fadeout scene.
But *Dodsworth* was not a box-office sensation. The crowds stayed
away from the smooth but serious film despite the hype of seven
Academy nominations—best picture, director, actor, supporting
actress, sound recording, art directing, and screenplay. It was Wyler's first Academy nomination, but only art director Richard Day
won an Oscar.

Two months after *Dodsworth,* Goldwyn released *Come and Get
It,* with reviewers reacting with the same adjectives. *Come and
Get It,* wrote Nugent, "is as fine in its way as those earlier Goldwyn successes of this year, *These Three* and *Dodsworth*. It has
the same richness of production, the same excellence of performance, the same shrewdness of direction. There is nothing static
about this one, thanks to Howard Hawks and William Wyler, the
directors, to Gregg Toland's photography and to the work of a
uniformly fine cast." [10]

151

An early cheer for ecology, *Come and Get It* was not exactly a happy instance of tandem direction. If anything, it was an example of raw producer power before the Screen Directors Guild—later, the Directors Guild of America—signed its first collective contract with the Motion Picture Producers Association in 1939.

Edna Ferber's novel was a gaze at free enterprise worship. Its subject was the "grand old boys" of her native Michigan of the 1880s. "Cutting and slashing, grabbing and tricking, they had seized and destroyed millions of acres of forest land with never a sprig replanted; they had diverted and polluted streams and rivers; had falsely obtained rights of way on either side of trumped up railroads and thereby got control of untold mineral wealth as well as woodland, water and farm lands. They in the North, were only the Wisconsin and Michigan reproductions of their brothers in the East—the Astors, the Vanderbilts, the Goulds, the Harrimans, the Morgans, the Fisks, the Rockefellers—oil, railroads, lands, forests, waterways, as in the West had been the Huntingtons, the Hopkinses, the Hills, all solemnly embalmed now in libraries and museums and hotels and boulevards," Miss Ferber wrote in her first autobiography.[11]

As screenplayed by Jules Furthman (the writer of Hawks' *Rio Bravo* and *The Big Sleep*) and Jane Murfin, *Come and Get It* was less the Ferberian sweep of a Wisconsin lumber dynasty than a father-and-son-in-love-with-the-same-woman story. Concentrating on the lusty, brawling life of Barney Glasgow (Edward Arnold), the lumber-camp boy rising to become a timber tycoon, the film reached its climax when, in middle age, Glasgow becomes infatuated with the daughter of the woman he once loved but spurned because she stood in the way of his ambition. Groping ridiculously for the ideal love of his youth, he loses the girl to his son (Joel McCrea).

With Frances Farmer playing both mother and daughter and Walter Brennan emoting as honest Swan Bostrom (for which he won the newly created supporting actor Oscar), Hawks was shooting one stage over from Wyler when Goldwyn was hospitalized for a combined gall bladder and appendix operation.

Suddenly Irving Thalberg, the boy genius with the weak heart, died. Two days after Goldwyn entered the hospital, Thalberg had attended a Jewish charity affair at the Hollywood Bowl and had caught a cold. It developed into pneumonia and he died September 14, three months after his thirty-seventh birthday. Goldwyn was still recovering from his operation and could not attend the funeral. Instead, the widow, Norma Shearer, visited his bedside.

The funeral at the Synagogue B'nai B'rith was the closest thing to a national mourning Hollywood had ever seen. The ushers who escorted the mourners to their seats were Clark Gable, Fredric March, Douglas Fairbanks, Sidney Franklin, Woody Van Dyke, Moss Hart, Sam Wood, Cedric Gibbons, Oaney Wilson, and Harry Carey. The Barrymore brothers, the Marxes, Charlie Chaplin, Walt Disney, Howard Hughes, Carole Lombard, Gary Cooper—all were there, the MGM leading men, past and present, and even Erich von Stroheim came to pay respect to his enemy from the Universal days. Gray with grief, Louis B. Mayer hurried past the respectful crowd and the rabbi read messages of condolence from around the world, including one from President Roosevelt. During the service, every studio observed a five-minute silence and MGM was shut down for the day. On *Dodsworth,* Wyler said a few appropriate words, telling his cast and crew of his first meeting with Thalberg during the early days at Universal.

When Goldwyn was released from the hospital, he ran everything Wyler and Hawks had shot. He liked *Dodsworth* but was not satisfied with the *Come and Get It* footage. He called Hawks in and the two of them had an argument over the ending of the film. Hawks, who had already signed with RKO to do *Bringing Up Baby,* had rewritten a number of scenes and filmed them. Goldwyn was furious—not so much over the changes as over the fact that Hawks had rewritten the scenes himself. "Directors are supposed to direct, not write," Goldwyn sputtered. Harsh words followed and Hawks walked off the picture.

Goldwyn was still recovering and Wyler was summoned to his bedside and told to do part of *Come and Get It* over. When Wyler refused, the producer exploded.

"He carried on like a madman about me having to do this, that I was legally obligated to do it and that he'd ruin my career if I refused. He got so furious that Frances Goldwyn took a flyswatter and beat it over his legs on the bed and I ran out of the room."

Later, Wyler had his lawyer go through the fine print of his contract. Goldwyn was right; there was nothing in the contract that allowed Wyler to refuse an assignment.

———

"At the end, I had to do it. I don't think it helped much. The best parts—the first half hour, were done by Hawks and the magnificent logger operations footage by second-unit director Richard Rosson. When I finished, Goldwyn still was sore at Hawks and wanted to take his name off the picture altogether and give me credit alone. I said, 'Absolutely no' and we had another blowup. The Directors Guild was just being formed but was not yet recognized by the studios and there was no way of appealing or bringing to arbitration such a decision.

"Goldwyn finally agreed to a half measure—putting both our names on the screen and I insisted that Hawks's name come first and that's how it appears—directed by Howard Hawks and William Wyler. Needless to say, I don't count *Come and Get It* as one of my pictures."

All of which didn't prevent Hawks from directing a Gary Cooper vehicle for Goldwyn in 1941—the smash success *Ball of Fire,* which Hawks and Goldwyn remade, shot for shot, in 1948 as *A Song Is Born,* this time starring Danny Kaye.

16

Direct attack on poverty and social injustice cropped up in a healthy proportion of New Deal films even if, in the fadeout, the brews were sweetened. To later generations, *Dead End* might exhibit "a genuine originality of conception," as one 1970s surveyor of the thirties would write.[1] To its 1937 audiences, the subject, not the medium, was the message.

Dead End was Goldwyn's answer to Warner Brothers' social gangster films, and from the Burbank studio he even borrowed the leading thug in residence, Humphrey Bogart. The project came about with usual Goldwyn panache. When Wyler and Sidney Howard were hanging out in mid-Manhattan inventing tabletop character insights for *Dodsworth,* the Goldwyns had come east, taking eight-year-old Sam Jr. on his first trip to Europe. Before sailing, Goldwyn had asked Wyler to come with Frances and him to see Kingsley's long-running play about East River slum children corrupted both by the rich and by crime. At the final curtain fall at the Belasco, Sam had asked his director what he thought. "Great!" Wyler applauded. The next day, Goldwyn bought *Dead End.*

"Just like that," Wyler remembered. "This was one of the sides of Goldwyn. He paid, I think, $140,000 for the rights, a tremendous price at the time. He just paid it and said, 'Okay, we've got it.' Then he engaged Lillian Hellman to do the script. I was delighted.

"There was one thing, however, I couldn't swing. I wanted to do the picture in New York, on the streets where the picture would be made today. I wanted to juxtapose a block in the East Fifties with the Sutton Place elegance. Goldwyn wouldn't let me do that. He was afraid I'd get away from him."

Goldwyn's *Dead End* set was the talk of the town. Richard Day had been spurred by his *Dodsworth* Oscar to create a magnificent complex of seedy apartment buildings, shops, a rear entrance, balcony of a lush hotel, a stretch of quayside and a tank-corner of a greasy East River for the Dead End kids to jump into and for Bogart to ponder by after dusk with Toland's camera catching water reflections in his face.

Goldwyn's own stars, Sylvia Sidney—the quintessential proletarian princess of the thirties—and Joel McCrea, took billing above Bogart's "Babyface" Martin role, but it was Bogey's (and the Dead End kids') picture. For the first time since he created Duke Mantee opposite Bette Davis in Archie Mayo's *The Petrified Forest,* Bogart was able to build a whole character ("I used to be the guy behind the guy behind the gun," he told reporters). As Babyface Martin, he played one of his more cherished scenes—the confrontation with his mother (Marjorie Main), a situation which reappeared in *Bonnie and Clyde* thirty years later. Bogey had marital problems and suddenly divorced Mary Philips, but the breakup and his liaison with Mayo Methot (soon to be his second wife) never spilled over on his performance. He kept such a good memory of *Dead End* that eighteen years later, he was to call Wyler and ask for the bad guy's part in *The Desperate Hours.*

The social thriller was well received. In an editorial, the *New York Post* said "the best thing that could have been done at the last session of Congress would have been to show the film *Dead End* to the committees which crippled the Wagner Housing Act." [2] The *New York Times* called it a "stout and well-presented reiteration of the social protest," although the Dead End kids were not taken too seriously as proof that slum conditions breed criminals.[3] "The show undoubtedly belongs to the six incomparable urchins, imported from the stage production whenever they are in view," the *Times* continued, "but the camera occasionally leaves them to their swimming and to their boisterous horseplay to discover Drina [Sylvia Sidney], footsore after a day on the picket lines; Dave [Joel McCrea] and Kate [Wendy Barrie] longing together for release from their respective imprisonments; Babyface snarling at life after his mother's hateful denunciation and his disillusionment on finding that the girl [Claire Trevor] hadn't waited." (Another Hays Office tonedown; his original disillusionment was over finding her with syphilis.)

Overseas, *Dead End* was seen as social criticism. Graham Greene called it "one of the best pictures of the year" and Bogart's Babyface "the finest performance he has ever given."[4] In Paris, critics were also impressed and in his big *Histoire du Cinéma mondial*, Georges Sadoul was to call it Wyler's best prewar picture and the film that began the foundation of his French reputation.[5] In Hollywood, *Dead End* was nominated for four Academy Awards but received none.

Next, Wyler was loaned out to Warner Brothers to direct the studio's top star in *Jezebel,* the story of an antebellum vixen named Julie Marsden, a blood sister, as it were, of Scarlett O'Hara.

The Owen Davis play, which Willy had admired in New York in 1934, was a consolation prize to Bette Davis for the missed *Gone With the Wind.* Jack Warner had had the first option on Margaret Mitchell's bestseller, but during his court feud with Bette, had dropped it. David Selznick had bought it and, at an early stage, had wanted to borrow Bette Davis and Errol Flynn from Warners. She had found the idea of Flynn as Rhett Butler so appalling that she refused "to be part of that parcel," as she said.

The Bette Davis against Goliath day in court was part of a general unrest in Hollywood. While Ronald Reagan was organizing the actors, John Howard Lawson the screenwriters, and King Vidor pushing for the first collective directors' contract, stars fought a contract system that made them virtual chattel of their studios. James Cagney was in court over his Warner Brothers contract, Katharine Hepburn was fighting with RKO, Margaret Sullavan was fighting the new Universal management, Carole Lombard was fighting with Paramount, and Eddie Cantor with Goldwyn.

The star system had always been based on contractual employment. What was new was that following a few poor decisions by a few stars, producers had become frightened and proclaimed no artist, no matter how big, had the right to decide what films he wanted to work in. The penalty for disobedience was, as always, suspension, which meant the particular artist was declared persona non grata on his home lot, was forbidden employment elsewhere, that his salary stopped, and the number of weeks or months of the suspension was simply tagged to the end of the running contract. A star, director, cameraman, composer, who had signed a two-year contract in 1933 might still be under the same contract eight years later. At Warners, which Olivia de Havilland called "a model prison," "doing solitary" meant suspension plus roles in "triple-B pictures." Among them, Cagney, Bogart, and Bette Davis had twenty suspensions.

Bette Davis had won the 1935 Best Actress Award for *Dangerous,* directed by Alfred E. Green, and had expected better scripts. When she was cast as a lady lumberjack in *God's Country and the Woman,* she revolted. Despite dire prophecies from friends and colleagues, she flew to Vancouver with her husband, crossed Canada to Montreal, and sailed for England, all to avoid being served injunctions by Warners' lawyers. In London, she signed with an Anglo-Italian producer, Ludovic Toeplitz, who caved in as soon as pressure built up from Hollywood and reneged on his contract with her. Warners served her with an injunction prohibiting her from rendering her services *anywhere* and prepared for a court battle.

Jack Warner came to London with William Randolph Hearst, whose newspapers treated Bette Davis as a wayward schoolgirl in need of a spanking. Warner had Alexander Korda testify on his behalf and the court turned down Bette Davis' lawyer's argument that the self-perpetuating nature of Hollywood contracts made them into "life sentences." Warners won a three-year injunction which, if the studio chose to pick up all its options, put Bette Davis into golden bondage until 1942. Gaumont British threw a victory party. Had Miss Davis won, everyone feared, all major stars would follow suit and the bottom would fall out of the contractual star system. The injunction was valid in Britain only, but Bette knew when she was defeated.

When she returned to Burbank, Jack Warner bent over backwards to forget and forgive and relieved her of the studio's share of damages. The publicity of her fight, however, paved the way for other court contests. In 1944, Olivia de Havilland won, on appeal, a California Superior Court ruling saying that time lost by a player put on suspension could not be added to a term contract after its expiration date.

To celebrate the return of the spoiled tizzy, Bette Davis got what she had wanted. Warner cast her in quick succession in three top pictures. The first was *Marked Woman,* costarring Bogart as a district attorney and directed by Lloyd Bacon, followed by *Kid Galahad* opposite Edward G. Robinson and with Michael Curtiz, Warners' top contract filmmaker, directing. Then Edmund Goulding directed her, Leslie Howard, and Olivia de Havilland in a comedy romp, *That Certain Woman,* a remake of *The Trespasser,* which Goulding had made with Gloria Swanson seven years earlier.

Bette Davis had an odd memory of Wyler and when Hal Wallis told her who would direct her in the upcoming *Jezebel,* she was stunned. It seemed that when she had been a newcomer at Universal in 1931, she had been considered for the part of the mail-order bride between Walter Huston and Kent Douglass in *A House Divided.* Despite her protest, the wardrobe department had given her a more than revealing cotton dress and sent her over to Wyler for the test. Next, she heard him wonder aloud to his assistant, "What do you think of these dames who show their chests and think they can get jobs?"

She had never forgotten.

"Mr. Wyler, not remembering me or the incident, was, to put it mildly, taken back when I told him my grim little tale of woe," she was to write in her autobiography.[6] "He was genuinely apologetic, saying he had come a long way since those days. I could not help believing he was sincere. With no revenge left in me, I started work on *Jezebel.* I became such a champion of his talent —and still am—that one would have thought I was his highly paid press agent. It was *he* who helped me realize my full potential as an actress. I met my match in this exceptionally creative and talented director." Wyler was to return the compliment. "We had three very good experiences together," he told *Cinema* in 1967. "She was a director's dream. If I dismissed her early one day, she would be unhappy and say, 'What's the matter, don't you want me anymore? You're all through?' She would go to her dressing room, change her clothes and come back to the set and stay until everybody went home. She wanted to be there, see everything." [7]

The first person Wyler ran into at Warners was John Huston and the first thing he did on *Jezebel* was to get John on the project for a rewrite of the script by Clements Ripley and Abem Finkel. Huston had become a contract writer at Warners a few months earlier. His father had married his third wife, Nan Sunderland, and John, himself, had married Lesley Black, "Marrying Lesley was probably the best thing that ever happened to him; she gave him standards to live by and the incentive to work," Henry Blanke, associate producer on *Jezebel*, said.

Huston tried to stick to the grindstone. His first job had been *The Amazing Dr. Clitterhouse*, in which Edward G. Robinson played a psychiatrist turning jewel thief in order to test criminal behavior. The picture costarred Bogart and was the first project together for the future director and star of *The Maltese Falcon*. The Dashiell Hammett classic was only three projects away. After *Jezebel* came Huston's *Dr. Ehrlich's Magic Bullet*, in which Robinson played the discoverer of a cure for syphilis, *Sergeant York*, and *High Sierra*, in which Bogart was a hunted criminal fleeing on foot into the Sierra Madre toting his machine gun in a violin case. After that, Warner felt Huston was ready to direct.

While Anatole Litvak shot *Clitterhouse*, John joined Willy on *Jezebel*. The background for the rather novelettish story was the New Orleans yellow-fever epidemic of 1853, which left eight thousand dead in the city, desolated the countryside, and—as southern writers would have it—"also steeled the spirits of men and women to endure when still greater devastation was loosed on them in the Civil War" eight years later. *Jezebel* was both a study of transition—southern society moving from the heyday of one era to the omens of a new one—and of Heraclitus' postulate that character is fate.

Julie Marsden is the reckless and resolute spoiled, wealthy, and imperious belle who destroys her chances for happiness by perversely flouting conventions. She is the kind of impulsive and complex girl whose flaming temper and all too soft depth have her admirers forever guessing and her family and servants pledging to her and clinging to her.

"It's hard to know which is Davis' 'big scene' in the movie—the painful flamboyant error of her appearance in red, or the breathtaking moment of her apology in white," Pauline Kael was to write. "She took the Academy Award of 1938 for this role, and rarely has it been awarded so justly." [8]

If the panorama of pre-Civil War southern society was nothing new in 1938, the portrait of Julie Marsden was an example of the rarest sort of movie—a genuine sketch of a complex individual. "Almost any sort of authenticity survives more easily on the screen than this: whether it derives from historical accuracy, observation of modern social condition, or merely from the straightforward exploitation of dynamic and desirable persons," Peter Galway was to write twenty years later. "Perhaps, a medium which depends on movement and has to keep moving is more naturally suited to the panorama than the portrait. In the close dissection of character, there may be something incurably static, depending on silence, intimacy, leisurely tempo. And then a film like *Jezebel* comes along to suggest the possibility of revealing character as effectively as in a good novel or play." [9]

Filming started October 21, 1937, and finished January 1938, the month the *Gone With the Wind* craze over the casting of Scarlett O'Hara reached its highest pitch. By the time *Jezebel* was world premiered at the Radio City Music Hall in New York in March, Katharine Hepburn, Susan Hayward, Frances Dee, and Carole Lombard's discovery, Margaret Tallichet, had been tested, and fourteen hundred young women interviewed before cameras at a highly publicized cost of $92,000. Selznick saw *Jezebel* in New York on one of his Search for Scarlett missions and was so impressed with Max Steiner's music, he hired the volatile Viennese, who had also scored *The Informer* and *King Kong,* to write the *Gone With the Wind* music.

Jezebel was three great months' work for Wyler. He didn't have Toland on the camera, but Ernest Haller's black and white photography was impeccable, even if without Tolandian "touches." And, best of all, he had a leading lady who appreciated him.

"After all these years, I had been given a high-budget film with all the trimmings I had fought for and a talented director that I had been begging for also," she was to write in her autobiography. "My first appearance was in a riding habit. As Julie entering her house, I was to lift my skirt with my riding crop. It sounds simple. Mr. Wyler asked me to take the riding skirt and the crop home and rehearse with them. The next morning, I arrived knowing he was after something special. I made my entrance a dozen times and he wasn't satisfied. He wanted something, all right. He wanted a complete establishment of character with one gesture. I sweated through forty-five takes and he finally got it the way he wanted, or at least, he said so, in his very noncommittal way." [10]

Bette Davis also was to marvel over a scene toward the end where Julie and Amy (Margaret Lindsay) fight over who will go with the stricken Preston (Henry Fonda) to Lazarette Island, and Wyler, making the point of the wife's proprietary air, moved into a closeup of Margaret Lindsay's left hand with her wedding band glistening with symbolism. And the "big scene," which was a bare paragraph in the script.

"Without a word of dialog, Willy created a scene of power and tension," she was to write. "This was moviemaking on the highest plane. Insisting that my correct escort dance with me—knowing that I am making him an accomplice in this gaucherie—and his refusal to stop, once the floor is cleared by the revolted dancers who consider us pariahs, is so mortifying that Julie wants to die. But now Press is relentless in his punishment. His own embarrassment is nothing to the shame he must inflict on her. Julie implores him to take her home. His grip on her waist becomes tighter, his step more deliberate, his eyes never meet hers. And always the lilting music, the swirling bodies and the peripheral reaction shots of the stunned pillars of society and Belle [Fay Bainter], who suffers with Julie. It is a scene of such suspense that I never have not marveled at the direction of it."

When Bette Davis received her second Oscar for *Jezebel,* she cried and told the Academy Award dinner party the joy was only lessened by the Academy's failure to give the directorial award to Wyler. And, in her memoirs, she was to write: "It was all Wyler. I had known all the horrors of no direction and bad direction. I now knew what a great director was and what he could mean to an actress. I will always be grateful to him for his toughness and his genius."

As Bogart's long marriage had floundered during *Dead End,* so did Bette Davis' first marriage, to Harmon (Ham) O. Nelson, come to a quiet divorce during the filming. *Jezebel* also witnessed happier occasions, however. The shooting schedule was juggled around to allow the leading man to go to New York for the birth of his first child, christened Jane, and, as ex-husbands of Margaret Sullavan who finally got to know each other, Henry Fonda and Willy Wyler discovered they were also both clients of the same agent—Maggie's third husband, Leland Hayward.

"I forget whose idea it was, but one of us said, 'Let's call Leland and pull one on him,' " Wyler recalled. "Fonda called him first and said, 'Leland, come out here. I've gotta see you immediately.' Then, I called and said, 'You have got to come out. I've got trouble.' "

The Fonda-Wyler stunt was elaborate and both managed to keep straight faces. When Leland Hayward arrived on the Burbank stage, Fonda was very upset.

"Get me out of this picture, Leland," he said, retiring to his dressing room, with a pale Leland following him and asking what had happened.

"You're over half finished, Hank," Hayward cried.

"Get me out of this picture. That sonofabitch Wyler, I don't want to work for him another day!"

"God!" Hayward asked Fonda just to sit tight while he went over to talk to Wyler, dramatically sitting on top of a camera crane.

"Get me another leading man," Wyler began before Hayward could say anything. "I want Hank out of this picture!"

"But you're almost through," Hayward pleaded, imagining himself breaking the news to Jack Warner upstairs.

"I don't give a damn. I'd rather reshoot the whole goddamn picture. Get him out of this picture!"

With the consummate skill of a high-powered Hollywood agent, Hayward got them to stop their threats, then, after another half-hour of delicate diplomacy between dressing room and camera crane, he managed to get them together. Then, on cue, Fonda and Wyler had the still man on the set snap a photo of all three. The photo was to be called The Maggie Sullavan Club, Hank and Willy explained. Hayward had to laugh also.

Wyler was soon to change agents. Old friendship was more important than playing jokes on Hayward, who was, with David Selznick's brother, Myron, the biggest of the independent talent representatives. Paul Kohner was opening up a modest shop on Sunset Boulevard, an agency which was eventually to specialize in European talent and represent such varied artists as Igor Stravinsky and Ingmar Bergman, Lana Turner, and Maurice Chevalier. The 1973 roster of Paul Kohner agency clients still included John Huston and William Wyler.

The two years since the departure from Uncle Carl's ruins and the dramatic midnight hiring by Louis B. Mayer had not been happy for Paul. The erstwhile chief of Universal's European production was resented at MGM and after preparing several projects for Thalberg, which he was not given a chance to produce, he quit and, with his own savings and money borrowed from Willy and Joe Pasternak, set himself up as an agent.

"I sat in my office and I didn't know what to do," he recalled. "I was so scared and so ashamed. Here I had been a producer and now I was an agent. Till today I sometimes have nightmares of finding myself sneaking around Universal studios that first day. That was what happened—I went to the only studio I knew, Universal, and made a Deanna Durbin script deal with Pasternak that made me enough money to carry me through the first six months."

Kohner's ability to "sneak around studios" was soon to bring Selznick's two-year contractee, Margaret Tallichet, to Goldwyn's to watch Jascha Heifetz play his violin before the cameras of a second-unit director called William Wyler.

17

"The trouble with directors," one of the less-celebrated Goldwyn-isms goes, "is that they're always biting the hand that lays the golden egg." After Willy's loanout to Warner Brothers, it was back to new and lively fights on Formosa Avenue.

This was the height of Samuel Goldwyn's long career. Between 1936 and 1941, he produced three or four pictures a year— between *These Three* and *The Little Foxes,* fourteen films all with his own money. Even if he didn't treat his premier director as a superstar, Wyler now had first pick. Or rather, only if Wyler refused to do a picture—utterly and completely and despite a heavy barrage of Goldwyn's inimitable psychological warfare—did Goldwyn assign another, and presumably lesser, helmsman. Goldwyn was a proud man. Even after a number of films refused by Wyler turned out to be box-office flops, Goldwyn still went ahead with other clunkers. When a newsman began a remark to him by saying, "When Wyler made *Wuthering Heights* . . ." he never got any further. *"I* made *Wuthering Heights,"* Goldwyn inter-rupted. "Wyler only directed it!"

Wyler's turndowns were totally illegal. There was nothing in the fine print that gave him the right to decide which Goldwyn pictures he would direct and which he wouldn't. He was paid $2,500 a week for forty weeks a year to *direct,* not to choose and pick. When Wyler refused—utterly and completely—Goldwyn's only weapon was suspension.

"I never did quite do as I was told and, as the saying went, I was 'suspended and extended,' " Wyler said. "I had a three-year contract that ran for almost five years. That means I wasn't paid for two years."

For the divorced director, who, unlike many of his confrères, wasn't saddled with astronomical alimony and child-support payments, a suspension was not the end of the world. He still lived in the rented house on Beverly Hills's Bedford Drive with his butler, Sam. When suspended, Willy simply took off. When he didn't go skiing with John Huston up in Running Springs, he was inaugurating Averill Harriman's new Idaho resort called Sun Valley or off to such mundane slopes as Switzerland's St. Moritz, where, in 1937, he switched to tobogganing, winning a second prize on the famed Cresta Run down a three-quarter-mile sheet of ice. If Goldwyn's suspension came during the summer, he was to be found on sailboats off San Diego. When the next project rolled around, Willy was back, tanned, willing, and ready. Goldwyn could have taken revenge, refused to take him back, and even sued for breach of contract. He never did.

The first picture Wyler refused to have anything to do with, but was conned into working on for a week, was a wacky farce that Dorothy Parker, her husband, Alan Campbell, and *Variety*'s Joe Bigelow had hacked out together—*Woman Chases Man*. The writing credits were long, meaning a lot of people had rewritten a lot of other people's rewrites. Lynn Root and Franklyn Fenton were credited with the original story and the screenplay credits went to three other unknowns—Joseph Anthony, Manuel Seff, and David Hertz. Basically, a switch on the wealthy-father/no-good-son routine, *Woman Chases Man* has Joel McCrea playing the practical son of erratic Charles Winninger. The boy has a million dollars and the father needs $100,000 to complete a nebulous real-estate development. Miriam Hopkins is an architect who wants a job and, after a first astonished stare, also wants her employer's son. So, woman chases man until, toward the end, Miriam Hopkins and McCrea find themselves, literally, up a tree.

The whole thing was more capricious than brilliant, a series of situations that failed to develop naturally because of lack of plot. Goldwyn asked Wyler to have a look at *Woman Chases Man*. "Just work on it for a few weeks and see," Goldwyn told him. "See if you can improve on it, work with the writer."

But Wyler found it hopeless. The material was scanty, too

many writers had had their fingers in it. After two weeks, he reported to the boss that he couldn't do anything with it.

"You've been drawing salary all this time," Goldwyn said.

"I'll give it back to you."

Wyler meant it as a joke. Goldwyn didn't. It cost Wyler $5,000, two weeks' salary.

Goldwyn replaced Wyler with John Blystone, a western and comics director, and made *Woman Chases Man* his summer release of 1937. "Reportorial accuracy compels recording that the Music Hall's first night audience laughed with approval of this picture for the first three-quarters of its running and then the giggles stopped," *Variety* wrote. "Laughs ceased when the action on the screen became so insanely illogical and dull, that the amazed disappointment of the house expressed itself in chilly silence." [1]

Next came a pair of Gary Cooper vehicles—*The Cowboy and the Lady* and *The Adventures of Marco Polo*.

Cooper was one of the stars Goldwyn had let slip through his fingers in the mid-twenties. The tall Montanan had been hired by Goldwyn's casting director, Bob McIntyre, in 1926 for the Henry King-directed *Winning of Barbara Worth*. Cooper made a deep impression on audiences as a youthful romantic figure (and the only genuinely western element in the film), but when Paramount offered him $150 a week, McIntyre let him go. In 1935, Goldwyn had made another bid for Cooper for a proposed picture on Maximilian of Mexico to costar Merle Oberon as Carlotta, but Paramount had Clifford Odets write *The General Died at Dawn,* the story of an American soldier of fortune in revolutionary China, and refused to loan Coop to Goldwyn.

When Wyler began *The Cowboy and the Lady* (with Toland on the camera), Cooper had just come from another comedy—Lubitsch's *Bluebeard's Eighth Wife,* written by Billy Wilder and Charles Brackett. Cooper had not been comfortable as the millionaire who had had seven wives before meeting Claudette Colbert in a Parisian haberdashery and *The Cowboy and the Lady* was closer to his screen image of the shy, whimsical boy who is a pretty nice fella until he's being made fun of and then all hell breaks loose. In *The Cowboy and the Lady* he was most appealing as the cowboy. Merle Oberon was the lady.

It was a breezy little comedy of a modern cowboy who travels with a rodeo, sprinkles bay rum on his hair and falls in love with the glamorous daughter of a rich Presidential candidate. When she marries him under false pretenses, he returns bitterly to cow country—only to find her waiting there for him in the fadeout.

Wyler showed little enthusiasm for *The Cowboy and the Lady,* but Goldwyn pressed him into service. The film had been scripted, again, by a bevy of writers—S. N. Behrman and Sonya Levien got screen credits—and by the time it was shot and reshot, the cost had escalated to $1.7 million.

To Wyler's relief, Goldwyn took him off the picture for being too slow after a few days of shooting. His replacement was H. C. Potter, who in 1936 had directed Goldwyn's Merle Oberon-starrer *Beloved Enemy* (and, in 1942, was to direct *Hellzapoppin*).

"When are you going to let me do *Wuthering Heights?*" Wyler asked.

"Get lost!"

Next came *The Adventures of Marco Polo,* which Wyler refused utterly and completely. John Cromwell, who had just directed *The Prisoner of Zenda,* had started the picture but quit after five days. When Goldwyn couldn't get Wyler to take over, he engaged Archie Mayo, the ex-gagwriter for Buster Keaton who had made *The Petrified Forest* with Bogart and Bette Davis.

"See, there's a fellow who helps you when you're down," Goldwyn told Wyler reproachfully.

"I'm not here to help, Sam," Wyler replied. "I'm here to make good pictures. I have, at least, to believe in it."

Goldwyn liked that answer and put Wyler on suspension.

The Adventures of Marco Polo was a mess. It was the first Goldwyn film since the Anna Sten triptych that failed to win *any* audience. Richard Day's glossy sets of Renaissance Venice and China were inferior to his *Dead End* decor and invariably compared to the Tibetan Shangri-La that art director Stephen Goosson created for Frank Capra's *Lost Horizon.* Opposite Cooper's Venetian explorer, Goldwyn cast a "Norwegian" discovery, Sigrid Gurie, who, it was soon discovered, was from Flatbush, New York. Cromwell had directed *Marco Polo* as a serious drama and Mayo never quite knew what to do with Robert Sherwood's tongue-in-cheek screenplay.

While Mayo struggled with *Marco Polo,* Wyler was in Europe and, on the way back, entertained the screen's real Norwegian star, Sonja Henie. The setting was the *Normandie* and included a dinner party in her honor. Since Joseph Kennedy, the U.S. ambassador to the court of St. James, was also aboard, Wyler invited him to join the little party.

"When it was time for dinner, Mr. Kennedy came and brought along two teen-age boys," Wyler recalled. "Nothing had been said about any kids, but we got a couple of more chairs and squeezed them in. The boys were the ambassador's eldest sons, Joe Jr. and John. They were both crazy to dance with Sonja but she didn't give them a tumble." In fact, nobody including me, gave them the time of day."

Goldwyn could be ruthless to men who didn't stand up to him. When *Marco Polo* turned out to be a disaster, life was made miserable for Mayo on the lot. Everywhere he was offended, told to come in at nine in the morning for no reason and treated like an office boy, all in an effort to make him break his contract.

Mayo was confused, upset, and in need of advice.

"Break the contract," Willy suggested.

"Break the contract?"

"You asked me for advice, don't take this insult."

But Mayo wouldn't. It was a three-year contract, he had bought a new house on the strength of it. He explained how he had everything figured out, down to how much he would make in three years. It gave him security.

"Your professional self-respect is worth more than security," Willy insisted. "You ask me for my advice, walk out and keep your self-respect."

Mayo hung on and Goldwyn somehow got rid of him anyway.

"From that point on, poor Archie went downhill," Willy recalled. "He ended up in Mexico. Shows you one year you're the golden boy, the next you're a bum, depending on what pictures you make. With Goldwyn I was always the hero, but much later I was sometimes the bum, then after the preview the hero, then if the picture was a failure, I was the bum again." Mayo's last film was *Angel on my Shoulder,* in 1946. He died in Mexico in 1968.

In the fall of 1938, Goldwyn started what was just called "the Heifetz picture" around the lot because its title was changed weekly, or so it seemed. It first appeared in the *Variety* listing of films in production as *The Restless Age.* It then went from *Angels Making Music* to *Music School* to its final title, *They Shall Have Music.* As written by Irmgard von Cube and John

Howard Lawson, the story line centered around a music school established by a kindly old master (Walter Brennan) on the Lower East Side of New York to give free lessons to slum kids. The sentimental tale has an underprivileged boy (Gene Reynolds) discovering music and landing in the lovable old maestro's school, which he finally saves by persuading Jascha Heifetz to come to and give a concert.

Heifetz's contract had a cutoff date and in order not to lose the maestro, Goldwyn put the picture into production even though the script was far from ready. Would Willy please film the concert finale?

"I shot it all on a stage at the studio," Wyler recalled. "I had Heifetz and the Peter Meremblum California Junior Symphony Orchestra and filmed the playing of Saint-Saëns' *Rondo Capricioso, Hora staccato* by Dinicu-Heifetz, Tchaikovsky's *Melodie,* and the last movement of Mendelsohn's *Concerto.* I loved it!"

So did the critics. The *New York Times*'s anonymous reviewer spent one of five paragraphs in lyrical ectasy over Willy's second-unit photography. "Perhaps a critic of music might better remark upon its excellence," the reviewer noted. "Suffice it for a journeyman of the films to comment enthusiastically that the crystal purity of Mr. Heifetz's playing, the eloquent flow of melody from his violin and the dramatic presentation of the artist commanding his instrument—closeups of his graceful fingers upon the strings, of the majestic sweep of his bowing arm and brilliant angle shots of the man before an orchestra—create an effect of transcendent beauty which is close to unique in this medium." [2]

Variety's reviewer was just as forceful: "Heifetz makes no pretense of being an actor; but when he faces the camera to start a number, his confidence in control of the instrument is easily discernible. His solos are tops, and although the camera remains on the virtuoso practically all the time he is delivering his numbers, it focuses attention in turn with rapid movement from closeups to medium shots of his fast-moving fingers, the flashing bow and rhythmic right arm to accentuate attention to his art." [3]

After *They Shall Have Music,* Wyler did *Wuthering Heights,* which Goldwyn was to call his favorite picture. Emily Brontë's story gave Wyler his second nomination, but 1939 was a hot year in the Oscar race—*Gone With the Wind, Goodbye Mr. Chips, Dark Victory, Ninotchka, Love Affair, Wuthering Heights, Stage-*

coach, and *Mr. Smith Goes to Washington.* President Roosevelt delivered the banquet address and, as Bob Hope quipped, the event turned out to be a "benefit for Dave Selznick." *Gone With the Wind—GWTW,* as the trade called it—took Best Picture, Best Actress (Vivien Leigh), Best Director (Victor Fleming), Best Screenplay (Sidney Howard), and Best Supporting Actress (Hattie McDaniel).

Willy was becoming a hot director and increasingly in demand. RKO had offered him *Having a Wonderful Time,* eventually directed by Alfred Santell. Selznick approached him and there was talk of another Bette Davis picture at Warners', a film for Darryl F. Zanuck, and one for Metro, the Olympus of studios.

"What do you do for an encore?" Selznick had laughed as he plunged into last-minute preparation for the "historic" Atlanta premiere of *Gone With the Wind.* He decided the followup would be *Intermezzo,* starring his new Swedish discovery, Ingrid Bergman, and his *GWTW* costar, Leslie Howard. The director would be Wyler.

If Sam Goldwyn was a maniac, Selznick—two months older than Wyler—was an obsessive madman, a twenty-hour-a-day Benzedrine-driven producer extraordinaire with a knack for firing his directors. He had replaced George Cukor on *GWTW* because he feared Cukor would "interpolate" into the script.

His New York scout, Kay Brown, had seen Gustaf Molander's 1937 *Intermezzo,* starring Gösta Ekman and a newcomer who had become an overnight sensation in Stockholm—Ingrid Bergman. Kay Brown had alerted her boss to this Swedish film and he had sent her to Stockholm to sign up property and star.

Ingrid and her doctor husband, Peter Lindström, had their reservations. She told Kay Brown that she had seen too many European actresses go to Hollywood only to have their names, personalities, and appearances changed and then to vanish within a short time, devoid of the attributes that had made them stars in their native countries in the first place. With telegrams flying between Miss Brown and the Selznick front office in Culver City, Ingrid finally agreed on the condition that Selznick provide her with a good script, director, and leading man. Selznick wired assurances that her first American picture would be none other than *Intermezzo* remade, William Wyler her director, and Leslie Howard her leading man. With such assurances, she said yes.

Meanwhile, Selznick ran Molander's *Intermezzo* for Wyler in his executive screening room and told him he wanted to make the film over with the same girl.

"One thing," Wyler said when the lights came back on, "does she speak English?"

"Sure."

"In that case, let's go."

"What about Leslie?" Selznick asked.

"Great."

"Leslie wants to be associate producer, I hope you have no objections."

"Not so long as he doesn't want to be associate director."

They left the screening room but didn't sign any contract right away. It looked like a happy assignment. Toland was borrowed from Goldwyn. It was, again, a violinist's story and Wyler began preproduction by recording a series of concert pieces with Toscha Seidl, a great Viennese who became a friend and who was to give Willy his first violin lessons since Mulhouse and become famous in the family for yelling in his inimitable Viennese accent, "Mr. Wyler, you do not vibrato by shaking your leg!"

One afternoon, Wyler and Toland got Ingrid Bergman (who resisted Selznick's attempts to change her name, recap her teeth, dye her hair, and "play down" her husband and two-year-old daughter Pia in his publicity) for a test. Her English was improving but still shaky. Before filming started, however, Wyler was out and Gregory Ratoff replaced him.

"I don't remember the reason," Wyler recalled thirty years later when Selznick had been dead for years (without coming up with his encore to *GWTW*). "Selznick had reasons to make things difficult for me and I said, 'To hell with this' and walked out. I worked about six weeks on it and never got a penny. That I do remember."

Intermezzo: A Love Story, as it was finally titled, received little attention from Selznick, who was involved in the completion and release of *GWTW*. Ratoff's heavy Russian accent added little to Ingrid's understanding of her first English-dialogue film. Leslie Howard did assume some production duties, but was impatient to return to England. It was his last Hollywood film; he was aboard an airliner from Lisbon to London shot down by German planes in 1943. *Intermezzo: A Love Story* proved "a disappointment but critics and audiences were impressed by the natural beauty and emotional depth of Miss Bergman." [4]

Intermezzo: A Love Story was not to be Willy's last "no-go" project.

18

When Margaret Tallichet married William Wyler in Walter Huston's weekend home in Running Springs, Saturday, October 23, 1938, the bride was called "Talli." Talli it had been since high school, and Talli it was to remain. Thirty-five years later, it was still Talli and Willy mellowing into grandparenthood. Nobody had given them a year back then.

"Starlet Weds Director," the *Los Angeles Examiner* headlined its society page notice the following Monday morning. The newspaper heading reflected most people's attitudes—another hasty Hollywood marriage that spelled anything but longevity. On Tuesday, the wedding rated a two-liner in Louella Parsons' syndicated column, below tidbits about Errol Flynn going to Hawaii and the possible casting of Henry Fonda in Darryl Zanuck's upcoming *Young Mr. Lincoln*. The society event of 1938 it wasn't.

Only a few friends were present at Mr. and Mrs. Huston's San Bernardino Mountains retreat Willy had had so much difficulty locating the first time. The groom's parents and brother were there, together with Lupi and Paul Kohner, Leslie and John Huston, and Willy's lawyer friend Mark Cohen. Melanie provided the tears, Leslie and John the wedding cake. None of the bride's relatives were present. She was to remember she was in a complete fog and that Willy was white as a sheet in his navy blue suit. The bride was twenty-four, the groom thirty-six.

There was no honeymoon. The newlyweds drove to Palm Springs for the remainder of the weekend and, on Monday morning, the groom was back on Formosa Avenue preparing his next picture, *Wuthering Heights.*

They had met five weeks earlier on Formosa Avenue. As a prospective new client, Paul Kohner had taken Margaret to watch and hear Jascha Heifetz play for the camera. That was the *in* thing to do in Hollywood that September.

Talli was always to remember: "When we arrived, there was indeed Heifetz and a full symphony orchestra on a stage. There was also the camera crew photographing him as the soloist and the orchestra. And there was the director. He was having a marvelous time riding on a camera boom, soaring up to high shots and coming down on Heifetz's hand on the violin fingerboard. I had heard a bit about Paul's friend. Anyway, we were introduced and he said, 'I've got tickets for the Southwest Tennis Tournament that's starting next week. Would you like to come?' "

Willy remembered nothing about the tennis tournament, but only that Talli was different and not too easy. "At first, she was just a pretty girl, another date. We went out a few times. It happened very quickly. In about four weeks. You can find out a lot in four weeks. I don't know what she saw in me, but I saw in her a bright, attractive, and intelligent girl. A college graduate and someone who wasn't like other dates. She was no pushover."

Talli had come to Hollywood in the spring of 1936 with a great-aunt who was spending a few months in California. She was a twenty-one-year-old graduate of Southern Methodist University in her native Dallas with a few months experience on the society staff of the *Dallas Morning News* and a blushing complex about her Texas drawl.

The Tallichets were an old French Protestant family chased from the kingdom of Louis XIV along with other Huguenots by his Revocation of the Edict of Nantes in 1685. The family had settled in Orbes, in French Switzerland. From there, Talli's great-grandparents had come to Alabama in 1822 and her parents had moved to Dallas in the 1900s. The common Swiss ancestry was later to amuse the Wylers as they realized their children were more Swiss than anything else, Talli being one quarter and Willy one half Swiss, although one was born in Alsace and the other in Texas.

Talli's Hollywood debut was right out of the fan magazines. "I had this desire, I thought at the time, to act and actually it was more restlessness than anything else," Talli remembered. "Since I had worked a little on a newspaper in Dallas, I got a job as a secretary with the Paramount publicity department. It was the first time I had ever seen the inside of a studio and before that I hadn't had the faintest clue of the world I was getting into. In the meantime, I was trying to prepare myself to become an actress. I took acting lessons and diction lessons trying to lose the southern accent that was so thick you could cut it with a knife. Part of the time I lived at the Studio Club. The whole thing was sort of traditional.

"One of my jobs in the publicity department was to take visiting press on the sets when they were in town. One day, Mr Boyd Martin of the *Louisville Courier-Journal* came out. He had an appointment to visit Carole Lombard and I was told to take him to her dressing room."

Talli had never been inside a star's dressing room and she just sat there wondering what a publicity department secretary was supposed to do during interviews. Suddenly, she heard Mr. Martin say, "This is a rather pretty girl, don't you think she should be in pictures?"

"Yes, I do," Carole Lombard answered. Talli tried not to turn too crimson.

With rare generosity, the actress set a few wheels in motion, got Talli an agent, coached her for tests, and when Carole starred with Fredric March in *Nothing Sacred* for David Selznick, she spoke to him. She also talked to Selznick's chief publicist, Russell Birdwell, and together they convinced the producer to give a small role to this Margaret Tallichet in *A Star Is Born*, directed by William Wellman (after a story he and Robert Carson had put together and everybody from Dorothy Parker and Alan Campbell to Selznick's junior scenarists, Budd Schulberg and Ring Lardner, Jr., had rewritten).

In an industry that revered ballyhoo as an art form, Birdwell was a genius and Carole Lombard his ideal accomplice. The former *Los Angeles Examiner* reporter had drawn Selznick's attention by his colorful, succinct crime reporting. "I don't want press agentry," Selznick had said when he hired the self-assured Texan, "I want imagination." Birdwell's first piece of publicity for Selznick was hiring dozens of painters to create the world's longest sign—a three-mile announcement of *Little Lord Fauntle-*

roy painted on a Culver City boulevard (upset city fathers' protests were part of the gimmick). For *The Prisoner of Zenda,* Birdwell discovered a hamlet in Ontario actually called Zenda and airlifted twelve of its thirteen residents to the New York premiere (Canadian news services took care of the thirteenth, an ancient lady deemed unsafe for travel, adding to the publicity). For *The Young at Heart,* he convinced Selznick's casting office to hire nine former stars as extras.

For the casting of newcomer Margaret Tallichet, Birdwell and Carole Lombard cooked up a couple of new tricks. For one day, Miss Lombard acted as makeup girl and hairdresser for Talli and Birdwell attracted further attention by insuring Talli's Texan accent with Lloyd's of London for a million dollars.

With *A Star Is Born,* Selznick put Talli under contract and shipped her to a drama school in New York to make her lose the southern accent and teach her acting. She was gone for almost a year and when she returned in the spring of 1938, she was loaned out for a couple of B pictures. Republic Studios had her in *A Desperate Adventure,* a painful attempt at keeping alive Ramon Novarro's career as a romantic leading man. In the film directed by John Auer, the original Ben-Hur played a Parisian painter and Marian Marsh and Margaret Tallichet two sisters vying for his attentions. For Columbia, she was in *Girl's School,* directed by John Brahm and starring Anne Shirley, Nan Grey, and Ralph Bellamy. Next, it was scouting-for-Scarlett-O'Hara time at Selznick International.

"Why don't we put on a nationwide search for a girl to play Scarlett?" David had suggested, "We did that with *Tom Sawyer.*" Birdwell was on top of the game from the beginning. He put his staff to work on a campaign to seek an unknown to play Scarlett in the upcoming filmization of *Gone With the Wind* and just sat back and waited. For months on end, mail poured into the studio from hopeful Scarletts who offered their physical attributes— some with photos of applicants in southern belle gowns, others with photos in the nude. On Christmas morning, Selznick had gone to his front door to find a seven-foot replica of Margaret Mitchell's bestseller. Out of it popped a hoopskirted girl who announced, "I'm your Scarlett O'Hara!" In time, Selznick hired extra guards and Birdwell reported these facts to the press.

The "unknown" campaign was just a warmup. Birdwell told

Louella Parsons and Hedda Hopper that Selznick just *might* consider an established actress if the scouting-for-Scarlett should fail. Irving Thalberg's widow, Norma Shearer, was the first star mentioned and in quick succession, Katharine Hepburn, Frances Dee, and Paulette Goddard—Charlie Chaplin's protégée—were considered and unconsidered. Next, Selznick invited other studios to submit their contract actresses for auditions, a stunt that brought forward Lucille Ball, Miriam Hopkins, Claudette Colbert, Jean Arthur, and Maggie Sullavan. Carole Lombard was also under consideration but a flaming affair with Clark Gable—*the* Rhett Butler—still married to Rhea Langham, disqualified her.

And then there was Margaret Tallichet. Birdwell whipped up a fast campaign. "I got an enormous amount of publicity," she recalled. "I was being tested for Scarlett about in the middle of the campaign. I've always personally felt that Birdwell was showing his boss how much publicity he could create for a total unknown. He did a fantastic amount of it and most of it came to absolutely nothing."

The next loanout was to RKO for a Peter Lorre thriller, *Stranger on the Third Floor,* the first picture of former screenwriter Boris Ingster. It had John McGuire and Talli acting halfway normal while Lorre was called upon to enact a flaying and grotesque imitation of a psychotic killer.

Then Talli met Willy.

They planned their wedding quietly. Only the Kohners and the Hustons knew about it in advance and to avoid newspaper gossip, they took out a license in San Bernardino. On his own, Willy rented a small house from Gladys Belzer, Loretta Young's real estate agent mother, on Beverly Hills' Tropical Avenue, beneath the Jack Warner's residence. During the wedding weekend, Willy's butler Sam and Sam's brother Leroy, who was now also working for Wyler, moved everything in and when the newlyweds returned from Palm Springs, the house was ready for them.

Without telling Melanie and Leopold that Talli was to be his new wife, Willy had taken her to dinner at his parents' house on Selma Avenue. He didn't often bring dates for dinner and Melanie had her driver take her to the main market downtown to get live trout for her specialty—*truite au bleu,* a recipe demanding that the fish be thrown live into boiling vinegar. The story of the trout broke the ice at the table. The way Melanie told it, she had brought along a water bucket so the fish could be kept alive until dinnertime. On the way home, the driver had made an energetic stop and several trout had leaped out of the pail. While he had accelerated again, sending more fish overboard, Melanie had been on the floor of the car catching the first fish and throwing them back into the bucket.

As everyone else, Talli was instantly charmed by Melanie. "I could never talk much to Willy's father because he never really learned English," she said, "but his mother . . . she was a marvelous woman. She had more verve and more energy than most people and the most outgoing nature. She genuinely liked people. She was the kind of person that if you mentioned her name or made a description of her, people would say, 'Oh, yes, I know *her*.'"

Talli was apprehensive about Margaret and David Tallichet in Dallas. She felt her parents would be less than enthusiastic and she kept pushing off the fateful phone call. On the wedding day, she could no longer postpone the call. "I'm sure my parents were shocked. I have always had a bad conscience about it. Except that I knew if I did call, they would try to dissuade me. 'Don't. Wait. You don't know him yet.' I knew they would only create problems and since I was in love with him and I wasn't able to cope with any of this, I didn't call until it was all over."

Shocked or not, the Tallichets came west for a Christmas visit to judge for themselves. Their son-in-law *was* a Hollywood director and, of course, utterly charming. He had just started *Wuthering Heights,* made $2,500 a week (when he worked) and had guided Bette Davis, Merle Oberon, and all sorts of stars in front of cameras. He was divorced, the former husband of a movie star, but the first thing he had done in marrying Talli was to buy off her contract with Selznick. And he had laid down the law—there wouldn't be two Caesars and only one Alp in this family. Which didn't mean Talli couldn't continue to act. In fact, he was trying to cast her opposite Gary Cooper in his upcoming *The Westerner.*

Mrs. Tallichet was an accomplished pianist. Soon, she and her son-in-law were playing together—Beethoven sonatas for piano and violin. He *was* Jewish, of course, but Talli and he said they would bring up their children in some sort of benevolent atheism. Talli would someday take them to church and he would take

---

179

them to temple so they would know. "Otherwise, we'll leave it up to them," Willy said. "We're not very religious."

Wyler was soon deep into *Wuthering Heights* and their first dinner guests were Vivien Leigh and Laurence Olivier. Since Talli wanted a woman in the house and they didn't want to fire Leroy, Willy and Talli managed to foist him onto the Oliviers, who had rented a house for the duration of *Wuthering Heights,* and, on Willy's recommendation, hired Leroy. "I remember a dinner at the Oliviers sometime later. Just a small dinner with Leroy serving. He didn't come into the dining room once without dropping a fork or a plate. It really got to be very funny and Larry ended up by saying it was all our fault."

On December 11, Selznick began shooting *Gone With the Wind* with the burning of Atlanta sequence and that night, as the flames licked one of Griffith's old sets, dressed up as Atlanta on the Selznick back lot, the producer's agent brother, Myron, presented his newest actress-client, Vivien Leigh. On January 13, 1939, Vivien signed the contract to play Scarlett O'Hara.

The Wylers gave their first party on New Year's Eve. Everybody was there, the Oliviers, the Hustons, publicist Mack Millar, who was moving to Hollywood finally but said he would continue to get Willy interviews in New York. Preston Sturges came with Louise Sargent Tevis, whom he was soon to marry. When Willy noted she was a bit cross-eyed and, in French mentioned it to his friend, Preston answered that the defect wasn't divergent strabismus but ocular flirtatiousness.* The year 1939 promised to be great for everybody.

Talli was a frequent visitor on the *Wuthering Heights* set. In Chatsworth, California, where five hundred acres were landscaped into a Yorkshire moor, Talli watched the filming of the meeting of the lovers at Penniston Crag. On Formosa Avenue, she saw Willy film Cathy's death scene and had tears in her eyes through every take. Later, she made friends with Alice Ehlers, who played the harpsichord in the party scene when Cathy married Linton.

When *Wuthering Heights* was in the can, Willy took Talli to Sun Valley. "I had never seen people ski because I had been brought up in Texas where snow, if it ever fell, would be gone in

---

* Willy: *Elle louche?*
  Preston: *Non, c'est une coqueterie de l'oeil.*

---

a few hours. Suddenly, I saw mountains covered with this white stuff and people gliding down slopes. I was pregnant and didn't want to take any chances, but I did get on the back of Willy's skis once and the three of us did fifty yards downhill together."

Goldwyn launched *Wuthering Heights* with a traditional Hollywood opening. Before the premiere, Frances and Sam gave a select dinner, attended by Eleanor Roosevelt, Irving Berlin, Norma Shearer, Merle Oberon, and a few others. Goldwyn helped the First Lady into his limousine for the drive to the theater, past the lines of screaming fans, angry police and "glorious pandemonium," as Frances Goldwyn remembered it.[1] This was not the era of the director as superstar and the Wylers were not invited.

In late April, Talli was walking two dogs on leashes on Tropical Avenue when one of them tripped her and she fell on the concrete sidewalk. She almost lost the baby and was forced to spend the last three months of her pregnancy in near-immobility. A girl was born July 25, 1939. She was named Cathy, after the heroine of *Wuthering Heights*.

19

It had taken Wyler almost two years to convince the mercurial Samuel Goldwyn to do *Wuthering Heights*. Although the film now drenched America in tears, Emily Brontë's dark romantic tale violated all accepted rules of successful screen entertainment. That, in a sense, was what Willy had found challenging.

Together with Gregg Toland, Wyler had continued to probe the inner reaches of filmmaking—that high-voltage core of drama which he felt held the secret to cinematic language, form, and style. They had agreed that to adapt *Wuthering Heights* was not so much a matter of filming breathless vistas of Yorkshire moors as of filming the wilderness of the mind.

Nineteenth century melodrama *was* treacherous. The sublime was only millimeters away from the ludicrous. The book by "the prettiest of the Brontë sisters," was a virgin's story. Its characters were harsh, their motives selfish and unbending, and the result without poetic justice. The love they felt for each other was a longing for absolutes, for a fierce, burning union. When she had managed to have the book published, it had been found to be "too abominably pagan even for the most vitiated class of English readers." "A disagreeable story" was what the 1847 reviewers had called the tale of the foundling Heathcliff who fell in love with his benefactor's daughter. After Emily Brontë's death, one critic had still regarded *Wuthering Heights* as an immature work of Currer Bell—sister Charlotte's pen name in the all-masculine world of Victorian letters—a novel written before *Jane Eyre*.[1]

It had been Sylvia Sidney who had drawn Wyler's attention to *Wuthering Heights*. During the filming of *Dead End,* she had told him Walter Wanger owned a very good script, actually written for her and Charles Boyer. "It's not right for me and I'm not going to do it although Wanger doesn't know that yet," she had smiled. "And if you ask me, nor is it right for Boyer."

Wanger, who had both Sylvia Sidney and Charles Boyer under contract, had hired the unlikeliest pair of infidels to turn Emily's book into a screenplay. Ben Hecht and Charles MacArthur were knocking out slam-bang movies and hit plays—lately, *The Front Page* and *Twentieth Century*. Alone, Hecht was about to be hired by David Selznick to lick the *Gone With the Wind* script (at $15,000 for one week's work) from a Sidney Howard outline discarded three years earlier. For George Stevens, MacArthur had just "hand-tailored" for Cary Grant Rudyard Kipling's poem *Gunga Din*.

The Hecht–MacArthur *Wuthering Heights* script was a clever job. While courageously preserving much of Emily Brontë's original dialogue, they had performed major surgery on the complicated plot and lopped off the book's entire second generation.

Writing the screenplay in Alexander Woollcott's summer cottage in Vermont, Hecht and MacArthur had eliminated the more unbelievable passages as well as the implications of incest. They had subdued some of Cathy's destructive extravagance and made her into little more than a petulant, headstrong girl. But they had coarsened the pallid Lintons—David Niven's Edgar and Geraldine Fitzgerald's Isabella, as it turned out. They had partially abandoned Emily Brontë's very cinematic flashback framework, but they had kept the aches and the angry restlessness. While strengthening the forward movement and drawing sparks from confrontations, they had also reinforced the romanticism and substituted a kind of sentimental haze for the clarity of the novelist's vision.

Wyler had taken the script to Goldwyn, who had read it and said, "No." Why?

"I don't like stories with people dying in the end. It's a tragedy."

"It's a great love story, Sam."

"No."

The script had come up again at Warners. When Goldwyn had

loaned his top director to steer Warners' top star through *Jezebel*, Bette Davis and Wyler had discussed the idea of doing another picture together. "Anything in mind?" she had asked during the shooting of the ballroom sequence.

He had given her the script. She had loved it and barged into Jack Warner's office. "Buy this for me!"

The ploy was as old as Hollywood. Wyler went back to his contractual employer and told him how hot Jack Warner and Bette Davis were on *Wuthering Heights*.

"Can Merle play it?" Goldwyn winced this time.

"Sure. She's even English."

Three months later, Goldwyn announced he had bought the Hecht–MacArthur screenplay, an announcement that aroused the London *Times* to a note of caution. "Mr. Goldwyn is a legendary figure who has a fine autocratic way with the English language and chronology and things like that," said the *Times* in an editorial, after acknowledging that a Hollywood film version of *Wuthering Heights* was indeed "a minor sensation." "Still, the title is not everything and its retention does not—witness among many others the conspicuous case of *Bengal Lancer*—at all imply that the film will be even remotely identifiable with the book." [2]

Before leaving for New York and London, Wyler had John Huston hired for some rewriting on the Hecht–MacArthur script. The changes were minor, but loud. So much screaming went on at the Goldwyn–Huston–Wyler story conferences that, at one of them, Huston apparently suggested a financial penalty for shouting.

"Let's make a wager, each one of us puts up fifty dollars and the first one who starts yelling loses."

"Fine, I'm with you," Willy agreed.

"I'm good for it." Sam nodded. He was too rich to carry money.

The trio had the quietest story conference in memory and when they got up, Goldwyn reached for the $100.

"Well, I win," he said, scooping up the money.

"What do you mean, you win?" Wyler asked.

"Well, I didn't yell."

It took Willy and John a long time to explain what the bet had been about.

Willy had wanted an all-British cast for *Wuthering Heights* and that had been one point where Goldwyn had agreed. Hecht had originally suggested Olivier for the part of Heathcliff and the more Wyler saw of him, the more he was convinced this young actor, who was unknown in America, was Heathcliff. Wyler went to dinner at the Christchurch Street townhouse where Larry and Vivien were living together discreetly—they were both still married to others.* Olivier was reticent about accepting. His previous brush with Hollywood had been humiliating. Being replaced on Rouben Mamoulian's *Queen Christina* after Greta Garbo had personally chosen him to be her leading man was not exactly an actor's triumph. In the face of Olivier's hesitance, Wyler tested Robert Newton for the Heathcliff role (and cast Flora Robson, Hugh Williams, and Leo Carroll).

What Larry wanted was a part for Vivien. One night, he took Wyler to see *St. Martin's Lane,* Vivien's last picture. Directed by Tim Whelan, it was a Cinderella story with Charles Laughton as a Cockney street entertainer and Vivien a street urchin living on petty theft until Laughton puts her into his act and, at the fadeout, has her on the first step of music-hall fame.

"Vivien, I'll give you the part of Isabella." Wyler smiled disarmingly at the next dinner on Christchurch Street.

"I want to play Cathy." She smiled back across the table.

Wyler explained that Cathy was already Merle's, that Merle Oberon—with whom Larry had starred in Whelan's *The Divorce of Lady X,* the year before—was a big star in America, and that Goldwyn was making *Wuthering Heights* just *because* he was looking for a picture for her.

"Then, I don't want any part."

"Look, Vivien," he tried patiently, "you're not known in the States, you may become a big star but for the first role in an American film, you'll never do better than Isabella in *Wuthering Heights.*"

That had been in July. Six months later, when Selznick cast her as Scarlett O'Hara, Willy's prediction turned out to be one of his lesser oracles.

Before returning aboard the *Normandie* and meeting Sonja Henie and the Joseph Kennedy family, Wyler had gone to France —to water-ski in San Juan-les-Pins and, in Paris, to look into production possibilities for him and Robert. Again, he tried to go to

* Olivier to Jill Osmond and Vivien to Leigh Holman.

Spain. He wanted to do a film about the Civil War, but again he was blocked. "It's a pity that we have to wait until such stories are history before they can be told to the public through the medium of motion pictures," he told the Paris *Herald-Tribune*,[3] adding that some "on the spot" color would be invaluable in making a film dealing with the Spanish war.

By the time Larry and Vivien arrived in Hollywood, Willy had filmed Heifetz, met and married Talli.

Wuthering Heights started out as an unhappy experience for Olivier. He went to Hollywood against his better judgment and was miserable during most of the shooting. Yet *Wuthering Heights* was to build him into a star of international popularity. Within a few months, a pleasant reputation among British theatergoers was inflated out of recognition. Under huge red lettering —"the mark of hell was in his eyes"—Olivier's face, tight-lipped, suffering, and with a touch of green about the jowl, stared with hypnotic fascination from billboards across the United States.[4]

As usual, Goldwyn knew how to spend money. He sent a cameraman to England to film Yorkshire moors so they could be matched: stone walls, crags, and heather, at Chatsworth in Ventura County. Besides the cast, he imported one thousand British panes of hand-blown glass for the interiors and a thousand heather plants. The greenery had him in trouble while the California Agriculture Department tried to decide whether it was legal to transport heather between Los Angeles and Ventura counties. Livestock was found in Chatsworth, but the ducks and geese were rented from an enterprising Hollywood trainer who had their vocal cords cut to guarantee against quacking. An equally enterprising Goldwyn publicist got Wyler in trouble with animal lovers when he put out a story saying the *Wuthering Heights* director had ordered the vocal cords of all the animals cut after the quack-quack of a goose had ruined one of his scenes. "I got letters from people, calling me a fiend, a sadist," Wyler remembered.

To bare Merle Oberon's shoulders once a bathtub scene was added and because Goldwyn didn't like her in Regency dresses, the period was switched from Emily Brontë's 1801 to 1841. Once the filming was completed and everybody had left, he ordered Wyler to shoot a new ending showing the cursed lovers reunited in heaven.

186

"I don't want to look at a corpse at the fadeout," Sam growled.

When Wyler refused, he had someone else make the shot—a double exposure of Olivier's stunt double and a girl, seen from behind walking on clouds.

"It's still there," Wyler said with a grin thirty years later. "It's a horrible shot but nobody seems to mind very much."

To put one of the most romantic films Hollywood ever made on the screen, Wyler and cast sweated bitter long hours.

Niven was unhappy, feeling he had been conned into playing Edgar. Two years earlier, Wyler had given him a break in *Dodsworth*. He was now under contract to Goldwyn, along with his recent girl friend, Merle, but playing a cuckolded husband was an insult to his off-screen life as Hollywood's man-about-town (along with his roommate, Errol Flynn). At first, he had refused to play Edgar and Goldwyn had put him on suspension.

"Why don't you want to play Edgar?" Wyler had asked him over lunch.

"Because it's such an awful part."

"There's something else, isn't there?"

"Honestly, Willy. I love you, I love being here with you, but I was so bloody miserable working for you on *Dodsworth*. I just couldn't go through it again. You're a sonofabitch to work with." [5]

Wyler grinned, saying that was the past. Niven had come back, but the filming of *Wuthering Heights* was tough.

Olivier found Wyler's constant correction of his acting to be almost persecution. A friction between Olivier and Merle developed into an open clash. It came during a love scene.

During the first runthrough of the romantic interlude at Penniston Crag, Olivier sputtered slightly on one of his lines. "Please don't spit at me!" Merle said and it seemed to him her tone was unnecessarily frigid. Once more they played the scene and the same thing happened. "You spat again!" said Merle. At this, Larry suddenly lost his temper and said a number of things which he afterward regretted. This magnified a trivial incident and both actors marched off the set.

Wyler sighed and, after a suitable pause, asked them back. In the best tradition of "the show must go on," Wyler made them play the same scene again. Still inwardly raging at each other, the lovers returned to the depths of mutual passion.

"Cut," called Wyler triumphantly when they had finished. "That's perfect!"

During the filming, Frank Nugent came west and, in his review of *Wuthering Heights,* remembered his setside visit with Heathcliff shouting "Cathy, come in to me! Cathy, my own!" into the cornflake flurries of studio-made snow while in a corner a German-speaking property man listened to Adolf Hitler on a tiny radio. Between takes, cast, director, and crew crossed to the radio corner where the prop man "was standing in newfound dignity, haltingly translating phrases that might have spelled a war, but did not." [6]

Goldwyn was behaving with his usual unpredictability. Among his less publicized examples of witty illiteracy was his penchant for garbling names. Louis Bromfield became Louis Bloomfield; Arthur Hornblow became Arthur Hornbloom or Author Hornblower; Joel McCrea was Joe McCrail; King Vidor became Henry King; and Shirley Temple became Ann Shirley. Perhaps even more galling was his real or affected forgetfulness of the names of his leading players. When Olivier twisted his foot, but nevertheless humped to work on crutches and Wyler began shooting around him in sitting position, the least everybody expected from Goldwyn was a smile and a cheer. But Goldwyn wanted all his pictures to look beautiful, his romantic leads to look handsome, even if the story line demanded the exact opposite.

Wyler had already fought Goldwyn on this in *Dead End.* Goldwyn would show up on the East River street set, where hopeless squalor was the whole dimension of the film, shouting, "Why is everything so dirty here?" On *Wuthering Heights,* he had already complained about Olivier in near black-face.

"Just wait," Wyler had grinned. "In the last part of the picture when Heathcliff comes back a rich man, he'll look just marvelous. But here he's a stableboy."

When stableboy Olivier limped by during a Goldwyn setside visit and was called over, he expected a pat on the shoulder and was all prepared to say, "It's nothing . . . the show must go on." Instead, Goldwyn turned to Wyler and sputtered, "If this actor continues to look dirty like that, I'm going to close the picture!"

The film *was* difficult. Wyler knew that to put on the screen a world where heather bloomed, larks trilled, and love was stronger than death could be disastrous. A line like "Why doesn't your hair smell of heather?" could be beautiful or a howler sending them roaring in the aisles. The difference was razor thin.

How could he delete the grandiloquence of Olivier's stage acting without, at the same time, rubbing out the magnetism and glow from this gifted actor's performance? The solution, it seemed, was to hone down carefully. He found it simpler to tone down a performance than to add to it if there was little there to start with.

Honing meant a lot of takes. It also meant impassioned discussions with Larry.

Olivier had always regarded realism as all-important on the stage. He hated as much as any young actor the tradition of mannered speech, bulging eyes, and declamatory gestures. As he talked and fought with Wyler, however, he began to realize that he had never bothered to *think* film, that realism had to be carried a step further because the camera, prying nearer than any audience, demanded the most delicate shades of acting. Olivier even realized that acting was only one facet of this synthetic art.

Wyler convinced his leading man that movies were a medium potentially as important as the stage, and Olivier was to remember these discussions all his life and, in an exceptional appearance on the Dick Cavett Show in 1973, tell TV viewers how Wyler had made him realize the potential of film.

Wuthering Heights received the New York Film Critics Award for best picture (John Ford was named best director for *Stagecoach*), with Goldwyn and Mayor Fiorello La Guardia attending the January 7 ceremonies. The film opened at Broadway's Rivoli Theatre April 13, this time with Willy in town "to get the verdict," as he told reporters.

The critics were polite. They spent more space on Emily Brontë's novel than on the movie, telling their readers what Hecht and MacArthur had left out, calling the film a test, hailing Goldwyn's courage, but saying very little. Two weeks later, the London premiere, attended by James Roosevelt and Ambassador Kennedy and his family, produced the same reserved praise. In *The Observer,* C. A. Lejeune summed it up when she said *Wuthering Heights* "proves to be so good that it's really a shame it isn't just that much better. With a little more courage, ruthlessness, and imagination on the producer's part, it might have been a great picture. As it is, the people who like it most are forced into

189

warmly defending it against its own mistakes." [7] The *Times* said that "if there must be a film version of a work that belongs so completely to its own medium, then this is a reasonable and even praiseworthy attempt." [8]

The critics' hesitation was echoed in the public's lack of enthusiasm. *Wuthering Heights* was a box-office disappointment, although with a reissue in the 1950s, Goldwyn did manage to get his money back and even make a slight profit.

If the hesitation has remained as to the film's place in history, Emily Brontë's tale of cursed love has continued to fascinate, perhaps not always for the best of reasons. The novel was celebrated by the surrealists of the 1920s as an early example of antibourgeois *amour fou,* magic and cult of the supernatural. Since *Le Chien andalou,* Luis Bunuel had in mind to adapt it for the screen. He did so in 1953 in the Mexican film variously known under the Spanish translation of the book's title *Cumbres borrascosas* and the later commercial tag, *Abismos de pasion.* With Irasema Dillian as Catalina and Jorge Mistral as Alejandro Heathcliff, this version had one convulsive Bunuel touch hinted at by Emily—necrophilia, with Heathcliff violating Cathy's grave on a dark night only to be surprised by Linton (a gravedigger surprised him in the book).

Feeling that Franco Zeffirelli's *Romeo and Juliet* had turned youth on to romanticism, American International Pictures (AIP) remade *Wuthering Heights* in 1970. The film was BBC documentarian Robert Fuest's first attempt at big-screen directing and starred Anna Calder-Marshall and Timothy Dalton. Despite location filming in Yorkshire, the film was a mangy look and a mean stab at Emily Brontë's book. This didn't prevent AIP from announcing plans for a sequel to "deal with the offspring," [9] a project quietly shelved when the Fuest version proved a box-office dud.

Reviewing its re-release in 1971, Charles Champlin found it dated only in Alfred Newman's "insistent, incessant music, which in the fashion of the time, was applied like body makeup" and in the obvious process photography of an un-English snowstorm that seemed right out of *Nanook of the North.* "As an embittered romantic hero, Heathcliff is almost shockingly up-to-date . . . and seeing the film again is to be struck by the magnetism and glowering intensity of the youthful Olivier." [10]

In 1939, Wyler bought his first house—on Copa de Oro Drive in Bel Air. The two-story house, across from the University of California, belonged to Frank Lloyd and after the Wylers outgrew it in 1946, it was bought by John Ford who was still living there in 1973.

Three weeks before Cathy Wyler was born, Leopold passed away. He had a sudden stroke and lingered unconscious for close to a week before he died. A month later, Carl Laemmle was dead.

After *Intermezzo* fell through for him and before the start of Goldwyn's next, Willy, Talli, and the baby spent two weeks with the Kohners in La Jolla, on San Diego Bay. One day, they went across the Mexican border to Tijuana to see a bullfight, meeting the cameraman Franz Planer, one of many Europeans waiting at the border for entry to the United States. It was a hot late-August day. They were all on the beach when, on the radio, they heard Hitler had marched into Poland.

Somehow, all Willy could think of was that he was grateful his father—and Uncle Carl, who had loved his native Germany so much—were not to see this second world war.

20

The Westerner was the first going-over of the story of Judge Roy Bean, a stocky, whiskey-sodden native of Mason County, Kentucky, who drifted into western Texas after the Civil War and, in the railroad tent town of Vinegaroon, managed to get himself appointed justice of the peace in 1882. Vinegaroon withered as fast as the road gangs departed and Roy Bean followed the rails to Langtry, a stopover on the Southern Pacific. The judge said he named the town after the girl of his wildest dreams—the English actress Lily Langtry; the railroad said the little oasis actually was named for one of its own dignitaries.

Roy Bean set himself up in business with the Revised Statutes of Texas for 1879, a strong will, and a shack complete with bar, poker table, jury box, and bench. It was a cozy arrangement; a man only had to cross the hardwood floor to spend what was left of his roll after a run-in with the "Law West of the Pecos," as Bean styled himself. He ruled over Langtry for twenty years, first by appointment, then by election (held in his saloon). His hated rival, Jesus P. Torres, won the office away from him in 1896 because of a lapse in Bean electioneering (the count of the one hundred-odd ballots showed he had more votes than there were people). Bean was unmoved by this foul device and went on handling cases originating on his side of town.

In middle age, Bean had acquired a child bride, Virginia Chavez, who bore him two sons and two daughters before quitting his company. After he set himself up as judge, his only love was a yellow magazine photo of Lily Langtry. He had only one look at the lady he had worshiped for years. When the Jersey Lily played San Antonio on her American tour in the spring of 1888, Bean got his Prince Albert out of his trunk, wiggled his beer-barrel midriff into the striped trousers, journeyed to San Antonio, bought a front-row seat to feast bloodshot eyes on his beauty all through the one enchanted evening of his life. The actress made a trip to Langtry in 1903, but Roy Bean had died eight months earlier from the combined effects of old age—he was in his eighties —and a prolonged battle with his own hootch. Like so many other tourists, Lily picked her way from the railroad depot to the famous saloon-courtroom, and the townspeople gave her the judge's pet bear. Not knowing the lady, the bear ran away and the townspeople made her a present of Bean's revolver, which she took home to England with her.[1]

In *The Westerner,* the old flea-bitten Roy Bean was played by Walter Brennan with such gusto that he stole the picture from Gary Cooper, a fictitious stranger accused of horse thieving and sentenced to hang by the judge, then paroled because he claimed to be an acquaintance of Lily Langtry.

Based on a story by Stuart Lake, the Jo Swerling-Niven Busch screenplay played free and easy with the judge's biography, particularly in killing him off in an apocryphal gunfight. After talking himself out of the noose, the lanky cowhand, Cole Harden (Cooper), and Roy Bean become friends. For a while. In the midst of a battle between homesteaders and cattlemen, Cole mediates trouble by convincing Roy Bean to declare peace between the factions. Cole becomes a closer ally of the settlers after he falls in love with Jane-Ellen Mathews (Doris Davenport), a farmer's daughter, and later turns against Roy Bean when he discovers the judge and his men are responsible for a fire that burns the homesteaders out of home and crops. The climax finds the two former friends shooting it out in a gaslit theater and the judge catching a glimpse of the famous Lily Langtry (Lilian Bond) before he dies.

Cooper had only to read the script once to realize *The Westerner* was all Walter Brennan's. "I couldn't figure for the life of me why they needed me for this picture," Cooper later related. "I had a very minor part. It didn't require any special effort. All the character had to do was exchange a few shots with the judge in the dramatic moment of the picture."

Cooper was a star (the U.S. Treasury Department reported him the nation's top taxpayer of 1939, on an income of $482,819) and the arguments to convince him to play second fiddle had to be persuasive. Wyler told him he might not have the greatest part, but the point of the whole picture was the curious friendship between judge and cowhand. He added that the judge's infatuation with Lily Langtry added a funny twist to the main situation and that although Cooper was to play a part he had done many times before, his juxtaposition with Walter Brennan would give this role a totally fresh sheen. Willy knew the script had its weaknesses, but he felt he could save it with subtle humor, especially in the beginning when Roy Bean prepares to hang the cowhand and at the end when the two friends square off. He wanted to give these scenes an undertow of humor and affection—Cooper playing with his usual standard of understated perfection bouncing off against Brennan's ruthless yet sentimental Roy Bean.

When it came to shooting the sequences, Wyler tried something dangerously taboo in Golden Era Hollywood—improvisation. "I got all kinds of ideas and these two actors carried them out marvelously. Cooper was a very subtle and fine comedian once he understood the humor of a scene."

Wyler had wanted Talli to play Jane-Ellen Mathews, the farmer's daughter Cooper marries. A tinge of bad conscience over old neglect made him outsmart himself.

Wyler had always hated to do tests and a few years earlier at a party had been painfully reminded of his early shortcomings as a director of screen tests. A woman had come over and asked if he remembered her. No, he had answered, he didn't.

"You should," the lady said, "because you're the man who ruined my life."

Wyler thought she was joking and offered to fix her another drink.

"Years ago, I was at Universal one day and I got a test," the woman continued. "The head of the studio wanted a test of me and it was my chance to become an actress."

"Let *me* get a drink."

As she talked, Willy began to remember, ever so vaguely at first. Because he was under contract, he had been told to do this test and he had hated it. It had been a Saturday afternoon and a test for some other director, some other picture for a stock contract.

"You made the test, but you were not interested, you couldn't care less. It was a bad test and that was the last time I was inside a studio."

Wyler had tried to apologize. He had felt terrible and had left the party early. A few years later, when Goldwyn had asked him to test a girl for him, Wyler had decided to make up for his Universal days. The girl was Doris Davenport, a very anxious and nice-looking girl who couldn't act. He had found an easy and very effective scene from one of his earlier films, told her to study it and not to worry.

"Even though she couldn't act for beans, I knew how to make the test effective for her," Wyler recalled. "Goldwyn saw it, was delighted with her, and signed her up. She was happy and I felt sort of exonerated from the previous experience."

When it came to casting *The Westerner* a year later, Willy thought Talli would be good as Jane-Ellen and tested her for the part. Goldwyn vetoed it. He didn't like the idea of one of his players and director being married and felt they might gang up on him. Grudgingly, Wyler began looking for another actress.

"I have the girl for you," Goldwyn said to cheer him up, "Doris Davenport!"

"No, no," Willy sighed.

"She's marvelous in your test. She was never good except with you. I had her in a couple of pictures."

"But she's not right for this," Wyler tried.

"Why not?"

Doris Davenport as Jane-Ellen in *The Westerner* was another drawn-out fight that Goldwyn won. She got the part and that was the last time *she* was inside a studio.

Producer and director had one other fight. Goldwyn had Alfred Newman completely rewrite Dmitri Tiomkin's score, delaying the picture's release from February to September of 1940. Otherwise, it was all Wyler's, a director's film all in the pacing and attention to characterization, a very individual film like the best of Wyler.

Contemporary critics saw these touches, the unusually realistic portrayal of the old West. The fights, for example, were deliberately clumsy, as they would be between cowhands and farmers, as opposed to western star and stuntman. "Wyler's direction is forceful and salty," *The Hollywood Reporter* wrote. "He has his principals do one remarkable thing never before seen, but often looked for by this reviewer of westerns—they stop to reload their weapons after the chambers have been emptied in an exchange of shots." [2]

The Westerner cost over one million dollars. Wyler went on location near Tucson (where John Huston filmed the story again over thirty years later as *The Life and Times of Judge Roy Bean,* with Paul Newman as the judge and Ava Gardner as Lily Langtry). Toland was on the camera, making his atmospheric landscapes compete with his closeups of Cooper's face, and Archie Stout filmed additional exteriors. It was Willy's first western since *Hell's Heroes* and he loved it.

Goldwyn gave the picture a rousing send-off in Fort Worth, Texas, on September 19. The premiere was preceded by a parade through downtown, people in their pet frontier "fancy dresses," an honor guard of eighty-five Texan gals, and three planeloads of Hollywood glamour and gentry flown in. Willy and Talli were in the parade, riding in a buggy behind the lead coach with Gary Cooper and Sam Goldwyn. Margaret and David Tallichet came over from Dallas.

The Westerner was underrated, perhaps because it followed such "slick and spectacular outdoor films as *Union Pacific, Stagecoach* and *Jesse James,*" as western historians George Fenin and William K. Everson felt.[3] In his first review of a Wyler film, the *New York Times's* Bosley Crowther found *The Westerner* a disappointment, saying the shift from the judge to the cowhand, to the homesteaders vs. cattlemen story, and, at the end, back to an affectionate study of Roy Bean prevented the film from hitting its stride. Crowther, however, loved the cross-conflict between Cooper and Brennan. "The scenes in which these two friendly and mutually respecting rivals square off are surpassing cinematic episodes—when they slowly and suspiciously fence with cryptic words for bits of information and oppose with no more than attitudes their dominating personalities. These scenes have been directed by William Wyler at the deliberate, suspenseful pace of a Texas drawl and are beautiful to see." [4] *Newsweek* said the film at its best presented "an arresting characterization of one of the most colorful and improbable figures of that era—Judge Roy Bean" and that Wyler had directed with humor and special attention to characterization.[5] *Time* said Brennan's penetrating personification of Judge Bean made the film "a cinema event," and correctly forecast he would win the 1940 Academy Award for the title role.

Despite *They Shall Have Music*, Wyler was interested in a musical film and during *Wuthering Heights* tried to sell Goldwyn on getting Marlene Dietrich to play the authoress in a George Sand-Frédéric Chopin "biopic." *La* Dietrich had just caused a sensation by appearing in a tuxedo at the Los Angeles opera. A hundred years earlier, the French novelist had been the first woman to wear men's clothes. Goldwyn didn't care for the idea, however, and Willy had his agent take the project to Columbia Pictures' Harry Cohn.

"Cohn *was* interested and later accused me of reneging on a deal," Wyler remembered. "When I left his office with my lawyer, he suddenly grabbed my hand saying, 'Okay, it's a deal.' I said, 'You have to talk with my lawyer and agent.'"

Cohn and the agents never got together on the finances and the rambunctious studio boss, with whom Frank Capra and almost everybody else had momentous fights, accused Wyler of walking out on a handshake. He, nevertheless, bought the story and Capra was to have made it. In 1945, Charles Vidor did make it for Cohn, with Cornel Wilde playing Chopin, as *A Song to Remember*. "It wasn't the way I had seen it," Wyler said later. "I was more interested in Chopin than in George Sand, I wanted to center the film on his music."

Following completion of the principal photography on *The Westerner* in January, Willy took Talli on a delayed honeymoon. Leaving little Cathy at home, they went skiing in Quebec (where *Wuthering Heights* was banned for immorality*). The Laurentian Mountains north of Montreal proved so cold they hopped down to New York to start a Caribbean cruise aboard the *Nieuw Amsterdam*. The war was everywhere, in the news and in the huge Dutch flags painted on the decks and sides of the ocean liner to mark its neutrality. They left the ship in Havana and, after a few days in Miami, hurried home.

Somehow, the times were not for vacations. In January, it was

---

* Goldwyn had been notified that, while there were no actual scenes of infidelity, in the opinion of the Quebec censors Cathy had not been punished enough for keeping the image of Heathcliff in her heart while she was married to Linton, nor had she died sufficiently repentant.

the "phony war." In April, Hitler invaded Denmark and Norway, and by the time Willy was shooting *The Letter* at Warners', cameraman Tony Gaudio listened between takes on shortwave radio to Benito Mussolini declaring war on Great Britain and France. "Son of a beeetch!" Tony exploded with his head halfway inside the radio before translating for the tense set.

In June, France fell and the ragged remnants of the Allied armies stood at Dunkirk while Britain desperately set up a rescue mission to get them across the Channel to Dover and Ramsgate. Britain admitted losses of thirty thousand men in the stupefying nightmare as the Luftwaffe hammered from the air, but three hundred thousand men, French and British, escaped what Britain's eloquent prime minister called "the jaws of death." In July, the Battle of Britain began.

Less than a year later, Willy was filming a fictitious story of a British family during the summer of 1940—*Mrs. Miniver*.

21

It was hard to concentrate on Somerset Maugham and Bette Davis in colonial Singapore when the world was on fire. Like his fellow directors, Wyler was trying to find topical subjects and should have had an inside track with Goldwyn to direct *Watch on the Rhine,* the play Lillian Hellman had just finished. *The Great Dictator* was the talk of the country. Alfred Hitchcock had made *Foreign Correspondent,* Frank Borzage *The Mortal Storm,* and Anatole Litvak, who had just directed Bette Davis in *All This and Heaven Too,* had been able to make *Confessions of a Nazi Spy.*

Not everyone was making war pictures. Not yet. Preston Sturges had finally conned Paramount into letting him direct and *The Great McGinty* was a success. He and Louise had given a party in his house above Hollywood Boulevard for his friends and Willy had been carried away and jumped fully clothed into the pool, which, as Talli observed, was all right except that his new wristwatch was not waterproof. For Selznick, Hitchcock had made *Rebecca* with Laurence Olivier, but Larry was anxious to get back to England. The entire British colony felt ill at ease being in California instead of sharing what Winston Churchill called their country's darkest hour. There were days on the *Letter* set when Herbert Marshall and James Stephenson didn't seem to be there.

The Letter was another loanout, or, as it turned out, a director-for-star swap. Warner Brothers got Wyler to direct their First

Lady in a remake of *The Letter* and Goldwyn borrowed Bette Davis for his upcoming filming of Miss Hellman's 1939 Broadway hit, *The Little Foxes*. *The Letter* was a remake of Jeanne Eagels' next-to-last movie, Somerset Maugham's trenchant 1925 play about sexual hypocrisy and sexual honesty, shared guilt and unacceptable compassion in the tropics—the story of Leslie Crosbie, the wife of an English plantation owner in Malaysia who can empty a gun into a lover and lie her way to acquittal because of her unimpeachable respectability. In London, Gladys Cooper had been the original Leslie; on Broadway, Katherine Cornell had played her.

Bette Davis was fascinated by Jeanne Eagels, the fiery carnival queen who had burst upon Broadway in 1922 in *Rain,* and for four years electrified playgoers with her vivid portrayal of Sadie Thompson, Somerset Maugham's South Seas harlot who seduces a missionary bent on saving her soul. Jeanne Eagels was an actress of irresistible freshness and a strangely corrupt beauty who had come to a blazing end in 1929, a drug addict who could barely finish her last film, *Jealousy;* when the work print of it was shown to her, she clawed at the screen and had Paramount reshoot it with a new leading man.

During her own climb, Bette Davis had admired and emulated Jeanne Eagels, watched her again and again, and felt she could herself be only a pale reflection of the flaming prima donna. Dead (of an overdose of heroin), Jeanne Eagels cast and ever-lengthening shadow. Although Bette Davis missed playing Sadie Thompson in Lewis Milestone's 1932 *Rain* (MGM imposed Joan Crawford opposite Walter Huston as the preacher), she won her first Oscar nomination in 1935 with *Dangerous,* directed by Alfred E. Green, the story of an actress whose career is eclipsed by alcohol, picked up, dried out, and given a second chance by an elegant young architect—a barely fictionalized retelling of Jeanne Eagels' life. In Wyler's *The Letter,* she incarnated a Jeanne Eagels role, and in 1946 she was cast in Irving Rapper's *Deception,* an Americanized remake of the Louis Verneuil play that had first become *Jealousy* (in 1957, Columbia did *The Jeanne Eagels Story,* a cleaned-up "biopic" directed by George Sidney with Kim Novak playing Eagels).

The director of both the 1928 *Letter* and *Jealousy* was Jean de Limur who, like Wyler, had come to Hollywood from France in 1920 and, like Wyler, had worked up to directing as assistant to

Rex Ingram, Chaplin, and DeMille. Unlike Wyler, however, de Limur had returned home in 1931 and made an even score of pictures in France during the 1930s and 1940s. Wyler knew de Limur as a member of the French crowd and remembered *The Letter* for two things—a frenzied scene toward the end when Jeanne Eagels tells her husband the truth and a morbidly fascinating metaphor that the new Society for the Prevention of Cruelty to Animals made impossible to duplicate in 1940—a fight between a mongoose and a cobra which had absolutely nothing to do with the story.

The Letter deals with Maugham's favorite themes—the individual in a situation for which his or her background has not prepared that person and, in a larger sense, the decline of colonial Britain. As the curtain rises on a planter's tropical bungalow, Leslie kills a man, pumping his body full of bullets as he staggers and finally falls. When Malaysian houseboys run in, she regains her poise, orders them to call the assistant district officer and, from Singapore, her husband, Robert. When the two men arrive hours later, she tells an entirely plausible story of a family friend arriving uninvited, getting drunk, attempting to rape her, and her shooting him in self-defense. The family lawyer steps in and helps to bring the whole painful matter through inquest and trial. To the Singapore British, Leslie is judged innocent in advance—everybody from judge to prosecutor is a friend of the Crosbies—especially as it becomes known that the dead man, also a Britisher, had been living with a Chinese woman. On the eve of the trial, the Chinese woman offers to sell a letter written by Leslie to the dead man on the day of his death. Meeting through Chinese intermediaries, the lawyer agrees to the sordid business of buying this incriminating evidence for ten thousand Hong Kong dollars, himself advancing the money for Crosbie. Besides its innate sordidness, the purchase is additionally distasteful as it is from people whose subservience the English have always taken for granted. Leslie is acquitted and when the matter of the hefty sum comes up, she tells her husband the truth—she had been the dead man's mistress for years. What had made her scrawl the incriminating letter and ultimately kill him was the fact that he acknowledged the Chinese woman and wanted to break off the liaison with Leslie. The husband manages to imagine forgiveness, but Leslie can only tell him she still loves the man she killed.

In de Limur's version, Leslie—not the lawyer—must go to a

native bordello, down long stairs and into a room with jeering native whores, and humiliate herself before the Chinese woman will let her have the letter. Paramount and de Limur had obtained the footage of the mongoose–cobra fight from a French documentary team which had filmed it in Borneo and intercut it with the brothel confrontation of the two women. The mongoose–cobra footage was so thrilling it was lifted right out of de Limur's film in 1951 and put into Ken Annakin's British film *Outpost in Malaya.*

If casting Herbert Marshall, who had played the lover in de Limur's version, as Robert Crosbie and Bruce Lister as the assistant district officer was a matter of course, finding an actor to play the lawyer proved a comical instance of an outside director telling a studio to use its own talent. Jack Warner had called Wyler in and told him he had a fine Englishman under contract that Wyler might think of using.

"I've got a terrific part, the lawyer, second most important role," Wyler said.

"Do you want to test him?"

"I'll be glad to."

After Wyler had tested James Stephenson, he told Warner the actor was marvelous and that he was going to cast him as the lawyer.

"Now, wait a moment," Warner began. "I didn't realize it was such an important part. I mean this fellow is just in stock here. Maybe you should use a better name."

"Jack, you asked me to test him. You said he was a good actor, you sent him to me. I tell you, he's excellent and that I couldn't possibly do better. . . ."

"Yes, but he's only a stock actor."

It was ludicrous. Willy found himself fighting for an actor the studio had tried to impose on him in the first place.

But James Stephenson gave more than stock acting. When *The Letter* was released, critics and public loved him. "James Stephenson is superb as the honest lawyer who jeopardizes his reputation to save a friend—a shrewd, dignified, reflective citizen who assumes a sordid business with distaste. He is the strongest character in the film, the one person who really matters," Bosley Crowther wrote.[1] Stephenson died of a heart attack nine months after this first triumph.

Casting the Chinese woman was another instance of putting

heavy makeup on a white actress (to play a Chinese general in Milestone's *The General Died at Dawn*, Akim Tamiroff was tortured with Oriental eyelids made from dentists' rubber). "Gale Sondergaard was very good," Wyler recalled. "Today, you would take a Chinese girl, but there weren't any then. Anna May Wong was the only Oriental actress I could have used and she was kind of a sex kitten and too young."

Howard Koch's script was a lean and intelligent rewrite of Maugham, providing strong characters and big scenes. Writing it and working with Wyler, Koch was to remember, was one of the more satisfactory experiences of his screenwriting career. As in de Limur's version, Koch's script had the Chinese woman stipulate that Leslie, herself, must come and barter for the letter.

A postscript had been added by the Hays Office. Maugham ended his play with husband and wife facing a loveless future together. The Hays Office, however, demanded "compensating moral values" to make Leslie pay for her deed. As she steps into the garden, an Oriental boy comes from the shadows and pinions her arm. Before she can scream, the slain man's widow appears, flashes a dagger, and stabs her to death. So that the Eurasian woman in turn is punished, she and the boy are arrested by two policemen in the fadeout.

Wyler set out to create mood from the first day. "I remember the first day's shooting, where we actually started with the first shot in the script. It said something like, 'We hear a shot and see Leslie Crosbie coming out and shooting a man.' I felt this opening shot should shock you. To get the full impact of the revolver being fired, I thought everything should be very quiet first. I also wanted to show where we were, give a feeling of the dank, humid jungle atmosphere of rubber plantation country.

"We had a nice set. The day before we started, I laid out the shot. The camera started in the jungle, went on to the natives sleeping, showed the rubber trees dripping and ended on a parrot awakened by the shot and flying away: all in one camera movement that took more than two minutes. This was the first day of shooting and since none of this really was in the script, we would end up with a quarter of a page in the can. You were supposed to do three or four pages a day. On the first day of shooting, I had one quarter of a page. Jesus, the whole studio was in an uproar, but it became a famous opening scene."

Wyler made strong scenes stronger by exploring new territory.

Although Tony Gaudio was no Gregg Toland, Wyler managed to infuse sultriness and putrefaction into the very air of the film. One way was by using extremely long setups–shots without cuts giving scenes extra smoothness and continuity and forcing audiences to pay more attention. This *mise en scène,* he realized, was also a fad, "to see how long you could run a shot." This meant sets filled with props, cues, chalk marks. "One such scene was the confrontation between Leslie and her attorney during her detention when he wants to know the truth. We rehearsed longer and longer stretches. Instead of cutting, I thought, 'Why not go on?' It was not done by design, but there was just no reason to stop. James Stephenson and Bette Davis were superb, every emotion was in it and every one came through. The scene ran on and on, for some eight minutes.

"We did it in one shot. When I saw it on the screen the next day, it was still fine except there was one moment in the middle where Stephenson had his back to the camera, a moment where an important reaction by him really demanded a closeup. That meant cutting the eight-minute scene in half. I sort of debated with myself. 'Hell. To have to cut up the scene, put in the close-up.' But does the audience care whether it's all in one shot? No. So I cut the scene and put in a closeup."

Wyler played the confrontation between Leslie and the Eurasian widow against the delicately ominous sound of a Japanese windbell. Silence when the two women faced each other, except for the eerie, soft tinkling.

The filming was not all clear sailing as director and leading lady clashed head-on over the ending. When Robert Crosbie offers a sad forgiveness and his wife rejects this pitiable gift of love and charity with "I still love the man I killed," Bette Davis felt she could not tell it to Herbert Marshall's face. She could not conceive of any woman looking into her husband's eyes and admitting such a terrifying truth. Wyler disagreed. Because of the very brutality of what she says, it must be said straight to his face. Turning away and saying it under her breath would soften the blow and, he felt, in that case, the line should never be uttered at all.

Bette Davis walked off the set, something she had never done in her career. "I could not see it his way, nor he mine," she was to write in her autobiography. "I came back eventually—end result,

I did it his way. It played validly, heaven knows, but to this day I think my way was the right way." [2] Wyler always remained convinced he was right.

Again, Wyler was nominated for an Academy Award. The 1940 director's Oscar, however, went to John Ford for *The Grapes of Wrath.*

After *The Letter,* Wyler went to Twentieth Century-Fox on a twelve-week loanout to do *How Green Was My Valley.* Darryl Zanuck had bought the rights to Richard Llewellyn's novel, a sudden bestseller in 1939, and had assigned Ernest Pascal, a Llewellyn enthusiast, to write the screenplay. The result had been disappointing and, in November, Philip Dunne replaced Pascal.

"I've always been sorry I couldn't do *How Green Was My Valley* but it couldn't be helped," Wyler recalled. "Zanuck had asked me to do it and had me read the book. When I started, he told me everybody at Fox, from Joseph Schenck down, was against it. But he liked it and I liked it so he said he was going ahead in spite of front office hassles.

"Philip Dunne and I went up to Lake Arrowhead and worked on the script for weeks and weeks, as it turned out. It wasn't easy to tell it all from the point of view of a ten-year-old. Darryl was convinced the boy should never grow up. He said he was bored with the strike business and starving babies in Welsh coal mines and we eliminated five or six characters. Dunne and I spent about eight or ten weeks while he rewrote the script and my loanout time was up. It was February and too early in the year to start filming since it was mostly an outdoor picture.

"Zanuck decided to wait until summer and then Jack Ford, who had done *The Grapes of Wrath* for Darryl, became available. One of the contributions I made was that I cast Roddy McDowell as the boy. I wanted an English boy and, at the time, they were sending refugees from England to Canada and New York by boat. It was the height of the Nazi bombings of London and the threat of a German invasion of England. I asked the Fox New York office to see if there was anybody on the next ship who was ten years old and could act. They found Roddy McDowell, made a test of him and he was just great."

While Wyler was at Fox (and Gregg Toland was at RKO shooting *Citizen Kane* for Orson Welles's directorial debut), Bette Davis did *The Great Lie* for Edmund Goulding, became the first woman president of the Academy, and joined her favorite director again on *The Little Foxes*. It was her first loanout since *Of Human Bondage* and Goldwyn had to pay $385,000 for her services.

For Wyler, *The Little Foxes* united, unexpectedly, the best of all the composites of filmmaking and allowed him a sudden quantum leap toward perfection. Suddenly, he was able to bring together all the elements of his deliberate direction with a force rarely matched in American film.

He was exceptionally well served by both actors and technicians. Bette Davis was on top of her career and her Regina Giddens is a flawlessly icy portrayal of ambition, treachery, and rapacity. The other little foxes were Charles Dingle, playing brother Ben, the effective head of the clan, with repellent charm; Carl Benton Reid as Oscar, the dark, sullen, and undependable other brother; and Dan Duryea incarnating villainy petering out in imbecility as the nephew Leo. Herbert Marshall is again Bette Davis' husband, here an invalid. In her screen debut, Teresa Wright plays their daughter, Alexandra. Patricia Collinge as Oscar's despised and ill-treated wife is painfully the faded flower.

The Little Foxes was the fifth film Wyler and Toland did together—*Come and Get It* didn't really count—and they worked increasingly in deep focus. The technique allowed Wyler to stage scenes in three dimensions as it were—deep into the background, which meant he could often have both action and reaction in the same shot. That, in turn, meant eliminating a lot of cuts—back and forth between antagonist and protagonist. Deep focus *was* difficult. It required, among other things, tremendous outputs of light, but the payoff was a new kind of dramatic geography. Characters could relate differently, relationships could become extremely complex and all sorts of shifting visual patterns by strong regroupings of characters within the shot were possible.

"It was not easy—physically, putting three, four or five people in such a way that you could see them all," Wyler recalled. "Somebody had to have his back to the camera, somebody else had to be less prominent than others, which meant camera movements were often very intricate. There had to be a great deal of rehearsing to have what was not natural appear very natural. Actors had to be very close to each other, for example, because the deep focus lenses made people in a distance look too far away.

"The technique, of course, allowed the audience to see *more*—action and reaction at the same time. Also, it made close shots more significant because the closeup now not only moved the audience closer to a person, it also eliminated everybody else. With deep focus, you could use closeups more sparingly and therefore more effectively."

There was yet another challenge and advantage—more acting was possible. Scenes didn't have to be chopped up in one-line closeups.

Behind Wyler and Toland was Daniel Mandell. It was the eighth picture Danny was cutting for Willy and their collaboration was smooth and efficient (except when pigeon-fancier Mandell had sat up all night waiting for one of his birds to fly home from Kansas City and was too bleary-eyed the next day to see much on the Moviola).

Wyler directed in long, ascetic setups that made Miss Hellman's best play even more terrifying with this controlled, compelling, and compulsive forward thrust. Style and subject matched perfectly. Since *The Little Foxes* was essentially a series of battles of perfidious willpower, Wyler's direction avoided closeups so as to underline the *duality* of the conflicts. As André Bazin was to write after the war, filmed theater like *The Little Foxes* "is assuredly not regression, but, on the contrary, evolution in film intelligence . . . the result of exceptional mastery or better even, an expression of inventiveness which is the exact opposite of passive recordings of theatrics. There is a hundred times more cinema, and of a better kind, in a shot in *The Little Foxes* or [Orson Welles's] *Macbeth* than in all the outdoor dolly shots, natural locations, exotic geography, and flipsides of sets with which the screen so far has tried to make up for stagy origins." [3]

The writing credits on *The Little Foxes* were to remain somewhat mysterious. The on-screen credits were: "Screenplay by Lillian Hellman, based on her stage play. Additional scenes and dialogue by Arthur Kober, Dorothy Parker, and Alan Campbell." The frontispiece of the typed script had "final script by Dorothy Parker and Alan Campbell." Kober was Lillian Hellman's ex-husband, an Austrian-born former journalist who apparently did write additional scenes on *The Little Foxes* before going on to become a writer for Otto Preminger. Years later, Wyler remembered the screenplay as being totally Lillian Hellman's. Dorothy

Parker had originally suggested the title and he suspected Lillian had helped her friend Dorothy and her husband to make a few thousand dollars by having them put on the payroll for a couple of weeks.

Set in the South of 1900, *The Little Foxes* concerns the setting up of a cotton mill to be run on cheap labor, for which Regina and her brothers, Ben and Oscar Hubbard, are to contribute a third of the capital. Regina sends her daughter, Alexandra, to Baltimore to bring her banker husband back from a sanitarium where he has been recovering from a heart attack. Arriving home, the husband remains firm in his refusal to give her $75,000 to finance the sweatshop venture. When Regina fails, their nephew, Leo, an employee in the family bank, steals enough negotiable bonds to finance the scheme. Suspecting the theft, Regina tries to blackmail her brothers into giving her a share of the new business, but her husband thwarts her by claiming he gave the securities to Leo.

Infuriated because he will not expose Leo, Regina abuses her husband until he suffers a coronary seizure and must beg her for his heart stimulant. He dies of a heart attack as he tries to climb the stairs to get the medicine that might avert his death while Regina sits by motionless. With the husband out of the way, Regina blackmails Ben and Oscar into letting her have two-thirds of the profits from the mill. Ben is forced to agree, though with the ominous hint that he is intrigued by the circumstances of her husband's death and intends to investigate. Defying them, she claims they have no evidence.

Alexandra overhears this and realizes how vicious her mother is. She denounces Regina and says she can no longer live in the same house with her. Outside, Alexandra's fiancé is waiting to comfort her. From the upstairs window, Regina watches them walk away. In possession of the power and wealth she schemed and killed to achieve, she is unloved and unwanted by anyone.

Because *The Little Foxes* was a recent Broadway success, the Hays Office did not impose "compensating moral values." Nevertheless, entirely new characters and scenes were added, including an opening sequence taking place before the curtain rises in the stage version—a family dinner. The formal conversation here introduced Regina and Horace Giddens and the rest of the family —the camera sweeping around to discover a soapy smile, a concealed nudge, a movement of impatience among the diners, undercurrents that would be lost in a theater. Another scene that critics and film buffs made famous has two men shave back to back in a narrow bathroom, each seeing each other in mirrors on opposite walls. At other moments, the camera enlarges, surprises, follows through shut doors and splits dramatic moments into their component parts.

Wyler worked hard at blocking the big scenes, expending the minutest care in perfecting every movement of players and camera. "Sometimes, I'd lay it out on paper at home, but nothing is really definite until you do it with the actors. With the real people, something happens. You have them sit down or stand up and the whole thing is changed. I didn't want technique to be noticed, but wanted to get the audience even more involved in the scene, with the characters and what they were doing."

A scene that has become a classic of the cinema is the death of the paralyzed Horace Giddens, intensified to horrifying paroxysm by Wyler's analytical staging. Wyler keeps the focus on Regina in the foreground as her wheelchaired husband drops his heart stimulant, begs her to fetch his medication, then, to save his life, tries to get upstairs himself, only to die on the stairs.

"I don't consider it such a fabulous invention. Because what is interesting here is the wife. The scene is her face, what is going on inside her. You could have him out of frame completely, for example, just hear him stagger upstairs, coughing, whatever. It was, of course, more effective to have him in the background, *out of focus* trying to get upstairs.

"Toland and I discussed having him in focus. Gregg said, 'I can have him sharp, or both of them sharp.' I said no, because I wanted audiences to feel they were seeing something they were not supposed to see. Seeing the husband in the background made you squint, but what you *were* seeing was her face."

The deep-focus technique inevitably imposed a greater burden on the actors to play scenes in long takes. It also added to the exaggerated folklore of "Forty-Take" Wyler as an actor's terror.

There was a lot of tension on *The Little Foxes*. Goldwyn was his interfering self, and this time the star–director clash over interpretation was not so easily smoothed over and settled.

"We fought bitterly," Bette Davis later wrote in her autobiography. "I had been forced to see Tallulah Bankhead's [Broadway] performance. I had not wanted to. A great admirer of hers, I wanted in no way to be influenced by her work. It was Willy's intention that I give a different interpretation of the part. I insisted that Tallulah had played it the only way it could be played. Miss Hellman's Regina was written with such definition that it could only be played one way. Our quarrels were endless. I was too young-looking for the forty-year-old woman and since the ladies of Regina's day had rice-powdered their faces, I covered mine with calcimine in order to look older. This Willy disagreed with. In fact, I ended up feeling I had given one of the worst performances of my life. This saddened me since Regina was a great part and pleasing Willy Wyler was of such importance always to me. It took courage to play her the way I did, in the face of such opposition." [4]

To Wyler, it was a repeat of the Ruth Chatterton quarrels on *Dodsworth*—an actress insisting on playing a villainess too rigidly evil and without the shadings that would make her human. "I wanted her to play it much lighter. This woman was supposed not just to be evil, but to have great charm, humor, and sex. She had some terribly funny lines. That was what our arguments were about."

Bette Davis refused to play it Wyler's way. Talli was to remember Willy so upset he would moan and toss in his sleep and literally gnash his teeth. There were also sleepless nights when frustrations ate at him.

"The filming was torture, the film was a smashing success both critically and popularly," Bette Davis was to write. "But Willy and I never worked together again. It was too bad."

Again, Wyler received an Academy nomination and again John Ford took the director's Oscar for *How Green Was My Valley*. *The Little Foxes* shocked Bosley Crowther, but the cruelest critic's jab came from James Agee who got the star–director difference all wrong. "So completely conceived was the stage play that its leading character, heartless, ambitious Regina Giddens is played by Tragedian Bette Davis with scarcely an accent's difference from gruff Tallulah Bankhead's interpretation of the original Broadway role," Agee wrote in *Time*. "This was not Miss Davis' idea. She quarreled with gap-toothed director William Wyler for her own version. He . . . or the play . . . won." [5]

If only Bette Davis had listened. Writing ten years later, Karel

---

Reisz found the characterization throughout to be too extravagant and too rigidly black and white to allow the film universality. "The material itself is, perhaps, not strong enough to provide the starting point for a masterpiece. But if *The Little Foxes* is not a great film it is, thanks to Wyler's achievement of a brilliantly apt fusion between pictorial style and writing, a perfect one." [6]

Wyler was to return to this technique again after the war, but with less satisfactory results because he wouldn't have the script —or the theme—matching the remarkable harmony of style and content of *The Little Foxes*. His significant films were to be the ones in which he would strike out in new directions.

22

During the uneasy period of "lend-lease" and "bundles for Britain," eighty Hollywood movies dealt in one way or another with the war, but *Mrs. Miniver* was everybody's favorite. Franklin D. Roosevelt ran it in his screening room and told everybody to see it. Two years later when Wyler screened *Memphis Belle* in the White House basement, the President was to tell him *Mrs. Miniver* had been of some help in getting public opinion in favor of self-sacrifice and going to the aid of England.

Mrs. Miniver was propaganda and an orientation course, introducing the American people to their future allies, exposing the nature of their future enemies, and inveighing against the powerful America First Committee isolationists. It was the most popular film of 1942 and *Time* called it "that almost impossible feat, a great war picture that photographs the inner meaning, instead of the outward realism of World War II." [1] It happily grossed $6 million and showered everybody with Academy Awards—Wyler included, although by Oscar time he was a slightly overage air force major walking open catwalks of B-17 bomb bays five miles above Germany, breathing through a walk-around oxygen bottle and pointing his hand camera at incoming flak.

Mrs. Miniver, a war film without battle scenes, started production November 11, 1941. Until the morning of December 7, the United States was technically neutral and whatever the sympathies of most Americans and the implications of the Roosevelt administration's pro-British politics, Hollywood walked a wary line, conscious that any open partiality in its films could lead to economic reprisals on the part of offended nations and outright bans in countries anxious to appear neutral. After Pearl Harbor, all such restraints vanished. Germans and Japanese immediately became stock villains and the new Russian allies, Communist villains before December 7, turned into brave and somewhat picturesque characters. At the height of the war, only Sturges had the temerity to satirize America at war.*

Mrs. Miniver meant working at Metro, the biggest, most glittering film factory of them all. It meant working for Louis B. Mayer, the stalwart, rambunctious, and most powerful figure in Hollywood. It also meant working with an intelligent producer.

Besides the Hollywood oddity of actually being born in Los Angeles, Sidney Franklin was a rarity—an erudite man of taste who had been ordered to stop directing and become a producer. As a director, he had made *Lady of Scandal, Soul Kiss, The Guardsman* (starring Alfred Lunt and Lynn Fontanne), and the successful but unfaithful film version of Noel Coward's *Private Lives.* On Formosa Avenue, he had directed the remake of *The Dark Angel* and to Wyler, the natty Goldwyn had once held him up as an example of a director who also knew how to *dress.* Pearl Buck's *The Good Earth* was the elegant Franklin's most famous, a movie started by George Hill (who died after collecting background footage in China), continued by Victor Fleming, and, when *he* fell ill, finished by Franklin. In the general confusion following Thalberg's death, Mayer had ordered Franklin off active directing and made him a producer. As such, his first acquisition had been a trio of writers of unequal background who complemented each other marvelously. They were James Hilton, the author of *Lost Horizon* (whose *Goodbye Mr. Chips* Franklin produced with Sam Wood directing), George Froeschel, a former Austrian cavalry officer and novelist, and a sprightly lady scenarist, Claudine West. Together, they wrote *The Mortal Storm* and *Random Harvest;* Hilton and Miss West wrote *Goodbye Mr. Chips;* and Froeschel wrote Franklin's latest production, *Waterloo Bridge,* directed, along with *Random Harvest,* by Mervyn Le Roy.

---

* In *Hail the Conquering Hero,* a comedy about Marines and the nervous respect civilians paid men in uniform, which led to Sturges' being publicly psychoanalyzed by a critic. James Agee felt Sturges' rather extraordinary childhood had led him to develop "a permanently incurable loathing for anything that stank of 'culture.' "

When Franklin called Wyler after *The Little Foxes* and asked him for lunch, Wyler pushed other appointments aside.

"I was glad to go and hear what he had in mind," Wyler recalled. "He had the script under his arm when we sat down in his office, but he wouldn't let me read it. He said, 'No, this I have to read to you myself.' Sidney was very precise, very good at story analysis, and so he began to read to me. Before he was halfway through, I jumped."

Wyler felt the fall of France very deeply. He had watched the newsreel reportage of German troops marching down the Champs Elysée with the swastika unfurling under the *Arc de Triomphe* and imagined Mulhouse, together with the rest of Alsace, annexed once more to the Reich.

Like most Americans, he realized that Germany, Italy, and Japan held control of Europe and Asia—with the exception of Russia—and Africa, and that if Britain collapsed, nothing remained between the United States and the totalitarian world. After the 1940 election, however, the split between isolationists and internationalists emerged more sharply than ever. In Congress, Senator Robert Taft of Ohio and Senator Burton Wheeler of Montana led the opposition to Roosevelt's foreign policy, while outside Congress, Colonel Charles Lindbergh and Robert McCormick, the publisher of the *Chicago Tribune,* gained wide support for the isolationists, who believed Roosevelt's "aid to the Allies short of war" would drag the country into it. They felt Britain was bound to lose and that the U.S. could live with victorious fascist nations, whose aggressive intent had been, they said, grossly exaggerated.

"To make propaganda, you must be successful and your film must be successful," Wyler said. "The most satisfaction I get out of a film aside from its critical and financial success, is its contribution to the thinking of people, socially or politically. In this sense, every film is propaganda. But, of course, propaganda must not *look* like propaganda.

"As I saw it, *Mrs. Miniver* was perfect as propaganda *for* the British because it was a story about a family, about the kind of people audiences would care about."

Hollywood of the "spaghetti factory" era knew how to work fast. Like Billy Wilder's *Five Graves to Cairo*—an espionage thriller taking place in the Libyan desert after the fall of Tobruk, which was in the can three months *before* Field Marshal Erwin Rommel lost North Africa—*Mrs. Miniver* was put into production at top speed. The script was quickly thrown together by Franklin's trio, augmented by a fourth scenarist, Arthur Wimperis, who had also worked on *Random Harvest.* Some of it was based on Scottish novelist Jan Struther's sketches of English life. Her *Mrs. Miniver,* however, ended with the blitz.* The film story was written by Hilton, Froeschel, Miss West, and Wimperis in two weeks, rewritten in one week. As filming progressed, Wyler and Henry Wilcoxon, who played the vicar, rewrote a sermon which was to become famous.

Greer Garson did not want to play Mrs. Miniver because, actually age thirty-two, she was to portray a woman old enough to have a twenty-year-old son (Richard Ney) in the Royal Air Force. She had been discovered in London in 1938, and had made her American film debut in *Goodbye Mr. Chips.* The red-headed actress had an initially disastrous meeting with Wyler. Before they started shooting, she presented her director with a pair of black velvet gloves with brass buttons. On one button, she had hand engraved, "For the iron hand," and on the other, "of William Wyler."

A couple of weeks into filming, Mayer called Wyler into his office to complain about the anti-German bias he had seen in the rushes. What particularly bothered him, he said, was a scene where Mrs. Miniver catches a German airman (ably played by Helmut Dantine) shot down and hiding in her garden. As written, the flier was a nice boy, but Wyler shot it differently, making him a fanatical young Nazi wanting to rule the world and destroy England.

"Look, maybe you don't understand," Mayer began, "we're not at war with anybody. This picture just shows these people having a hard time and it's very sympathetic to them, but it's not directed against the Germans."

"Mr. Mayer, you know what's going on, don't you?" Wyler asked.

"This is a big corporation. I'm responsible to my stockholders.

* Jan Struther, *Mrs. Miniver,* Harcourt, Brace, New York, 1940. Under the somewhat false impression that the slim little volume was the written version of the MGM film, book buyers went through thirteen printings of *Mrs. Miniver* in less than two years.

We have theaters all over the world, including a couple in Berlin. We don't make hate pictures. We don't hate anybody. We're not at war."

"Mr. Mayer, if I had several Germans in the picture, I wouldn't mind having one of them sympathetic. But I've got only one German and as long as I only have one, he's going to be one of Goering's little monsters. That's the way he's been brought up. Maybe it's not his fault, but . . ."

Mayer looked at Wyler for a long moment, then quietly told him to go ahead but don't "overdo" it. "I think I could see what was going through his mind, 'It's just the one scene. Let him finish the picture. I can always have another director shoot it over if I don't like it.' "

Wyler was assigned Metro's top cinematographer, Joseph Ruttenberg, who was to remember *Mrs. Miniver* with affection.

"Wyler has a marvelous way of directing," the Russian-born cameraman said. "He sits next to the camera and watches the rehearsal without saying a word. Actors have no idea *what* he thinks."

Ruttenberg, who had behind him thirty-six features and had worked with Griffith, Vidor, Borzage, Cukor, and Le Roy, recalled how Willy had remembered a gesture in rehearsals and had waited for his actor or actress to repeat that gesture on camera. "In one scene, Greer Garson was on her stomach and Walter Pigeon gave her a tap with his slipper on her behind. It was in rehearsal, but Willy caught the gesture and had it repeated in the take. Another example: at one point, the maid closes the kitchen door with her foot and nobody notices this detail. Later in the film, however, when the majordomo, in love with her, has dinner with her a last time before going off to war, she closes the door again with her foot. A very cute detail that wasn't thrown into the audience's face. That's how Wyler works, never giving precise indications so that the actor's instinct has a chance."[2]

One Sunday morning, Wyler and John Huston went to Anatole Litvak's house in Malibu to meet a travel agent. Talli was pregnant again and the baby would be due in May, almost three years after Cathy's birth. Willy, John, and Tola were meeting with the travel agent for the final plans for a trip to China. John's first picture, *The Maltese Falcon*—written by Dashiell Hammett—had opened in October to raving reviews and his next was to be *In This Our Life,* to star Olivia de Havilland and Bette Davis. It was midday when the radio flash came that the Japanese had attacked Hawaii. That was the end of their China trip.

A couple of days later, Wyler was again told to report to Mayer.

"You know what you wanted to do there with that scene," he grimaced. "You just go ahead. You do it the way you wanted."

The Dunkirk operation of June, 1940, was shot in the big tank on Stage 30, where Esther Williams was soon to start her aquatics. The battleship and little fishing and pleasure boats, including the motor launch of Clem Miniver (Walter Pidgeon), were all miniatures.

To simplify dramatically, Wyler eliminated the part of the captain on the bridge of the battleship telling the civilians in their small craft what their mission would be. "I don't want to look at a man, I want to look at the battleship," he told Franklin. "It doesn't matter what the captain looks like. I want to show the people standing and listening in their little boats, with the voice coming over the loudspeaker."

One of the best things in the script, Wyler felt, was the twist of fate of the Minivers' twenty-year-old son and his young bride. "The whole story builds and builds to the inevitable death of this young man in the Royal Air Force. He is the slight-hearted young man. His mother has the scene with the downed German pilot, trying to get information about combat flying, and you *know* young Miniver is going to get killed. And what happens—he returns and his wife dies in a bombing raid."

After Pearl Harbor, Wyler felt the vicar's sermon in a bombed-out church at the end of the film was too tame and, together with Wilcoxon, he rewrote some of it and reshot it. The sermon so impressed President Roosevelt that he had the text reprinted in leaflets in many languages, dropped over German-held territories and broadcast over Voice of America. *P.M.* and *Look* magazine reprinted the text *in toto:*

> We, in this quiet corner of England, have suffered the loss of friends very dear to us. Some close to this church—George West, choir boy; James Ballard, stationmaster and bellringer;

and the proud winner, only an hour before his death, of the Beldon Cup for his beautiful Miniver Rose. And our hearts go out in sympathy to the families who share the cruel loss of a young girl who was married at this altar only two weeks ago. The homes of many of us have been destroyed and the lives of young and old have been taken. There is scarcely a household that hasn't been struck to the heart. And why? Surely you must have asked yourselves this question. Why, in all conscience, should these be the ones to suffer? Children, old people, a young girl at the height of her loveliness. Why these? Are these our soldiers? Are these our fighters? Why should they be sacrificed? I shall tell you why. Because this is not only a war of soldiers in uniform, it is a war of the people—of all the people—and it must be fought, not only on the battlefield, but in the cities and in the villages, in the factories and on the farms, in the home and in the heart of every man, woman, and child who loves freedom. Well, we have buried our dead but we shall not forget them. Instead, they will inspire us with an unbreakable determination to free ourselves and those who come after us from the tyranny and terror that threaten to strike us down. Fight it, then! Fight it with all that is in us! And may God defend the right!

A few weeks later, Wyler was in Washington and, together with Lillian Hellman, ready to go to Moscow and prepare *The North Star,* an original story and screenplay by Miss Hellman telling in passionate terms of Russian suffering under the invading Nazi armies. The news had been bad during the winter. On December 14, 1941, German armies had been within twenty-five miles of Moscow. "All of America was moved and bewildered by the courage of a people who had been presented to two generations of Americans as passive slaves," Miss Hellman was to write in her autobiography.

"Both Wyler and I were wild to do the picture," she continued, "and so Goldwyn flew East to consult with us, and the famous cameraman, Gregg Toland, agreed to come along. Wyler and I went to Washington to see [Soviet] ambassador Maxim Litvinov, whom I already knew and liked. But Litvinov said our plan was impossible, wouldn't work without full cooperation from the Russian government, and that they were too hard pressed to give it. When Litvinov described the horrors of the German sweep through White Russia to Moscow, Leningrad and Stalingrad, we felt like young school children who had heard of *Oedipus* and thought it excellent to stage in their lunch hour." [3]

The next afternoon, things had changed. Stalin's foreign secretary, Vyacheslav Molotov, had arrived for consultations with President Roosevelt. To Litvinov's surprise, Molotov had liked the idea of *The North Star* and said the Soviet government would guarantee a bomber, a camera crew, and whatever else was needed.

The North Star was eventually made—on Formosa Avenue, directed by Lewis Milestone as "a big-time, sentimental, badly directed, badly acted mess," as Lillian later wrote.

Mrs. Miniver opened at New York's Radio City Music Hall June 4, 1942, the second anniversary of Winston Churchill's "we shall go to the end" address. In ten weeks at the Music Hall, almost one and a half million people saw it (1,499,891 was the unheard-of attendance figure). The critics didn't spare their adjectives. "It is hard to believe that a picture could be made within the heat of present strife which would clearly, but without a cry for vengeance, crystallize the cruel effect of total war upon a civilized people," Bosley Crowther began. "Yet that is what has been magnificently done in Metro's *Mrs. Miniver*, which came to the Music Hall yesterday. Perhaps it is too soon to call this one of the greatest motion pictures ever made, perhaps its tremendous impact is too largely conditioned by one's own immediate association of one's torn heart with the people so heroically involved. But certainly, it is the finest film yet made about the present war, and a most exalting tribute to the British." [4]

The *New York Herald Tribune* said Wyler was "chiefly responsible for the sincerity and overpowering emotional intensity of this picture . . . concentrating on the essential personal drama and suggesting the larger drama of the work by consummate indirection, he has achieved a reconstruction of significant and enduring human experience which is certain to leave you shaken for a long time." [5] *Look* called it "the most important motion picture to come out of this war." [6] *Life* ran an eight-page picture spread. "In *Mrs. Miniver*, there are no spectacular battle scenes," *Life* wrote. "The judging of one prize rose is almost as momentous as the retreat from Dunkirk, but William Wyler directs these family affairs with such warmth and good taste that *Mrs. Miniver* packs more emotional wallop than any other fictional war film to date.

Wyler's secret is simple. He makes his Minivers, unlike most movie characters, the sort of people you really enjoy knowing for two hours." [7]

Mrs. Miniver was released a month after Talli gave birth to the Wyler's second daughter, Judy. Greer Garson married her son in the picture, Richard Ney. Six Oscars resulted from the film—Best Picture, Best Actress, Best Direction, Best Supporting Actress (Teresa Wright), Best Screenplay, and Best Black-and-White Photography (Joseph Ruttenberg). The Academy Award dinner was held at the Ambassador Hotel's Coconut Grove and was remembered as the event where Miss Garson thanked practically everybody but her manicurist in a marathon acceptance speech. Talli was in the audience, sitting with Frank and Lucille Capra until Frank left the table and reappeared on the stage to announce the director's award. "And the winner is . . ." he said, grinning, opening the envelope, "William Wyler, for *Mrs. Miniver!*"

Willy was in London with the newly formed Eighth Air Force putting together an outfit called a combat camera unit when Talli went up to accept the Oscar. "I was told I couldn't have directed it better," Willy said years later, "because her speech was subtle yet emotional, not sloppy and that she gave a most marvellous performance."

PART FOUR

War and Aftermath

23

"You Hollywood bigshots are all alike, all a pain in the ass," was the way Colonel Schlossberg, Signal Corps, Army Pictorial Service, had it figured out after a couple of weeks with Major Frank Capra and Colonel Darryl Zanuck. President Roosevelt and his chief of staff, General George C. Marshall, had it figured differently. They knew that the large armies—around eight million men—the country was raising, had to be told *why* and that movies were the best way. America's citizen armies, where drafted civilians would outnumber professional soldiers fifty to one, were up against a highly trained and highly indoctrinated enemy. In General Marshall's judgment, Americans, used to doing and thinking for themselves, *could* be equal or superior to totalitarian soldiers if they were given answers as to *why* they were in uniform and if the answers they were given were worth fighting—and dying—for.

The Army Pictorial Service made thousands of training films on every conceivable subject from venereal disease to spotting enemy aircraft and assembling M-1 rifles, but, as Capra realized after one week in Washington, "colonels were automatically hostile to the power of ideas."

Colonel Schlossberg had made a trip to the Coast with Sy Bartlett, erstwhile screenwriter (*Road to Zanzibar*) and now Signal Corps captain. Bartlett recommended Capra, John Huston, Anatole Litvak, and William Wyler to Schlossberg. Only Capra was free immediately as the others were in the middle of productions.

When *Mrs. Miniver* was finished, Wyler called Colonel Schlossberg in Washington, saying he was ready.

"Yes, well you just take it easy," Schlossberg said over the long-distance phone.

"Jesus, the war is going to be over . . . ."

"We'll call you, Mr. Wyler. You just sit tight."

Schlossberg was waging a major battle with Capra in Washington and wasn't anxious to have more Hollywood types telling him how documentaries should be made.

Wyler sat tight until after Judy was born, May 21, then he took off for Washington on his own. When he arrived, Capra had won the jurisdictional squabble. With the help of a couple of generals, the energetic Capra had first requisitioned from the Treasury Department's Alien Property Custodian warehouses of German and Japanese newsreels and had screened miles of footage to study psychological warfare. (Years later, Dr. Hans Traub, chief of UFA's Lehrschau at Berlin's Babelsberg was to tell how UFA board members ran American films and were most impressed by *Mrs. Miniver*.) The first scripts for Capra's *Why We Fight* series had been parceled out to seven Hollywood civilians, but turned out to be too left-leaning for Capra and his superiors.

"We all realized the project was so sensitive it could only be carried out with controllable men in uniform," Capra was to write in his autobiography.[1] On May 2, Capra got the power to enlist and commission his own film personnel, setting up the 834th Photo Signal Detachment "under the jurisdiction and direct control of the chief of Special Services."

When Wyler arrived in Major Capra's "cooling tower" in the Department of Interior building, Tony Veiller, Robert Heller, Leonard Spiegelgass, and Litvak were already working—pending their induction into the army—on seven one-hour "must see" *Why We Fight* edited documentaries.

"Anything I can do for you, Frank?" Wyler asked.

"Wanna make a picture for the army?" Capra asked, pushing a list of subjects across his desk. "Which one do you want to do? Pick one out."

Wyler picked *The Negro Soldier*. A few days later, still a civilian, he was on his way to Alabama together with journalist-dramatist (and *Green Pastures* author) Marc Connelly and a black writer, Carlton Moss.

Wyler had never been in the Deep South and some of the scenes were right out of *The Little Foxes,* if not of *Jezebel.* Moss couldn't stay in the same hotels as Wyler and Connelly. After Charlotte, North Carolina, he could no longer ride the same railway car. It was an irony that hurt. Here they were on their way to the Negro university in Tuskegee and the nearby Air Force base, where the only squadron of black fighter pilots was in training to do research for a government film on why it was also a black man's war. In March, a black man had been held for treason in Philadelphia when he told a Negro army sergeant, "This is a white man's war, and it's no damn good."

They did their homework. Blacks had fought in every American war since the Revolution. In the Civil War, the Union had 170,000 black soldiers under arms. But when the first Negro leader, Frederick Bailey Douglass, asked why they were paid less than white soldiers, President Lincoln temporized. Since World War I, the black man's status as a U.S. fighting man had gone backwards. Of the 1,078,331 Negroes registered for the draft in 1917, some 380,000 Negroes served as soldiers—ten percent of the whole army. The 292,000 Negro troops the army expected to have at the end of 1942 would come to eight percent of the U.S. armed forces. In spite of the shortage of skilled labor, black citizens were unwelcome in many war industries and a year earlier President Roosevelt had been obliged to issue an executive order forbidding racial discrimination in defense industries. He had since set up a Committee on Fair Employment Practice.

There were also brighter spots. If only four blacks had ever graduated from West Point, the army had two regular black line officers—Brigadier-General Benjamin Oliver Davis and his West Pointer son, Lieutenant B. O. Davis, Jr., military instructor at Tuskegee Institute. It was the young Davis that Wyler, Connelly, and Moss wanted to see, along with the university's famed Dr. George Washington Carver.

When they visited the Air Force base, they met with Lieutenant Davis, who was to retire a three-star general. The colonel in charge of the base was the only white man and Wyler asked him how things were.

"Fine, sir," he answered. "These boys are doing very well. They are anxious to see action."

"Don't they have any . . . problems?"

The colonel eyed the civilian and then explained, delicately, that the population around the base was white and unhappy about seeing airplanes flown by black boys. "They feel it's the last thing in being uppity," he said with a grin.

Since Wyler also smiled, he got it all off his chest. "It could happen, of course."

"What?"

"Some fanatic getting on the phone one day and calling the local Ku Klux Klan and having them all come charging in here."

Wyler was to remember impressions and moods of Alabama, 1942, when he shot *The Liberation of L. B. Jones* in Humboldt, Tennessee, twenty-eight years later.

When they got back to Washington, the situation had changed. Capra and his editors at the cooling tower were clipping from feature films, newsreels, and combat footage to create a panoramic background of the events leading up to World War II. Wyler, like John Ford, who also blazed through town, wanted to film overseas action *now,* do on-the-spot war reporting and combine powerful images with thoughtful commentaries. All Capra's Hollywood professionals plus some twenty civil service personnel worked like tightly packed ants, translating and rephrasing German and Japanese films, cataloguing and cross-filing film scenes, while Capra and Veiller did most of the writing. Eric Knight and *Mrs. Miniver* coscripter James Hilton had joined them. They were all too cramped in the two floors of the Interior Department building and there was talk of transferring the whole operation to Fox's old Western Avenue studio in Hollywood.

"Your project still has top priority," Capra drawled, explaining that Secretary of War Robert Patterson was pressuring for the film to buck up morale among black soldiers. His advisers had opened a dossier of sickening acts of discrimination against black troops in the South. "Patterson doesn't think it's exaggerated," Capra added significantly.

"It isn't."

Wyler celebrated his fortieth birthday in his room at the Statler Hotel talking to Talli on the phone. It suddenly looked ridiculous. *Mrs. Miniver* was the rage of the country, seen by millions every week, and here he was letting himself be talked into joining the army so he could go back to Hollywood and, in a dilapidated studio, make a documentary saying exactly the opposite of what he had seen in Tuskegee and elsewhere in the South. He could think of all sorts of heroics and hardships he was willing to suffer except working on Western Avenue for ten dollars a day. The phone rang. It was Lillian Hellman.

In ten minutes, *The North Star* came into focus. In one week, it was out of focus again, although Miss Hellman still flew to Moscow, via Alaska and Siberia, as a war correspondent.

Willy ran into Sy Bartlett. The former newsman had managed to transfer out of Colonel Schlossberg's Army Pictorial Service and had become aide to Army Air Force General Carl Spaatz. Bartlett invited Willy to be his "date" at a reception at the two-star general's home. The occasion was significant and hush-hush, but, by the time they got there, Wyler had an impressive respect for General Spaatz and knew the general and his staff were leaving the next day for "overseas" to set up the newly formed and still top secret Eighth Air Force. Bartlett said Spaatz was a strapping, tough, and taciturn man. There was the story about a lieutenant training to become a pilot and given a physical examination. "Do you ever see spots in front of your eyes?" the doctor asked. "I see that sonofabitch everywhere I go," the pilot answered.

Spaatz was indeed impressive. He looked like an eagle with his hawk nose and keen blue eyes. He sipped his bourbon standing. This was the chance, Willy thought. He asked Sy to introduce him and to tell their host who he was. The right moment came when Spaatz was alone with General Claude E. Duncan, his chief of staff. Sy's introduction to the two gentlemen was brief and to the point.

"General," Wyler began, screwing up his courage, "I don't know where you're going and I don't know what for, but whatever it is, I think it should be on film."

Spaatz arched an eyebrow. Wyler explained what movies could do and should do. The general listened, sipped his bourbon, and turned to his chief of staff.

"Take care of him," he told Duncan, turning to talk to other guests.

"Come out to Bolling Field, day after tomorrow," Duncan said.

For the next two days, Wyler ran around Washington with Miss Hellman, from the War Secretary's office to the Soviet embassy. He also drove out to Bolling Field. Duncan filled out the induction papers himself, but, at the heading "rank" hesitated.

"Rank," the one-star general said, looking up thoughtfully. "Er . . . would you like to be a major?"

Willy thought he was kidding but said yes. An hour later, he was a major in the United States Army Air Force.

"No training, nothing," Wyler recalled. "I was sent someplace to buy a uniform. Next thing, I put on this uniform that didn't fit and walk down the street with my cigarette, my briefcase, and here comes a general. Jeez, what do I do? Swallow the cigarette, throw the briefcase away. I threw away the cigarette and saluted. The general saw me and laughed."

Washington was full of men who had never been prepared for what they were suddenly doing. General Marshall had told Capra, "I have never been chief of staff before. Thousands of young Americans have never had their legs shot off before. Boys are commanding ships today, who a year ago had never seen the ocean. We are all being asked to do what we never dreamed we could do."

Wyler was, as he told Talli on the phone, "in business." His orders were clear—make a documentary about the Eighth Air Force, which meant form a film crew and proceed to England where the new United States Army Air Force was being assembled.

When General Spaatz and the USAAF arrived in Great Britain in mid-1942, there was sharp disagreement between English and American planners on the feasibility of proposed daylight bomber offensives. The Americans believed their Flying Fortresses, the ten-gun B-17's, would prove up to the test. As it turned out, neither British nor American commanders were right. Heavily armed American bombers proved more formidable than others that had been used before, but not so much that they could roam German skies without fighter escort. American authorities never called off the offensive, but, in late 1943, it became clear that the losses were murderous. Of the three hundred and fifteen B-17's that reached the target of Schweinfurt and Regensburg in the first heavy American bombing raid, sixty were shot down (six hundred men) while the Luftwaffe lost only twenty-five one-man fighters.

For Willy, it was back to Hollywood first to recruit his crew, get equipment, and make arrangements for editing and laboratory. He decided to shoot the film in color—16mm Kodachrome.

Talli thought he looked like a filling station attendant in his ill-fitting uniform, but they had two precious weeks together.

The personnel he enlisted for his Eighth Air Force combat camera unit included three cameramen—William Clothier, Harold Tannenbaum, and William Skall. His writer was Jerry Chodorov. He organized camera and sound equipment and arranged for military transport of all personnel and gear.

He flew ahead himself, stopping over in New York and running into all sorts of people. At the Plaza Hotel, he was introduced to Ferenc Molnar and told the Hungarian he had directed the screen version of *The Good Fairy.* Molnar congratulated him and talked warmly of the picture. When Willy asked where Molnar had seen the film, the aging author smiled and said he had never seen it. The last night in the new world was spent in exquisite company from the old, at a dinner with Paul Jacob and leading Frenchmen in wartime New York—Professor Maurice Wolff, Maurice Pregel, Georges Wilkenstein, Jacques Maritin, and the physicist Francis Périn. Paul had escaped to England in January and joined the Free French in London; Charles de Gaulle had sent him to New York as his personal representative. It was both funny and moving, as they thought of it, two childhood friends from Mulhouse in a Manhattan restaurant, one a *capitaine* in the *Forces françaises libres,* the other a major in the USAAF, both fighting in a war against a dictatorship that had arisen from the ashes of what had been their homeland.

One of the last purchases on American soil was a little pocket calendar for 1943. He had never kept a diary, but now he would. Well, maybe; jot down a few impressions, perhaps, of this momentous war.

Willy flew to Europe in a PBY flying boat via Ireland. "We had to wear civilian clothes to respect Ireland's neutrality," he remembered. "If we were caught in Ireland, we would have been interned. We stayed several days and were finally transferred to England.

"There were still very few Americans, just Spaatz and his people. Kids stopped on the streets to day, 'Look, an American!' We were a sensation in London in 1942."

24

"Willy had this brand-new uniform and his military experience consisted of that—a change of wardrobe," Beirne Lay remembered. "I was immediately struck by his warmth, his intelligence, and his enormous inferiority complex at being completely out of his element. He had been a general on Hollywood sets and here he was completely lost, supposedly an officer, and rather appalled by the difficulties facing him. He had been ordered, in effect, to make a picture about the Eighth Air Force and all he had was one 16mm camera in a shoulder strap he had brought along himself."

Beirne Lay was a strapping West Virginian with both a military career and experience with movie people. He had graduated from Yale and had entered the Army Air Corps in 1933 and been on active duty since. He had written the novel *I Wanted Wings,* as well as the subsequent screenplay of the Paramount picture directed by Mitchell Leisen (after the war, he was to write *Twelve O'Clock High* for Henry King, with Sy Bartlett, and alone, *Strategic Air Command* for Anthony Mann). A lieutenant colonel, Lay had been ordered by Ira C. Eaker, the commanding general of the Eighth Bomber Command, to take temporary charge of the combat camera unit, get the men quartered, and organize equipment and basic training for combat photography.

"Willy had nothing to start making pictures with, not even a paperclip, just this Eyemo camera on a shoulder strap. I got him and his people quartered somewhere in Old Audley Street and got him a little office on Davis Street, off Grosvenor Square."

Willy was not interested in desk space. He was soon out at the Eighth Air Force headquarters at High Wycomb and, twenty miles farther away, at the Ninety-first Bomb Command at Bassing-bourne, getting a first look at the Boeing B-17's and talking to fliers and ground crews.

"Naturally, I was very excited, but my equipment didn't arrive. I stood on the field and saw the first American bombers clamber into the air for target across the Channel in France. I had no film, nothing. My equipment had very low priority, of course, and was coming across on surface vessel. Suddenly, John Ford showed up, eyepatch, cigar, and all. He was in the navy and his equipment was *flown* over by the air force! I don't know how he did it. He and Gregg Toland had been over on Hawaii filming Pearl Harbor a week after the attack. When my stuff arrived, half of it had been sunk by the Germans."

The frustrations were not only over equipment. There were also military rules and reasons. Suddenly he learned he was not allowed to go on mission, even if he had his equipment. Why? Because he was not a gunner. No man could hop on a B-17 unless he was an emergency gunner and could take over a machine gun in case a man was hurt.

"Photography was not considered a useful job," Wyler remembered. "I always ran into people saying, 'Come on now, this is not Hollywood!' So, we all went to a gunner's school in Bovington. We learned to take a machine gun apart and put it together again and we learned 'aircraft recognition' so we wouldn't shoot down friendly planes. That was the most difficult part, identifying aircraft in a fraction of a second from any position when the sky would be full of Spitfires, Focke-Wulfs, and Mustangs."

Aircraft recognition was taught in a domed building where Fred Waller, a trick cameraman who had worked for D. W. Griffith, had rigged a series of 16mm projectors together. The student gunner sat in the middle with a simulated machine gun and was told to shoot down the right plane as it flashed across the multiple screens of the dome. After the war, Waller took out a patent and called it Cinerama.

Friends and imposed mundanities fleshed out the long wait. He was happy to see Larry and Vivien, but not very hot on Olivier's suggestion that he direct *Henry V.*

"I don't know enough about Shakespeare," Willy said evasively.

"You don't have to," Larry said with a smile. "I know Shakespeare and you know cinema."

Larry offered to have Winston Churchill pull the necessary strings to have Willy out of the Air Force long enough to direct *Henry V*. The only epic Wyler was interested in putting on film, however, was the ongoing war, and Olivier ended up directing *Henry V* himself.

The mundanities included a top-brass screening of *Mrs. Miniver*. Willy wasn't interested—it all felt so distant and unreal, shot on Culver City stages and now to be shown in bomb-scarred London. As his commanding officer, Lay had to threaten Willy with near court-martial before he agreed to attend the affair.

"Willy told me he couldn't bear to watch this now," Lay recalled. "He said, 'I made this picture and I didn't know what I was doing. Now, with an audience like this!' He almost chickened out because he feared it wouldn't ring true. Well, halfway through the picture it was a handkerchief job. You could hear people sobbing and sniffing. I sat next to Willy and when the lights came on, I turned to him. Tears were on his cheeks and he said, 'Christ, what a tearjerker.'"

After gunner training and the arrival of equipment and raw stock, Clothier, Tannenbaum, and Wyler went on their first mission, each aboard a different B-17. The missions were not to Germany as Wyler had hoped, but over St-Nazaire and Lorient on the southern coast of Britanny, dangerous bombing runs of naval yards as the yellow-nosed Heinkel He51's—"Göring's Squadron"—were in Britanny and considered the best Luftwaffe fighter fliers. They were all alive at New Year's, 1943, celebrated at Claridge's.

Willy wanted to fly missions to Germany, but to find out the next day's target proved the toughest thing to arrange. He had made friends with Colonel Stanley Wray, the commander of the Ninety-first out at Bassingbourne. After a lot of high-power persuasion, Wray agreed to have someone phone Wyler in London in the evening as soon as the next day's target had been determined. If Wyler was asked, "How's the weather in London?" it meant the target was Germany. The combat camera unit took off in the middle of the night to reach Bassingbourne over wintry, blacked-out roads before the dawn briefing.

U.S. heavy bombers made their first daylight raid on Germany on January 27, and, although the bombing of Wilhelmshaven was not one of the great aerial attacks of the war, the mission was significant because it was the opening of the daylight bombing offensive against Germany itself. The combat camera unit was on board for the next weeks' runs—Kiel, Hamburg, Schweinfurt, and the Messerschmidt plants in Regensburg. The B-17's penetrated the German air space alone. Escort fighters did not yet have the range to accompany bombers all the way to their targets and no B-17's bombed Berlin until November 1943.

"The escorts went halfway across the North Sea with us then turned back," Wyler recalled. "The flak was terrific. We'd fly through entire belts of it, so thick that at twenty-six thousand feet the blue sky looked like a punctured sieve."

Regensburg was raided by 147 B-17's commanded by General Curtis E. LeMay. Later that same morning, 168 Fortresses roared out for the ball-bearing industry at Schweinfurt. Sixty bombers were lost in this combined operation, almost twenty percent of the total force, and later evaluations indicated the sacrifice did not justify the result. Schweinfurt was hit again, in a raid where sixty B-17's of a force of 291 were shot down. Six more crashed attempting to land in England. "Much damage was inflicted on the German plants, but it did not completely justify the wholesale sacrifice," military historian Arch Whitehouse was to write. "The morale of the Eighth Air Force was very low and the Germans were jubilant as their fighter pilots ran up fantastic scores. General Henry H. Arnold later admitted, 'No such savage air battles had been seen since the beginning of the war. Our losses were at an all-time high but so were those of the Luftwaffe. Nevertheless, our bombers were not being turned back from their targets." [1]

Vincent Evans, bombardier of one of the B-17's Wyler flew on, the *Memphis Belle,* remembered the director-cameraman walking the open catwalk of the bomb bay five miles above Germany, breathing out of a walk-around oxygen bottle, his body clothed in bulky flying equipment, the temperature at forty-five degrees below zero, pointing his hand camera at flak bursts and at German fighters trying to break up the formation.

"We could hear him cuss over the intercom," Evans recalled. "By the time he'd swung his camera over to a flak burst, it was lost. Then he'd see another burst, try to get it, miss, see another, try that, miss, try, miss. Then we'd hear him over the intercom, asking the pilot if he couldn't possibly get the plane closer to the flak."

Captain R. K. Morgan's response remained unrecorded.

The intercom often crackled with dialogue that stayed burned in Willy's mind. Bombardier Evans once interrupted a long-flight explanation by the pilot with a bitchy, "Yeah, you know everything, don't you." And Morgan's voice coming back, "You're alive, ain't ya."

Filming at 29,000 feet was not easy. The B-17's were not pressurized and to withstand the lack of oxygen and the 60 below temperatures of the near stratosphere, the airmen were dressed in electric suits under fur-lined clothes, heavy boots, and special gloves. Besides being hooked into oxygen and intercom, their gear consisted of Mae West lifejackets, parachutes and, when they moved, portable oxygen tanks. If not kept close to a man's chest, an Eyemo camera would freeze up in a few minutes. Also, the cameras had 100-foot spools (at 24 frames a second only 2.8 minutes of filming). To reload, a camera operator had to take his gloves off—but fast. Hands were frostbitten after about two minutes. On pure oxygen, to move from the "waist" to the nose of the plane felt like running a mile.

One feature of the Flying Fortress that more than intrigued Wyler was the ball turret which allowed to shoot 180 degrees vertically and 360 degrees horizontally under the plane. For example, if an enemy fighter zeroed in from the front the ball turret gunner, strapped into his totally mobile seat, could fire back as it passed under the ship, until at the end he was hanging upside down shooting out backwards. Wyler saw the possibilities the ball turret offered and told Morgan he'd like to film a landing at Bassingbourne from the turret. Regulations made the turret off limits on landings since anyone sitting in it would be squashed instantly if the landing gear had been damaged by enemy fire and collapsed on touchdown. Morgan found a solution—landing on a British field where such rules didn't exist.

A spectacular fire in a munitions dump at the U.S. base at Alconbury had Wyler ask Morgan to fly over the field with open bomb bays so he could film the holocaust. Inexplicably, Morgan failed to clear with the tower below or answer radio calls when he buzzed the field and every anti-aircraft gun was trained on them. The Luftwaffe was known to have refurbished several

B-17's that had crash-landed in Holland. The Memphis Belle sailing overhead must be one of them, the base commander was almost sure, why else would she fly with open bomb bays? Later, Morgan and Wyler were told that if it had been a British field, they *would* have been shot down.

To Talli, Willy wrote reassuring letters, telling her not to worry. In his pocket diary, he was a little more candid. Under May 19, 1943, he wrote in his neat and legible handwriting, and with space-saving abbreviations, about one mission: "Kiel— learned a lot about it in school—and the Kaiser Wilhelm Canal —never thought I'd see it this way—counted 160 B-17's in perfect formation—it's a sight I'll never forget. I feel like now I've seen everything. Got good pictures—could have gotten more but was saving the film for the target—and the fighter attacks. Then passed out (bad show) good thing I came to—don't know how either happened—but the latter was lucky, was so dopey I thought I was dead—strange feeling—don't think I like it—thought of Talli and Cathy—naturally and what a fool I was to go—who asked me? When I came to I found myself in the bottom of the ship between the pilots and the nose. Decided to move from the nose to the pilots' compartment because the nose was too cluttered up with guns and sights & since we were leading—the bombardier was bombing for the whole group [91st]. It's only 2 crawls and 2 steps but on oxygen carrying camera, bottle, chute, etc.—it's a 5-mile run—I guess because I didn't make it when I woke up we passed the target and got into a short fight. They missed us but I think our [No.] 1 waist [gunner] got one FW 190."

A couple of entries later, Willy wrote: "Yesterday's sortie was made with Capt. Gaitley, Pilot of Our Gang on his last mission. Radio operator passed out, too—he's a big husky kid about twenty-four—now I don't feel so bad."

On Friday, May 21: "Tough day. Didn't get up for briefing (Clothier came in my room & told me target was Wilhelmshaven —I been there—so I rolled over & got more sleep). Lucky stiff, they came back at 4 P.M., all shot to hell—3 [planes] missing from the 324th alone—and Fisher among them—with all of Gaitley's crew 5 of them on their last mission—one of our cameras & long lens lost too."

After each mission, Wyler collected the exposed film from

Clothier and Tannenbaum and discussed the footage. It began to look as if they had a film. One evening, Tannenbaum's "crate" didn't come back. He was killed on a bombing mission over France. Writing to Tannenbaum's family was Wyler's saddest moment of the war.

If Wyler didn't find the going too scary, General Eaker did. The commanding general of the Eighth Bomber Group felt that, as a Jew and as the maker of *Mrs. Miniver,* a film which, as President Roosevelt said, had been instrumental in getting United States public opinion in favor of going to war against Germany, Wyler would not have an easy time if he were shot down and captured. Eaker passed the order to Lay.

"I passed it on directly to Willy—no more combat missions!" Lay recalled. "The next morning, he didn't show up in the office, so at ten o'clock, I called Bassingbourne and they said, 'If you want to get hold of Major Wyler, he's probably over Hamburg.' When Willy got back, I said, 'This is in direct violation of orders. You can be court-martialed for that.' He said, 'I've got to get the film. If anybody wants to court-martial me for doing what I think is my job, I'm willing to leave that to the judgment of the readers when they see the headlines.' "

Cockeyed Hollywood parlance, perhaps, but Lay, Wray, and the boys out at Bassingbourne began to have an odd respect for this crazy civilian-in-uniform. Because he *could* stay in his office in the West End and order a bunch of cameramen to get the film, because he didn't have to go. "If he had no other qualities, he had enormous guts," Lay said. "This wasn't easy. Someone on a set might think he was a sonofabitch, or a sadist, because he wanted twenty takes of a scene, but here was the acid test—with his own skin on the line, he went out there because he wanted the picture to be right."

Lay did not tell Eaker that the flying filmmaker was violating direct orders and Wyler went on one last mission, the roughest of them all.

On May 25, Wyler and Clothier filmed the visit of King George and Queen Elizabeth to Bassingbourne. "Talked with Queen about 5 minutes while King and generals waited," Willy wrote in the daybook. "Spoke of *Mrs. M,* going on missions, RAF, etc., she was charming, interested—loved *Mrs. Miniver.*"

With his tin cans of film, Major Wyler flew to Hollywood—the long way, via military cargo planes to Iceland, Greenland, Halifax, and across the United States, hitching rides on other military planes from air base to air base. The meeting with Talli was strange and awkward, almost scary. They both felt like strangers. Their first meeting at opposite ends of a long hallway was to provide the model for Fredric March's homecoming in *The Best Years of Our Lives*.

Willy set to work quickly at "Fort Roach," as Hal Roach's studio had been dubbed since its takeover by the Air Force. Before leaving London, General Eaker had asked him how much time he would need to edit the film and he had said ninety days.

"I had to have this film blown up from 16mm to 35 and I couldn't get it finished in three months. It needed sound effects, a narration had to be written, a score. So, when I realized this, I sent a cable asking for sixty days more. General Eaker's return wire said, 'Come back or send replacement.' I didn't want to send replacement so I went all the way to England to explain what I had to do to finish the picture—in a bucket seat of a C-54 transport, again from Los Angeles to New York, then via Greenland and Iceland. Eaker gave me another sixty days and I flew back."

The return trip, again aboard a C-54, got recorded in a new pocket daybook he bought in New Bond Street, including a critical takeoff from Prestwick, Scotland. "Took off at 2:30. Engine No. 3 blows out on runway, ship thrown sideways but straightens out—pilot takes her up fast but wobbly—good decision—had too much speed and not enough runway to stop—a bad minute. Circled and came back. Finally took off 5:30 p.m. Iceland 9:30 overnight at the Hotel de Gink. In the sky aurora borealis—moving and changing constantly a beautiful phenomenon of nature would look wonderful on film—with airplanes. Took off from Iceland Saturday 23rd, 9:30 A.M., saw Irving Berlin in Newfoundland, arrived New York midnight—DEAD (tired). Sunday saw Goldwyn, attended dinner to honor Walter Lippman—by Freedom House and Wendell Willkie—drink at Herbert Swope's, long talks with Elsa Maxwell—long speeches & shows to get money from all the rich for the war. It's depressing to think that's the only way they can get it with a big dinnershow and lots of glamour."

Memphis Belle became a personalized account of the twenty-fifth and final mission of the Flying Fortress *Memphis Belle*, recording in forty-three minutes the experiences of the plane's crew on its last raid on Wilhelmshaven before being ordered home.

Memphis Belle begins with glimpses of a peaceful English countryside and, as the commentator cautions that "this is a battlefield—a battlefront like no other in the long history of mankind's wars," the camera pans to an airfield where green-brown bombers sit on broad runways. The documentary shows the preparations for the mission—loading of bombs, pilots' briefing, crews boarding their crates, and the planes lifting into the sky. The *Memphis Belle* and other bombers fly eastward. Ice forms on windows, fliers don oxygen masks, and feathery trails of vapor stream back from engines of other planes in the formation. As they approach their target, bursts of flak appear—deadly black puffs which grow more and more frequent as the *Belle* levels off for her bombing run. The planes are now on the target, fat yellow bombs are dropped and from 9 o'clock the first fighters come sweeping in to attack. "The first half of the mission is over—the easy half."

"Perhaps the most absorbing part of the picture is the subsequent sequence, taken within the *Belle,* showing the battle against the enemy fighters, with dubbed dialogue of the crew on their interphones," Bosley Crowther wrote in his front-page review of *Memphis Belle.* "From voices even but tense, you hear—and then see—'There's four of 'em, coming in at nine o'clock. They're breaking at eleven. Get that ball turret on 'em'—and then the angry chatter of machine guns. Or heartbreakingly, you see a giant Fortress fall dizzily off below, with black smoke billowing behind her, as a voice notes, 'B-17 out of control at three o'clock'—and then follows a few moments later with an urgent appeal to stricken friends, 'Come on, you guys—get out of that plane! There go three chutes. There go two more.' "[2]

Back at the base, ground crews sweat out the mission, smoking and waiting, to hear the drone of their planes coming home. The first of them comes in. Some drop flares to warn of wounded men aboard. The bombers flop down on the runway, some of them torn with great holes, others not a scratch. At last, "the ship which we'd all been pulling for, the *Memphis Belle,* comes home." The film ends with decorations being pinned on the *Belle*'s crew by King George and the Queen and by General Eaker. Then the *Belle* takes off for the United States.

With the finished film, Wyler went to Washington to show it to

General Arnold, the supreme commander of the Army Air Force. A screening was arranged for the President in the White House basement.

On the appointed day and time, the White House screening room filled mostly with Navy brass, an admiral nodded to Wyler to start the film.

"Is everybody here?" Wyler asked, hoping someone would say they'd better wait for the President.

"Yes, everybody's here. You can run it now, colonel," the admiral said, settling back in his seat.

Wyler knew nothing of the service rivalry for the President's attention and had the film started. *The Memphis Belle,* which at one point said Air Force bombings of enemy submarine pens meant more Allied ships would get through and that lives of many seamen would be spared, ran to a less than benevolent audience. When the lights went up, a senior officer said "Very nice," thanked Wyler and everybody filed out.

"I'll leave the print here, sir," Wyler tried.

"No, no, you can take it with you."

"It's no problem, sir. I can leave the print in case somebody else *might want* to see it."

"That won't be necessary, colonel," the officer said. "You can take the print with you."

An elderly civilian with a kind face was the last to leave.

You'd like the President to see it, wouldn't you?" the little man said softly.

Wyler nodded. The man smiled and left.

The next day, Wyler got a call from the Air Force liaison officer at the White House telling him to bring the print back. The little man was Judge Samuel I. Rosenman, Roosevelt's adviser on defense reorganization.

"This time everybody was there except the navy guys," Willy recalled. "They wheeled in the President and he said, 'Okay, which one of you did this?' 'I did, sir.' 'Okay, you come and sit here.' "

Wyler sat down next to Roosevelt. He had been told not to put his hands in his pockets, that this was protocol. The picture started and Roosevelt was full of questions.

"What kind of bomb is that, a thousand pounder?"

"No, sir, that's a five-hundred pounder," Wyler replied.

"Oh, yeah?"

After two minutes, Roosevelt took out a pack of Camels and offered Wyler one. Watching the screen, the President waited for someone to light his cigarette. Wyler remembered he had been told not to put his hands in his pockets, but hauled out his matches and lit Roosevelt's and his own cigarette. After five minutes, the President stopped asking questions.

"He was very enthusiastic," Wyler remembered. "He said it had to be shown right away, everywhere."

As Talli joined him in Washington, Willy was recommended for the Distinguished Service Medal. The National Press Club sponsored a preview where General Arnold introduced *Memphis Belle* and, over a special radio hookup, General James H. Doolittle addressed the newsmen from London. "I consider this film an important piece of documentary history which has caught the spirit of our air and ground personnel in true and memorable fashion," General Arnold wrote Paramount Pictures' president, Barney Balaban, when Paramount agreed to distribute the film for free and show it in three-quarters of the nation's sixteen thousand theaters.

Together with John Ford's *Battle of Midway* and John Huston's *San Pietro, Memphis Belle* was the most famous of the on-the-spot-reporting documentaries. "These films spoke the language, made facts significant, dramatic," Arthur Knight was to write. "And perhaps because they were created by civilian soldiers rather than the military itself, they never suggested that war was a heroic, glamorous business. It was always a means—a nasty, sordid, murderous but necessary means to a vital end—the preservation of democracy. What was even more laudable, the democracy that they extolled was implicit in the films themselves, ingrained in the spirit of the men who made them." [3] They served a different purpose than Capra's series backgrounding the events leading to the war and the issues at stake.

The war was not over and Wyler was anxious to get back and make another movie. The night before he was to leave for the Italian front, he was waiting in front of the Statler Hotel in Washington for a rare cab when someone got into an argument with the bellhop. The someone apparently won the argument and took off in the only available taxi.

"Goddamn Jew," the fuming bellhop told the next guy in line for a taxi.

"Look, you're saying that to the wrong fellow," Willy told him.

"I didn't mean you, I meant *him,*" the bellhop answered, pointing toward the disappearing cab.

"That doesn't make a goddamn difference," Willy said as he slugged him.

The bellhop was on the sidewalk, people stopped and looked. He picked himself up and disappeared into the lobby. Among the onlookers was a rather stern-faced officer. Willy tried to smile, but the officer asked for his name and went into the hotel also.

When he told Talli what had happened, Willy tried to brush the incident off. As they left together for New York and the last goodbye, Talli had visions of her husband spending the rest of the war on some obscure atoll in the Pacific. "It was nothing," Willy kept saying.

When he was ready to leave for Italy, he was handed a telegram cancelling his orders and telling him to return immediately to Washington. It was signed by General Arnold.

Back in the capital, Wyler was told to report to an air force base, where a stonefaced captain paraphrased his enquiry with the words, "Everything you say here may be held against you."

"You know the articles of war," the captain began, nodding to a private taking everything down in shorthand.

"No."

The captain registered surprise and asked how Wyler had become an officer. Willy told him.

"Sir, did you ever hear the expression, 'Conduct unbecoming an officer and a gentleman?' "

"Yes."

"What does that mean to you?"

"Well, it means what it says, but I'd like to state for the record that I have been a gentleman long before I became an officer."

The captain remained expressionless and asked whether Wyler felt he had legal provocation.

"I sure did, the man said, 'Dirty Jew.' "

"No, *legal* provocation, sir. The only legal provocation for an officer to hit a civilian is self-defense. Would you say this was self-defense?"

"No, I can't say it was."

"Do you wish to add anything, sir?"

"Yes, this kind of thing is one of the reasons I am in uniform and subject to these articles of war."

"Thank you, that's all."

It was not all. Wyler could not join General Eaker in Italy. The next day, he received a firm letter from General Arnold's staff outlining the charges and saying he could choose between court-martial and official reprimand. His first reaction was for court-martial, but officer friends told him he wouldn't have a chance because he *had* hit the man and "without legal provocation."

"Everybody told me to accept the reprimand," Wyler recalled. "Also, a court-martial was going to take a long time. The Allies had just invaded Sicily. I decided to take my friend's advice, received an official letter of reprimand from General Arnold, which was made part of my record, and was finally allowed to take off."

Via Casablanca and Algiers, Wyler flew to Naples where Eaker was now commanding general of all Allied air forces in the Mediterranean. "When I got there, he and other officers *had* heard about the incident. They joked about it. I could sense they understood what had happened and that they rather respected my attitude."

But the Distinguished Service Medal never came through.

25

The use of tactical, as opposed to strategic, air power in support of ground troops was what *Thunderbolt* was about. The documentary was to show how Allied air power, by strafing and bombing enemy lines of communications and supplies hundreds of miles behind the front, broke the stalemate that for months held up the U.S. Fifth and the British Eighth Armies. The Italian campaign was never "the walk in the sun" Winston Churchill had hoped. The Allies landed in Sicily in July 1943, but didn't get to Rome for almost another year. At war's end, hunks of northern Italy were still in German hands.

Thunderbolt wasn't as easy to put together as had been *Memphis Belle* for the simple reason that in a one-seat fighter plane, no one could ride along to film the action.

The Republic P-47 Thunderbolt, which had been in the war in both the USAF and the RAF since 1942, was, together with the Luftwaffe's latest Focke-Wulf 190, the toughest of the fighters, a radical-engined, air-cooled, snubnosed plane which could take more punishment than most fighters and did. Strafing pilots often brought their beloved "seven-ton milk bottles" back full of holes. Toward the end, when most of the high-scoring Luftwaffe aces were either dead or training Hitler's last-stand teen-age pilots, P-47's followed FW-190's to the deck and fought it out, if necessary, at treetop level where the American planes could outturn the German fighters.

When Wyler joined Major General Ira C. Eaker's command at

Caserte, near Naples, he brought with him Lester Koenig, the writer of the *Memphis Belle* narration, and John Sturges, a former David Selznick cutter who had already edited scores of Air Force training films. The trio immediately set to work to rig 16mm cameras on P-47's of the Twelfth Air Force's 57th Fighter Group, based on Corsica during the early stages of the campaign. The Thunderbolts were already fitted with cameras to verify pilot reports of downed enemy aircraft, cameras hooked to the machine-gun trigger. Whenever a pilot began firing, the camera filmed what he was firing at. Wyler's unit, which soon possessed a complete camera shop and a jeep, rigged Eyemo cameras on tails, under wings, and in cockpits with start and stop buttons on the instrument panels so the pilots became camera operators themselves. Wyler's installations were voluntary. Some airmen objected. Cameras, they claimed, brought bad luck.

It was a painstaking way of making a documentary, but exposed footage did trickle in. The points of view were somewhat monotonous and Wyler & Co. tried to figure new places to attach cameras. The ground fighting was bitter and brutal and P-47s were thrown into the battle every day. Field Marshal Albert Kesselring's divisions fought stubbornly and when Supreme Allied Commander Sir Harold Alexander was unable to dislodge German units, he authorized the outflanking maneuver—a landing behind the German lines near the port of Anzio. At first, the tactic seemed successful, but Kesselring launched a furious attack against the Anzio beachhead and the Allies were forced to renew their pressure against the main German positions—including the almost impregnable stronghold near Monte Cassino. The decision in February 1944, to bomb Monte Cassino and the fourteen-hundred-year-old Benedictine monastery on its summit was one of the most controversial of the war. The monastery was reduced to rubble by B-17's, but for weeks the American infantry got no farther.

P-47's were thrown into the battle with new fury. They were equipped with five hundred-pound bombs under each wing and sent farther north to cut railways and to block roads used by the Germans to get men and supplies south.

The camera unit's big difficulty was to get reaction shots—footage of what the Thunderbolts accomplished, and, more daring, footage of the fighters coming in for a strafing or bombing attack. Together with John Sturges, who twenty years later was to direct World War II suspense in *The Great Escape,* Wyler hopped into the jeep to get up to the front and film destroyed bridges and, hopefully, Thunderbolts hammering away on a nearby target. These expeditions for reaction shots took them through shell-scarred olive and fig groves on terrace hillsides to outposts of Alpine-trained U.S. and Canadian troops climbing snowy slopes toward German machine-gun nests. One day in the British sector of the front, Wyler and Sturges persuaded a Yorkshire colonel to take them to his foremost observation post.

"Hit the dirt!" the colonel suddenly yelled, throwing himself to the ground. Artillery shells hit closer and closer. All three men bored their faces into the mud in a ditch. Fifty yards, thirty yards, twenty. The enemy was getting their range. The next one would be it. But the next shell never came. Wyler always had the vision of the German artilleryman asking the man next to him for a match and lighting his cigarette.

Wyler also needed footage of Thunderbolts in the air. He managed to convince General Eaker to assign to the camera unit a North American B-25, a sturdy twin-engined plane which, under General James Doolittle, had become famous for a token bombing of Tokyo in April, 1942, taking off from an aircraft carrier and landing in China. As a "camera ship," the B-25 was ideal. With doors and windows out, cameras could be pointed in almost any direction. The only inconvenience of flying without windows was that the engine noise was deafening.

With the B-25 came Captain Barnett Bartlett, a crazy daredevil of a pilot who had done two tours of combat flying and was now assigned to the low-risk headquarters squadron. Flying a movie director around was not exactly what Bartlett found the most exciting and any chance to do stunts was welcome. To establish their working relationship, Wyler felt a note of caution was necessary. "Look, I don't know anything about flying," Wyler told him. "You know flying. I tell you what I want. I don't want us to get killed and you tell me if you can do it. If you can't, say so. It's not an order when I say what I want."

Bartlett nodded. Since they had no copilot on the camera ship, Wyler usually sat up front next to Bartlett and via the intercom (and over the engine din) did his best to alert the cameraman in the back or the one in the bombardier's seat underneath to upcoming action.

Bartlett's chance to do some "creative flying" came when Wyler decided to film the awesome sight of hundreds of ships in Naples harbor preparing for the invasion of southern France. Going through the proper channels, he got permission from the navy to film the armada.

"I thought it would be a good shot to come from behind Mount Vesuvius, to have the active volcano fill the screen, and coming over it, discover the harbor. I told Bartlett to get behind Vesuvius. He said okay and began to circle the mountain to gain altitude. I didn't tell him *how* high over Vesuvius I wanted to go so when he got on level with the mountain, he just went straight toward the crater and, at the last moment, just over the edge. Maybe eight or ten feet from the crater. What he didn't count on was that over the crater, there was a difference in air current or temperature and the plane dropped. I saw him pull the stick and just make the rim on the other side. All the time, the cameraman below was filming as far back as he could. It was almost the end of us—*our* Arlington cemetery burial in the crater of Vesuvius."

The invasion fleet in the harbor had blimps overhead to guard against air attacks and a strong wind had the balloons pull their cables sideways. When Wyler said he wanted some closer shots of the ships, Bartlett flew the B-25 between the near-diagonal cables, lower and lower until they skimmed the water and Wyler's cameramen filmed *up* at the ships. "There was just enough room to fly between the ship and then there would be a cable and he would tip the plane to avoid having the cable clip a wing off. The goddamndest ride I ever had, but we got some good film."

In late May, the Allies broke Kesselring's defenses and cracked their way beyond Monte Cassino to avenge the humiliation of Anzio. Alexander announced "we are going to destroy the German armies in Italy" and his polyglot troops began preparing for the battle of Rome.

As soon as rumors of Rome's eminent fall reached Caserte, Wyler, Koenig, and Sturges piled film cameras and themselves into the jeep and headed north. Although Hitler and Kesselring cheated them of a major battle by deciding to spare Rome, declaring it an "open city" and abandoning it without a fight, Wyler, Koenig, and Sturges rolled across the city limits on Via Casilina on June 4, only hours behind the first armor and infantry. Before sundown, they reached Piazza Venezia and filmed themselves in martial poses under the Mussolini balcony. Two days later was D-Day, the invasion of Normandy.

In July, the Germans backed into the Umbrian Mountains where they were expected to make a major stand along natural defenses more formidable than the Gustav Line they had held for so long below Rome. Kesselring still had an estimated twenty divisions and the battle of Italy was far from over even if it was overshadowed by the Normandy invasion.

In the fall, Wyler felt he had enough film, at least for a rough cut. With Koenig and Sturges, he flew to London to get into a cutting room and blow up the usable footage to 35mm. The flight was almost their last. The unarmed transport was flying low over liberated France when it was fired upon from the ground. When they landed in London, they were told there were pockets of Germans around the Normandy peninsula who still had food and, obviously, ammunition.

The film looked good and Wyler ordered Koenig and Sturges to Hollywood to cut it and write the narration. As on *Memphis Belle,* Wyler could have gone back to Fort Roach himself, but he didn't want to miss the fall of Berlin. He was living a momentous war and had no difficulty convincing himself he needed additional footage, perhaps of the French campaign. Under Supreme Commander Dwight Eisenhower, Field Marshal Bernard Montgomery was driving north through Amiens toward Brussels and General George Patton was pushing his Third Army toward Reims, a mere hundred miles from the Rhine. On August 15, the Allies had opened the new front with the *débarquement de Provence* and were pushing up the Rhone Valley toward Lyons. In the back of his mind grew the idea of taking part in the liberation of Mulhouse.

With Koenig, Sturges, and the film safely aboard a States-bound cargo plane, Willy obtained orders to proceed to Paris, "enroute to Caserte and General Eaker's command." Paris had been liberated August 25.

After a sentimental trek down Rue de Rivoli past the recent Paris headquarters of German commandant Dietrich von Choltitz to the 100,000 Chemises, he dropped in on Colonel George Stevens. The director of *Gunga Din* was filming for the Sixth Army and welcomed a fellow filmmaker-colonel. They hadn't seen each other since Frank Capra's cooling tower.

"What can I do for you?" Stevens asked after they had told each other what everybody was doing.

"I want to go up to the front and shoot some more film. Do you have anybody you can assign to me, a driver and a jeep?"

"I got a fellow, yes, Leicester Hemingway."

"Hemingway?"

"The kid brother."

The next day, a jeep loaded with film and a camera from Stevens' Sixth Army film unit headed north toward Laon and the front on the Luxembourg-Belgian border. Wyler was in the passenger's seat and Leicester Hemingway was the driver. Seventeen years younger than Ernest, the novelist's brother was a tall daredevil who was never happy unless he was being shot at. As they drove, he told how Ernest was also around somewhere, a war correspondent for *Collier's*. Ernest's part in the liberation of Paris, Leicester proudly related, had consisted of taking possession of the Hotel Ritz in the Place Vendôme. The writer had made no attempt to cover the formal surrender of von Choltitz to General Jacques Leclerc at the Gare Montparnasse, but he had lent his typewriter to the *New York Times* correspondent for the historical dispatch. Although they never ran into the Hemingway party, Leicester and Willy constantly came across people who had seen the author and his irregulars, who included the London *Daily Mail's* Peter Lawless, the Brazilian correspondent Nemo Lucas, Red Pelkey, Jean Décan, and two other Frenchmen, all traveling in a cavalcade of two cars, two jeeps, and a motorcycle. Leicester was proud of his brother and tried to correct the wilder stories— how Ernest had tried to get Patton to give him explosives to mine a road no German traveled or how he shot heads off chickens and had villagers make chicken fricassee. Where there was a war, Ernest would go—and Leicester would try to follow.

When they heard warplanes overhead, Willy and Leicester stopped to turn the camera skyward. Sometimes, the front was solid; at other times, the countryside was a vast no-man's-land. At one point, Willy left Hemingway on the road and, with camera in hand, crawled behind a GI toward an eagle's nest observation post. From up there, they told him, he could see planes coming in to pulverize German positions. The soldier crawled back again, leaving Wyler with another GI inside the observation shack, equipped with a field telephone.

"Nothing happened," Wyler recalled. "I looked out over lovely countryside. I said it looks beautiful. He said, 'It's crawling with Germans.' But you couldn't see anything moving."

Suddenly the phone buzzed. The soldier picked it up and after listening, "Oh shit!" he said.

"What's the matter?"

"We're surrounded."

When Willy could finally speak he managed to ask, "So what do we do?"

"Nothing. We wait."

They waited, scanning the peaceful hillsides and valley below. Half an hour later, the field telephone rang again.

"Yes?" the GI whispered into the mouthpiece. "Okay, thanks!"

Wyler looked at him as he hung up.

"We're not surrounded anymore," the soldier drawled.

The incident stayed burned in Wyler's mind and if he had ever made a war movie, the scene would have been there. "It shows you what suspense is. A momentous war, but not a shot. No planes, no shelling, just quiet. Nothing happens, just two phone calls."

The military situation became confusing. Patton's Third Army wormed its way deeper into Lorraine, but the welcoming crowds thinned out and hostility increased. Among the civil population were thousands of diehard Nazis planted there after 1940 when 35,000 French-speaking citizens had been expelled or deported. Slowly, the war of movement that General Omar Bradley had ushered in after Paris turned into a war of position. It became evident that the closer the Germans were pushed toward home ground, the harder they would fight.

The rains started in October and, it seemed, never stopped. All around were signs of enemy delaying action to harass the flanks of advancing American columns. The Germans sowed mines and set up ambushes. To the north, a daring British push into Holland proved costly. Patton's steamroller got stuck in the mud around Metz.

In December, the Battle of the Bulge was on. Hitler's major and carefully conceived offensive to avert defeat was a blow to the Allies of unsuspected strength. On December 16, 200,000 Germans attacked through the snow with all they had, from specially souped-up tanks to spoiling side attacks, making deep penetrations before Eisenhower in Versailles and Bradley in his Luxembourg headquarters knew what to make of the situation. The German high command accurately assessed and hit the weakest point on the 400-mile front—the eastern Belgian market town of Bastogne. It was not until mid-January that the Battle of the Bulge was won—at a cost of 176,000 casualties, 76,000 of them on the Allied side—and the push through the snow to the Rhine was resumed.

Willy and Leicester were right behind. With blue fingers on steering wheel and camera rewind, they made dolly shots through what was left of Bastogne and interviewed members of the 101st Airborne Division who had parachuted into the beleaguered ruins. Wyler then had Leicester turn the jeep south and head for Bradley's Luxembourg headquarters, which they reached a few days after Ernest had pulled out.

In Luxembourg, Wyler met General Hoyt S. Vanderberg, the young commander of the Ninth Air Force, who immediately wanted a *Memphis Belle* about his force. "One day of good weather and we broke the German offensive," Vandenberg said, and told how his airmen had taken film of their pinpoint bombardment of Bastogne.

"A great picture, I tell you. You can make a great picture for us," the general repeated. Before Wyler could talk himself out of anything, Vandenberg had him on a plane taking captured German officers to London to look at the Ninth Air Force footage (and Leicester put up for an unexpected rest). The film was not impressive and there was not enough footage to make anything. Wyler hitched a ride right back to Luxembourg, apologized to Vandenberg for being unable to make another *Memphis Belle,* and told Leicester to get the jeep ready. The last German resistance around Mulhouse was crumbling, he had heard.

Willy and Leicester rolled south to Strasbourg, where they met another gun-toting novelist with a passion for war—André Malraux. The U.S. forces were making a strategic retreat when Willy and Leicester approached the city, but the French regulars and irregulars refused to pull back for fear of reprisals against Strasbourg and its civil population. The situation was confusing, but Willy was told that a few miles down the road, a "Colonel Berger" and a bunch of Alsatian *maquisards* were holding a part of the front and that what was interesting was that Colonel Berger was really André Malraux.

ABOVE, Willy against a telling
background

LEFT, Charles Bickford in
Hell's Heroes

ABOVE, shooting with padded camera booth in the desert, August 1929

LEFT, Willy with William Boyd and Lupe Velez on Truckee siding where *The Storm* was filmed

ABOVE, *A House Divided* triangle—Walter Huston, Kent Douglass, and Helen Chandler

RIGHT, with John Huston, Long Beach, 1931

ABOVE, Zasu Pitts and Slim Summerville in *Her First Mate*

BELOW, with Elmer Rice on return from Mexico City

The Wylers united in California—Willy and Gaston standing behind Leopold,
Melanie, and Robert, 1929

ABOVE, with John Barrymore in *Counsellor at Law*

BELOW, with Preston Sturges

ABOVE, with Herbert Marshall, Uncle Carl, and Margaret Sullavan on *The Good Fairy* set

BELOW LEFT, Maggie in garden after honeymoon

BELOW RIGHT, Miriam Hopkins, Merle Oberon, and Joel McCrea in *These Three*

ABOVE, with Sam Goldwyn

OPPOSITE PAGE TOP TO BOTTOM, with Gregg Toland; with Walter Huston on *Dodsworth* set; directing Joel McCrea, Allen Jenkins, and Humphrey Bogart in *Dead End*

ABOVE, the "Maggie Club" on *Jezebel* set: Wyler, Leland Hayward, and
Henry Fonda

BELOW, the East Side set in *Dead End*

LEFT, actress Margaret Tallichet

BELOW, with Bette Davis and Fay Bainter on *Jezebel* set

ABOVE, newlyweds and Paul Kohner, 1938

BELOW, Laurence Olivier and Merle Oberon in *Wuthering Heights*

ABOVE, directing Gary Cooper and Walter Brennan in *The Westerner*

BELOW LEFT, the streets of Fort Worth, for *The Westerner* opening

BELOW RIGHT, Bette Davis in *The Letter*

ABOVE, Dan Duryea and Carl Benton Reid in the shaving sequence in *The Little Foxes*

BELOW, deep focus, Herbert Marshall and Bette Davis in *The Little Foxes*

ABOVE LEFT, clowning with Greer Garson on *Mrs. Miniver* set

ABOVE RIGHT, *le repos du guerrier;* with Cathy and Judy, 1943

BELOW, martial Hollywoodites in new uniforms: From left, Wyler, Sy Bartlett, John Huston, and Anatole Litvak

LEFT, with Queen Elizabeth, Bassingbourne, 1943. From left, Wyler, Brig. Gen. Haywood S. Hansel, the Queen, Maj. Gen. Fred Anderson

MIDDLE, with a flier and John Sturges, Corsica, 1944

BOTTOM, the *Memphis Belle's* twenty-fifth mission is completed. Wyler is at center.

The author of *Man's Fate* and his Brigade Alsace-Lorraine were indeed holding a piece of the front on the Rhine, a wild bunch of men all dressed differently. They had one tank and loved their commander.

"Malraux got his supplies from the Americans or the French army, but he would have nothing to do with either of them," Wyler recalled. "He ran his own war. He took me to several of his posts and together we crept to the edge of the Rhine and looked across at the Germans on the other side. There was a fierce loyalty to him wherever we went; all these fellows with old-fashioned rifles and that one tank showed they loved him. I got a feeling that Malraux, too, like Ernest Hemingway, loved war. Anyway, we talked about movies and he was very interested in making a documentary about the war. He said we must meet again after the war. We did, a few times, but nothing came of it."

To talk Alsatian was both funny and moving and Willy was impatient to cover the last 120 kilometers to his home town. Central Alsace, including the Maginot Line stronghold of Colmar, however, was in enemy hands and the 80-mile drive proved to be a 300-mile detour around the Vosges Mountains.

The First French Army had reached Mulhouse November 20. The enemy, however, had quickly recovered and held on to the suburbs of Lutterbach, Pfastatt, and Bourtzwiller. A frozen front was established north of the city proper, and for two months, nothing moved. The civil population lived with artillery thundering overhead. Shells had hammered gaping holes in scores of Old Town houses although Mulhouse came through without total destruction.

As Leicester and Willy snaked in and out of French columns toward town, the First French Army engaged the battle for Colmar. The fighting around Mulhouse flared up, and in a blinding snowstorm the French launched an attack against enemy pockets to the south near St. Louis and the Swiss border. When Willy reached his birthplace, the Germans still held Lutterbach, where fifteen hundred persons had lived sixty feet underground in the old brewery cellars during the two months' shelling.

Willy had Leicester drive right up to the Magasin L. Wyler on Rue du Sauvage. The store was still standing and peering out was Henriette Helm, or Madame Henriette as the Wylers always called the caretaker. The old lady and her family thought it was the most natural thing that Willy should come as an American officer. With Leicester looking on, Madame Henriette kissed the prodigal son and invited them inside.

There was so much to tell, but she became a little sad when she realized Willy was in the Air Force. Why? he asked. Well, one day, long before D-Day and everything, somebody had run down Rue du Sauvage yelling, "The Americans are coming!" When they had asked if he was crazy, he had pointed toward the sky. "Up there, American planes!" The sirens had wailed and the Germans had told them to get into the cellars, but everybody had run out in the street.

"We got a bedsheet, a big bedsheet, and waved it to say hello and then you drop bomb on us."

"Did you think we were coming just to wave to you?" Willy tried. "What did you think?"

"We wanted to welcome you."

"You know you've got factories here working for the Germans, that this is a big railway depot. We're fighting a war, Madame Henriette. We sent leaflets saying get out in the country."

"Yes, but it killed a lot of people. Some bombs fell on the hospital and killed some babies."

She had managed to save the store because Leopold Wyler had been a Swiss national. The authorities had harassed her, but she had carefully obeyed every law. On Hitler's birthday, she had displayed the Führer's picture in the store windows as the law required, but she had always managed to choose the smallest of the pictures the Hitler youths came around and sold every April.

In the evening, she took Willy by the arm and, in the backroom, handed him a bundle of French money. "It belongs to you, to the family," she said. When Willy looked astonished, she explained the money was the Wylers' part of the profits since 1939. At the risk of her life, she had falsified the books and every year buried the money—illegal profits for enemy aliens—under a tree.

The trip to war-ravaged Mulhouse was a voyage into the past and into pain. He went looking for old friends and soon found himself asking information at City Hall.

"I went to see the mayor and asked him where people were. He said, 'Take my advice, don't look for anybody. If you see people you know, be glad they're alive, but don't look for them because you won't find them.' "

When he drove out to Lutterbach, he was told that a week earlier the Germans had gone down into the brewery cellar and picked out sixty men for the Volkssturm. He drove on to the French army roadblock behind Lutterbach and looked across a snowy no-man's-land at the German roadblock a few hundred yards farther away. Between them were a few dead soldiers. Nobody paid attention to the frozen bodies, not even the children.

He went around 43 rue de Brubach to ask for Edmond Cahen. The childhood friend wasn't there, but he was alive, the neighbors said, somewhere in the *maquis*. When Cahen returned two months later, the neighbors told him an American colonel had been looking for him.

Although the temple on Rue de la Synagogue was still standing, the little Jewish community was gone. Some, like Cahen and Paul Jacob, were in the French armed forces; others had disappeared into the camps of the fatherland to which Alsace had been forcefully attached in 1940. The extent of the Jewish holocaust was not yet known—the discovery of Buchenwald, Belsen, and Dachau was still three months away—but Willy felt the chill of empty ranks. Like the Auerbachs. There was no one left of his mother's vast family. Willy followed the mayor's advice and stopped looking for people.

Willy and Leicester wound their way back to Paris where they said good-bye. Hemingway had been on a loanout and rejoined the George Stevens film unit (which was soon to record the concentration-camp horrors).

Willy went to General Carl Spaatz's headquarters only to be told he had been reported missing in action. Nobody had heard from him, he was told, and the missing-in-action report had even appeared in the *Hollywood Reporter*. Frantically, Willy wrote to Talli.

With her friend Mary Loos, a niece of Anita Loos, Talli had taken a trip to Mexico and had never even heard that he was missing.

Spaatz invited Willy to a dinner where Moet & Chardon '28, labeled "Reserviert für die Luftwaffe," was served. Willy took it as an omen of imminent victory that it was the American Luftwaffe that was drinking the champagne.

By the time Willy reached the Eaker headquarters, the home base was no longer outside Naples but two hundred miles to the north, at Grosseto, midway between Livorno and Rome. Everything was there, including the B-25, Captain Bartlett, and—among the letters from Talli—a message from Sturges specifying what kind of shots would enhance the final cut: Corsica and Rome from the air.

The front was above Florence and Pisa, stretching from La Spezia on the Ligurian coast through the Apennines to Ravenna on the Adriatic. The Allies flung out their air force daily in an all-out push toward Genoa and Venice. Once they sent more than two thousand planes over German positions, a welcome sight for infantrymen slogging endlessly up mountains in some of the dreariest and most discouraging fighting of the war. Elsewhere, the news was more heartening. In January, the Russians had taken Warsaw, in February, Budapest, and now the Western Allies had crossed the Rhine into Germany.

Wyler crawled back aboard the B-25 with Bartlett and two cameramen and began making film runs over Corsica and Rome. "Atmosphere shots," he called this footage that wasn't essential to the film but, like the Naples harbor shots, would add to its dimension.

One day shortly before Easter, they had a passenger along, Pilade Levi, a native Roman in the U.S. Army who had earned his captain's stripes planning the battle of Rome that never happened. Since he knew every piazza, street, and alley by heart, he had been attached to the Office of Strategic Service (OSS). He had sketched instant maps for commanding officers during the only skirmish of the taking of Rome, the four-hour fighting at Via Casilina. Levi loved to fly over the Eternal City, down to the coast, and across the shimmering sea to Corsica. They flew back to land at Rome's Ciampino Airport. It was the eve of Passover and Levi wanted to be home by sundown.

The cameraman in the waist of the plane had not managed to get the footage Wyler wanted—shots of Rome, the coastline, and Corsica without distracting wing tips and engine cowlings in the frame and Willy climbed back to shoot the stuff himself.

He stayed in the waist all the way back to Grosseto. Due to engine noise and whining wind, he lost his hearing at one point. It had happened before and the deafness always went away once the plane landed. When they sat down at Grosseto, the hearing didn't pop back. Also—and this was new—he couldn't walk straight. He grinned to airmen hanging around the field who mimicked his drunken walk, but the base flight surgeon didn't think it was funny. The next day, Wyler was flown to the big navy hospital in Naples. After doctors examined him, a nurse scrawled on a piece of paper that he would be sent home. He was deaf.

The next months were to be the low points of his life. How could he direct? And, if his career was over, if he was never to make another picture, how could he live? Deafness, he felt, was worse than blindness since a deaf person was totally cut off from his fellow man.

The nine-day voyage to Boston was aboard a ship filled with war casualties, a floating nightmare of maimed flesh. To keep his sanity, he got the thickest volumes from the ship's little reading room and tried to read the nine days away.

Once on U.S. soil, he lingered at Air Force hospitals in the East, too depressed to write Talli, too deaf to phone her. Slowly, the hearing began to return in the left ear, first noise, then, if people shouted, voices. The diagnosis was the same everywhere—the nerve had been damaged and there was, and still is, no cure for nerve deafness. One doctor suggested the removal of the adenoids to save what hearing was left.

Talli was in the kitchen with Cathy and Judy when the long-distance call came. "Instead of hearing a happy voice, I heard an absolutely dead voice, toneless, without emotions, totally depressed," she recalled. "I was stunned and shocked and couldn't imagine what had gone wrong. It was not the cheerful phone call I had expected for more than a year. He said he was going to have his adenoids removed in hope of improving the hearing. He didn't want me to come East."

When, weeks later, she picked him up at Union Station—he was no longer allowed to fly—nothing had improved. If people were to his left, spoke loudly and only one at a time, he could hear. Melanie was there also, fussing over the returning son.

"It was difficult getting adjusted," Wyler recalled. "You never knew whether the hearing difficulty might affect the marriage. I wasn't sure whether what had worked before might work again. Like in *The Best Years of Our Lives,* the uneasiness of people coming together again, of not feeling comfortable with each other. It was tough getting adjusted, particularly with an injury. It took me a long time to get settled and to make the best of it."

The consultations continued, but all doctors said there was

nothing that could be done. "A nerve is a nerve and that's that," they said. The nerve in the right ear had been destroyed. If only he had had cotton in his ears, anything, on that forty-five-minute flight from Rome to Grosseto. In fact, he should count himself lucky that he could hear at all. With Talli, he visited an Air Force hearing rehabilitation center in Santa Barbara where he was given a sodium pentothal treatment, in case the deafness was caused by emotional shock. "When I came to the hospital to pick him up, he was in a padded cell," Talli remembered. "I had to hold him as he staggered up and down to come out of it. The psychiatrist said firmly that while under the influence of sodium pentothal, Willy had heard what somebody had said two rooms away." Only years later did Talli come to the conclusion that to lie to the wife was part of the treatment.

The hearing never improved. Wyler learned to live with the handicap and even to turn it into a professional advantage, plugging himself into his soundman's microphones. "It's a better way to direct a scene and I recommend it to all directors, even if their hearing is perfect," Wyler said years later. "With no trouble at all, you can hook yourself into the recording and hear the scene on a set of earphones. This way, instead of hearing the scene from behind the camera, you hear it as it appears on the soundtrack.

"Aside from that, being hard of hearing is a big bore. Anyway, I get sixty dollars every month from Uncle Sam—tax free."

26

Few movies have been so well loved by their contemporaries as *The Best Years of Our Lives*. Wyler's most famous film came out of its time and gave voice to what Americans had been saying to themselves without knowing whether others shared their doubts, regrets, and hopes. It was the drama of war's end, of three men's collisions with the realities of the postwar world, and it reflected the tensions, anxieties, and expectations of men and women trying to find each other again. To Wyler, *The Best Years of Our Lives* was a film where he never had to lean back and imagine how his characters would think or react. For the understanding of pain and embarrassment between veterans and their well-intentioned loved ones, he could draw from his and Talli's emotional life—as he did when a wife, unexpectedly seeing her returning husband on the doorstep, exclaims, "Oh, but I look terrible!" He had not, like Harold Russell in the film, lost both hands, but like the amputee, he had come back physically diminished.

The Best Years of Our Lives became a classic of the American screen, a unique glance in the national mirror that was not to be possible a few years later when cold war made self-criticism unpatriotic. It was a film that traced the outer limits of Hollywood filmmaking. It was a worldwide success, even in Germany, where it also rang true. It won prizes everywhere, including seven Academy Awards, and established Wyler as the equal of any director in postwar Hollywood. "The picture was the result of the social forces at work when the war ended," Wyler said in a rare piece of writing published under his name. "In a sense, it was written by events and imposed a responsibility on us to be true to these events and refrain from distorting them to our own ends." [1]

Like his characters, Wyler had come home feeling everything had changed. The war, he said, had been "an escape to reality." This was suddenly another era, imposing another tone, other beliefs and values, other tastes and demands. The movies he and others had made before the war now looked dated, fake, out of touch.

There had been no money in the war, only relationships totally devoid of phoniness. "The only thing that mattered were human relationships; not money, not position, not even family," Wyler said years later. "Only relationships with people who might be dead tomorrow were important. It is a sort of wonderful state of mind. It's too bad it takes a war to create such a condition among men."

World War II was a conflict fought with movies—obsessively. On the homefronts of both sides, audiences flocked to the only existing diversion and movies were shown not only in theaters, but in factories, schools, and union halls. Tens of millions of men at war saw movies endlessly, aboard ships, in barracks and mess halls. Moviegoing was not a habit; it was a compulsion.

Wyler had felt the gap between the reality of war and screen warfare at air bases everywhere. In Corsica, he and a couple of hundred zonked-out airmen sprawled every night to boo the heroics of noble Air Force officers or to howl with lust as Betty Grable or Rita Hayworth crossed the bedsheet screen in bikinis. The airmen were a fantastic audience and the showings an exhilarating twilight trip to total honesty. If anything on the bedsheet became the least corny, the flyers would boo; if anyone was called a war hero, they would laugh or walk out.

Wyler felt that American war journalism was sharp and penetrating. News coverage and photographic techniques, he felt, had practically created a third dimension, giving significance and meaning to the flow of information, from country to country and people to people. Movies were the most international of media, yet they seldom achieved the accuracy of reporting of press and radio.

Like his fellow moviemaking veterans, he found adjustment difficult. At home, however, things were falling into place. In the spring of 1946, he and Talli had their first son, William, Jr., who soon became known to everyone as Billy.

If he didn't share George Stevens' apprehensions about finding a place in postwar Hollywood, Wyler shared his friend's reluctance to plunge head over heels into "civil production." Another ex-colonel, however, couldn't wait—Frank Capra. To Stevens, Wyler, and others, Hollywood was still in the hands of the wrong people. They resented those who had holed up in the studios during the conflict and they saw too many new faces. Tinseltown was at its zenith and 1946 was to be the biggest year in history— eighty million Americans went to the movies every week and the annual box-office gross was edging toward an incredible $2 billion. During the war, when over four hundred movies had rolled off the assembly lines every year, it had been quantity over quality—eighty percent B pictures and twenty percent A. Everybody had made money: cigars waxed fatter and longer than ever and mediocre talent had become as important as quality talent.

Capra was rolling up his shirt sleeves, ready to take on the whole town. The day after VE-Day, he, producer Samuel Briskin, and attorney David Tannenbaum filed papers to incorporate a company they called Liberty Films, Inc. The idea was to unite producer-directors of stature into an independent combine. Everybody listened. To be independent was everybody's dream.

Wyler still owed Samuel Goldwyn a picture and there was *Thunderbolt* to finish. John Sturges and Lester Koenig had assembled a rough cut and the trio quickly finished the documentary even if there was little interest in it. "The damn war stopped on us," they joked to friends as they checked out of the army, Wyler a lieutenant colonel on October 31, 1945.

If writing to the widow of Harold Tannenbaum to tell about her husband's death had been the saddest moment, hearing that Beirne Lay was alive and behind a desk in Washington had Wyler rushing to the telephone.

"It's me, Willy!" he shouted excitedly into the phone when he heard Lay's familiar voice.

"Yeah Willy," Lay drawled matter-of-factly. "What's on your mind." To Beirne, there was nothing extraordinary in having been shot down over France, in having lived as a guerilla with the *maquis* until the Liberation, and to be back behind an army desk again.

259

The War Department offered the forty-four minute *Thunderbolt* to theaters for free, but it sat on the shelf for two years before Monogram Pictures gave it a limited distribution. By 1947, Cassino and Anzio were long, long ago and Wyler could only reflect that he had given one ear for nothing.

Goldwyn was happy to see his premier director back and Wyler was eager to go to work. In 1946, the Wylers had found a new and larger home on Beverly Hills's Summit Drive. It had been Fred Astaire's house and even if they couldn't really afford it, Talli and Willy bought it.

Charles and Oona Chaplin were the next-door neighbors and, until the anti-Communist hysteria drove Chaplin into exile, Cathy and Judy played with the Chaplin daughters while the adults organized Sunday afternoon tennis tournaments. Between sets, Willy told Charlie about his student days in Lausanne and his discovery, with the other boys from the *pensionat,* of Chaplin movies, all rolling with laughter even before the shows started. The tennis afternoons were both fun and play. Years later, Wyler kept, among the Oscar statuettes and other trophies in his study, a plain kitchen mug, decorated by Chaplin, and, in his neat handwriting, inscribed, "The Chaplin-Wyler courts, 1949. Ladies Singles. 1st National Cockamamie Tournaments. Winner Talli Wyler."

Since *The North Star,* which nobody was proud of, Goldwyn's "touch" had not been the most dazzling. In 1944, he had produced—and Elliott Nugent directed—*Up in Arms* and, with David Butler directing, *The Princess and the Pirate.* The following year, Bruce Humberstone had made *Wonder Man* and, as Wyler returned to Formosa Avenue, Norman Z. McLeod was finishing *The Kid from Brooklyn.*

Goldwyn let Wyler pick and choose among projects and properties. One planned feature was an Eisenhower biopic, which, like *Patton* twenty years later, Wyler almost made. Robert Sherwood, who had been the head of the Office of War Information's overseas division and an aide to Franklin D. Roosevelt, was working on a screen treatment. There was a possibility that he and Wyler would go over to Germany to spend some time with Ike. The film would be a feature with an actor playing Dwight Eisenhower. Another project was Robert Nathan's novel *The Bishop's Wife,* but Wyler wasn't interested. The comedy became a Goldwyn produc-

260

tion, with Cary Grant playing the angel sent down to earth to save the marriage of Anglican bishop David Niven and his wife, Loretta Young. George Seaton was fired and rehired several times and the final director credit went to Henry Koster. Wyler read MacKinlay Kantor's *Glory for Me* and told Goldwyn this was what he wanted to make.

Kantor was a prolific journalist and novelist whose specialty was historical fiction, particularly about the American Civil War. In 1940, Leslie Fenton had directed a screen version of *Arouse and Beware* and in 1945, Andrew Marton, who was to be Wyler's most valuable collaborator on *Ben-Hur,* had adapted *Gentle Annie,* a novel set in Oklahoma circa 1900 (adaptations of Kantor's *Andersonville* were to come much later). The writer had been a civilian in the war. According to Goldwyn press agents, the genesis had started with the August 7, 1944 issue of *Time.* The magazine had carried a photo showing a group of homecoming Marines leaning out of windows of a railway car on which had been chalked "Home Again!" The news story suggested that the boys might be returning to their families and jobs with mixed emotions. With that intuitive flash which proverbially strikes movie moguls, Goldwyn snatched up his phone, called Palm Beach, Florida, and, for $12,500, commissioned Kantor to dash off a story treatment. The result was a novel in blank verse, *Glory for Me,* the story of three men coming back to face civilian life.

Kantor had delivered *Glory for Me* to Goldwyn in January 1945. Nine months later, Sherwood and Wyler set to work on a film. Kantor had his three men return to a town he called Boone City (the model was Cincinnati). One of them is Captain Fred Derry, an Eighth Air Force bombardier who was a soda jerk before the war, lived on the wrong side of the tracks with a weak, alcoholic father and a slovenly stepmother. While in training in Texas, he married Marie and had only a few days of marriage before being shipped overseas. His first night home, he finds her making love to an ex-Marine and gives her enough money to get a divorce. Al Stephenson, the second veteran, is a middle-aged man who has been an infantry sergeant. His first night home, he realizes how soft his life will be with his model wife, grown daughter, and teen-age son. He was a banker and will have no difficulty making a living. But the war has changed his outlook and his problem becomes that of reconciling business ethics with a new social conscience. The third serviceman is Homer Parrish, mechanics mate second-class, a nineteen-year-old who became a spastic as a result of combat injuries. Unable to coordinate his movements, he finds himself grotesque and home sheer misery because no one understands him. He also fears that Wilma, his high-school sweetheart, will go through with their planned marriage out of pity. When he drinks, he can coordinate his jerky movements a little better and is on the verge of becoming an alcoholic.

Fred falls in love with Peggy Stephenson, Al's daughter, almost robs her father's bank when he can't find work, and eventually goes into partnership with the drugstore owner for whom he had worked before the war. Al makes a GI loan to a veteran with a shaky credit rating, bringing down the wrath of the bank president about his ears. Al resigns from the bank and goes into partnership "to grow things" with the veteran he has given the bad-risk loan. Homer drinks more heavily, fights with his parents, tries to shoot himself but because of unsteady hands, bungles the attempt. Wilma's love becomes apparent to him and the story ends on a note of hope, with Wilma studying medical texts in order to understand and help him.

With Kantor's novel as a guide, Sherwood and Wyler began to explore the general postwar scene, picking up and discarding aspects they felt could best be ventilated on the screen. Goldwyn was sympathetic and enthusiastic although he cautioned them not to be too radical. At one point, he vetoed a sequence Sherwood had written where GIs stage a riot over lack of decent housing.

Because Wyler wanted to change Homer's war scars, he and Sherwood visited veterans' hospitals. Spastic paralysis, Wyler felt, had to be acted and would always look acted and unconvincing. At a hospital in Pasadena, they were introduced to amputees, including four armless men living together in a bungalow with a male nurse tending to all their needs.

"So you're gonna make a picture about fellows like us," one of them said. "You gonna make a lot of money, eh? Exploit this thing?"

Sherwood said he and Wyler understood the men's feelings and talked about the total honesty they were after for their film. Wyler mentioned an Army Pictorial Service documentary he had seen about Harold Russell, a sergeant who had lost both hands when a dynamite charge exploded prematurely during maneuvers in North Carolina.

"Ah, Harold, we know him!" one of the amputees said. "Lucky guy."

"Why?"

"He's got his elbows. When you've got your elbows, they can put claws on you."

Russell was finally chosen to play Homer, not because he had been fitted with strap-on artificial clamps, but because he had adjusted to what had happened to him. Like Homer, Russell resented anyone feeling sorry for him.

In Ontario, twenty-five miles east of Los Angeles, Wyler had spotted a "graveyard" of bombers and fighter planes constructed too late to be used in the war. "We've got to use this," he told Sherwood, describing the rows of hundreds of stripped-down, engineless Flying Fortresses and other military craft that had never flown. From Broadway, Wyler got hold of George Jenkins to design sets that looked lived in. Jenkins made the sets actually smaller than life size.

Sherwood rewrote Fred Derry's story. Instead of having him discover his wife with another man on the first night, Sherwood allowed the love story between Fred and Peggy Stephenson to develop. Marie would be kept throughout, not so much as the third side of a triangle but as a mute symbol of changed feelings and sensibilities.

"We had to be honest in ending the three stories," Wyler wrote in *The Screen Writer*. "We could not indicate any solution which would work only for a character in a movie. Sherwood felt, for example, that it wasn't a fair solution to let Al Stephenson quit his job at the bank and go into something else where he could avoid 'problems,' because millions of other veterans would have no such easy alternative to a job they did not like. Most men would have to stick with the job and try to change it for the better. So we left Stephenson still working at the bank, having thrown down the gauntlet to the president, and announcing his intention to fight for a more liberal loan policy toward veterans.

"Homer's story demanded a particular resolution in terms of a man who has no hands. We wanted to have a scene in which Homer tells Wilma the reason he has been avoiding her is not that he doesn't love her, but that he doesn't feel it fair to her to

263

marry her. 'You don't know, Wilma,' he says, 'you don't know what it would be like to live with me, to have to face this everyday—every night.' Wilma replies, 'I can only find out by trying, and if it turns out that I haven't courage enough, we'll soon know it.' This was intended to lead to a scene in Homer's bedroom in which, in order to prove his point, he demonstrates his difficulty in undressing, removes his hooks, and explains how helpless he is once they are off.

"The scene affords a good example of how writer and director can function together, for I had to decide whether or not I could do such a scene on the screen. There were delicate problems in bringing a boy and a girl to a bedroom at night with the boy getting into his pajama top, revealing his leather harness which enables him to work his hooks, and finally, taking the harness off. After discussions with Bob, we solved the problems and felt we could play the scene without the slightest suggestion of indelicacy and without presenting Homer's hooks in a shocking or horrifying manner. As a matter of fact, we felt we could do quite the opposite and make it into a moving and tender love scene. Wilma meets the test squarely, makes Homer see that she doesn't mind the hooks, and what she feels for him is not pity, but love."

Director and writer also felt the film should tell veterans not to expect special favors from society. Fred could not, as in *Glory for Me,* fall into a good job, almost by accident. The change allowed Wyler to use his airplane graveyard in Ontario and to create a sequence that was to go straight into the history books. "When Fred decides to leave town in defeat, unable to get a job, no longer married and at odds with Peggy, whom he loves, he goes to the airport to hitch a ride on an army plane," Wyler wrote. "While he waits, he wanders around among endless rows of junked combat fighters and bombers. In long moving shots, made on location at the Army scrapheap for obsolete planes at Ontario, California, we found Fred Derry as he moved through the gigantic graveyard. At once, the parallel was apparent: for four years Fred was trained, disciplined, and formed into a precise human instrument for destruction. Now his work is done, and he, too, has been thrown to the junk pile.

"At this point, we wanted to have Fred Derry relive one of his war experiences, and, as a consequence, have him realize that in order to win his personal battles as a civilian, it was necessary to

264

apply courage and strength of character that he and twelve million others applied to win the war. This was the climax of Fred's story; unlike most movie stories, it had to be resolved in terms of a basic change of attitude, which is always difficult to handle in such an objective medium. 'You'll have to do something cinematic here,' Bob told me. 'I know just what we want to say, but it isn't to be said in words—it must be said with the camera and that's your business.' "

Script and casting were completed by spring of 1946. Although neither Fredric March nor Dana Andrews had been in the war, Wyler agreed they would be right—March, as the middle-aged sergeant-banker and Andrews as Fred Derry. March took the part only because William Powell had been chosen over him for Michael Curtiz's *Life with Father*.

Goldwyn personally undertook to persuade Myrna Loy to play Milly Stephenson. He and Frances had her over for dinner and Sam talked and talked. Actresses made a great mistake to think only of their own roles. What was important, he said, was the whole picture, even if, in this case, she was asked to portray a woman old enough to be Teresa Wright's mother and she would be seen more than heard because her lines were few and far between. Miss Loy surprised the Goldwyns by cheerfully agreeing. She wouldn't mind playing Teresa Wright's mother, she didn't care if the part was small, but . . . William Wyler as the director? "I hear he's a sadist."

Goldwyn rose to Wyler's defense.

"That isn't true. He's just a very mean fellow."

Teresa Wright was given the role of Peggy Stephenson. Virginia Mayo was cast as Marie, Dana Andrews' two-timing wife (and throwback to the vanished world of fly boys, WACS, one-week courtships, and three-day honeymoons of 1942–43). Roman Bohnen and Gladys George were cast as Andrews' father and stepmother, while Cathy O'Donnell, who was soon to be Wyler's sister-in-law, was the "new face" as Wilma.

On the technical side, Gregg Toland was on camera, Daniel Mandell was back in the cutting room, and Gordon Sawyer was the soundman, rigging a headset for Wyler into his recorder. Joseph Boyle was first assistant and Wyler got Lester Koenig a job as production assistant. Filming began April 15 and ended August 9.

Best Years was Toland's first black-and-white film since the war and he and Wyler decided it demanded simple, unaffected realism. "Willy had been thinking a lot, too, during the war," Toland told Koenig in an interview also published in *The Screen Writer*. "He had seen a lot of candid photography and lots of scenes without a camera dolly or boom. He used to go overboard on movement, but he came back with, I think, a better perspective on what was and wasn't important." [2]

Wyler carried the quest for revealing honesty a step further. Myrna Loy, Teresa Wright, and Cathy O'Donnell were sent to department stores with costume designer Irene Sharaff to buy the kind of clothes they would buy and wear in their screen lives, and Wyler asked them to wear them for a few weeks so that the clothes wouldn't look too new.

The Best Years of Our Lives was not cheap. By the time it was finished, Goldwyn had $2.1 million invested in the film. In production over three months, Wyler shot 400,000 feet of film, edited down to 16,000. It was deliciously hard work.

Wyler changed his work method with his actors, and before going into major sequences rehearsed them around a table for a whole day. After reading and discussing a sequence until everyone understood it, he staged each setup, letting the actors indicate which way they felt most comfortable acting it out.

"On the set, before shooting, I rehearse the scene as a whole and each time we go through it, I try to make suggestions for improving it," he wrote in *The Screen Writer*. "I very rarely give actual 'readings' of lines, but rather try to show the actor where he was missing some shade of meaning the writer had intended. Sometimes, the actor shows me where my concept could be improved. I try not to hurry, or give the cast a feeling that I am impatient with them. This is not merely diplomacy. It is a recognition that it is not easy to play a scene well, and that a director cannot hope to go through a brief rehearsal, shoot a take, and let it go at that. I try to be patient because I recognize that filmmaking is a long, slow, detailed process. I have been called a perfectionist, but that hasn't actually been intended as a compliment. I do make a great many takes, when necessary, but there is always a reason. I may not always communicate the reason to the actor, but then, for that too, there is a reason."

Toland had been on the location scouting and sometimes he

and Sherwood went off by themselves to look for exteriors. The writer was happy when he was shown the dilapidated structure that was to be the home of Fred Derry's father and stepmother. One shot of the wretched exterior and there was no need for explanatory dialogue.

The airplane graveyard scene *was* difficult. Sherwood's script described how Fred Derry would climb into the abandoned B-17, then added, "and here Mr. Wyler will have to invent something cinematic." What he invented was, finally, simple and direct.

"We did nothing in the interior of the B-17 except show Fred Derry seated and staring out through the dusty plexiglass," Wyler wrote. "Then, we went to a long exterior shot of the plane, in which we could see the engine nacelles, stripped of engines and propellers. As we panned from nacelle to nacelle you heard motors starting up as though there really were engines in them, and the plane was starting up for takeoff. Then we made another long shot, on a dolly, and also head on. We started moving our dolly in toward the nose of the B-17, through which we could see Fred Derry seated at the bombardier's post. This shot moved in, from a low angle, and, as it moved in, it created the illusion of the plane coming toward the camera, as if for a takeoff. To these shots we planned to add sound effects of engines starting and then let the musical score suggest flight. We then cut inside to a shot of Fred's back, and as we moved in, we saw his hand reach for the bomb release. We continued moving until we reached an effective closeup of Fred, framed against the plexiglass nose of the bomber.

"What made this scene give the audience the feeling that Fred was reliving a specific combat experience was a scene immediately preceding which was designed for the purpose. This was a scene in Fred Derry's home, in which his father was reading aloud from a citation for the Distinguished Flying Cross. The citation gave us not only a capsule form of exposition, but allowed us to make a sharp and ironic comment on Fred's reward for his war record being discouragement and hopelessness, and defeat as a civilian. The reading of the citation tells the audience the story of Fred's determination and courage and the audience remembers it subsequently while Fred sits in the nose of the wrecked B-17. As a result of reliving this experience, Fred decides to take a job as a laborer, which isn't well paid, but which may lead to a future in the building business. And so his story is resolved, not by letting him have a good job, but by a change in his attitude to a realistic appraisal of himself in relation to the time in which he lives."

Talli visited the set with the girls. Seven-year-old Cathy and four-year-old Judy made their screen debut, two little girls in the drugstore scene with Dana Andrews.

As in *The Little Foxes,* Toland's deep focus meant action and reaction in the same shot, which, in turn, meant fewer and longer scenes. As André Brazin noted when *Les Plus belles années de notre vie* reached Paris, it contained fewer than two hundred shots, whereas the average film would have three to four hundred shots per hour. Wyler felt that conventional staging would be dishonest, that his function was to allow his audiences to make up their own minds about where to look. Honesty meant playing with the cards on the table. It meant being explicit and staging everything with transparent clarity. If script, camerawork, costumes, and sets were honest, his own *mise en scène* would also have to be, yes, democratic. They were making a movie about returning soldiers and the collision of their ideals with a less-than-perfect world in peace, not civilian propaganda.

Deep focus and longer scenes made it possible to put currents of feelings and opposing sentiments on the screen in almost geometric patterns. More important, such staging allowed several simultaneous pools of interests. If audiences had to divide their attention, they would have to apply critical judgment to the screen. They would have to think. To make people think was the whole purpose of *Best Years.*

Two scenes were to become famous—the bar sequence where Fred phones to break up with Peggy Stephenson and the Homer–Wilma wedding. In the first, Al Stephenson, Fred Derry, and Homer Parrish are together, Al and Fred at the bar where Al persuades the former airman to break with his daughter and Homer at the piano, trying to play with his hooks. Al urges Fred to call his daughter right away and Fred crosses to the booth at the other end of the bar to phone her. Al leans on the piano and appears to be interested in Homer's musical exercises. The famous shot starts on the piano keys and Homer's hooks, tilts up to frame Fredric March in a foreground close shot and, in the background, Dana Andrews in the booth. The shot is constructed with two dramatic centers of interest—Homer's odd piano playing and, in the depth of focus, the real dramatic crux—Fred on the telephone.

Traditional direction would demand a cut to the booth to hear what Fred is telling Peggy and to see his emotions (many directors would even cut to Peggy's face at the other end of the line), but Wyler stays—interminably, in the master shot, and makes March in the center an odd pivot of apprehension. Wyler has March look toward the booth a few times as if trying to guess what is going on. At the end, Andrews hangs up and, without coming toward March and Russell, leaves the bar.

At the wedding of Homer and Wilma toward the end of the film, Fred and Peggy are among the guests. It is their first meeting since the breakup. Peggy is there with her parents and Fred is the best man. In the beginning of a long shot in which Wyler has two equal actions coexist until one overwhelms the other, the audience's attention is quite naturally on the ceremony—Wilma, all in white and nervous, Homer painstakingly passing the ring onto her finger with his articulated hooks. After a while, the attention veers toward Teresa Wright and Dana Andrews toward the left of the frame. Wyler moves his actors with consummate skill and plays much of the dramatic shift on Miss Wright's eyes, pulling Fred and Peggy out of the mass of guests and making us feel they *must* be thinking of the same thing.

Wyler had *Best Years* ready in November, with music by San Francisco-born Hugo Friedhofer, and Goldwyn arranged a January booking at the Hollywood Pantages.

"My God, aren't you going to get it out to qualify?" Wyler asked Goldwyn, referring to the Academy rule that to qualify, a film must play two weeks for paying audiences in greater Los Angeles before the end of the calendar year.

"I have a good booking. Do you think it'll win anything?"

"Let's try, maybe."

Goldwyn changed his booking.

Best Years opened in New York November 22, replacing Laurence Olivier's *Henry V* at the Astor, with especially jacked-up prices ($2.40 on weekends for reserved seats). It became a phenomenal success with critics and public alike, earning $11 million in the U.S. and Canada during its first years in release and, in Great Britain, outgrossing *Gone With the Wind*. "It is seldom that there comes a motion picture which can be wholly and enthusiastically endorsed not only as superlative entertainment but as food for quiet and humanizing thought," Bosley Crowther wrote. "Having to do with a subject of large moment—the veterans home from war—and cut, as it were, from the heart-wood of contemporary American life, this film from the Samuel Goldwyn studio does a great deal more, even, than the above. It gives off a warm glow of affection for everyday, down-to-earth folks." [3] Crowther returned to *Best Years* the following Sunday, and on December 30, the picture received a New York Film Critics Best Movie of the Year award. On March 11, President and Mrs. Harry Truman attended the Washington premiere with Robert Sherwood and Willy's wartime commander, Major General Carl Spaatz, also in the VIP audience. Two nights later, *Best Years* nearly swept the entire Oscar slate. Besides Best Picture, Academy Awards went to Wyler, Fredric March, Harold Russell, Bob Sherwood, Daniel Mandell, and Hugo Friedhofer.* The next day, the congratulatory telegrams began pouring in from friends and studio bosses, wires signed Preston, Bette, David Niven, Vivien and Larry, David Selznick, Darryl Zanuck, Dore Schary, and Jack Warner. Newspaper editorials continued. "*The Best Years of Our Lives,*" the *Los Angeles Times* said, "represents the better American spirit. It deserves to be seen by people throughout today's chaotic world. It typifies the kind of life most people know and understand in this country. It is not linked with the gangsters and racketeering so often exploited in the homegrown cinemas, and which give such a false idea of America."

The honors and affection continued abroad. The film received the first British Academy Award as Best Picture, British or foreign, and the French Victoire Award. It ran sixty weeks in London, seventeen in Stockholm, nineteen in Rio de Janeiro, twenty-nine in Sidney, and seventeen in Buenos Aires.

James Agee wrote a review so long it had to be printed in two successive issues of *The Nation,* saying Wyler "has come back from the war with a style of great purity, directness and warmth, about as cleanly devoid of mannerism, haste, superfluous motion, aesthetic or emotional overreaching as any I know; and I felt complete confidence, as I watched this work, that he could have

---

* Olivia de Havilland won the Best Actress award for Mitchell Leisen's *To Each His Own. Best Years* was also nominated for Best Sound, but Gordon Sawyer was the only miss.

handled any degree to which this material might have been matured as well as or even better than the job he was given to do."[4] Agee didn't like the story and reasoned its shortcomings were Sherwood's. "At its worst, this story is very annoying in its patness, its timidity, its slithering attempts to pretend to face and by that pretense to dodge in the most shameful way possible its own fullest meanings and possibilities," he wrote, while at the same time praising Sherwood's lines. "Although the dialogue has a continuous sheen of entertainment slickness, it is also notably well-differentiated, efficient, free of tricks of snap and punch and overdesign, and modest in its feeling for how much weight it should carry on the screen; and most of the time, there is an openness about the writing which I don't doubt every good screenwriter tries for but which few achieve. By openness, I mean simply that the scenes are so planned, and the lines so laid down that every action and reaction, every motion and everything that is seen, is more centrally eloquent than the spoken lines. The movie thus has and takes its chance to be born in front of the camera, whereas the general run of screenplays force what takes place before the camera to be a mere redigestion of a predigestion.

William Wyler has always seemed to me an exceedingly sincere and good director; now he seems one of the few great ones," Agee said, concluding, "I can hardly expect that anyone who reads this will like the film as well as I do. It is easy, and true, to say that it suggests the limitations which will be inevitable in any Hollywood film no matter how skillful and sincere. But it is also a great pleasure, and equally true, to say that it shows what can be done in the factory by people of adequate talent when they get, or manage to make themselves, the chance."

Best Years became a touchstone in the evolution of French criticism and provoked one of the most penetrating critical essays in film history.

While Roger Leenhardt shouted *A Bas Ford, Vive Wyler!* and Georges Sadoul called *Les Plus belles années de notre vie* the most characteristic of American postwar films, André Bazin wrote a twenty-two page critique that was to reverberate through *cinéphile* circles and little magazines during the 1950s as a textbook essay looking beyond content to form and structure.

Form over content was a Gallic discovery. Whereas Anglo-Saxon critics continued to grade movies according to their social values, the French looked with increasing fascination on film form. Too much attention, they said, was paid to grand humanistic themes (à la Welles and Chaplin) and not enough to style, to the way things were said, to *how* the medium was used. In Paris, the "grammar" of cinematic language was reexamined with both scholastic vigor and arduous enthusiasm, and even in disagreement, French critics often came closer to understanding how movies worked than many professionals. Gilbert Cohen-Séat would write that the movies' special suggestivity created a state of emotionality that, instead of heightening the mental level of their audiences, enslaved human faculties with a series of psychological "tensions" and miseries. Jean Carta postulated that this degrading effect could be overcome. "A movie is humanistic," he said, "when it is made in such a way as not to enslave its spectators but, on the contrary, when it gives them a chance to free themselves from its spell so they can judge." Eisenstein, who was still the chief theoretician, was declared the chief villain. Eisenstein and his followers saw in movies the supreme tool of manipulation, of thought control. Adding the voyeur impulse to the director's arsenal of audience control, Alfred Hitchcock was found to be another Stalinistic paternalist.

The means of humanizing the movies was found in the theories of a Marxist playwright. Bertolt Brecht had not wanted to "fascinate" his proletarian theater audiences, but on the contrary, to make them sit up and criticize. To achieve this, he deliberately "alienated" his theatergoers, breaking whatever fascination for the characters they might have with direct speech to the audience, songs, placecards, etc. But the Brechtian *Verfremdungseffekt* was hard to transpose to the screen because any deliberate break of what Cohen-Séat called the projection-identification had the effect of a power failure—the magic was destroyed and management alerted by whistling and catcalls. The key to lucid participation and humanism was found in the films of Orson Welles and William Wyler. Both forced audiences to judge between simultaneous actions. By making two actions conflict, they forced their audiences to choose—to apply critical judgment to the screen. In his long essay, Bazin put Wyler ahead of Welles.

Bazin's essay—inexplicably omitted from Hugh Gray's translated collection of his work—was called *William Wyler ou le jan-*

272

*seniste de la mise en scène.** Analyzing Wyler's body of work, Bazin finds that each film is different, that the plastic form of *Best Years* has little in common with that of *The Letter,* and that the ingenuity with which Wyler stages "climactic scenes" varies with the dramatic content. Unlike Ford, with his hell-bent-for-leather rides, Tay Garnett, with his fist fights, or René Clair, with marriages and chase sequences, Wyler does not try to accumulate permanent and repeated themes. He has neither favorite sets nor favorite landscapes, but does seem to prefer psychological stories playing on a background of social conflict. Despite the disparity of Wyler's source material, says Bazin, it is simple to recognize a Wyler film in a few shots because his "signature" is as visible as Ford's, Fritz Lang's, or Hitchcock's. Capra, Ford, and Lang are not above imitating themselves. "There is a John Ford style and a John Ford manner. Wyler only has a style, which protects him from aping, even by himself. The only way to imitate Wyler would be to embrace the directorial ethics of which *Best Years* offers the purest results. Wyler cannot have imitators, only disciples."

Bazin admits that the directing in *Best Years* is styleless, that Wyler's direction tries to cancel itself out, but that carried to its own extreme, such stripping away (*dépouillement*) allows the dramatic structure and acting to shine with maximum force and clarity. Bazin spends two pages on the Herbert Marshall–Bette Davis scene in *The Little Foxes,* saying that because Wyler does not move the camera or cut to the dying husband stumbling upstairs, the shot is twice as effective. A lesser director, he says, would have tried to "cinematize" the Lillian Hellman play, but that such efforts would have lowered, not heightened, the dramatic voltage. Thanks to the framing and the ideal coordinates of

*An unyieldy title since Jansenism in contemporary French thought refers less to the theological principles of Cornelius Jansen, the seventeenth-century Dutch churchman condemned as heretical (for maintaining that human nature is incapable of good and for emphasizing predestination over free will) than to René Descartes' desire for austerity and ordered, if slightly subversive, behavior. By calling Wyler a directorial Jansenist, Bazin meant to qualify him as a filmmaker of stern virtues, order, and a certain artistic *hauteur*. André Bazin's *What Is Cinema*, Vols. 1 and 2, selected and translated by Hugh Gray, was published by University of California Press, Berkeley and Los Angeles, in 1967. *William Wyler ou le janseniste de la mise en scène* first appeared in *Revue du Cinéma*, in 1948, and appeared in the first volume of the 1958 edition of *Qu'est-ce que le cinéma*.

the dramatic geometry, it is the camera that organizes the action.

Coming to *Best Years,* Bazin says the deep focus liberates its audience, that deep focus here is democratic and therefore worthy of the subject. He analyzes the difference of the *mise en scène* that Welles, Jean Renoir, and Wyler use. In *La Règle du jeu,* Renoir used simultaneous and "lateral" staging in the castle sequence to make audiences feel the interaction of various intrigues, while Welles seeks either a "tyrannical objective à la Dos Passos" or a kind of rubber-band effect, by which he can first extend reality then let it slap in our faces. In *Citizen Kane,* says Bazin, Welles uses Toland's deep focus to heighten the suspense with fleeing perspectives, low-angle foreshortening, etc., in order to provoke and torture. "Welles' sadism and Renoir's ironic anxiety have no place in *Best Years.* The point is not to provoke the spectator, to put him on the rack and torture him. All Wyler wants is that the spectator can (1) see everything; and (2) choose as he pleases. It's an act of loyalty toward the spectator, an attempt at dramatic honesty."

Bazin feels Wyler's *mise en scène*—"liberal and democratic as the conscience of American audiences and the heroes on the screen"—is the filmic equivalent of what André Gide and Roger Martin du Gard tried to accomplish in literature—perfect neutrality and transparency of style without coloration or refraction between the reader's mind and the story. This demands a new kind of *découpage,* of cutting scenes up into shots. Cutting a dramatic unity into shots is always an arbitrary operation, says Bazin, and long setups force a director to concentrate all his efforts on the direction of his actors.

Bazin analyzes in detail the bar sequence and the Homer–Wilma wedding and finds that Wyler's directing—the staging of the action and the positioning of the actors within the frame—are like an equation, that the dramatic punch is drawn in geometrical lines. This is nothing new, Bazin says; everybody knows that in directing conflict, the dominating character is placed higher than the character he dominates. Wyler, Bazin contends, has discovered his own laws and managed to give deep focus a fresh dimension. The Herbert Marshall–Bette Davis scene in *The Little Foxes* is an example of how Wyler manages to make a scene "turn" entirely on the actors. In the Homer–Wilma wedding scene, Bazin believes he has found the key to Wylerian *mise en scène.* The skeleton of Wyler's direction is in the characters' eyes, in *where* they look. Following the actors' glances is following the author's intentions. "All the dramatic joints are so fine-tuned that the direction of a pair of eyes shifted only a few degrees is not only legible even for the dullest of spectators, but capable of toppling a whole scene," Bazin wrote about *Best Years.*

"What is perhaps the innate nature of perfected directing is that it knows how to avoid building on pre-established aesthetics. Here, Wyler also incarnates the opposite of Orson Welles who leaped onto cinema in one bound with the intention of using it for certain effects. Wyler toiled a long time on obscure westerns, whose titles nobody can remember. It is through professionalism, not as esthete but as craftsman, that he has become the consummate artist, which *Dodsworth* already asserted. When we talk about his direction, we must keep in mind that this is conceived for the spectator, that his first and only worry is to make audiences *understand*—as strongly as possible—what is going on. The immense talent of Wyler lies in his knowledge that to simplify is to clarify and in his humility toward both subject and audience. When it comes to things cinematic, he has a kind of professional genius which allows him to carry his sparing means to the point where he can invent, paradoxically, one of today's most personal styles of cinema."

When, shortly before his death in 1959, Bazin went over his text again in preparation for its inclusion in a book of his essays, he felt he had to readjust his enthusiasm downward, as it were. Yet, he wrote, it was still possible to distinguish the inherent values of Ford and Wyler, for example, and to make an abstraction of their individual aesthetics. "It is thus possible still to prefer the 'written cinema' [cinéma-écriture] of certain Wyler films over John Ford's spectacular cinema," Bazin said.

PART FIVE

Eclectic Patterns

27

Liberty Films was a noble failure. It was an attempt at tilting financial windmills in favor of creativity instead of money; it ended with a sellout because one picture didn't make it. In historical perspective, Liberty Films' only fault was being ahead of its time. Twenty years later, independent production companies were the rule, not the exception.

Liberty Films started as "the great experiment" in freedom when Frank Capra, George Stevens, Wyler, and Capra's business associate, Sam Briskin, went into partnership and made a deal with Radio-Keith-Orpheum (RKO) to make nine films independently, involving expenditures of over $15 million. The new company provoked much comment and many imitators. Others sought to affiliate with the four ex-colonels—president Capra, vice-presidents Stevens and Wyler, and secretary-treasurer Briskin —and the new company was offered deals by MGM, J. Arthur Rank, Goldwyn, Selznick, United Artists, and RKO. They signed with RKO for three films from each producer-director. Wyler, Stevens, and Capra each received $3,000 a week from the day RKO signed and Briskin received $1,500 a week as business head for the company. President Capra owned thirty-two percent of the company stock, Stevens and Wyler had twenty-five percent each, and Briskin eighteen percent. But the voting rights were equal. It took three out of four votes to resolve such major decisions as hiring a star or buying a story. Once purchased, however, the story was assigned to Capra, Stevens, or Wyler who, from that point, worked autonomously, functioning as producer–director without interference from the others. RKO advanced the cost of physical facilities—rental of offices, studio space, and equipment—and Liberty Films moved into a swank bungalow on the center court of RKO's studios.

Goldwyn tried to stop Wyler. "I guess he believed I'd never leave him; he had a sort of father complex," Wyler recalled. "I just wanted to join Capra, Stevens, and Briskin in this very attractive new idea. For years, Goldwyn came back to me with some of the films he made after that; *Porgy and Bess,* I remember. He offered his projects to me first, but I was engaged elsewhere and I didn't want to go back to the old Goldwyn days."

The first Liberty film was Capra's *It's a Wonderful Life,* a Christmas comedy in Capra's prewar vein, which went into production a week after Wyler started *Best Years* for Goldwyn. To launch the first Liberty film, Capra, Wyler, Stevens, and Briskin invited all the stars and near-stars they had ever used in their films to a dinner-dance and a showing of *It's a Wonderful Life,* starring James Stewart and Capra's prewar stock company—Thomas Mitchell, H. B. Warner, Beulah Bondi, and Frank Faylen. *Time* called it "a pretty wonderful movie," saying that for the upcoming Oscars, it had only one formidable rival—*The Best Years of Our Lives.* Capra's exuberant and sentimental film opened "soft" however, and remained a box-office disappointment.

One down and eight to go. Capra put down a hefty deposit on the Howard Lindsay–Russell Crouse stage hit, *State of the Union,* and bought Jessamyn West's novel about Quakers, *Friendly Persuasion.* He soon had two writers on *State of the Union* and another doing a first-draft screenplay of *Friendly Persuasion.* Wyler was thinking of taking Talli on a trip to Europe and Stevens felt that although he wasn't ready, it was his turn.

"I went to work on a comedy, a social comedy, which was to star Ingrid Bergman," Stevens remembered. "It wasn't what I felt like doing, but I thought that this was the kind of film that I should do. And Ingrid was ready to do a comedy."

Jo Swerling—Wyler's coscenarist on *The Westerner* and Capra's cowriter on *It's a Wonderful Life*—was knocking Stevens' comedy into shape. Working on the script on the train to New York, Stevens took it to Miss Bergman, starring on Broadway in

St. Joan, but when he met her, he told her the project didn't feel right. He returned to his partners in Culver City and told them he would have to be honest with himself and do a picture he had real feeling for, something "that my present state of mind will allow me to believe in."

That something turned out to be John Van Druten's 1944 play *I Remember Mama,* set in the San Francisco Stevens had been raised in. "I knew what the city looked like and I knew who these people were, and it was a story of the confirmed period of the past and disassociated from all of the unresolved present."

Meanwhile, Liberty Films developed into an expensive proposition.

Wyler had been handsomely paid for *Best Years,* but besides the lieutenant colonel's pay, it was the first money since 1941. Wyler had twenty percent of the profits and Goldwyn had given Robert Sherwood five percent, but in 1958, Wyler sued for $408,356 which he said was due him. The highly technical suit was over Goldwyn's bookkeeping. The producer added the percentages of the profits paid to Sherwood and Wyler to the film's negative cost, meaning that the more money *Best Years* made the higher the "break-even point" and the less the actual percentages of the earnings going to writer and director. Goldwyn claimed Wyler got $1.4 million for *Best Years,* but nevertheless settled for an undisclosed sum shortly before the suit was to go before the courts in 1962.

While Capra and Briskin wrestled to get *State of the Union* off the ground, Wyler took Talli on her first trip abroad. Leaving Cathy, Judy, and Billy in the care of a nurse and both grandmas, the Wylers took the train to New York, bought a new '47 Buick and had it put aboard the ship with them to Southampton.

"There were few cars in Europe in 1947," Wyler remembered. "The Buick was the first car with automatic transmission, power windows, and roll-down top. When a cabdriver in Paris came over to give me hell, I pushed the button. The window went up in front of his face and he nearly fainted. In little towns, I'd wait until there was a good crowd, than I'd press the button and the top would go back. It was pandemonium, people came running. A kid once asked me if the car was amphibious, too."

The itinerary was over familiar ground as husband showed wife the echoes of his war experiences, retracing the route from London to the Alsatian byways Leicester Hemingway and he had traveled behind General Patton's armor and André Malraux's freebooters two years earlier. In London, it was a reunion with old friends, Larry and Vivien, Carol and Pempie Reed. Olivier took them with him to Denham studios where he was producing, directing, and starring in *Hamlet,* allowing Willy a crack that reached the columnists at home. Willy asked him, "How does it feel to come on the set and start the day with, 'Okay, camera here, three inch lens. Big closeup of me!'"

In Paris, it was the discovery of the Italian cinema—Roberto Rossellini and Vittorio de Sica. *Rome, Open City* and *Shoeshine* especially impressed. Neorealism was what he, himself, had been after in *Best Years,* but the Italians had gone much further in their search for voracious immediacy and rough narratives. This was putting a country's experience on record, it was building a national cinema out of recent history.

In southern France, some bridges were still bombed out and the Buick had to be pulled across rivers on barges. The summer was hot and the country roads so empty, the Wylers often stopped at rivers and lakes, took off their clothes, and went swimming. In Mulhouse, it was introducing Talli to people and places she had so often heard about.

They rolled north toward Strasbourg and, in Riquewehr, where Willy wanted Talli to taste the Gewürztraminer wine, they ran into Malraux's former chief of staff. Germany was across the Rhine, but it was only in April 1950 that they made it to the Berlin that the "tin ear" had made Willy miss on VE-Day.

"In London now and then you'd see a bombed-out building, in Berlin now and then you'd see a house standing," Wyler recalled. "People hadn't learned anything. They complained about our bombing and about how the Russians acted, and never seemed to realize they had started the whole thing themselves. They hated the Russians and could only think of Russians raping some of their women and stealing their wristwatches, when they had killed millions and millions of Russians." Wyler wanted to push on to the Soviet Union, but was not to visit Moscow until 1962.

On Kurfürstendamm, he couldn't help plunking down two marks to catch a glimpse of *Die Besten Jahre unseres Lebens.* "The dubbed version was very good. You got the impression it was about German soldiers returning home. I wanted to see one reel only, but sat through the whole picture. It was like a different film altogether."

When the Wylers returned to Hollywood, the future of Liberty Films looked less than promising. When RKO had backed off the $2.7-million budget of *State of the Union* over Spencer Tracy's salary, MGM picked up the project. "We'll loan Tracy to Liberty Films," Louis B. Mayer told Capra, "if Liberty makes the picture at our studio. We'll release it as an MGM picture and that'll still keep Tracy under our banner." When Claudette Colbert, Capra's leading lady from *It Happened One Night,* refused to sign the contract unless Capra guaranteed she would never work past five o'clock, she was replaced by Katharine Hepburn. The other stars were Adolphe Menjou, Van Johnson, and Angela Lansbury.

But it was not to be the year for political satire. President Harry Truman's course had been set when he established his Temporary Commission on Employee Loyalty in November 1946, when he needed not only spiritual but tactical backing for the devil theory of communism. He sought the advice of Arthur Vandenberg, the only paladin he trusted in the Senate. Vandenberg's counsel was famous; "Scare the hell out of the country, Harry." Truman was to regret the excesses four years later, when anti-Communist hysteria had produced not only Joseph McCarthy but McCarthyism.

Not to be outdone, the House Committee on Un-American Activities (HUAC) remembered Hollywood's prewar radical chic, rallies for Spain, the near-underground organizing of the Screen Writers' Guild, the Federal Theater and Writers' Project, which HUAC chairman J. Parnell Thomas had termed "sheer propaganda for Communism or the New Deal." On October 18, Thomas assembled his committee in Washington to conduct "an investigation of Communism in motion pictures." The hearings gave HUAC what it needed most—publicity. Among the all-star cast there was the impeccably tailored Adolphe Menjou telling committee member Richard Nixon that anyone who listened to Paul Robeson "singing his Communist songs" ought to be ashamed, that Hollywood was "a world center of Communism" and that a Communist invasion might be imminent, aided and abetted by certain stars, writers, and directors. Gary Cooper declared that Hollywood Communists had dared to tell him, "America would be better off without a Congress," a remark that brought the house down. Ronald Reagan delivered an eloquent speech against Communist infiltration in California, and Robert Taylor defended himself by declaring that "Roosevelt aides" had instructed him to play in MGM's 1943 *Song of Russia* because it showed little children smiling, "one of the stock propaganda tricks of the Communists." Most memorable was the testimony of Ginger Rogers' mother, who criticized Dalton Trumbo's *Tender Comrade* as subversive because her daughter had been compelled to say: "Share and share alike—that's democracy." Mrs. Rogers further testified her daughter had turned down *Sister Carrie* "because it was just as open propaganda as [Clifford Odets'] *None But the Lonely Heart*." Four years later, Wyler brought the Theodore Dreiser classic to the screen, but he never offered the role of Carrie to Ginger Rogers.

Of the nineteen "unfriendly" witnesses, only eleven were called to the stand—the Hollywood Ten plus Bertolt Brecht, who, in some German-English mumblings, completely bewildered the committee. Some of the best material never got a hearing because testimony of the Ten was barred, although Trumbo managed to yell into network microphones that this was the beginning of concentration camps in America and John Howard Lawson, the first president of the Screen Writers' Guild, shoehorned in the remark, "I'm not on trial here, Mr. Chairman. This Committee is on trial before the American people. Let's get that straight."

Within days, Dmytryk, who had just directed *Crossfire* about anti-Semitism in the U.S. Army, and Adrian Scott, who had produced it, were fired by RKO. Twentieth Century–Fox announced it would "dispense with the services" of Ring Lardner, Jr., and MGM fired Lester Cole and Trumbo. The other five—Alvah Bessie, Herbert Biberman, Albert Maltz, Lawson, and Sam Ornitz—could not be fired since they were not under contract. In November, the studio heads—Mayer, Goldwyn, Harry and Jack Cohn, Dore Schary, Spyros Skouras, *et al.*—met at the Waldorf Astoria in New York and agreed on a blacklist which eventually grew to about two hundred and fifty names. On December 5, a Washington grand jury indicted the Ten for contempt of Congress, and six months later they all went to jail, after the Supreme Court, peppered with some of the most eloquent briefs in legal annals and pleas from everyone from Laurence Olivier to George Bernard Shaw, refused to review appeals by Trumbo and Lawson. The Ten had one wonderful moment—to the Danbury Penitentiary in Connecticut where Lardner and Cole served their ten months was sent HUAC chairman Thomas for embezzlement of public funds.*

At the conclusion of the Washington hearings, Menjou reported back to *State of the Union.* He now called Katharine Hepburn a do-gooder. "Scratch do-gooders like Hepburn," he muttered, "and they'll yell *Pravda.*" [1] To cool tempers and get on with the shooting, Capra closed the set, but Menjou managed to give the *Los Angeles Examiner* a setside interview in which he "resumed his explosive assaults on producers, directors, writers, and actors who have reputedly become involved in subversive activities." [2] In early December, they all foregathered at Forest Lawn cemetery to bury the greatest nonpolitical subversive of them all—Ernst Lubitsch, felled by a heart attack at fifty-five. Together with Walter Reisch and Marlene Dietrich, "the sultan of satire" was to have seen *Le Diable au corps* at the Wylers'. Marlene, whose instinct for casting made Lubitsch listen, had described Gérard Philipe in Claude Autant-Lara's daring new film and Talli had organized the screening for November 30. Friends had called friends, Billy Wilder and Charles Brackett were there, together with the Paul Kohners, Mervyn Le Roy, Mary Loos, Otto Preminger, Gottfried Reinhardt, Walter Wanger, Miklos Rozsa, and Michael Romanoff, but Lubitsch didn't come. He had died in the afternoon. They had run *Le Diable au corps* and sadly agreed that Philipe would have been perfect for the part of the young Octavian in Lubitsch's planned remake of *Rosenkavalier.*

As Menjou predicted, the witchhunt tore Hollywood wide open. At stormy Directors' Guild meetings, Cecil B. DeMille was the rallying point of the right-wingers. Leo McCarey had testified in Washington and Sam Wood repeated his allegation that Katharine Hepburn had helped raise $87,000 for a very special political party, which, he added, "certainly wasn't the Boy Scouts." To hunt down leftists of every creed, Wood organized the Motion Picture Alliance for the Preservation of American Ideals.

Wyler, John Huston, and Phillip Dunne were the less conspic-

---

* MGM, Warners, Columbia, and Universal eventually settled the suits of Trumbo and Cole, but the Ten had spent $150,000 in three years in the courts. In 1955, Fox settled Lardner's breach of contract suit for $10,000—the only individual victory. With the exception of Dmytryk, who recanted after his release from prison, all had to survive on a black market, where credits were pseudonymous and bargaining positions the weakest.

uous counterforce. They formed the Committee for the First Amendment—an organization soon listed by the California Un-American Activities Committee as a "Communist front."

Wyler was appalled, especially at the foreign-borns like himself —Jack Warner, Goldwyn, and even Capra—wrapping themselves in the righteous mantle of superpatriotism. The grand fight within the Directors' Guild was over DeMille and his group of right wingers trying to get control.

"With our Committee for the First Amendment, we tried to defend the *principle* of the secret ballot. We tried to defend not so much the Ten as a person's right to keep his political beliefs to himself, that no one would have to disclose whether he was a Communist. We tried to stand up and defend political affiliation. I remember we did try to urge some of the Ten to disclose their political beliefs to the press, but not to the Un-American Activities committee, before going to jail. I knew we were on the right side of things, but we were not able to fight the whole mood of the McCarthy era." The committee's credo said, "Any investigation into the political beliefs of the individual is contrary to the basic principles of our democracy. Any attempts to curb freedom of expression and to set arbitrary standards of Americanism is in itself disloyal to both the spirit and the letter of the Constitution."

State of the Union was a box-office disappointment despite upbeat reviews and a Washington world premiere with Harry Truman in attendance. George Stevens was loaned out to RKO to make *I Remember Mama,* with Irene Dunne, Barbara Bel Geddes, and Oscar Homolka. This restrained immigrant saga, Stevens' first postwar picture, was also less than a financial success although it also was a very good film.

Imperceptibly, the Golden Era was drawing to a close. Theater attendance continued to slip and exhibitors began complaining as loudly as New York critics that Hollywood stories were too slick, empty, and superficial to please war-hardened audiences. In September, Louis B. Mayer had cut his MGM staff by twenty-five percent, the Cohns followed suit at Columbia, and cost cutting was the order of the day. By eliminating seventeen days of shooting, Capra had slashed $500,000 from the *State of the Union* budget. By early 1948, Hollywood was in the middle of a new crisis. If the slippage in movie attendance (from eighty to sixty-two million a week over the 1946–1948 period) and foreign currency restrictions weren't enough, the U.S. government's old antitrust moves to break up the majors' control of both production and exhibition came to a head. "Block booking" was the core of the fight, a practice dating back to the days of the Motion Picture Patent Company when the movies had become big business. It basically meant that if a theater owner wanted the winners, he had to buy the turkeys, also. In France, lead films were eloquently called "locomotives" since they pulled the second-grade pictures, routine westerns, *séries noirs,* specialized curios, and works of "independents." As early as 1933, the Department of Justice had looked into these monopolistic trade practices. Will Hays, the former postmaster general and autocratic head of the Motion Picture Producers Association (MPPA), tried to intercede with President Roosevelt in 1938, when the Justice Department named Loew's; MGM, Paramount, RKO, Warners, Fox, and United Artists in a suit accusing them of "gross violations of the Sherman Act." The litigation dragged through the courts for years, with batteries of MPPA lawyers obtaining postponements and extensions. Bent on wresting, once and for all, every movie house from the majors, the Truman administration reopened the entire case in 1948, winning a series of so-called consent decrees, which, in effect, forced the majors to sell their chains of theaters. Legally speaking and in terms of strict idealism, the government's action was perfectly sound and a desirable result of Rooseveltian liberal thinking, but, as Charles Higham was to write, "in practical terms, the victory of the Department of Justice and the independents over wicked Hollywood had incalculably disastrous effects on the film industry and the very character of film entertainment itself. For confidence in a product, the feeling that it could flow out along guaranteed lines of distribution, was what gave many Hollywood films before 1948 their superb attack and vigor. Also, the block booking custom, evil though it may have been, ensured that many obscure, personal and fascinating movies could be made and released, feather-bedded by the system and underwritten by more conventional ventures." [3]

RKO was now owned by Howard Hughes, but he and his production chief, Dore Schary, were barely on speaking terms. In the spring of 1948, Hughes canceled Schary's patriotic *Battle-*

ground (eventually directed by William Wellman) and three other projects. Schary resigned and went over to Metro.

In April, Willy took time out to attend the wedding of his brother. Robert was forty-eight and Cathy O'Donnell twenty-three when they married in Las Vegas. Melanie had practically given up the idea of ever seeing her eldest son married, but she liked Cathy—real name, Ann Steely, a native of Siluria, Alabama —and the marriage, the only one for both of them, was to be a lasting union. Cathy had just starred in Nicholas Ray's *They Live by Night,* and she and Farley Granger had been termed "a gifted team of young players." Robert was to live increasingly in his brother's shadow, sometimes cowriter, often associate producer, but always involved in Willy's films. Cathy O'Donnell, who had gotten her break in *Best Years,* was also to end her minor career with her brother-in-law, playing Tirzah in *Ben-Hur.*

Less happy occasions also marked 1948. Gaston, who had lived with Melanie all his life, died at the age of forty-five. He had remained gently retarded and spent only the last months in an institution. In August, it was Gregg Toland. Returning from a location trip to Sonora, California, the cameraman was fatally stricken by a heart attack. He was forty-four.

In Paramount, Briskin found an out for Liberty Films. "He urged us to accept Paramount's offer," Wyler recalled. "We had other offers and had discussions with Louis B. Mayer among others, but Paramount's offer was the best. They assured us we would have the same independence as before, which didn't turn out to be true. We still had to have their approval of subject and budget. I guess there is no such thing as complete independence unless you put up your own money."

Capra felt he had to take all the blame and joined Briskin in pulling in favor of the Paramount offer to buy the Liberty stock, valued at about $4 million. Briskin was delighted with the idea (Paramount was to give him a five-year executive producer contract), but Stevens was against it. "It's wrong, it's immoral to sell out," he told the others. "It's a colossal sellout of our artistic freedoms."

Wyler agreed, but felt they had to be practical and take the best offer, which was Paramount's. When Liberty Films threw in the towel, others followed—Mervyn Le Roy's Arrowhead Productions, the Cary Grant–Alfred Hitchcock unit, James Cagney

Productions, and many other independents dropped from the "active" lists.

Besides, the Paramount offer didn't mean perpetual slavery. The deal was that each make five pictures. "What we sold was actually the contracts Liberty had with us individually," Wyler remembered. "In exchange for these contracts, we received Paramount stock and actually made a good deal of money. The five films each of us had to make, however, would be on salary without participating in their eventual profits."

It was to take Wyler seven years to work off the contract and of the three ex-partners, he was the only one to do so. Capra never managed to regain his prewar status (he was only to make four more pictures) and Paramount never allowed him to make the projects he really loved. Ironically, Stevens was on the verge of both critical and popular success, but before *Shane* had a chance to prove itself, Paramount bought off his contract and he went over to Warner Brothers to make his most famous film, *Giant*.

28

Although he was never to make any of them, Frank Capra had his quota all lined up. His first would be *Friendly Persuasion,* to star Paramount's Bing Crosby and Jean Arthur. His second would be *Roman Holiday,* the story about a runaway princess and an American newsman for which he had already contacted Elizabeth Taylor and Cary Grant, to be followed by *A Woman of Distinction,* a Liberty Films property that had been part of the sale. Numbers four and five could be *The Flying Yorkshireman,* with Victor Moore in the title role, and *Westward the Women,* a big western ideal for Gary Cooper. Allotting four months to each and shooting them back to back, he could be out of the Paramount contract in less than two years.

The Paramount story department contained fascinating properties, but, as Capra was told when he offered to remake James Cruze's silent epic *The Covered Wagon,* "when covered wagons need remaking, *we* will make them. We didn't pay you a bundle to pick plums from Paramount's tree, but to bring us new stories and fresh new faces." [1] If Capra wasn't allowed to pick Paramount plums, however, Stevens and Wyler were and they both chose politically sensitive material—two of Theodore Dreiser's forgotton classics. Paramount had paid $150,000 for *An American Tragedy* in 1930, when Dreiser was at the height of his tortuous career, and had originally engaged Sergei Eisenstein to convert the notable novel into film. The following year, Adolph Zukor had handed the project to Josef von Sternberg, who had directed an

American Tragedy that so infuriated the novelist that he took Paramount to court—and lost. Nine years later, when Dreiser's reputation and finances were on the skids, his agent had managed to sell the screen rights to his first novel, *Sister Carrie,* for $40,000, but no one had been able to lick the story. If the second witchhunt caused Paramount to scissor *Carrie* and hold up its distribution for almost two years, Stevens' *A Place in the Sun* (as *An American Tragedy* was called) made amends, even if Dreiser was never to see either film. The old left-wing writer had died in total obscurity on a Hollywood side street in 1945 (with John Howard Lawson delivering the graveside eulogy, Charles Chaplin among the mourners, and Joseph Stalin the only chief of state to send condolences).

But Wyler wasn't at *Carrie* yet. He was undecided about several projects, including *Twelve O'Clock High* (which the studio vetoed), when Olivia de Havilland—fresh from her triumph in Anatole Litvak's *The Snakepit*—proposed that he direct her in a screen version of *The Heiress.*

The Heiress was a successful stage adaptation of another American classic—Henry James's *Washington Square,* the story of a wealthy physician's daughter favored by neither beauty nor brilliance, her proud and unbending father, and her fortune-hunting suitor. One of the few Jamesian novels set in his native land, *Washington Square* was written in 1881, the same year as *The Portrait of a Lady,* the masterpiece that culminated James's first period and made his early reputation. Like *Portrait, Washington Square* has a heroine who is the victim of a domestic tyrant and someone who has been deceived in her generous affections. Like *Portrait,* the short novel is a study of Victorian rectitude and suppressed passion, a provincial story, revealing a corner of the past, "medieval New York," with a light and caressing irony. In the 1880s the novel's modernity was its form, observing consciousness rather than telling an intricate plot, a sketch of what Marcel Proust was soon to call *le pathétique de l'existence* and a bittersweet statement of the incompatibility of the demands of the individual and those of society. James's psychological lyricism was, in another medium, also Wyler's.

Curiously, the story of Catherine Sloper, her father, and suitor Morris Townsend had started in the theater. In the Haymarket Theatre in London, an actress, Frances Anne Kemble, had told

James the story of her handsome brother's engagement to a dull, plain girl, the only daughter of the master of King's College, Cambridge, with the handsome private fortune of £5,000 a year. "She was very much in love with H. K., and was of that slow, sober, dutiful nature that an impression once made upon her, was made forever," James wrote in his notebook, February 21, 1879. "Her father disapproved strongly, and justly, of the engagement, and informed her that if she married young Kemble, he would not leave her a penny of his money. It was only in her money that H. was interested; he wanted a rich wife who would enable him to live at his ease and pursue his pleasures." James's notebook outlined the basic story of *Washington Square*—how the girl turns to her suitor's sister for advice and is told not to marry against her father's will because if she is disinherited, her handsome husband will turn against her; how she, nevertheless, decides to defy her father, only to have the suitor disentangle himself and run away when he realizes there will be no money; and how, ten years later, after her father's death has made her a rich and still-unmarried heiress, the dubious swain makes a clumsy attempt at winning her, only to be spurned in turn by her.

Ruth and Augustus Goetz brought the James story to the stage in 1947, writing a workmanlike yet arresting drawing-room adaptation variously called *The Doctor's Daughter* and *Washington Square* before *The Heiress* became the definite title. (Once settled in London, James had written several plays, and their failure, when Oscar Wilde was at his height and *An Ideal Husband* was playing to full houses every night at the Haymarket, was one of the most poignant episodes of his life.) Despite near-fatal pre-Broadway tryouts, the Jed Harris production settled into a healthy New York run, opening at the Biltmore, September 30, 1947, with the new British actress Wendy Hiller playing Catherine Sloper, Basil Rathbone her father, and Peter Cookson the fortune-hunting suitor. In London, John Gielgud staged *The Heiress* with Peggy Ashcroft and Wendy Hiller alternating in the title role and Ralph Richardson becoming famous as Dr. Sloper.

Wyler went to New York and, after seeing the play, had Paramount buy the rights. After grappling with contemporary themes since *The Little Foxes,* he was enthusiastic about a careful and close adaptation of a period play. With his brother Robert and Lester Koenig as associate producers (as per the Liberty

Films swallow-up agreement, Wyler was his own producer), he set to work. Ruth and Augustus Goetz wrote the screenplay, hewing closely to their play and, when Montgomery Clift was cast as Morris Townsend, softened the suitor's character.

To create the New York of the 1850s, Wyler counted himself happy to have Harry Horner as art director—so much of the Jamesian manners, conventions, and emotional frustration were in the sets, in the atmosphere of Sloper's residence in Washington Square. Olivia de Havilland was enthusiastic, and from London Wyler got Ralph Richardson, who was to repeat his honed portrayal of Dr. Sloper.

But Leo Tover was no Gregg Toland. Wyler ordered deep focus setups that Tover would take half a day to light. More important, what was a liberation from convention with Toland, here began to look formula, a prop for dialogue. Also, Wyler was without Daniel Mandell in the cutting room.

Richardson was his own perfection. His first scene had him come in and, silently, hang up his cane and take off his hat, coat, and gloves.

"How would you like me to play this?" he asked his director.

When Wyler wondered if there was more than one way of making an entrance, hang up a cane, and take off a hat, coat, and gloves, Richardson gave him a virtuoso demonstration of half a dozen different interpretations. "He gave me a display, laying out his merchandise," Willy remembered. "He entered this set as if he had lived there twenty years. I suspect that all the time he knew which way he wanted to do it. That's an actor for you!"

Miss de Havilland worked hard. To play an ungainly girl and at the same time give undertones of color and excitement was difficult, but she presented no particular problems. The climax of what on the stage was the first act, in which she is jilted because her suitor thinks she will be cut off from the $20,000 income, was ruefully echoed in the ending. Opposite thirty-three-year-old Olivia, twenty-eight-year-old Clift incarnated a somewhat frailer Morris Townsend than the Jamesian suitor but a no less ambiguous and sometimes charming character.

"His character was a subject of controversy—should he be charming and believable to her or should he be a fortune hunter," Wyler recalled. "I was told after the film came out that people were disappointed at Townsend turning out to be a fortune hunter, that they had expected a happy ending because he had been charming through most of the picture. Well, of course they didn't expect it. Neither did Catherine Sloper. If she had, she wouldn't have fallen in love with him. The way I played Townsend was rather straight so that you would believe, as she believed, that he was honest and straightforward. When I saw the play in New York, it was so obvious, the way he was leering and estimating the value of everything in Dr. Sloper's home. He was clearly, heavily, and awkwardly established as being there only for the money. I decided I wouldn't do that. It became an argument, but I still think I was right."

To score *The Heiress,* Wyler got the idea of asking Aaron Copland. To his surprise, the composer said yes. Music had been Wyler's first love and his relations with writers of film music had been better than those with other film craftsmen and technicians. Copland had scored Sam Wood's *Our Town* and Lewis Milestone's *Of Mice and Men* in 1940. In 1943, he had written the music for *North Star* for Milestone and Goldwyn, which now made him "red-tinged," but Wyler got him on the picture despite rumblings from Paramount's studio chief, Frank Y. Freeman.

The Heiress opened at New York's Radio City Music Hall in October, 1949, and Wyler made a promotional swing east, which included an evening with the Yale University drama students. After the screening of *The Heiress,* the students asked questions and Wyler told them more universities should take up the study of film, saying that if "drama" departments include comedy, their curriculum should also include movies, which led him right into a trap. "Colleges prepare students for working on the stage alone, but there is much more opportunity for work in other fields, such as radio and motion pictures," he said. When a student wanted to know if this meant they could get jobs in Hollywood, Wyler had to be cautious. "There is always room for talent in the creative end—if you have talent," he said.

Hollywood's current economic woes were also the subject in San Francisco. The economic plight, he told the *San Francisco Chronicle* reporter, was largely Hollywood's own fault because people wanted to see good films and weren't getting them. What was needed, he said, was adult movies, films created and designed for the mature mind. Hollywood's coming of age depended upon its recognition of the fact that it must make pictures for adults and pictures for children and not try to cater to all intellectual levels at one and the same time. He believed it was the job of parents to protect their children from movies emotionally beyond them, rather than to place responsibility for censorship upon the industry. "I value my children more than I value my pictures," he said. "And, as a parent, I do not insist that the picture industry assume full responsibility for their entertainment."

Wyler said he found hope in the lifting of screen taboos. "The word 'Jew' is no longer forbidden," he said, adding that he hated blatant "message" pictures as much as he hated films that had nothing to say. "A movie should not be an advertisement. Drama lies in the subtle complexities of life—in the grays, not the blacks and whites." [2]

Wyler was home by mid-November. For Thanksgiving, the Wylers and their three children drove to Palm Springs, one hundred miles east of Los Angeles. Everyone was comfortably settled for the four-day weekend when three-and-a-half-year-old Billy became ill. At first, Talli and Willy didn't pay too much attention—children often get sick, they reasoned. When Billy began to throw up, Talli called the family pediatrician in Los Angeles. The doctor had a broken leg. With the leg in a cast, he was in no mood to have himself driven to Palm Springs.

Little Billy looked worse and worse. When he began to vomit bile and blood, they took him to the hospital. The local doctor didn't know what to do and his perplexed looks alarmed Talli and Willy even more. Shouldn't the boy be flown to Los Angeles? But how? It would take hours since there were no scheduled flights, a long weekend, and a little charter plane would have to come from L.A. It became Willy's decision not to attempt a transfer but to keep Little Billy at the hospital.

The big scare of 1949 was poliomyelitis and, by nightfall, it was decided to test for polio, a near-operation which involved extraction of spine marrow. The test was negative and the relieved parents were told to go and have dinner. When they returned toward midnight, Billy's condition had worsened, all his body fluids seemed to be leaving him. The doctors were as baffled as before and Willy got on the telephone to Los Angeles. Within minutes, he had chartered a plane and had the game-legged doctor flown to Palm Springs. When the pediatrician arrived, it was too late. Little Billy died at two A.M. of what the local doctors thought might have been an acute lymph gland infection. "We were so stunned we had an autopsy performed," Talli remembered. "They couldn't find anything. It was a question of a doctor not knowing then how quickly a child can dehydrate and just go. That was what happened."

Billy's death put more than a damper on the Wylers' interest in the fortunes of *The Heiress*. Louella Parsons' column carried a short paragraph announcing that Dashiell Hammett would adapt *Detective Story* for Wyler, adding, "I'm glad William Wyler is throwing himself into a heavy work schedule. He and Margaret Tallichet were so broken up over the death of their little boy, and work is the only solace for Willy right now." To escape similar columns and the ensuing enquiries and condolences, the Wylers left with Cathy and Judy for Sun Valley until early 1950, followed by a private trip to Europe, which ended in Switzerland.

The Heiress became the first Wyler film to please more abroad than at home. American reviewers ranged from polite to enthusiastic. Bosley Crowther gave the film a glowing review—"Mr. Wyler has taken this drama, which is essentially of the drawing room and particularly of an era of stilted manners and rigid attitudes, and has made it into a motion picture that crackles with allusive life and fire in its tender and agonized telling of an extraordinary characterful tale"[3]—and followed up with a Sunday *Times* analysis, defending Wyler's softening and expansion of the characters' natures. In this way, "their conflict is more persistent, though the actual collisions are less intense. This is mainly a matter of definition within the frame of the motion picture medium, which permits of more intimacy."[4] In the *New York Herald Tribune*, Wyler wrote a commentary. Under his own byline, he outlined the whys and therefores, calling *The Heiress* a departure and an experiment.

"There are many reasons why I chose it—I liked it, of course, as a play and felt that it would make an unusual and highly entertaining film," he wrote. "I believe that the emotion and conflict between two people in a drawing room can be as exciting as a gun battle, and possibly more exciting. For some years, I have wanted to make a film with a deliberately slow unfolding of character in dramatic conflict rather than a rapid-fire unfolding of plot in pictorial action. I saw in *The Heiress* an opportunity to study the characters of interesting people, with special emphasis on the heroine, Catherine Sloper. Unlike so many films which leave their characters pretty much as they discover them, Catherine Sloper would undergo a series of experiences which would change the very texture and inner structure of her personality." [5]

Max Youngstein, Paramount's chief of publicity, went all out on *The Heiress,* personally touring thirty-one cities and setting up merchandising campaigns that included "tie-ups" with Whitman's Chocolates and *Good Housekeeping* magazine. Several New York fashion designers displayed "the Heiress Look." For the West Coast premiere, Talli arrived with Montgomery Clift and Elizabeth Taylor and four hundred other movie "names."

The first week's "take" at the Music Hall was a big $155,000, but the matinees were sluggish. Youngstein kept the heat on, but Paramount president Barney Balaban and the sales department had to admit to themselves *The Heiress* was not going to be a stupendous success. Wyler was unfazed. What Hollywood needed was not less but more courage. He had meant every word of it when he had told the Yale students that there was a crying need for writing, producing, and directing talent. In the steady stream of interviews Youngstein's men set up, he repeated that movie audiences liked to discover things for themselves or "even to speculate a little" and he used the media exposure to hit the Production Code, saying the industry must shake off the shackles of censorship if it hoped to offer the public quality films based on adult themes.

The Heiress was nominated for six Academy Awards, from Best Picture to costume design, and won four. Olivia de Havilland received the Best Actress award, Edith Head and Gile Steele got the costume, Harry Horner and John Meehan the art direction, and Copland the music Oscars (Robert Rossen's *All the King's Men* was 1949's Best Picture and Joseph Mankiewicz the Best Director).

In history's rear-view mirror, *The Heiress* was to come off increasingly well. While Karel Reisz in 1951 said the film was directed with an intensity that the writing could not meet and Andrew Sarris in 1969 called it warmed-over theatrical melodrama, Charles Higham in 1973 called it Wyler's most underrated

---

film. Its *mise en scène* impressed Arthur Knight in 1960 because Wyler had developed to perfection "a technique that might best be described as cutting within the frame."

"Realizing that dialogue imposes a slower edition pace than obtained in silent days, he has sought to create the effect of shifting visual patterns by strong regroupings of his characters within the shot, or by sudden changes of background," Knight wrote. "In the scene of Fredric March's homecoming in *The Best Years of Our Lives,* for example, March enters close to the camera. His wife, Myrna Loy, runs toward him down a long corridor. As she approaches, their daughter, Teresa Wright, moves in from the side and the trio shut out the view of the corridor. Similarly, in *The Heiress,* the constant closing of doors, shutting off room after room as the camera passes through, accomplished very much the same effect. Testing out his dialogue, Wyler felt that repeated cuts would detract both from the importance of the words and the emotional flow of the performances. His solution proved an ideal technique for sound films. And, as *The Big Country* (1958) testifies, for widescreen films as well." [6]

29

Dashiell Hammett, on the Coast with Lillian Hellman, wasn't getting anywhere with the adaptation of Sidney Kingsley's *Detective Story,* but the *Carrie* screenplay Wyler had assigned to Ruth and Augustus Goetz was in shape.

"We're in the gambling business and we just have to take chances," Wyler told *Variety.* "You can't call any picture until its completed. There is no such thing as a safe story." [1]

Theodore Dreiser's *Sister Carrie* was by no stretch of the imagination "a safe story," but it was not necessarily riskier than *Sunset Boulevard* or Tennessee Williams' *A Streetcar Named Desire* that everyone was trying to get. What had appealed to Wyler in the turn-of-the-century story of a beautiful, materialistic girl who accepts a liaison in preference to the conditions of sweatshop labor was the background, Dreiser's intense feeling about poverty and social injustice, his description of the abject poverty during the triumph of American capitalism, his compassion for human suffering and tolerance for transgression. *Sister Carrie,* written in the winter of 1899–1900, was suppressed by Frank Doubleday after the publisher's wife had found it offensive. Lust and vice were allowable only if punished in the end—as they had been in Frank Norris' violent *McTeague* (which Erich von Stroheim made into *Greed* for MGM in 1923). Instead of punishing Carrie as a "fallen woman," Dreiser seemed to say she was justified in seeking her welfare as best she could. Carrie played fast and loose with two sinners and ended up in luxury, a successful actress, with audiences' cheers ringing in her ears as she collected a huge salary—a dénouement that could be construed as advocating unchastity as a way of life. The novel, as W. A. Swanberg was to write, could also be indicted for dealing with uneducated people, for being vulgar and "steeped in a pessimism that offended the national taste for sweetness." "Carrie, Hurstwood and all the rest appeared almost as helpless creatures adrift on ships in a stormy sea, devoid of will, unable to steer any course, able only to seize whatever comfort was washed their way (precisely as Dreiser had intended)," the biographer wrote. "This flew in the face of the moral doctrine of free will that each individual could choose his own path for good and evil." [2] Compounding his crime of obviously *liking* his characters, Dreiser showed great sympathy for the plight of his vulgar heroes. On film, as it were, the story was just as offensive fifty years later. In 1950, Americans were rallying around demagogues telling them a worldwide cold war was on between good and evil, and that the crusade against godlessness was fought not only in the rice paddies of Korea.

Sister Carrie—the first half of the title was dropped to be sure the public wouldn't think it was a nun's story—was not easy to adapt for the screen. For screenwriters, the novel's demerits were many—clumsy writing, loose construction, and a mass of realistic detail, but the Goetzes were getting there. Casting was a bigger headache, it seemed. Jennifer Jones was set for the title role, but who would play George Hurstwood, the reckless Chicago gentleman of America's raw past whose gradual collapse and suicide was one of the most impressive passages of the book?

After an unrelenting courtship, David Selznick had made Jennifer Jones his second wife. The thirty-year-old actress (née Phyllis Isley, renamed Jennifer Jones by Selznick, and recently divorced from actor Robert Walker) and the forty-seven-year-old producer were married aboard a yacht off the Italian Riviera. Selznick was in the habit of loaning out his leading contract player (lately to Columbia for John Huston's *We Were Strangers* and to MGM for Vincente Minnelli's *Madame Bovary*), and Paramount could have her too for *Carrie*. Selznick worshiped his new wife and announced he wanted to devote himself, now that he was freed from the burden of running a studio, to her further glory. Aside from being the leading lady's husband, Selznick had no business in *Carrie*, but Wyler had already received one of the celebrated Selznick memos, urging him to run the Selznick production of *A Star Is Born* because of the similarity of plot (ambitious girl rising to the top while supporting and adoring man goes to the bottom), and approving the choice of Laurence Olivier for Hurstwood. Wyler feared the worst of Selznick interference and, before filming, had the erstwhile producer promise not to visit the set. Selznick promised and kept to his word.

Larry as a Chicago embezzler? Willy felt current American stars —Kirk Douglas, Humphrey Bogart, Gary Cooper, James Stewart, Spencer Tracy (Cary Grant had turned down the part)—did not have the suave sophistication. When Elia Kazan clinched *Streetcar Named Desire* and cast Vivien Leigh as Blanche, Larry was also willing to come to Hollywood.

Carrie went into production in August when Larry arrived. It was his first time in the United States since his knighthood and a certain amount of confusion was created by his request that he should *not* be called Sir Laurence on posters or the *Carrie* credits (in billings, his name was above Jennifer Jones's). It led to the assumption by Hollywoodites that he was making a concession to republican sentiment and to good-humored jokes at Paramount. Bob Hope, shooting *Fancy Pants* for George Marshall a couple of stages over, fixed a notice on his dressing-room door: "Sir Robert Hope—peasants keep out."

As had happened with Frances Dee in 1935, Jennifer Jones turned out to be pregnant. When Wyler asked her why she hadn't told him before, she answered, like Frances Dee, that she had been afraid it would cost her the part. "Here, it was much more difficult because *Carrie* was period and she always had herself strapped into corsets to have the smallest possible waist," Willy recalled. "I told her, 'When it's a closeup you don't have to do it, I'll tell you when we see the full figure.' But she always had herself strapped in. Just watching her made me uncomfortable. She lost the baby after the picture. How much the strapping of her waist had to do with it, I don't know."

Carrie demanded something of Larry he had never done and was always to refuse—speak American. He was soon deep into the study of Chicago speech patterns, refusing to be disturbed by such trivialities as seeing newsmen and gossip columnists. The Paramount publicity department was unhappy and, with Wyler's help, finally managed to convice Sir Laurence to hold one joint session with the entire Hollywood press corps.

"He agreed on one condition—that Sheila Graham couldn't

attend," Wyler recalled. "He was absolutely firm about that. I said 'But she's a compatriot of yours.' No! I don't know what she had written about him and never found out. Paramount publicity was, of course, up in arms. How could they *not* invite her? But he stuck to it."

Larry enjoyed himself, making friends with all the crew, carefully studying new film techniques. Since he had become a director himself, he was very interested in production methods. He continually picked the brains of engineers on innovations, a far cry from the days of *Wuthering Heights.* Only one thing marred his second Hollywood experience—*why* were they making *Carrie?*

"I don't think Larry had much faith in the story," Wyler remembered. "He kept asking me, 'Why are you doing this picture?' I saw *Carrie* as portraying a period of America that was very interesting. As it turned out, Larry was right."

Carrie was a tragedy, with an even darker ending than *The Heiress,* and a kind of hopelessness settled around the film. Jennifer Jones was good and Selznick kept his promise about not showing up on the set, although he did send Wyler a twenty-page memo suggesting three different endings. The shooting finished with a sigh of relief from everybody, and Robert Swink—an editor who had been recommended by George Stevens—began cutting the picture.

On November 25—almost a year to the day after Billy's death —Talli gave birth to a girl, named Melanie after her grandmother.

What Wyler needed professionally was a tonic, a change of pace to get the seemingly endless eight weeks of gloom of *Carrie* out of his system. When Hammett had failed to write anything on *Detective Story* and had returned his advance to Paramount, Wyler had given the play to his brother Robert and Philip Yordan, who had come up with a quick, slam-bang adaptation of Kingsley's 1949 Broadway hit. Gratefully, Wyler put *Detective Story* into production.

"I really decided to step on it on this picture," he said. "Not a lot of takes and closeups, just sail through it fast. It was excellent due to that, it had speed and spontaneity."

The biggest tonic of *Detective Story* proved to be Lee Garmes. The veteran cameraman, who, with Josef von Sternberg, had created rippling shadows in *Morocco* and provided a "northern light" to shine in the face of Marlene Dietrich, said *Detective Story* could be shot in thirty-six days if . . . . "I told [Wyler] to find a stage with smooth floors at Paramount," Garmes recalled. "If there were any holes in them, he must fill them up with putty and sandpaper them. I told him I'd use the crab dolly; he'd never used it before, and he was delighted with the idea of a camera he could move wherever he wanted it without tracks. 'Jeez,' he said, 'that will be fantastic!' And I told him to rehearse the actors while I rehearsed the camera and lights at the same time; if I made too much noise, he was to tell me." [3]

Detective Story is of the stuff the nascent television was to make into innumerable series—an ultramodern morality play of power, comedy, and pace, acted against the shabby, turbulent background of a Manhattan police station. It has everything from a caricature of a man who kills unborn babies (he'd be an abortionist, as he was in the play, if the Production Code didn't consider that profession unsavory) to a detective who hates his crooked father so much that he has worked up an impossibly rigid system of moral values. When the detective discovers that his wife's past includes a carnal romp with a gangster that led her to becoming a client of said abortionist, all hell, of course, breaks loose. Other characters include a boy who embezzles $400 to take a girl to the Stork Club and winds up in love with her sister; a kindly detective mourning a son killed in the war; a pair of wonderful burglars long past redemption; and an understanding lady newspaper reporter.

Wyler had Robert and Philip Yordan cut out the play's long speeches designed to draw parallels between Detective McLeod's rigid zeal and the evils of the police state and cautioned them to open it up without destroying the construction. As he had done with Kingsley's *Dead End* fourteen years earlier (and with *Counsellor at Law* eighteen years earlier), he intended to sacrifice "cinematics" for construction by adding to the police station decor—a station-house roof, upstairs, sidewalk, and restaurant interior across the street.

Kirk Douglas played Detective McLeod. His first "job" on the production had been at a dinner at the Wylers'—carrying pregnant Talli upstairs in preparation for the birth of Melanie, which was to become a running joke in the Douglas–Wyler friendship.

His second job was to go to Tucson, Arizona, and, for one week, play McLeod in a road company version of the play (Ralph Bellamy had played the detective on Broadway). Eleanor Parker was cast as his wife and the remainder of the playbill was filled with top performers. Lee Grant played the hilarious man-hungry shoplifter, Horace McMahon made the squad commander true to life, Joseph Wiseman played the degenerate fourth offender with feline depravity.

The witch hunt was raging and Freeman one day called Wyler in to tell him he had noticed one of the policemen was a black. Why? "Why not?" Willy smiled. "There must be a reason," Freeman said "No, no reason." It never occurred to the studio chief that there were no subversive reasons buried behind the choice of one black cop in a lineup of a dozen New York policemen.

The second wave of the witch hunt was pounding Hollywood with the reopening of hearings by the House Committee on Un-American Activities. This time, personal friends were scooped up. Lillian Hellman was ordered to appear and, like Michael Wilson (who had written the first *Friendly Persuasion* script for Capra), she took the Fifth Amendment. She said she would tell the committee anything its members wanted to know about herself but refused to talk about other people. She refused to say whether she knew a screenwriter named Martin Berkeley, a "cooperative" witness who had helped get her in trouble. Meetings at the Directors' Guild of America turned into emotional outbursts and newly elected president Joseph Mankiewicz had his hands full. At one meeting, Cecil B. DeMille proposed that directors begin keeping files on allegedly subversive actors.

"Joe Mankiewicz really stood up for the Guild and defied the forces that DeMille had gathered around him," Wyler remembered. "At one time, DeMille said something to the effect that some of us were traitors and not good Americans. I remember getting up and saying that if anybody doubts my loyalty to my country, I'll punch his nose 'and I don't care how old he is,' looking directly at DeMille when I said it." Wyler added that he considered the superpatriots bad Americans since they were ready to tear up the Bill of Rights. "I often thought it would be good for many native Americans to go through a naturalization course as I did, because it teaches you to realize the value of this heritage and the meaning of the Constitution and the Bill of Rights." At another meeting, he suggested they help Edward Dmytryk—the only one of the Hollywood Ten who belonged to the DGA. "I said he was a member, that he needed help, and I felt it was time where the Guild should stand up for its members. I got some applause from the left and contempt from the right."

Freeman always stood up for Wyler. An ultra-conservative and a staunch anti-Communist, the studio chief told Willy how he handled demands for the Wyler scalp. "I tell them you're not a Communist," the studio chief would laugh. "I tell them you're just a bleeding heart, a do-gooder, a peace monger, in short a damn fool, but no commie." Willy often wondered which was worse: to be called a Communist or a damn fool.

Detective Story finished shooting in five weeks—six days ahead of schedule, a record for Wyler. Seven months later, it opened and was a solid success. Bosley Crowther called it a brisk, absorbing film: "Long on graphic demonstration of the sort of raffish traffic that flows through a squadron of plainclothes detectives in a New York police station-house and considerably short on penetration into the lives of anyone on display, it shapes up as an impeccable mosaic of minor melodrama." [4] *Newsweek* said that if there was anything wrong with *Detective Story,* it was "the very virtuosity of the proceedings. Sometimes, the brilliance of the fiddling is a good deal more obvious than the music." [5] *Time* said that although the film rarely ventured out of the station set that housed Kingsley's play, *"Detective Story* makes an even better movie than a play,"* [6] a pronouncement Kingsley himself endorsed. "It's obviously hard to compare two different mediums," the playwright told the *New York Times,* "but on the whole, I'd say that the impact of the film is greater than that of the play." [7]

Carrie was still unreleased, but the next film was decided on and in the works. Ian McLellan Hunter's short story, "Roman Holiday" had been part of the Liberty Films assets, but Frank Capra had abandoned it because of Balaban's 1948 dictum that no Paramount picture was to cost more than $1.5 million.

The property was passed around and Wyler said he would like to make it on one condition—that he could make it in Rome. Freeman was against "location filming" and that was almost the end of *Roman Holiday.*

"You can go to Rome and do the second unit, longshots with

doubles, process plates," Freeman relented, "but the rest we'll do here; we'll build you the sets."

"You can't build me the Colosseum, the Spanish Steps. I'll shoot the whole picture in Rome or else I won't make it."

Freeman gave in. After signing Gregory Peck to play the American journalist, Wyler left for Rome, stopping over in London to look for an English girl to play the princess.

While Wyler was preparing *Roman Holiday* in the Italian capital, Balaban and Freeman moved to get *Carrie* off the shelf. The maneuver was classic. Cables began arriving in Rome saying *Carrie* would not be released unless Wyler agreed to cuts. As per Wyler's producer–director contract, Paramount could not cut the picture without his approval, but the contract didn't say the film had to be released.

"The reason for the cuts, as it turned out, was the McCarthy era," Wyler remembered. "*Carrie* showed an American in an unflattering light, a very sophisticated and cultured man who sinks to the depth of degradation, becomes a derelict and ends up sleeping in flophouses and begging in the street. This, the superpatriots said, was un-American, even if it happened every day on the Bowery and even though the story took place forty years earlier."

Telegrams flew back and forth. Balaban and Freeman promised the cuts would be in the best of taste and draped themselves in the flag, saying the cuts were in the best interest of the country. What cuts? A page-long cable arrived with the suggested deletions —the elimination of Hurstwood's suicide and general restructuring to make the tone less depressing.

Rather than see the picture shelved, Wyler gave in. *Carrie* was released in August 1952—a violently sentimental version of Dreiser's tale. Despite the mutilations, Olivier's Hurstwood retained critics' attention. "When the word first came through that Mr. Olivier had been cast in the difficult role," Crowther wrote, "there were those who regarded the selection as a perilously chancy choice, likely to lead to a distortion that would throw the whole story askew. The eminent British actor was thought too elegant and alien for the role of Mr. Dreiser's middle-aged hero who went to ruin out of love for a pretty girl. As it turned out, however, Mr. Olivier gives the film its closest contact with the book, while Miss Jones' soft, seraphic portrait of Carrie takes it furthest away." [8]

Wyler strongly disagreed with Crowther, thought Jennifer Jones was excellent and, in the overview of his career years later, tended to put the blame for *Carrie* on his own shoulders, feeling that the Dreiser novel was the wrong film for the wrong period and that Paramount's cuts made little difference. "It was the choice of the original material, not the Goetzs' screenplay, that was not popular, and that was entirely my doing."

30

Who would think a romantic comedy could have an unhappy ending? Wyler's happiest film is a fairy tale, where, for once, the shepherd doesn't marry the princess.

The royal lark was the first feature he made outside the United States, the first time he tore himself loose from studio stages, the first out-and-out comedy since *The Gay Deception,* a film that made his unknown actress an overnight sensation and brought out all the adjectives—elfin, exquisite, ravishing, moving, wistful. "The newcomer, named Audrey Hepburn, gives the popular old romantic nonsense a reality it has seldom had before," *Time* wrote in a cover story. "Amid the rhinestone glitter of *Roman Holiday*'s makebelieve, Paramount's new star sparkles and glows with the fire of a finely cut diamond. Impertinence, hauteur, sudden repentance, happiness, rebellion and fatigue supplant each other with lightning speed on her mobile face." [1]

Wyler got Audrey Hepburn because the signing of Gregory Peck satisfied Paramount's demands for a star with marquee value.

At first, Peck turned it down. The girl in the script obviously had the starring part.

"You surprise me," Wyler told Peck. "If you didn't like the story, okay, but because somebody else's part is a little better than yours, well, that's no reason to turn down a film. I didn't think you were the kind of actor who measures the size of the roles."

That did it. Peck signed.

"According to Hollywood mathematics, now that I had a male

star, I didn't need a stellar leading lady. I wanted a girl without an American accent to play the princess, someone you could *believe* was brought up as a princess. That was the main requirement: besides acting, looks, and personality.

Wyler looked around in London and interviewed several girls. One was the stick-slim Audrey, a Brussels-born dancer (of Dutch mother and English-Irish father) who had played the cigarette girl in the opening scene of Charles Crichton's *Lavender Hill Mob* and, while acting in Jean Boyer's *Nous Irons à Monte-Carlo* in Paris, had been chosen by Colette herself to play the title role in the future Broadway musicalization of *Gigi*. Leaving for Rome, Wyler ordered a test of the twenty-three-year-old Audrey, telling the British test director to play a trick on her and to keep the camera rolling *after* she played her little scene and he called "cut" so that Wyler *could* see her natural self when not acting. "That was the film we received in Rome," Wyler recalled. "She was absolutely delightful. First, she played the scene from the script, then you heard someone yell 'Cut!' but the take continued. She jumped up in bed relaxed now, and asked, 'How was it? Was I any good?' She looked and saw that everybody was so quiet and that the lights were still on. Suddenly, she realized the camera was still running and we got *that* reaction too. Acting, looks, and personality! She was absolutely enchanting and we said, 'That's the girl!' The test became sort of famous and was once shown on TV."

Shooting in Rome was a delight and Wyler loved his new freedom. No sets, no back transparencies, nothing of the style of "Hollywood romance." Since newspaperman Peck is anxious to get the exclusive rights to the princess's adventures in Rome and since he is also anxious to keep her in the dark as to his own identity, a Cook's tour of the Eternal City was practically built into the story—a motorscooter ride through streets, alleys, and marketplaces, a dance on a Tiber river barge, sidewalk cafés, the Pantheon, the Forum, and such landmarks as the Castel Sant' Angelo, Brancacci, Barberini Palazzo and the Spanish Steps. Wyler had only one regret—that he thought of color too late. "I tried to switch, but in those days, making pictures in color was unusual. I would have needed new filmstock, had to fly exposed film every day to London, and reorganize the production. It was just too late."

Journalists and paparazzi swarmed over the locations and Peck fell in love with a French reporter, Véronique Passini. Since he was still married, it had to be kept halfway secret and elaborate plots were hatched. Once, the lovers and the Wylers had lunch on an island in the middle of a lake outside Rome. They had been told they would be alone, but paparazzi photographers soon came out of the bushes. A year later, Véronique became the second Mrs. Peck.

Wyler had rented an apartment on Piazza Elvezia and Talli and the girls joined him—Talli to bear the Wylers' last child, Cathy and Judy to play schoolgirls at the Trevi fountain (when Gregory Peck suddenly needs a camera, it's Judy's that he borrows). David was born during postproduction, September 25, 1952, at the Salvatore Mundi hospital following a phone mixup and a taxi race through Rome that belonged to the screen. The drive from Piazza Elvezia to the hospital had been carefully rehearsed. If it became necessary to rush to the hospital during the day when Willy was at the studio at the other end of Rome, the chauffeur of the Venezuelan legation to the Vatican, also located on Piazza Elvezia, was to take her. When it did happen, Willy was at the studio, the chauffeur was out to dinner, and Talli reached Salvatore Mundi fifteen minutes before the baby was born. Willy got there ten minutes late. A boy at last.

"It was a happy picture," Talli remembered, "for the whole family, a gay and wonderful period."

The first cameraman was Franz Planer, whom Talli and Willy had first met in Tijuana on the eve of World War II. When Planer fell ill, Henri Alekan (René Clement's and Yves Allegret's cinematographer) replaced him. "It was marvelous to shoot in Rome," Willy remembered. "There were practically no automobiles in 1952, only scooters, and it was a lot easier than today. I had a choice of four locations for each scene, each better than the other. If I chose one, it meant giving up the other three. A director's dream, l'embarras du choix. I was happy I hadn't listened to Freeman."

Paramount had blocked funds in Italy and wanted to use the money for the production. To free the lire, the government had to approve the script. Wyler had a translation sent to the proper authority, Annibale Scicluna at the Ministry of Entertainment and Tourism, and when it was turned down, presented himself.

"You can't use blocked money to make fun of Italy," Scicluna told him. "You make fun of Italian police, of the Italian people."

"That's right," Wyler interrupted, "but we also make fun of an American newspaperman, of American tourists. We make fun of royalty. We make fun of everybody. It's a comedy!"

Scicluna remained suspicious.

"I promise you that I'll not do anything that would demean the Italian people," Wyler continued. "I promise you that you'll love the film."

At considerable risk to himself, Scicluna gave in. Months later, Mario Ungaro, the Italian consul-general in Los Angeles, pinned decorations on Freeman and Wyler's chests at a ceremony at Paramount studios—Star of Italian Solidarity first class for Freeman, second class for Wyler. "I looked at Freeman during the ceremony, but he never cracked a smile."

Robert Swink was again the editor and *Roman Holiday* was completed in Rome, with Georges Auric writing the music. "We sent the finished picture back and spent the next summer in France, renting a house in St. Jean-de-Luz on the Atlantic coast. A lot of people visited us there that summer. John Huston, with his new wife, Ricky Soma, was there, fresh from *The African Queen,* Irwin and Marianne Shaw, Peter Viertel. At one point, Paul Kohner came to visit, bringing with him Harold and Lotti Mirisch and their daughter. Cathy and Robert Parrish were there. It was great fun that year."

Roman Holiday opened at New York's Radio City Music Hall the last week of August 1953 to rave reviews and instant fame. A week later, *Time* had Audrey Hepburn on its cover. Inside, the magazine, after describing the opening sequence where the princess receives noblemen and diplomats in her palace and slips off one high-heeled shoe, quoted Billy Wilder—slated to direct her next in *Sabrina*—as saying, "This girl, singlehanded, may make bosoms a thing of the past," and told the story of the sly screen test in London. In its October 21 issue, *Look* gave the screen test a four-page spread.

William Wyler, Billy Wilder. Through their careers the two directors were complimented by people for the wrong films. "It often happened to me that people came over and said how much they had enjoyed *Some Like It Hot,*" Willy said somewhat later. "I had to tell them that, regretfully, this was not my picture and this always embarrassed the person. When I told Billy about it, he told me the same thing happened to him occasionally. So we made an agreement that every time somebody would say something nice about the other's picture, we'd be very gracious, accept the compliment and say, 'Thank you very much.' "

When Talli and Willy visited Japan in 1955, the Paramount publicity department in Tokyo told them *Roman Holiday* had been as big a success as *Gone With the Wind*. To help with the language in the provinces, a bilingual member of the publicity department accompanied the Wylers on a train ride through central Japan. At a station, the Wylers found themselves on the rear platform of the train facing an emormous crowd of cheering people, a reception the publicity department had organized. Scores of girls pointed to their own heads. They all had Audrey Hepburn hairdos, the rage of Japan that year.

While the millions rolled in and Paramount showered Wyler with compliments and new scripts, Audrey picked up an inevitable Academy Award (Wyler was also nominated, but the directing Oscar went to Fred Zinnemann for *From Here to Eternity*). Wyler leaned back, taking his time to choose the next film.

Robert suggested an adaptation of Thomas Wolfe's 1929 novel *Look Homeward, Angel*. It was a powerful story, ending in an insane moment when a father, mother, sons and daughters of a passionate, embattled, and hopelessly bound North Carolina family turn with unholy wrath on the home that has held them together.

Yes, perhaps. But Willy had a better idea—a biopic on the Duke of Reichstadt, the tragic son of Napoleon and Marie-Louise. Dutifully recognized emperor at his father's downfall when he was three years old, François-Charles-Joseph Bonaparte—l'Aiglon, or Little Eagle, as passionate Bonapartists called him—spent his short, feeble life in Schönbrunn Castle in Vienna, a pawn of his grandfather, Emperor Franz II of Austria and his crafty Chancellor Metternich, and died at the age of twenty-one. Years earlier, Wyler had seen and read Edmond Rostand's 1900 dramatization, *L'Aiglon*. The author of *Cyrano de Bergerac* had made a strange and compelling hero of the adolescent craving for a measure of his father's glory but unable to escape Metternich's web.

"I want to make it with Audrey playing Aiglon," Willy told Barney Balaban and Freeman.

"Audrey Hepburn, oh fine. And who's the boy?"

"*She* is the boy," he told them.

"That's crazy," Balaban said and laughed.

"You mean a boy who turns out to be a girl masquerading?" Freeman asked, hopefully.

"No, a boy."

Wyler told them the part was traditionally played by a girl, Sarah Bernhardt and Maude Adams had played him, and that Audrey would look stunning in uniform. They looked at him and with pained expressions began to talk about other things.

Frank Capra had made two Bing Crosby vehicles—*Riding High* and *Here Comes the Groom*—and had wanted out as early as 1951. After his release from the Paramount contract and his "self-exile," he had wanted to make the break complete and had sold whatever story properties he still owned. Stanley Kramer had bought *The Flying Yorkshireman* but never made it, while William Wellman took *Westward the Women* and made a routine western out of it.

Wyler set *The Desperate Hours* in motion, a chilling story of three escaped convicts invading a suburban home and holding a family hostage. The idea was not new—there had been Archie Mayo's *The Petrified Forest,* starring Humphrey Bogart as the gangster, Richard Thorpe's *Night Must Fall,* and, recently, John Sturges' *Kind Lady*—but Joseph Hayes's story had a twist that *was* new. Members of the terrorized family were allowed to go to work by their captors, knowing that if they talked, the hostages at home would be murdered. It was terror with open doors of a kind political extremists were to discover a decade later.

Wyler was intrigued by this premise of ultimate blackmail. *The Desperate Hours* had been a novel and a play and Wyler got author Hayes to write the screenplay. On Broadway, newcomer Paul Newman had played the young punk leader of the three escaped convicts, and mentally Willy was casting the picture in the James Dean–Marlon Brando vein when he got a call from Bogart saying he would like to talk about *The Desperate Hours.* Willy was a little puzzled but invited Bogey over.

"You really want to play this part?" Willy asked when they were comfortably seated in Wyler's Paramount office.

"Sure."

"It's not really your type."

"Why not?" Bogey asked.

"Well, he's a family man, children . . ."

"Hell, I don't want to play *that* role; I'm talking about the gangster!"

"The gangster, but he's a kid!"

"Why does he have to be a kid?"

Why indeed, Willy reflected. Usually by the time an actor reached stardom, he wanted roles with redeeming qualities, even when portraying villains. But Bogart wanted to play the absolute heavy without a shred of humanity in him.

The Desperate Hours was to be Bogart's next-to-the-last film and his last as a snarling killer. Shortly after starring in Mark Robson's screen adaptation of Budd Schulberg's *The Harder They Fall,* Bogart died of what he and no one around him would admit he suffered from—cancer of the throat. During the filming of *The Harder They Fall* in New York, he let off steam about young actors, telling newsmen from under his fedora that they were all a drab lot. "I defend my right to cut a caper if I feel like it, a man had the right to get rotten drunk and raise some trouble. The trouble with these young male stars today is that they have no color, no imagination."

To play the father of the terrorized family, Wyler wanted Spencer Tracy. After reading the script, Spence said yes, but no deal was to be consummated. Neither Bogart nor Tracy would take second billing. "It's stupid, but each said, 'My name always goes first,' " Wyler recalled. "We tried all sorts of things—one half of all posters would have one name top right and the other lower left so you wouldn't know who was first, and vice versa on the other half. But we just never could get them together."

The picture went before the cameras with Fredric March incarnating the able and courageous father and with Arthur Kennedy portraying a taut detective. Bogart's henchmen were Robert Middleton and Dewey Martin, the latter playing a youthful, troubled thug, while Martha Scott was cast as Fredric March's wife, Mary Murphy as their daughter, and Gig Young as her fiancé. Little Richard Eyer, who was to steal scenes from adults in *Friendly Persuasion,* played a loud and bratty son of March and Martha Scott.

Bogart ran effortlessly over familiar ground. He had played a fugitive criminal holding hostages at the point of a gun in *The Petrified Forest.* Wyler directed him with gusto in what was to be his last brutal role (in *The Harder They Fall,* he was an out-of-work sports writer who allows a ringside racketeer to talk him into promoting a boxer who can't box). When newsmen visited the Paramount set and asked how he acquired his hard, dry-mouthed look, Bogey replied, wide-eyed, "I don't know what you mean," giving the hard, dry-mouthed look.

Wyler again had Lee Garmes on camera, giving the film a good harsh documentary look that everybody, Garmes included, loved. Robert Swink was in the cutting room and Gail Kubik, who had scored *Memphis Belle* when both he and Wyler were in the army, turned in a rather avant-garde score.

A paragraph in the fine print of the contract between Paramount and the Broadway producer of the stage version of *The Desperate Hours* held up the release of the film. Meanwhile, Wyler tried his hand at a new medium, directing a live television version of *The Letter.* Taped in New York, the TV special had Siobhan McKenna playing Leslie Crosbie and John Mills her husband.

When *The Desperate Hours* opened at New York's Criterion October 5, 1955, Andrew Stone's *The Night Holds Terror* had had a four-month headstart in the ruthless-convicts-seizing-suburban-family market. Bosley Crowther liked *The Desperate Hours* moderately, saying Wyler had turned the Hayes story into a "crafty and crackling" screen thriller in every respect save one— the credibility of the characters. "With a stalking and searching camera that peers into people's eyes and pinpoints the monstrous menace of a hoodlum's snarl or a suddenly drawn gun, he [Wyler] has created a visible picture of the sense of helplessness and doom that takes hold of the peaceful family when the fugitive criminals move in," Crowther wrote. "He has caught—for a while —the horrible feeling of suffocation that these people have when they find themselves strangely isolated by their captors from the world outside. And, in the top villain, played by Humphrey Bogart, he has etched a fearful symbol of brute force, impervious to pity or regard for the rights of other men . . . but, when Mr. Hayes' audacious plotting has the 'brains' of the captors permit the father and daughter to leave the house and go to business, on the assumption that they'll be too scared to tell (because the mother and little son are still held hostages), then the strain is switched to the viewer's credulity." [2]

Where does credulity snap? In private, Wyler tended to agree. He had not had enough violence, not enough white terror in the first half to make the "audacious plot" stick. But that was the gamble and excitement of the genre—the very thinness of the narrative. The next time he was to strain credulity but *not* have it snap was to be in *The Collector*.

31

The basic appeal to Wyler of his next three films and the theme of one he was never to make was something running deep in him. Born of parents of the same creed but of different nationalities in a borderland with allegiances to rival cultures, he had offered coffee and bread to soldiers in different uniforms when he was twelve, but had kept his father's neutral nationality through the four years of war. He had been schooled by both sides and, at twenty, had emigrated to a third country and married outside his faith. When the guns had hammered again and the culture of his childhood had become the opprobrium of civilized men, he had become a uniformed maker of documentaries, not a civilian maker of war movies. When crusaders had hunted for galled sheep and foreign-borns had become "more Catholic than the Pope," he had opted for sanity and reasonable doubt.

Man was an odd creature, aggressive, often selfish, generally shortsighted, sometimes noble, but inclined to run in packs. Yet there were those from the border marshes, those from the no-man's-lands, the halfbreeds with blood from both sides, those of the diaspora, those who congenitally had to understand, conscientious objectors, *Kosmopoliten* and *apatrides,* outcasts, and holy men.

How to portray goodness on the screen? Wyler was increasingly fascinated by this other outer limit of filmdom. The movies had always been full of striking villains and dull good guys. The challenge, it seemed, was to make films with "good people" as heroes. *Friendly Persuasion* was a loosely woven account of a clutch of Quakers on the edge of a civil war that their faith forbade them to take part in, and its hero was a man in whom nothing—not even goodness—was hardened. *The Big Country* was a western about a man who refuses to shoot. *Ben-Hur* was many things, but it was also the story of the destruction of the amity between two men and childhood friends of clashing beliefs. The film Wyler always wanted to make would have been about a child of war.

"Not just a child in war, that's appallingly common, but a child in a place where loyalties are divided," he said later in life. "Because it's always the same in all countries, isn't it—patriotism and flag waving. You see them here parade with flags, hundreds of flags, and in the Soviet Union or Nazi Germany, all the same. Where I grew up, you didn't know. You heard one thing at school and another at home. Some people were on this side and those who were on the other side were not traitors. One neighbor was on this side, another neighbor on the other. It was not simply everybody waving the same flag, right or wrong. I never found the story that would tell that. But it must have been like that in Vietnam."

But during Hollywood's decade of disruption and at the height of the East-West confrontation, Wyler got to make two remarkable pacifist movies.

Friendly Persuasion was not to be a Paramount picture. With *Desperate Hours,* Wyler had finished his five-picture deal at Marathon Street. As he looked around, Allied Artists came to him with an attractive offer. Restructured in 1953 (and dropping the Monogram Pictures tag which denoted B pictures), AA wanted to attain major studio status. Under Steve Broidy, vice-president Harold Mirisch (whom Wyler had met in St-Jean-de-Luz in 1952) shopped around for name directors. In early 1955, he signed Wyler, Wilder, and Huston to make major-budget films for the company.

Money, again, obsessed the Hollywood mind. Television had proved to be a major threat after all, and, if the alarming slump in cinema attendance was to be stopped (in the United States, it had slid from eighty to thirty-five million a week in a decade), corporate wisdom had it that only size could do it. The wide-screen revolution had begun in 1952, and the following year Cinerama and 3-D seemed to prove the sock-it-to-'em school to be right. Twentieth Century-Fox acquired the rights to Henry Chretien's quarter-of-a-century-old process, which Spyros Skouras christened CinemaScope. Instead of rushing to the market with a hastily produced trick film, Fox introduced the new process with a $5-million biblical spectacle, Henry Koster's *The Robe* (which grossed $18 million in the United States and Canada alone). As CinemaScope installations fanned across the country and theatermen installed screens that were two and a half times as wide as they were tall (and directors invented dirty jokes about filming people lying down), the other studios dropped 3-D in favor of wide-screen processes. Paramount refused to go along with Chretien's "squeezed" image and came up with double-width 70mm VistaVision, which allowed tremendous blowups without the loss of intensity of color and crispness of focus that marred anamorphic projection. But 70mm prints meant new projectors in every moviehouse and exhibitors balked—which didn't prevent Mike Todd from fast-talking a good part of the industry for a while with 65mm Todd-AO.

For Wyler, outsized screens were to be postponed until *The Big Country* (shot in Technirama) and *Ben-Hur* (MGM Camera 65), but with *Friendly Persuasion,* he began filming in color.

John Huston's Allied Artists release was to be either *Typee,* another Herman Melville novel, which would reunite him with his *Moby Dick* star, Gregory Peck, or another Stephen Crane yarn, *The Blue Hotel* (written a year after *Red Badge of Courage,* which Huston had put on the screen in 1951). He was to make neither, but Wyler and Wilder made theirs—two expensive propositions, as it turned out, starring Gary Cooper.

Friendly Persuasion was budgeted at $1.5 million and slated to shoot in its native habitat, southern Indiana. It was actually filmed in Hollywood—on the estate of Rowland V. Lee in the San Fernando Valley and at the old Republic studios—and was completed at a cost of over $3 million. By 1960, its world gross had reached $8 million. Cooper had wanted to do a picture with Audrey Hepburn since he had seen *Roman Holiday,* and Wilder found a vehicle in Claude Anet's slim novel *Ariane,* a Parisian story of romance between a very young girl and a mature man. Giving it a title with appropriate Wilderian resonance, *Love in the Afternoon* was shot during the summer and fall of 1956 in its natural habitat, in and around Paris. Bad weather marred exterior shooting and drove the film over budget.

Friendly Persuasion was a long story. Michael Wilson—now a blacklisted writer because of his refusal, in 1951, to answer questions by the House Committee on Un-American Activities—had written the original screenplay from Jessamyn West's collection of Quaker stories in 1946. By the time Wyler's new assistant, Stuart Millar (who was publicist Mack Millar's twenty-six-year-old son), drove to Napa in northern California to ask the middle-aged Miss West to come down to Hollywood to talk about her book, it had been ten years since she had sold the screen rights to Frank Capra and Liberty Films. Quaker existentialism was not routine screenfare and she had long since stopped believing press clippings sent to her saying that Bing Crosby, James Stewart, or Spencer Tracy was going to play her Jess Birdwell. She was more than skeptical when Millar asked her why in her book she had never confronted her Quaker hero with the *need* to fight. Neatly, she replied that in mankind's long history of war, the question had not been to fight *or* see your house burn down and your wife attacked, but to fight *and* see your house burn down and your wife attacked.

Despite her initial unwillingness to probe again her Indiana Quaker childhood, despite her misgivings about Hollywood and her forebodings of betrayal, the steadfast assistant (she later called Millar Wyler's "altar boy") convinced her to come down and meet the producer-director who was finally going to turn her *Friendly Persuasion* into a movie. The meeting led to her spending nearly a year on the making of the film, commuting between her husband and home in Napa and the Beverly Hills studio apartment Wyler rented for her. It also led to a wise, humorous, and vivid account of her experiences—*To See the Dream.*[1]

The circumstances surrounding her first meeting with Wyler were sad—his mother had died two days earlier. Melanie passed away February 13, 1955, at the Cedars of Lebanon Hospital, surrounded by her two sons and their families. She had lived in the Hollywood Boulevard apartment house she and her lady friend had owned for over twenty years. Until recently, Melanie had been active and lively—still the opera enthusiast she had been in Mulhouse when the boys were small, taking her friend and Robert's business manager, Hilda Walls, to a Los Angeles performance of *La Tosca,* and very much involved in Jewish charities. She was seventy-seven.

Jessamyn West was intrigued. After a dinner at the Wylers', where Cooper told her his persona demanded that he pull the trigger, she settled down to write what Wyler called "the story of what the camera sees." This led to Robert, "smaller, frailer, grayer than his brother," she observed. "William Wyler's face looks solid enough to push through a situation. This doesn't mean that W. W. has a tough mug—but he does have a compact one. If the brothers' faces were hands—William is a hand curved inward, self-protectively. Robert's lies open. William Wyler, however, can focus, does focus more attentively upon the person who faces him. Robert is open but what he is open to is not necessarily the person in front of him. William either focuses upon you or gets rid of you."

Together Jessamyn West and Robert Wyler wrote the script, establishing their friendship and their routine (*To See the Dream* was to be dedicated to Stuart Millar and Robert). Robert even warned her about his brother. "When Willy comes back from New York, he'll go over the script with you. Now, we've got a good story line. Don't let Willy touch that. Willy gets carried away. He enriches the scene, but that scene, if it gets too big and heavy, will pull the whole design out of shape."

Cooper still pressed for changes allowing him to fight in the Civil War battle that was to climax the picture.

"Some Quakers have fought, haven't they?" he asked Miss West.

"A lot of them," she answered. "Your son in this picture does."

"But not me?"

"Not you."

"Action seems to come natural to me."

"I know it."

"There comes a time in a picture of mine when the people watching expect me to do something."

"I know it. You'll do something."

"What?"

"Refrain. You will furnish your public with the refreshing picture of a strong man refraining."

"It doesn't usually film well—strong men refraining. Strong man puts hand toward doorknob, fingers quiver, then strong man lets hand fall from doorknob, shakes head slowly, and walks away, head bent. That's not what I do best."

"How do you know? You always kick the door down."

"I reckon that gets old, too," Cooper sighed.

Jessamyn sat in on casting conferences and saw Maureen O'Hara and Eleanor Parker being tested for Eliza, Jess's wife, and heard Margaret Sullavan, ("a former wife of Mr. Wyler's"), Ingrid Bergman, Vivien Leigh, and Eva Marie Saint mentioned for the part before Dorothy McGuire was chosen. She sat in on costuming conferences and fought for less severe and dark clothes, she took Cooper to a Quaker meeting in Pasadena, saw the title changed to *Mr. Birdwell Goes to Battle,* apparently a publicity department echo of Cooper's *Mr. Deeds Goes to Town* for Capra in 1936. She marveled when Robert Middleton, reading for the part of Sam Jordan, gave her lines breath and was astonished when Wyler told her to overwrite. "I like choices. I like room to turn around in in the dialogue. Give me more than I need," he told her.

A choice *Friendly Persuasion* audiences preferred not to hear about was the fact that a flock of geese played Samantha.

Goose directing was not easy. "You try one goose and she won't do it right so you take another." Willy said. "They all look alike —all white geese. You try a third goose, she goes the wrong way. Try the next one. Finally one of them would do it right."

The Birdwells' goose is not only the bitter enemy of little Jess (Richard Eyer) but also the protagonist of a highly charged and significant scene. When, toward the end, a starved rebel soldier tries to strangle the goose, Eliza hits him with a broom, showing her spontaneous defense of something she loves but also a gesture she immediately feels ashamed of. At previews and premieres Wyler attended, people were so charmed by Samantha as a "scene stealer" they wanted to know more about her. "Who was that goose?" they asked. Patiently, he told them several geese had actually played Samantha. The disappointment, if not downright hurt, he read in peoples' faces soon made him drop the truth in favor of a touching story of fowl love.

During the feverish preproduction period, Wyler felt an urge burrow deeper into his subject. "One Sunday, we went alone to a Quaker 'meeting' in Pasadena and came away impressed and moved by the Society of Friends, which—in addition to violence, rejects ritual, formal sacraments, a formal creed, and priesthood."

"They knew I wasn't part of the congregation, but I was welcome and we all sat down on chairs and benches," he remembered. "The doors closed and everybody sat there and just did nothing. Nobody spoke, nobody got up. We all sat in silence. This went on for a long time and I realized that people like myself never do this. I was so busy I never sat down and really thought.

"After a while somebody spoke and told about an experience he or she had had. Somebody else got up and told of traveling to another town and attending another meeting of the Society. That was about all that happened. A few people got up and said what was on their mind. After about twenty minutes the children were asked to go. Children get impatient, so they were let out to play in the courtyard while the congregation remained there and occasionally someone got up and talked.

"I must say that it was the closest feeling to religion that I had felt in a long time. I was simply involved and had nothing to do but to think—about myself, my family, about my work."

Jessamyn West observed Wyler grow more intense as the shooting start approached. She saw him express hopes for the picture but also flashes of doubt. She went out to the Rowland Lee Ranch and saw southern Indiana sprout out of scorched California brush —1860 barns, farm houses, the Quakers' "meetinghouse." She fought to retain the Quaker habit of addressing each other as "thee" and "thy" (and won). When the filming started, Robert went to France "partly because of business, partly, I think, because he doesn't want to be around while his brother has *his* say." Stu Millar took her out for the first day's shooting and she felt that "Wyler works like a sculptor, molding script, actors and locale into a form which strikes him at the moment as being significant."

Her chores were not over. Convinced that she must stay over as technical adviser (and receiving salary as such), she faced new crises and new joys as the filming progressed. Suddenly, Wyler wanted to know what Josh (Anthony Perkins), the elder of the Birdwells' sons who goes to war, stands for. "We know what Josh is against, what is he *for?*" Wyler's dislike of time lapses led to a rewrite that led to one of the film's funniest scenes. But the pressure was still on Wyler—and not only from Cooper—to change the ending and have Jess avenge slaughter with slaughter. She found herself in the incongruous position of defending the script against John Huston.

"Mr. Wyler spoke to me last night about a talk he'd had with

John Huston. Huston has read the script. He likes it. Others have read it and liked it, but Huston's liking, I could see, was special. 'Huston likes the script,' Mr. Wyler said, 'but he thinks Jess shouldn't touch that gun. He says that when he saw that Jess was going to pick up his gun . . . he had to stop reading. He said it was painful for him to watch Jess, a man whose whole life has been given to nonviolence, waver. John's a fine director. His feeling about this troubles me.' "

For an hour, the Quaker novelist had to defend Jess's picking up his gun, telling Wyler their leading character must be tempted to violence. "We have promised the audience that. And he must have the means of killing in his hand at the moment of his temptation. And we must see him decide, in spite of the provocation and in spite of the means, to refrain. Even though the refraining may lose him his life. Otherwise, we don't have a drama—we have a chronicle. Give the audience what it must want at this juncture—and Huston says he wants—a Jess who does *not* pick up his gun. Will Jess fight? You can answer the question in a vacuum here in Jess's bedroom as he looks at his rifle. Or you can answer it in action, where Jess is willing to test it—and would test it. He did not refuse to fight because Quakers say it is wrong to fight. That's imitative action, and Quakers despise it. He refused to fight because as a human being, he could not bring himself to take a human life. We must see him make that decision as an individual; we must see the individual and the Quaker become one."

Wyler was still not convinced, saying Huston was a very sensitive, very bright man, and Jessamyn answering that Huston was too mixed up with "that whale of his" to take on Quakers, too.

"Johnnie isn't limited in the number of things he can consider simultaneously," Wyler said.

"Maybe he doesn't want any competition for *Moby Dick,*" she answered. Wyler stared at her, unable to believe she could have such a black thought.

Miss West got the title of her book about the making of the film from little Melanie. When, together with Bob Swink, again the editor, the novelist had gone to the Wylers' to see the dailies, four-year-old Melanie called, "Daddy, can I see the dream?" When Miss West asked Swink what the child meant, he said, "That's what she calls looking at rushes."

324

"A movie is a guess at an echo," Jessamyn West reflected toward the end of her chronicle. "Writing, as opposed to script writing, does not aim at this echo. One writes, when one is 'writing, not scripting,' to give form to a world, a life, which seems significant. . . . The danger in moviemaking is even greater than in writing or living (if the last two can be separated) of not being 'a thing in itself' but always only a means, a guess at an echo."

Dmitri Tiomkin scored the picture, working at the same time on George Stevens' *Giant*. Both directors, Tiomkin laughed later, were jealous of his time.

Friendly Persuasion opened at New York's Radio City Music Hall November 1, 1956, to polite reviews. Bosley Crowther said that, inspired by a lovely group of stories by Jessamyn West and spurred by the sympathetic talents of Gary Cooper and Dorothy McGuire, Wyler "has brought forth a picture that is loaded with sweetness and warmth and as much cracker-barrel Americana as has been spread on the screen in some time." [2] *The New Yorker* said the film "doesn't delve very deeply into Quaker philosophy but by the time it reaches its climax—in a look at a Civil War battlefield—it has demonstrated that one needs a lot more courage to seek the goal of peace then to seek the goal of victory," [3] while *Time* dismissed the film as "a nice, folksy costume comedy that tried to say something serious about the relations—and the lack of it—between private morals and public life." [4]

Allied Artists got more attention than it bargained for when *Friendly Persuasion* was hit with a lawsuit. Asking $250,000 in damages, Michael Wilson charged "conspiracy" on the part of AA and William Wyler to keep his name off the film. Also listed as defendants were Jessamyn West, Robert Wyler, Liberty Films, and Paramount, which previously owned the movie rights. Wilson's suit alleged that the defendants kept his name off the screen because he "was an unfriendly witness" before the HUAC in 1951. The suit was aimed less at Allied Artists, Wyler & Co. than at the film industry and a 1953 Writers' Guild of America amendment of its bylaws permitting producers to withhold screen recognition from a writer who failed to defend himself when asked to do so by an employer or duly constituted Congressional committee. The suit presented the first court test of the Guild's so-called "credits escape clause."

Wyler was all in favor of including Wilson in the screen

credits. With the exception of one racial incident blown out of proportion (in Jessamyn West's original, a black escapee coming to the Birdwell farm telling them *his* conscience tells him he must fight), Wilson's 1946 script for Capra was quite good. Also, it was what Jessamyn and Robert had started from.

"We felt the screenplay credits should be given to all three, that all three had contributed substantially," Wyler recalled. "We went to the Writers' Guild for arbitration and they gave solo credit to Wilson. I think it was a kind of backlash against the whole McCarthy trauma, with the Guild leaning over backwards so it couldn't be accused of refusing Wilson anything on political grounds."

The solo credit, Wyler felt, was not only unfair to Jessamyn West and to his brother, it also caused Allied Artists to balk. "I got the contract out, got my lawyer to look into it," Wyler remembered. "I had artistic control over the picture. This, they said at Allied Artists, was not an artistic matter, but a commercial one and I could not possibly win in court. They said that if Wilson's name was on the picture, especially now with the adverse publicity, *Friendly Persuasion* would be picketed by the American Legion and the results would be a financial loss. So it *was* a business matter.

"If only the Guild had agreed to a three-way credit, Allied wouldn't have objected and perhaps the American Legion would have overlooked it. It was a damn pity because I think all three might have gotten Academy nominations, because that was the year Dalton Trumbo won under a false name." *

Friendly Persuasion went into release without *any* writing credits. Wilson, who had won the 1951 writing Oscar for George Stevens' *A Place in the Sun,* was to work ten more years without credits, the unnamed coauthor of David Lean's *Bridge on the River Kwai* and *Lawrence of Arabia,* before surfacing, ironically with Wyler, on *The Sandpiper.* The deal to have Wilson write the script of producer Martin Ransohoff's original story was announced "up front" in May 1963. Postponement of the production until Richard Burton was sprung from Huston's *Night of the Iguana* and Wyler's lack of confidence in the story led him to bow

---

* Alias "Robert Rich," Trumbo won for *The Brave One,* directed by Irving Rapper.

out (and Vincente Minnelli to become the director of *The Sand-piper*).

The political crossfire and internecine Writers' Guild warfare in which *Friendly Persuasion* and the Wyler brothers were innocent bystanders left Willy embittered. The brouhaha had cost his brother his best chance also to earn an Oscar and the American Legion threat smacked of Fascist bookburning, even if the super-patriots were to look increasingly pathetic. "Their chief contribution to the film industry has been keeping Chaplin's name off Hollywood Boulevard for twenty years," Willy said in 1972 when the Academy brought the aging comedian to America for a belated tribute and the Hollywood Chamber of Commerce finally dared put his name in a star on its "walk of fame."

An adaptation of Terence Rattigan's *The Sleeping Prince* was a possible next for Wyler but Wilson's lawsuit and the high cost of *Friendly Persuasion* cooled relations between Allied Artists and the producer-director. As Geoffrey Wolf was to write, the blacklist "died of terminal stupidity" around 1960 and Dalton Trumbo was to be the first writer up from the underground. Kirk Douglas was instrumental in getting Trumbo a credit on Stanley Kubrick's *Spartacus*, but it was to be Otto Preminger who stole the publicity thunder by announcing *before* production that Trumbo would be his screenwriter on *Exodus*. The American Legion picketed both films (Senator John F. Kennedy was one of the few legislators to brave the cinema pickets). As Preminger had shrewdly foreseen, *Spartacus* and *Exodus* were too successful at the box office and the Legion grip was broken.

To help sell *Friendly Persuasion,* Wyler took it to the 1957 Cannes Film Festival. It was the first time he was there as a contestant (competing films included Ingmar Bergman's *Seventh Seal*, Andrej Wadja's *Kanal,* and Jules Dassin's exile picture, *Celui qui doit mourir*) and he and Talli had to follow the festival etiquette laid down by Metro's Paris publicity office (MGM distributed Allied Artists' films in Europe).

After showing *La Loi du Seigneur*—as *Friendly Persuasion* was majestically titled in French—and the obligatory press conference, the Wylers settled down at the Carlton, meeting old friends and making new acquaintances. They were enjoying themselves when the publicity chief told Willy he had to get out of town.

"Why!" Willy wanted to know.

"You're a contestant. If you stay here now it looks as if you're waiting for the Palme d'or."

"Well, aren't we?"

"Of course, but we must not *look* as if we are."

Willy suggested they go home, but the publicist told him he couldn't do that. "Just move down the coast a bit, to Monte Carle or Beaulieu for the remainder of the festival. Then on the night of the awards, I'll find out. If we win, I call you and you come back."

The Wylers went around saying *au revoir* to old and new friends before spending several wonderful days at the Hotel Réserve in Beaulieu. On the big night, they didn't hear from Cannes and started packing to leave for California, when suddenly the publicist called. "Come back, *Friendly Persuasion* had won the Palme d'or first prize!"

"Back we went, feeling ridiculous because a few days earlier we had said goodbye to everybody," Willy remembered. "But not one person said, 'I thought you had left.' They all knew I hadn't."

The Big Country was a United Artists release. It was coproduced by Wyler and Gregory Peck, who spared no expense or trouble to make the film live up to the operative word in the title. Big it was.

Westerns had come a long way since *Crook Buster* and the other Mustangs Willy and the others had conceived, written (if that was the word), shot, and cut in one week on Uncle Carl's back lot. Recently the genre had become fashionable and significant, beginning with Fred Zinnemann's *High Noon* in 1952 and, the following year, George Stevens' *Shane*. Not everybody liked the new "significance." In the mid-1950s, André Bazin felt John Ford was repeating himself, that Howard Hawks represented a healthy transition, that Anthony Mann was the young hopeful, and that, with *Seven Men from Now*, Budd Boetticher was becoming the greatest western director.[5]

Wyler thought the new giant screen was eminently suited for the western (Bazin felt Henry Hathaway had started using CinemaScope without much imagination in *The Kentuckian* but that Preminger had been inventive in *his* wide-screen debut, *River of No Return*) because the whole idea was to have space. With *The Big Country*, story and screen size should be of the same dimensions. The wide screen, he soon discovered, was awkward in intimate scenes because it tended to let the audiences' eyes wander from principal characters toward incidental "bits." To shoot *The Big Country,* Wyler chose Franz Planer. Together, they chose Technirama and Technicolor.

The story was as bone-hard and uncluttered as a 1928 Wyler five-reeler—two feuding families, their cattle, their need for water belonging to a school mistress (Jean Simmons), and their settled conviction that as big as the country is, there is no room for both of them. The Terrills, led by the Major (Charles Bickford), stand for culture and live in luxury, but they are as brutal in their own way as are the Hannasseys, who live in squalor under the patriarchal domination of Rufus (Burl Ives).

What made *The Big Country* a western with a difference was its hero, James McKay (Gregory Peck), a man who refused to act according to accepted standards of behavior, the western code of ethics.

McKay is a gentleman sailor from Baltimore coming west to wed Patricia Terrill (Carroll Baker), whom he had met and wooed while she was attending a New England finishing school. McKay is a man out of place in the west, it seems, and the Major's spoiled and uppity daughter is not long in coming to the conclusion she has made a mistake. Her fiancé does not bother to answer back, hit back, or try to prove his courage unless it suits him to do so. He rides the unridable stallion with no one watching him except the Mexican stable hand, he fights the sardonic Terrill foreman (Charlton Heston) alone in the moonlight.

Enraged by the Hannasseys' rough stuff and spurred on by the foreman, who himself cottons to Patricia, the Terrills pillage the Hannassey ranch. Reprisal bounces back on reprisal until the scattered feud pulls together into one pitched battle for control of Big Muddy, the schoolmarm's ranch. Now it must be held by one or the other. The Hannasseys make their own bid by kidnapping the schoolmistress. To stop the bloodletting, McKay has already bought Big Muddy so that everyone can continue using its water. All is to no avail. Patricia refuses to understand and the Terrills and Hannasseys fight it out in a long bloody battle between the walls of a sand-white canyon. Old man Hannessey kills and is, in turn, killed by old man Terrill and, in the fadeout, Patricia is ready to marry the foreman while McKay rides into the sunset with the schoolmistress.

For a simple story, *The Big Country* had the lengthiest writing credits of a Wyler movie—screenplay by James R. Webb, Sy Bartlett, and Robert Wilder; adapted by Jessamyn West and Robert Wyler from the Donald Hamilton story *Ambush at Blanco Canyon*. Webb was a prolific western writer, the scripter of such Robert Aldrich yarns as *Vera Cruz* and *Apache,* who had just written *Pork Chop Hill* for Lewis Milestone (he was also to write the Ford–Hathaway–George Marshall Cinerama western *How the West Was Won* and Ford's *Cheyenne Autumn*). Bartlett was the former newsman who had helped Wyler get into the Air Force, now a screenwriter-producer forming a partnership with Peck (in 1967, he was to hire Wilson to write *Che*). Wilder was a novelist friend of Robert's, the author of *Flamingo Road,* which Curtiz had adapted in 1949, and of *And Ride Tiger*. Increasingly, credits were "arbitrated" by the Writers' Guild of America (WGA), the successor to the old Screen Writers' Guild. Wyler was to remember little of who wrote what on *The Big Country* and even to express astonishment at finding Jessamyn West among the names. His fights with the WGA over who should have his or her name on the screen were far from over.

"It was a good story and I got a big cast together," Wyler recalled. "Secondary people were all top actors and actresses. We built a whole western town near Stockton, California. We needed wide open stretches but also fertile country. The canyon battle was shot in the Mojave Desert and Red Rock Canyon, some of the same locations as *Hell's Heroes*."

Charles Bickford was another throwback to Death Valley and the Mojave Desert, 1929. Then Charlie had been a pain in the neck, Wyler reminded Bickford's agent when the "ten-percenter" sat down in his office to offer his client's services. Charlie would like to play the Major, the agent said, a perfect role for him.

Wyler smiled. "I thought, 'Old Charlie wants to make up and he doesn't get the parts he used to.' So, I asked the agent to bring Charlie in."

At the next appointment, Bickford was eager and pleasant. They never mentioned the old days. Wyler did want to know one thing—how was Charlie in the saddle these days?

"Oh, you remember how I ride." Bickford grinned with a telling gesture.

"In that case, the part is yours."

Once in the Mojave, Wyler had to double Bickford in equestrian scenes as the actor could hardly get on or off a horse. One day in a scene with Peck, the company had to wait for one hour until Charlie came back from his private lunch.

"Charlie, you're late," Wyler said.

"Yes, what are you going to do about it?" the actor replied.

"I guess you've got me there. I can't fire you, you're in half the picture."

"So let's cut the bullshit and get to work."

The Big Country started in August 1957. Wyler loved his big screen and Technicolor and lovingly shot a lone tree in a yellow-brown prairie, horsemen tracing their arabesques against dusty plains, bone-white canyons and cruel mesas. He had Planer put the wide-angle lenses on the camera and film muted hues—browns, faded yellows, early dawns, and perspectives stretching to the horizon. At the screening of the dailies—Bob Swink had been upped to "supervising editor" and the cutters were Robert Belcher and John Faure—he realized there was a danger, that the open country was *too* big, that it actually dwarfed the actors and, in a sense, made the story puny and irrelevant.

He worked painstakingly, demanding perfection from actors and technicians alike. The premise was as tough as the theme of *Friendly Persuasion*—just how much violence must a peaceable man use to preserve peace—and his *mise en scène* would have to say that also. To make the point, violence had to be expert. It also had to carry the exact weight. When McKay rouses the foreman out of bed to fight him with no one to watch them in the moonlight, the script had it ending in a draw and McKay, gasping for air, say, "Well, what has it proved?" Very simple on paper, but once fleshed out by Peck and Heston, the scene didn't necessarily have the same weight. And now this huge screen. Shot in closeup, the fisticuffs looked ugly. Wyler chose to shoot it in long shots that made the fight pointless, tiny figures in the expanse of the landscape.

The scene was an example of the camera expressing an action by the choice of setup. It underscored the superb machinery at the command of a modern filmmaker and the technological perfection of the medium. Willy couldn't help comparing this fine-tuned tool to the means at his disposal back in the Blue Streak days with Art Acord or Ted Wells and the leading lady changing wardrobe behind a reflector. A quantum leap separated the two.

But weren't movies becoming the most cumbersome way of communicating an emotion? Wasn't this gigantic apparatus, this marvel of calibrated lenses, miles of cables, sync motors, cranes, and trailers on this barefaced mountain mesa, and the backup technology in labs and studios hundreds of miles away yielding forever diminishing returns? If *everything* had become possible, it had also become difficult and expensive. The power was now equally divided between management and union, as in any noodle factory. If producers, agents, directors, and stars decided *what* would be on the screen, the unions decided *how*. To get the silhouettes of two horses on a cliff above the canyon for the next morning's first shot was an exercise in ruinous logistics. It involved wranglers and the Teamsters' Union. The two wranglers would get up at four in the morning to breakfast and be at the stables at five, there to be driven in production cars to the location, there to feed the two horses and take them to the designated cliff. The horses were in place by nine when the day's first shot was lined up and the wranglers behind boulders safely out of camera range. By noon, these men behind the boulders were on double time, by two P.M., on golden time, and by "wrap"-time they had earned more than the first assistant director. If two men were to sit on the horses up on the cliff, other unions became involved and if the horses were the principals' mounts, the number of wranglers automatically doubled.

In setside interviews with visiting press, Wyler made fun of traditional westerns and tried to get newsmen's reactions to the pacifist theme with provoking statements. "I have never seen any great virtue in the American tradition of punching a guy in the nose if he said something you didn't like," he told one group of visiting Hollywood correspondents. "It only proves who can punch the quickest or the hardest—nothing else. The problem that intrigues me is whether people can have faith in a man who doesn't punch." The newsmen grinned and hurried on to interview the stars. Rumors of clashes with Bickford had filtered down from the location. "I have been an independent spirit since I was that high," Charlie told the press with a glint in the eye toward Wyler. "It's a characteristic of mine and there's nothing I can do about it, even if I wanted to. I have never been unreasonable at any time, merely firm." [6]

It was a big picture. By the time it opened at the Astor on Broadway, October 1, 1958, it was a $3.1-million production and a two-and-three-quarter-hours-long movie that United Artists was nervous about. Would it click? The reviews ranged from disastrous to sublime. Bosley Crowther said that despite its mighty pretentions, *The Big Country* did not get "beneath the skin of its conventional western situation and its stock western characters. It skims across standard complications and ends on a platitude. Peace is a pious precept but fightin' is more excitin'. That's what it proves." [7]

The *New York Herald Tribune* said the film was "astutely and enthusiastically made" while *Newsweek* felt it "strongly suggests that there is absolutely nothing wrong with westerns that plenty of money and an offbeat hero can't cure, or at the very least ameliorate." [8] *Time* went all out and called *The Big Country* "a starkly beautiful, carefully written classic western that demands comparison with *Shane*." [9]

On their way back from Rome and *Ben-Hur,* Heston, Talli, and Willy attended the London premiere and the opening of a British Film Institute "season of four Wyler films"—*Detective Story, Carrie, Jezebel,* and *Roman Holiday*. Heston told a news conference he was happy, whether playing a villain or a hero. "Change is healthy; an actor thrives on diversity," he said, adding that "Willy's poorest film is good by any other standard."

The *Times* called *The Big Country* "not quite an epic but touched with the epic quality," but found Wyler "a director of understanding and sympathy who yet has a touch that is strangely fallible and uncertain." [10] *The Guardian* felt the only saving grace of this massive treatment of a slight theme was Wyler's irony, while *Film and Filming* saw the picture as an allegory, Major Terrill a Fascist dictator, and Hannassey running "his less prosperous community like a Communist dictator." [11]

Perhaps the most perspicacious notice came from veteran critic C. A. Lejeune, who put her finger on what Wyler himself had feared: *"The Big Country* is too big for its little people. The actors struggle to make their own affairs seem important, but they are dwarfed by the immensity that the camera has brought into the field of vision.

"I remember some years ago there was an exhibition of modern American paintings in London," Miss Lejeune wrote. "One picture called, I think, 'Joanna's World,' has always stayed in my memory. I don't know the artist's name, but I do know I wished then and have often wished since that I had been rich enough to buy it for my own, or provident enough to save a newspaper reproduction. It showed a very young girl lying in a field of long grass, looking up meditatively towards a small, white frame house in the heart of nowhere. I thought it quite beautiful and it said, with an economy of strokes, everything I have longed to feel assured of about America's size and space and peace. Because it put me in mind of that picture, every now and then, I am grateful to *The Big Country*. It may not be much to think about, but it is often a lovely thing to see." [12]

32

If *The Big Country* was big, *Ben-Hur* was gigantic, a colossal
gamble by Metro-Goldwyn-Mayer to redress the fortunes of a
company weakened by years of debilitating proxy fights, hardened
arteries, and a sorry record. For Wyler, *Ben-Hur* was a film that
took two years out of his life, a picture that made him feel less
like a director than a general and eventually gave him financial
security.

Everything was outsized. For the better part of a year, *Ben-Hur*
was the biggest movie in production anywhere, using more people and bigger sets and inspiring more news bulletins than the
rest of the industry put together. Metro's re-creation of ancient
Rome was visible from afar on the outskirts of the Eternal City.
The story of the Judean aristocrat who falls into the hands of
Roman conquerors, becomes a galley slave, and rises to help his
people as Rome's greatest athlete took nine months to film. Five
hundred newsmen visited the locations during 1958 and the interest was compounded by VIP chic. Everyone who was anyone
wanted to ride chariots that summer. For years, prime ministers,
diplomats, and "beautiful people" would tell Wyler they had, of
course, met on *Ben-Hur*. "Of course," he would say with a smile,
not knowing who they were. To him. *Ben-Hur* has been a sixteen-hours-a-day, seven-days-a-week galley.

In 1958, *Ben-Hur* was the costliest movie ever made. Yet it was
not the financial madness of *Cleopatra,* which Fox started in late
1959 on a $3.4-million budget and wrapped three years later at a

cost of $44 million. As they go, *Ben-Hur* was not the tightest-run movie in film history, but it *was* managed and, in financial terms, it was a vindication of president Joseph R. Vogel's gamble. Ironically, MGM's husbanding was thrown to the winds two years later with the $30-million disaster *Mutiny on the Bounty* that wiped out most of the profits of *Ben-Hur.*

Excess was nothing new. D. W. Griffith had started the trend in 1915 with *The Birth of a Nation,* an epic that was almost three hours long, cost over one hundred thousand 1915 dollars, and over the next decade, grossed an estimated (but never verified) $50 million.* Metro's own 1926 *Ben-Hur,* on which Willy had worked as a $10-a-day assistant, had been one of the biggest box-office hits of its day, earning more than $9 million, even if distribution costs and the "crazy" Frank Godsol deal (giving the original stage producers fifty percent of the profits) left Metro with a million less than the $4 million it cost.

To compete with television, size had worked again. *The Robe* and CinemaScope had shown the way and *Around the World in 80 Days* confirmed the hunch. Mike Todd's 1956 extravaganza had pinned its faith on a mixture of lavish expenditure ($7 million), exotic locations, clever back-lot shooting, and big-screen treatment. Michael Anderson had shot the Jules Verne classic on Fox, MGM, and other studio back lots with acres of permanently built sets which Todd, forebodingly, had simply rented. *Around the World* had grossed $23 million domestically and Cecil B. De-Mille's *Ten Commandments* had just brought over $40 million into Paramount's coffers (even if King Vidor's *War and Peace* had been a disappointment). Currently, Joshua Logan's *South Pacific* and David Lean's multinational *Bridge on the River Kwai* were doing it for Fox and Columbia Pictures. MGM, of course, owned the all-time box-office champion—Victor Fleming's *Gone With the Wind,* which since 1939 had made over $80 million.

But Metro was falling apart. Early in the 1950s, MGM stockholders had become restive, noticing dwindling profits (a $1-million loss in studio operations was declared in 1953), and the apparent inability of tired old men—Nicholas Schenck at the presidency of Loew's Inc. and Louis B. Mayer at the studio—to

---

* Griffith poured his personal earnings of over $1 million into *Intolerance* and lost it all.

revitalize the companies, now nominally "divorced." In 1955, seventy-four-year-old Schenck stepped down in the face of possible proxy fights by large stockholders and was succeeded by Arthur Loew, the son of the founder and a long-time chief of the successful foreign operations. A year later, Loew backed down and the presidency went, unexpectedly, to Vogel, a competent, if colorless, sixty-one-year-old theaterman.

Although largely inactive, Mayer began to scheme for Vogel's downfall. Mayer's fortunes had not been the best. When shareholders had started to question the studio's losses between 1947 and 1951, Mayer and Schenck had appointed Dore Schary head of production, with Mayer acting in a supervisory capacity. But Schary, who, in 1951, first thought of remaking *Ben-Hur,* made movies too often out of touch with the times and, by 1956, MGM's annual losses were approaching $5 million. Schary was fired.

An increasingly bitter battle of factions continued through 1957 as Vogel cleaned out cells of nepotism, caused some economies, and initiated plans for bolder movies. Mayer had never liked the cool theaterman and had allied himself with Joseph Tomlinson, a tough Canadian contractor who, with five percent of outstanding stock, was the holder of the biggest block of shares. In March, Tomlinson issued a statement to the board condemning Vogel outright and demanding that Mayer be given the presidency. Vogel feared a coup d'état and, for an irregular board meeting of the Tomlinson-Mayer group in New York, had the Loew's building filled with armed guards. After four directors resigned, Vogel decided to bring the war to a head at a stockholders' meeting October 15. Eleven hundred stockholders filled the Loew's State Theater on Times Square. The struggle proceeded for over ten hours as Tomlinson clashed furiously with Vogel. At the end, the stockholders overwhelmingly voted confidence in Vogel and completed the rout of the Mayer group. Vogel rushed out announcements of forthcoming projects—William Wyler would start production at once on a lavish new version of *Ben-Hur,* Yul Brynner and Maria Schell would star in a screen version of *The Brothers Karamazov,* Paul Newman and Elizabeth Taylor in *Cat on a Hot Tin Roof,* and Frank Sinatra in *Some Came Running.* The "vault" of MGM movies would be leased—not sold—to television, perhaps Vogel's wisest move, since it meant

Metro retained ownership of its magnificent library and could continue to reissue *Gone With the Wind* and *The Wizard of Oz*. Two weeks after the stockholders' meeting, the humiliated and drained Louis B. Mayer died. "This is the end of a volume, not a chapter," Rabbi Edgar Magnin said in his eulogy at the sparsely attended funeral. At Mayer's death, the era of the movie mogul had been gone for several years.

The remaking of Lew Wallace's biblical saga—first published in 1880 and an MGM property since 1923—was a spur-of-the-moment decision by Vogel, although Sam Zimbalist had had it in mind since he produced (and Mervyn Le Roy directed) *Quo Vadis* in 1951. Fifty-six-year-old Zimbalist was an obscure, if literate, house producer, a "Mayer man" during the early rounds of the first fight between Schenck and Mayer (*Quo Vadis* had been a Dore Schary–John Huston project before it became a Zimbalist–Le Roy production). Zimbalist's most famous producer credits were the 1942 *Tortilla Flat*, directed by Fleming, Le Roy's war propaganda, *Thirty Seconds over Tokyo,* and, in 1950, *King Solomon's Mines,* a film with two directors, Compton Bennett and Andrew Marton.

Zimbalist came to Wyler in mid-1957 saying he wanted him to direct a hush-hush project—*Ben-Hur.* Wyler thought the producer was kidding.

"Why don't you go after DeMille or somebody like that," Wyler wondered. "I've never done a spectacle, that's not my style at all."

"That doesn't matter, Willy," Zimbalist interrupted. "The spectacle will take care of itself. What we want, what we're interested in, is good intimate stuff. Intimacy is the meat of the story and proportionately, the spectacle is, perhaps, one tenth of the whole film."

"Nevertheless, it's not my kind of a film."

"Won't you read it?"

Wyler did and found the script a good but primitive and elementary story. Zimbalist kept after him but Wyler remained uninterested. One meeting was held in Zimbalist's office, where the producer showed Wyler a meticulous storyboard layout of the chariot race. Wyler looked and listened and realized that more time and effort would go into this sequence than into any movie ever made.

"Now *that* intrigues me," he told the producer. "I'll direct the chariot race. That, I can see, will be terrific."

"Come off it, Willy."

"I'm an old western director. I'd love to do a horserace of this size."

"The chariot race is second unit," Zimbalist tried to reason.

"I know, but that's what I'd like to do. Pay me what you like and you don't have to give me any screen credits."

Zimbalist tried another tack, telling the reluctant director he was just plain chicken and didn't have the courage to tackle something of this size.

"You may be right there," Willy said.

At home, Wyler read Wallace's book. He reasoned with himself that this *was* new, something that would be a challenge, bring him a lot of money, and be fun besides. There was, perhaps, also a deeper reason. There was something in the clumsy, naïve, and nearly unreadable Victorian fiction that appealed to the Jewishness in him.

As many men of his generation, temperament, and political background, he wore his Jewishness with nonchalance and distance. Somehow, it only came up in him when it was challenged. His children were not brought up in even Reform Judaism, only made aware of his and Talli's different upbringings (he refused the word religion). Although he had never been there, he had applauded the creation of Israel and given generously to the cause. His empathy for Israel had just been roused. In 1956, the Jewish state had started a preemptive war against Egypt, a *blitzkrieg*, as it were, actively backed by England and France, but condemned by President Eisenhower and the United States and, therefore, stopped in its tracks.

Ben-Hur told the same story—Jews fighting for their lives and their freedom. What had changed in two thousand years? Nothing. Instead of Romans, it was now Arabs; but the fight for a homeland hadn't changed.

Wallace's old bestseller was an attack on Rome, on the militarist state. To Wallace, the crime of Rome had been that it became decadent, that it had no longer governed but oppressed. The hero was right out of storybook fairy tales—rich, handsome, and aristocratic. He dressed well, admired women, was a brave hunter and prepared to gamble, not only with money but with his life as well. Above all, he was resourceful and had learned to survive. The perils of the plot were designed to measure his strength. Exile, slavery, the chariot race, and the attempted seduction by Messala's mistress (mercifully left out of the script) were the obstacle course Odysseus and all folk heroes had always faced.

Wyler felt he could make a picture out of *Ben-Hur*. Wallace's tale didn't have to be altered; only judicious pruning and polish was necessary. What was needed, he decided, was a sure narrative and dialogue that wasn't Hollywood archaic.

"The more I thought about it, the more I saw the possibilities. There were interesting elements. The tremendous enmity between hero and villain was nothing new, but here the antagonism grew out of a great childhood friendship. Ben-Hur and Messala had grown up together and their reunion after many years offered the possibility for a great emotional scene. On the other hand, Ben-Hur and the commander of the Roman fleet started as the bitterest of enemies only to become the best of friends. In fact, as the custom had it, Quintus Arrius adopted Ben-Hur and made him his foster son. There was a kind of switch here which intrigued me. Basically, of course, it was an adventure yarn."

He talked it over with Talli. Saying yes meant disrupting the girls' education. It meant moving to Italy for a year or more. The whole family was enthusiastic, however (Willy included), since *Roman Holiday* had been such a gratifying experience. Nineteen-year-old Cathy, seventeen-year-old Judy, seven-year-old Melanie, and five-year-old David would come over with Talli. The pre-production budget was $7 million. Willy's salary would be $350,000 plus expenses. Metro wouldn't skimp on the frills for its director. The Wylers would have a villa, complete with servants, for the length of the production, plus limousine and chauffeur. *Ben-Hur* would be headquartered at Cinecitta studios.

"My God, I said to myself, I'll make *Ben-Hur* and see if I know how to make a picture like this."

Wyler's yes set the dinosaur in motion. He was still working on *The Big Country* when Vogel made the announcement and Swink had to finish editing and mixing the UA release. Charlton Heston was immediately set for the title role (he was doing retakes at Paramount on *The Buccaneer* when they signed), and to play Messala, Zimbalist and Wyler chose Stephen Boyd, a virile Irishman who had starred in several British and French movies and recently completed his first Hollywood film, Henry King's *The Bravados*. Wyler left for Rome, where a diplomat's villa on Via Appia Antica and a flock of servants awaited him. Within days, he was on a sixteen-hours-a-day, seven-days-a-week schedule that was to go on for nine months.

Key people were already in place. Andrew Marton, who had co-directed *King Solomon's Mines* and done second-unit work on *Quo Vadis*, had already been picked by Zimbalist to film the chariot race with Yakima Canutt—"the ex-greatest stuntman in the world," as Heston said—training drivers and setting up the race. Robert Surtees was named director of photography and writer-director Mario Soldati (*Il sogno di Zorro, La Donna del fiume*, and other workaday Gina Lollobrigida, Sophia Loren, and Alberto Sordi movies) headed the Italian contingent. William Horning and Edward Carfagno shared the art direction responsibilities, and Hugh Hunt did the set decorations. The main set, the eighteen-acre Circus Maximus of Antioch, was far from ready when Wyler arrived, but everything was advancing on schedule.

Heston arrived April 13 with press conferences at the Stazione Termini and a safari by Cadillacs to another villa with five gardens, frescoed ceilings, marble floors, and statues in the hallways. With him were Lydia, their three-year-old son, Fraser, and twenty-three pieces of luggage. The next day, Heston began training with Canutt and head wrangler Glenn Randall's horses, brought to Rome from Yugoslavia. Heston decided to keep a diary of *Ben-Hur*. "Considering we are not shooting, workday is certainly full—three hours chariot practice, one hour javelin practice (I'll never make the Olympics). I was very cowardly at doctor's office. PM—the fourth fitting for contact lenses designed to protect eyes from flying stones during race sequence. Frankly, they hurt like hell! Inclined to think I'd prefer stones." [1] When Heston wasn't with Canutt, he was with Elizabeth Haffenden, the London couturière who headed the costume design.

While thousands of Romans grew beards in the hope of being hired as extras, Wyler and Zimbalist were off to London to persuade Christopher Fry to work on Karl Tunberg's original script and to cast the picture. Tunberg, who had been the Screen Writers' Guild president in 1951, was a prolific writer whose efforts included *A Yank in the RAF, Beau Brummell* and *My Gal Sal*. He had delivered the *Ben-Hur* script to Zimbalist years earlier and the producer had had S. N. Behrman and Maxwell Anderson try their literate hands at it. Tunberg's screenplay was a quasi-western morality play and it was hoped Fry could give it the neoclassic tone and literary lift that Zimbalist's (and MGM's) decision to hire Wyler was predicated on.

Wyler felt strongly about the film's language. No one could speak informal American in a Biblical drama. The dialogue would have to have the *sheen* of the period—speaking Latin and first-century Hebrew was of course out of the question—and the speech would have to be colloquial, but neither *modern* colloquial, nor archaic. It was all a matter of nuances. As Martha Scott exclaimed when she first heard Cathy O'Donnell read the line "Dinner is ready!", "that sounds like Andy Hardy."

Fry delivered. A line by Sheik Ilderim when he feeds Ben-Hur in his tent had read: "Did you enjoy your dinner?" In Fry's typewriter it became: "Was the food to your liking?" Throughout, Fry—who was to write *The Bible* for John Huston—gave the spoken words a *classical* sound.

With second billing—ahead of Boyd—Jack Hawkins was persuaded to play Quintus Arrius and both Zimbalist and Wyler were excited about Haya Harareet, an unknown Israeli actress they signed to play Esther. Hugh Griffith was cast as Sheik Ilderim—the man who puts Judah Ben-Hur into the chariot race —and Sam Jaffe as Ben-Hur's loyal steward. Martha Scott, who had played Heston's mother in *The Ten Commandments,* repeated her maternal role as Miriam. There was no official slot on the picture for Robert, but sister-in-law Cathy O'Donnell was given the part of Tirzah. In all, the script had forty-five "principals" (MGM publicity somehow managed to count 360 speaking parts).

The majority of the speaking roles were divided between British and American actors, following Wyler's decision to have all Romans represented by Britons, and the Hebrews (with the exception of Miss Harareet) chosen from among Americans. Boyd's Irish fitted well into this linguistic scheme since Messala was a Roman brought up in Judea.

Back in Rome, Soldati and Wyler's French-speaking second assistant, Alberto Cardone (later to become a director of spaghetti westerns) lined up background actors and extras while Miss Haffenden's dressmakers turned out Roman togas *en masse.* By the end of April, Heston had soloed in a chariot and Boyd had joined him in the training. Heston's experience in westerns made the driving comparatively easy, but Boyd's hands were torn to ribbons in the initial tryouts.

Christopher Fry arrived early in May. Under May 13, Heston wrote in his diary that he had had a long conference with Wyler about his role. "His ideas on making Judah Ben-Hur more than a lay figure in a costume picture are becoming clearer and clearer to me," Heston wrote. "Main areas of work here seem to lie in the beginning when we must make him an untried, uncommitted man, thus allowing room for change at slave galley and on Calvary."

Four days later, Heston spent the morning rehearsing Fry's rewrite of a quarrel scene with Messala. "This is crucial scene of whole first half of story since it motivates everything that follows," he noted. "Christopher's version vast improvement and Willy brought out its virtues in his usual manner as we worked . . . picking, carping, nagging, fiddling; a reading here and a gesture there until you are trammeled and fenced in by his concept. Rehearsals not nearly as trying, however, as dinner interview with one of those lethal London journalists who strain everything you say through an acid ear."

Principal photography started May 20 with a scene with Griffith and Heston, followed four days later by the first spectacular —the entrance of the chariots in the Circus Maximus. Eight thousand extras were at hand. Before he yelled "Action!" for the first time, Wyler had Cardone translate the story of how he had been one of Fred Niblo's assistants thirty-three years earlier.

"It was a fabulous day, the chariots came out into the arena, thousands of people, and Pontius Pilate (Frank Thring) were supposed to give the charioteers the signal to start the race. I thought this was too fast. I knew that once the race started, there would be no longshots. In order to sustain the race, the audience would have to be *in* it, not up in the stands among the spectators, where there would be little chance to see this magnificent set, as it should be seen, in longshots from all angles. So I decided we should have a parade of the charioteers going around the stadium once, in perfect formation, like a ballet. Go around once, then come to the place where Pontius Pilate makes his speech and they're off!" Heston recalled the day as long and difficult, observing, "Willy seems to be succeeding in vital task of injecting details of small reality in huge canvas he has to color before we are done."

On May 29, the principals moved indoors to the Castle Antonio set for the first meaty scenes—the opening-sequence meeting of Ben-Hur and Messala. "Got very little on film, but Willy established thoroughly just exactly amount of pains he's prepared to take with scene," Heston wrote. Eight days later, Heston scribbled: "Today, one of the toughest days I've ever had professionally. Willy really bore down and it was *not* an ego-boosting experience. He's unhappy not so much with what I've done so far in part, but with my potential for part."

Whenever Heston or Boyd were not in a setup, they were sent over to Marton, Canutt, and Soldati for closeups of the race, which was established as being run by nine charioteers. Each chariot was drawn by four horses and since certain teams had to be duplicated and there had to be understudy teams for the star teams, it added up to nearly eighty horses. The surfacing of the track proved a major problem. Research in Roman libraries turned up nothing on the composition of circus grounds. "The surface of our track had to be hard enough to hold the careening chariots and horses, had to have a drainage system in case of rain, and had to have a sanded top because cement would lame the horses," Marton wrote in an account of his filming.[2] "So, we started with ground rock debris, which had to be steam-rolled. That was covered with ten inches of ground lava—against my and Yakima Canutt's judgment—and *that* was covered with eight inches of crusted yellow rock. This lasted only one day when actual shooting began."

At the end, they decided to leave only a one and one-half inch layer of lava. Marton's charioteers were mostly elite stunt and rodeo riders from the States, but there were also Italians. Despite the best precautions, accidents did occur. Two chariots smashed into two of the 65mm cameras. The camera operator and his assistant were only bruised because they were behind a wooden barricade, but the production schedule suffered. Canutt's twenty-two-year-old son, Joe, doubling for Heston, took the heaviest spill when he and his chariot sailed over another charioteer's wreck and he was thrown out between his horses.

From Heston's diary June 11: "Shot till nearly eight tonight on short scene with Mother and Tirzah after Messala quarrel. I've little to say in scene, but this precisely situation where Willy likely to be digging for nuances of reaction . . . flicker of response to someone else's lines. As the fellow says, 'Acting is reacting.' "

June 25: "Finished first scene with Esther, closest to real love scene we have. She played, in my opinion, very simply, very well. She worked with intense, grinding concentration with Willy, but each take seemed to progress and there wasn't that dead-end feeling of nowhere you sometimes get. Poor Haya, having started so well on her first scene, will now have to wait several months before she works again, while Judah is off in the galleys and whatnot."

June 27: "Still on Stage One trying to escape from that damned prison cell. We did, in all, thirty shots of fight with guards and attempted escape. At lunchtime, Willy came up with really brilliant idea that escape at this point should only be attempt that fails. Audiences have seen Errol Flynn do too many spectacular escapes in old Warner movies to try that one again. Today, Willy didn't like it early, Lord knows, but he liked it a lot when we finally got it. He even, surprisingly, asked me for ideas on how to manage fight. I left a lot of sweat, not to mention drop or two of blood, on floor of that cell, though. Propman, very pleased at fulfilling Willy's exacting standards of detail, proudly produced some two dozen bugs to crawl on wall of cell. Willy watched them gravely, then deadpanned, 'Yeah, but all crawling *downwards!*' "

July 12: "Started retakes of dinner for Messala scene with Martha Scott now playing my mother (again!); good to work with her once more, we were getting to be old hands at mother-son relationship after *Ten C.* We didn't get too much shot; after long session with Fry, Willy came back to sound stage with not a word about changes they'd obviously been making. When we asked him, 'What about new scene?' he grinned wicked Willy-type grin and said, 'I'm not going to throw out this one till you get it right.' "

The big negative was awkward and time consuming. Everything was in the frame and Wyler had to fight empty screen space. He either had to film two people in a void or fill the screen with superfluous and distracting elements. To light a scene was another problem. Since the camera "saw" too much, light could not be brought down too close. Scaffolding had to be built to put projectors up and out of the frame. Moving them farther away meant more projectors were needed to give the same candle-power. The 65mm cameras had other drawbacks. Their sheer weight made moves complicated—it took four men with steel bars to lift a camera and Wyler ended up keeping his camera on a crane much of the time. Marton had other problems. In standard 35mm, he would use a four-inch (100mm) lens for closeups. In the 65mm medium, however, this became a 200mm lens and the 200 could not be focused closer than fifty feet. He ended up using a 140mm lens and moving himself and crew closer to the horses, the hooves, and danger.

Since both Heston and Boyd were blue-eyed, Boyd was fitted with contact lenses making him a black-eyed Messala. As the months went by, the lenses hurt him so much, scenes had to be switched to give his eyes a rest. As Heston wrote September 5, "It's very difficult to achieve staring into blazing sun, blazing re-flectors, equally blazing 10-K spots."

Exposed film piled up in the cutting rooms of Ralph Winters and John Dunning, as did the cost in the accounting office. Zim-balist and Wyler sat up one night pouring groggily over figures.

"You know what's going to happen if we make a flop?" Zimbal-ist sighed.

"No," Wyler yawned.

"Metro will go bankrupt and the MGM lot in Culver City will disappear," the producer said.

"And once Metro goes under, other will follow," Wyler added.

"The whole American film industry will vanish."

"Hollywood will become a desert again."

"And it will all be the fault of Wyler and Zimbalist."

They knew they were exaggerating but it didn't sound so un-reasonable. *Ben-Hur* was now over the $10-million mark.

Vogel came over from New York and confirmed rumors that the stockholders were far from pacified, that he was in constant collision with the board and with Benjamin Thau, whom Vogel had appointed head of the studio on the Coast. Thau believed in sumptuous spectacles typical of MGM's heyday—massive musicals and historical dramas, while Vogel was so cautious he hesitated to approve outlays for studio repairs. Vogel had been very nervous about approving even a $10-million budget for *Ben-Hur*.

Vogel was given a VIP tour and taken to see Wyler on his cam-era boom directing a scene with Hugh Griffith.

"Is there anything I can help with?" Vogel asked the director during a moment of relative privacy.

"No, thank you," Willy replied. The MGM president watched politely for a while, then said good-bye.

For some reason, the scene didn't satisfy Wyler. After a couple of rehearsals, he thought it would be a better idea to shoot something else. Excusing Griffith for the day, he moved the company to an alternate set.

"Vogel was going around Europe attending to company affairs," Wyler remembered, "and when he came back five weeks later, I was picking up the same scene with Griffith, with some improvements made by Fry. Again, Vogel stood and watched. Finally, he said, 'Haven't I seen this scene before?' No doubt he thought we'd been filming the same thing for five weeks."

Pace, scope, and heat took their toll. Although casualties weren't so numerous they required a twenty-bed hospital staffed with two Italian physicians and two nurses, as MGM publicity claimed, the August and September heat did fell a number of people. The heat was unbearable, especially when added to the caloric output of projectors. Marton's horses could take only seven or eight runs a day. In his diary, Heston called September 9 the hottest day ever. "This damned slave galley is exactly that. Hottest set I've ever worked in and those oars are *heavy,* especially at six P.M." A week later, a cold wave set in and he and Hawkins spent days bobbing around wet and half-naked on a chilly raft.

The first major casualty was Henry Henigson, the picture's efficient general manager, who, back in 1933, had introduced John Barrymore to Wyler. Henigson had been active in all MGM films produced in Europe since 1950. He never stopped working and one of *Ben-Hur*'s two doctors warned Zimbalist and Wyler that Henigson would not last through the summer. Producer and director packed the manager off to a forced vacation on Capri while Maurizio Lodi Fe, the assistant general manager, ran the office. Both Henigson and Lodi Fe had been with Willy on *Roman Holiday* and it had been Helena Lodi Fe who had helped Talli to the hospital when David was born. Henigson couldn't stay away from *Ben-Hur,* however, and four days later was back in his Cinecitta production office.

On November 4, Zimbalist collapsed and died of a heart attack forty minutes after leaving the set with chest pains. No one had realized he was ailing or that the pressures were that high.

During the night, calls went back and forth across the Atlantic. By morning, tentative arrangements were made. Wyler still had at least a month and a half to go and it was agreed he would simply take over as producer while Joseph Cohn, a good administrator, would be sent over. Later in the morning, Willy called everybody together on Cinecitta's Stage 5 and said some appropriate words about Sam Zimbalist, who had worked on *Ben-Hur* since 1952. "Then we plunged back into scene," Heston wrote in his diary, "Willy exploring it with usual flexibility and insight, but through the afternoon, he seemed to lose heart a little, as well he might, and we stopped fairly early tonight." Three days later was a clear beautiful autumn day and they began filming Christ (Claude Heater) carrying the cross. Wyler wanted the Crucifixion to be both strong and real and to give a feel of dark political intrigue. "Huge, restless mob coiled and stirred through vast square Eddie Carfagno designed for scene, ready to howl derision on cue," Heston noted. "We shot avidly until the light went around four-thirty, even skipping lunch."

Many pictures have their "running gag," a tongue twister or line of mispronounced dialogue that becomes an in-joke insanely repeated by the whole crew during filming and always remembered. On *Ben-Hur* it was a centurion's command, uttered by an American actor who had lived a little too long in Rome. When exhausted slaves on their way to the galleys were led through Nazareth and allowed to drink from a fountain, the centurion suddenly pointed toward Ben-Hur and roared, "No water for *heem!*" Years later, Wyler and Heston would greet each other with that line. On *Jezebel,* it had been an eager shout by a little black boy, telling Miss Marsden, "Carriage comin'" and, a beat later, "Man on horseback, too." Soon everybody said "Cadge comin' " instead of "How are you?" and answered "Man on horseback, too."

The stream of visitors never stopped. Though not everyone was admitted to all the working areas, company policy was to try not to turn anyone away. Some five thousand persons were formally asked in and shown around, but many others saw some aspect of the filming. For the Wylers, the most welcome visitors were friends and family. Willy's cousin Lucien Wyler, his wife, and sister, Dorely Picard, came down from Basel, visiting the day they began filming the Passion. Lucien always had a sharp sense of humor and, in the middle of Jesus' cross-carrying scene, leaned toward Willy, whispering: *"Mach'sch risches!"*—a Yiddish expression roughly translating as "So, you're making anti-Semitic propaganda!"

Everybody from the Wyler and Tallichet clans was invited. The Wylers were spoiled on Via Appia Antica, but *Ben-Hur* was not the happy picture that *Roman Holiday* had been. It was an endurance contest, and Willy had little time for aristocratic leisure.

Since Cathy and Judy had appeared ever so briefly in *The Best Years of Our Lives* and in *Roman Holiday,* Talli wanted to get Melanie and David in *Ben-Hur.* "But the film was just too big and so much was going on, we never made it," she remembered. "The responsibilities were so heavy, it was so hot in Rome, and it was all too complicated."

Both Lydia and Talli were pressed into service as hostesses to what Willy called "diplomats, ambassadors, and bigshots from everywhere," but the location lives of Mrs. Heston and Mrs. Wyler were not the glamorous succession of fascinating people and parties every night their friends at home imagined. "They have visions of you leading marvelous lives in Rome and Paris; actually, it's more like entering a monastic order," Talli said. "Social life is confined to the day because everybody is in bed at nine. What it really comes down to is finding something to do during the daytime—fortunately, I'm a passionate sightseer—and being home at night. I don't want Willy to stumble in the door at eight-thirty to have dinner with the butler."

To Metro's gratification, the media interest was so overwhelming that *Variety* even interviewed the picture's publicist, Morgan Hudgins. "No less than five hundred correspondents from around the world showed up," Hudgins told the trade paper.[3] Wyler usually had the excuse of being too busy for anything but a two-minute setside interview, but he had to get used to never rehearsing or shooting a scene without visitors behind his back. On his January 25, 1959, show, Ed Sullivan had a film clip of himself learning to ride a chariot on the *Ben-Hur* set.

Marton's most difficult shot was toward the end of the race when the wheels of the two rivals' chariots are interlocked and Messala starts to whip Ben-Hur. "In order to show the immediate danger in which they were, I decided to pan from the interlocking and splintering wheels to the two antagonists in vicious combat," Marton wrote. "To get this effect, we had to chain the camera car to the two chariots. I didn't have time to realize that if one horse stumbled, the whole contraption—horses, chariots, stars, camera car—would crash and pile up in disaster."

Wyler was not to remember any "most difficult shot." To him, the constant pressure was what he could never forget. He was fast ruining MGM. The latest cost estimate Cohn brought over was a grand total of $15 million—the chariot race alone was costing $1 million. At current projections, *Ben-Hur* would have to gross $30 million just to break even.

Wyler was still not happy with the final scene and had Fry back on his typewriter reshaping Pontius Pilate. Heston took more punishment than most. "Ty Power's shockingly sudden death on set in Spain yesterday made me suddenly aware of my mortality," he reflected November 16. "Appropriate time to think of it since we were shooting on our day off to take advantage of continuing fine weather. We did last closeup after sun had gone, really. I was, perhaps, too tired to react quickly in struggle with Roman legionnaire while trying to give Christ water. Was flung heavily against well curbing on hip still unhealed from pirate scene and then slipped over the eye with spear. Neither blow disabling, but both gave me pause, thinking of Ty. This racket sure not padded refuge for idle boozehounds Hollywood novels make it out. Have been shooting ten and twelve hour days, six days every damn week, not to mention a few Sundays, since May."

The end was in sight. In early December, Wyler had to give in to a persistent flu and spend two restless days in bed, but on Christmas Eve, he began shooting pickup shots and on January 7, yelled "Cut!" for the last time. The very last shot was of Ben-Hur watching Christ's body being taken down from the cross.

Heston was to remember Wylerian directing with both candor and awe. "Doing a scene for Willy is like building one of those towers of toothpicks on top of a milk bottle," he was to write several years later. "He'll ask you to do take after take, but it is not true that he'll just say do it again. He'll tell you something every time and often they are contradictory things. But that doesn't disturb him at all. Indeed, one of his best weapons is that he doesn't mind changing his mind. All of us have a certain egotistic allegiance to the decision we have once made. You know, once we have committed ourselves to a certain point of view we feel morally obligated to stay with it. Willy doesn't.

"He can spend a whole morning working on one version of a take. And then he can come back to the set after lunch and say, 'You know, Chuck, we've got to do this—cut out the first line and don't turn on her at all.' And you say, 'Well, gee, Willy, we were flailing away at this all morning to build up the necessary fury when I take her by the arms . . .' and Willy says a bit impatiently, 'Yeah, but I was wrong, all wrong, we'll go to the other way!' And that doesn't disturb him at all. And it really doesn't the actor either. I doubt he likes actors very much. He doesn't empathize with them—they irritate him on the set. He gets very impatient, but invariably, they come off well. The only answer I have is that his taste is impeccable and every actor knows it. Your faith in his taste and what it will do for your performance is what makes casting a Wyler picture a cinch . . . doing a film for Wyler is like getting the works in a Turkish bath. You darn near drown but you come out smelling like a rose." [4]

By the time the last negative was shipped to Culver City, one million feet of film had been exposed. The end of the shooting had Vogel sigh with relief and dispatch a congratulatory wire. It was not the end of expenditures, however. The cost of dismantling the sets alone came to $150,000. Under a special arrangement with the Italian government, almost everything could be exported duty free, and MGM sold whatever it could from ten miles of steel tubing used to erect the stands for the chariot race, to seventy-eight horses. A backing for the artificial lake built at Cinecitta for the sea battle went back to Culver City, while galley and pirate ships and standing sets were dismantled to prevent cannibalizing by epic-prone Italian producers.

A new deal was worked out for Wyler. Vogel wanted him to stay on through postproduction and supervise the cutting, scoring, and release. The new contract gave Wyler another $100,000. He already had a percentage of the profits and his "up front" earnings were now $450,000.

With Talli, Willy went skiing for two weeks in Switzerland. "We had no sooner left Rome, then he began getting migraine headaches," Talli remembered. "The headaches continued all through the summer and the cutting of the film and until *Ben-Hur* opened in November." In London, on the way back, they attended the opening of *The Big Country* with the Hestons. Passing through New York on the way home, the Wylers learned of the death of Preston Sturges. He had died in the Algonquin Hotel, his New York home, two years after his last film, the unfortunate vapid *Les Carnets du Major Thompson* (also known as *The French, They Are a Funny Race*). Since he had left Hollywood in 1949, Preston's work had inexplicably and shockingly deteriorated. Talli and Willy had last seen him in Paris in 1956.

Wyler plunged into the cutting, reducing the six hours of film to less than four. Zimbalist had put Miklos Rozsa under contract to write the music a year earlier (the Hungarian composer had scored *Quo Vadis*) and November 18 was the target date for the premiere at Loew's State Theater on Broadway. MGM's advertising-publicity department swung into high gear. By mid-summer, ad-pub expenditures of $3 million had been approved by a harried Vogel. Paid newspaper space was penciled in at $1.5 million. A grab-bagful of merchandise tie-ins were lined up. Designer Ceil Chapman tucked a couple of Ben-Hur creations into her line of gowns, toymaker Louis Marx whipped up a miniature arena complete with an array of chariots. Acorn Industries had a counter of junior-size Ben-Hur swords, helmets, scooter chariots, and breast-plates. F. W. Schrafft & Son obliged with a Ben-Hur candy bar and Bantam Books, Dell Publishing, Pocket Books, and Signet rolled out paperbacks while Random House issued a hardback souvenir book, to be sold in lobbies as well as in bookstores. The Forum of the 12 Caesars, a New York City restaurant, hoped to stage the premiere party.

Industry interest was high. With movie attendance again down from the previous year, exhibitors scrambled for *Ben-Hur* in hope that it would be a powerful box-office attraction. Almost daily, theatermen trooped to the Loew's building with offers—give us *Ben-Hur* and we will spend $50,000 on renovating our picture palace. "We are being besieged by theater owners from all over the world," Vogel told the *Wall Street Journal* in a front-page interview that outlined Metro's efforts to sell the "costliest U.S. movie."

"The company will spend another $2 million to $3 million on prints of the films and advertising," the *Journal* said. "Distribution costs will run into additional millions of dollars. As a result, Loew's Mr. Vogel figures *Ben-Hur* won't begin making 'any real money' until Loew's receipts from film rentals top $30 million." [5] Vogel announced admission prices would be higher than usual. At Loew's State, the top price would be $3 a seat on weekends.

A telephone call to MGM was answered, "Good morning, this is MGM, and *Ben-Hur* is coming." One wit noted the merchandising would include Ben-His and Ben-Hur towels, and the *Wall Street Journal* mentioned the company was licensing "a hair ornament manufacturer to put out tiaras and combs for women with a Ben-Hur motif." MGM Records issued three recordings of the sound track.

"This shows you what a company can do when it really gets behind a picture," Wyler reflected in sympathy with Tom Laughlin in 1972 when the producer-director launched a lawsuit against Warner Brothers, charging neglect in promoting *Billy Jack*. "While I was in New York, one of the studio producers came in from the Coast, telling me how nobody at Metro was paying any attention to *his* Metro picture. It was nice for me to be on the *Ben-Hur* side, but I knew what it felt like to be in the other shoes. Paramount had been busy promoting DeMille's *Samson and Delilah* when I came to New York to show *Carrie*."

A month and a half before the scheduled opening, the Writers' Guild of America (WGA) went into an emotional tiff over Wyler's request that Christopher Fry be given credits along with Tunberg. Charging that Wyler was attempting heavy-handed armtwisting and trying to wreck Guild rules, the WGA took out trade ads defending its arbitration committee's ruling that only former WGA president Tunberg's name could be on the screen.[6]

"It's true, Fry didn't do a major part but he did contribute substantially," Wyler recalled ten years later. "I wanted to have some sort of credit for Fry and suggested his name in second, or *any* position on the credits. Verbally, Tunberg agreed. Then the arbitration committee decided Fry hadn't contributed twenty-five percent of the screenplay. I don't know how you measure these things. Zimbalist was no longer alive, I wrote a letter to the Guild. *Ben-Hur* got twelve Academy Award nominations, including screenwriting—the highest in history—and all but one received the award, a record which still stands. That one was the writing Oscar, because of the controversy.

After "sneaks" in Denver, Dallas, and San Diego, *Ben-Hur* opened on schedule to a first-night audience of Wall Street and

Manhattan society leaders. Reviews were nearly unanimously up-beat (Dwight Macdonald in *Esquire* was about the only really acid pen). Bosley Crowther set the tone: "Within the expansive format of the so-called 'blockbuster' spectacle film, which gener-ally provokes a sublimation of sensibility to action and pageantry, Metro-Goldwyn-Mayer and William Wyler have managed to engi-neer a remarkably intelligent and engrossing human drama in the new production of *Ben-Hur*," he started out, adding that Wyler's "largely personal and close-to direction design" transcended the spectacle. "His big scenes are brilliant and dramatic." [7]

The film received flak from religious groups. Although the Catholic Legion of Decency gave *Ben-Hur* its top rating, Jesuits panned it, saying all Romans were portrayed as being both stupid and ignoble. Forgetting for a moment Judeo-Christian doctrine of the world in the throes of a cosmic fight between good and evil, they said the film possessed the subtlety of a third-class western quickie, with good guys and bad guys.[8] *The Christian Century* suggested that Protestants challenge "that promotion of lurid dis-tortions of the Bible," to which Wyler answered in a United Press International wire story that *Ben-Hur* was not a biblical film but first-century fiction. In matters theological, Macdonald hit closer to home when he analyzed the film as shifting the blame for Christ's martyrdom from Jews to Romans.

The most heavily publicized picture of the year, *Ben-Hur* won the record-breaking eleven Oscars—Wyler picked up his third di-rectorial Academy Award—the New York Film Critics' award, the Directors' Guild award, the British Film Academy award, and countless other prizes.

In financial terms, *Ben-Hur* was a triumph for Vogel. It was ob-vious that the picture had saved the studio. Because the cost of "roadshowing" proved cheaper than anticipated, the break-even point was scaled down to $20 million, considerably less than dou-ble the $15-million negative cost Vogel had forecast six months earlier. Once launched, *Ben-Hur* simply stayed. By the time of its first reissue in 1969, it had brought in $66 million and until the 1972 phenomenon of *The Godfather*, it was the fourth biggest "all-time grosser" in the United States and Canada (behind *Gone With the Wind*, *The Sound of Music*, and *The Graduate*).

News of its success excited the industry into a whirl of activity and MGM into a policy of remakes of its past hits. Vogel did not survive the *Mutiny on the Bounty* disaster, however. In 1962, he resigned and Metro limped on from hit to sporadic hit, saved from the ruin the next time by Lean's *Dr. Zhivago* and every so often by another desperate reissue of *Gone With the Wind*.

Intellectual disdain for *Ben-Hur* hurt Wyler. When interviewed by *Cinema* in 1967, he chided film buff magazines for attacking *Ben-Hur* with leaky arguments. The story dictated the size. If size meant pretentiousness, *Ben-Hur* was pretentious, but he didn't make up the size. The story required it. *Ben-Hur* was an adventure story, a very elementary, commercial story and if he had tried for an "artistic" film, he would have failed on both accounts—artistic and commercial.

"I don't think it is more pretentious than the story dictates," he told *Cinema*'s editor Curtis Lee Hanson in 1967. "If you have to have a chariot race, you have to have stands of people around it and you have to fill the stands with five or six thousand people not because you want to, but because you can't have empty stands. We would have much preferred to have a cross-country chariot race; it would have been much cheaper. We could have gone across the hills of Rome and down dirt roads and along beaches, and we could have saved a couple of million dollars." [9]

A decade after making the epic, Wyler felt it had been something worthwhile to wrestle with and that he had proved to himself his versatility.

With *The Collector,* the intellectuals were to forgive him for *Ben-Hur*.

33

Broadening the mind of the movies was to preoccupy Wyler during his maturity as a filmmaker. The development of a wholly personal cinema was, for the most part, still in the future in America, but the New Wave explosion made Hollywood directors strain at the leash. Wyler's first two movies of the 1960s were shots at censorship. The first proved to be a misaimed dud and the second a bull's-eye hit.

Wyler started the 1960s—a decade of shattering change in a once comfortable film industry—by addressing the National Press Club in Washington on March 15. "Has anyone ever identified a picture, or a scene or a word, that is Communist propaganda?" he asked the press luncheon. To underline the absurdity of the blacklist, he disclosed that Ian McLellan Hunter had been blacklisted and called a Communist, yet his original story *Roman Holiday* was, if anything, a royalist fairy tale immensely popular everywhere, including, of all places, the Soviet Union. "Royalists everywhere loved it."

Wyler had taken a long holiday after *Ben-Hur* (which, out of competition, opened the 1960 Cannes festival). He had been looking for a small film, something entirely and totally removed from *Ben-Hur,* when it occurred to him to do *The Children's Hour,* not the way he and Samuel Goldwyn had done it in *These Three,* but as Lillian Hellman had actually written it as a play. The subject of lesbianism, however, was as much taboo in 1961 as it had been in 1936.

If, in retrospect, the death of the Motion Picture Producers

Association (MPPA) self-censorship was both predictable and inevitable in the onrushing permissive society, the old handbook of screen proprieties was still the law when Harold Mirisch and Wyler decided to make an unexpurgated version of the Hellman drama.

With the exception of a minor revision in 1956, the Production Code had remained unchanged since its inception in 1930. Hollywood had long since discovered that married folk—and some couples who were not thinking about matrimony—slept in double beds rather than the twin beds the Code office insisted on. Yet this and other specific strictures remained in force, mainly to head off righteous bluenose attempts to push for state censorship. Also, it seemed the intent was not so much to spare filmgoers from obscenity and bad taste as to impose an idealized view of the world. This limitation contributed, perhaps, as much as specific taboos to the Code's final demise in 1968, when "to tell it like it is" was a generation's war cry.*

In 1961, the only way to deal with sapphic love on the screen was to change the Code or release the picture without its seal of approval. Five years earlier, Otto Preminger and United Artists had done just that. When the Code office had refused a seal to *The Man with the Golden Arm,* UA had scared the censors into revising the Code by a clever act of high treason—releasing the film *without* a seal. Mirisch, Wyler, and UA planned to do the same thing, or at least to threaten to defy the industry's self-censorship system, with *The Children's Hour.*

"We haven't attempted to make a dirty film," Wyler told an August news conference designed to help soften up the Code office. "We plan to do everything possible to keep [children] away, even to telling them: 'We don't want your money if you're under sixteen.' " Mirisch told the press he was "working" on a change in the Production Code, but refused to say how he, Wyler, and UA planned to make the blue-pencil board give in. Their trick was disarmingly simple—to sweeten their own brew. They had the sting written out of Miss Hellman's drama and decided never to use the word "lesbian."

---

*On November 1, 1968, the MPPA, National Association of Theater Owners, and International Film Importers—still fearing the old nightmare of conflicting censorships in fifty different states—agreed to classify all films as to their suitability for young audiences.

In 1934, Goldwyn had bought *The Children's Hour* from the new young playwright for $35,000. This time, Mirisch paid Goldwyn $350,000 for a ten-year lease on the drama. Miss Hellman, who after the witchhunt smear in 1952 had been forced to sell her farm, was quietly teaching at Harvard and had no regrets about her original outright sale. "After all," she said, "thirty-five thousand dollars was a lot of money then."

Wyler wanted her to write a new script and she had finished a first outline when the death of Dashiell Hammett on New Year's Day, 1960, made her lose all interest. Wyler turned to an older pro. John Michael Hayes had turned out excellent screenplays, including such Alfred Hitchcock items as *Rear Window, To Catch a Thief, The Trouble with Harry,* and *The Man Who Knew Too Much,* and easily turned out a workable script. Miss Hellman read his final draft and scrawled a lot of "no good— L. H." over it, but Hayes's work had been subordinated to the nervousness of Wyler and the Mirisch brothers sparring for a Production Code seal before going into filming.

To play the schoolteachers, Wyler chose Audrey Hepburn for the part of Karen Wright and Shirley MacLaine for Martha Dobie. Miriam Hopkins played "her own aunt," as publicity releases had it. In *These Three,* she had been Martha Dobie and now she was Mrs. Lily Mortar. James Garner, who had just broken out of television cowboyhood and starred in Joseph Pevney's *Cash McCall,* was cast as Miss Hepburn's fiancé (the role Joel McCrea had played in 1936). Fay Bainter, who had won her first Oscar under Wyler in *Jezebel,* was Mrs. Tilford, and after a nationwide search, Karen Balkin, a vivacious twelve-year-old from Houston who had been acting since she was seven, was cast as little Mary.

Entitled *Infamous,* the picture went into rehearsals May 22, 1961, at the Goldwyn studios on Formosa Avenue. The shooting went smoothly with a lot of horseplay from Shirley MacLaine, who spent hours off-stage discussing "latent homosexuality in women," as she was to write in her autobiography.[1] Audrey Hepburn, who had just finished Blake Edwards' *Breakfast at Tiffany's,* liked the change of pace and the flock of schoolgirls hired to play her boarding-school wards. Between takes, the twenty little girls chatted or played ball, sometimes raising their voices to the point were they had to be shooed off into an alley because their voices filtered onto the sound system. Wyler loved directing the kids.

"You just have to be patient with children," he told Murray Schumach, the *New York Times* Hollywood correspondent, during a setside visit. "But then there are plenty of adults with whom you have to have patience, too. Generally, children are good actors because they don't know enough to be bad and they have quick imaginations. This, you understand, is no reflection on any adults in the cast." [2] He added that he didn't think it was difficult to explain to children what their parts meant, even when the role was as complex as that played by Karen Balkin. "You tell the children what to think," he said. "You guide them in their thinking. Children are not involved with big psychological problems. Their emotions are very simple. You must always remember to tell children why they are being corrected."

The acting was the film's chief virtue. Miss Hepburn effectively laid on her special brand of wide-eyed reserve and Miss MacLaine gradually built tortured uncertainty into agonizing portrayal. "Audrey, like most actresses, will require a moment to get herself in the proper mood for the scene, but Shirley—she will make jokes and clown it up until the last second," he told *Newsweek* when the film was released. "And then, when the camera starts, she will be right in it. It's often disconcerting for the other people around." [3]

Wyler used the occasion of a national magazine interview to try and correct the public's idea of a director. "The function of a director is widely misinterpreted," he said. "Some people think it has just to do with the mechanics of picturemaking—the camera and the photography. Camera work, script, cutting, editing, music—all that goes into it. But people who separate directing from acting make a great mistake, because I consider the first function of a director to be the acting. There's no such thing as a bad performance and a good director. They don't go together."

When asked how he went about mining Oscar-winning performances, he said no director could *make* people act. "I think guiding an actor's thinking is the most important thing. You can't say, 'Make this kind of a face, make that kind of a face.' If you and the actor agree on what goes on inside the character, then he will have the right expression."

The shooting ended September 1 and Robert Swink cut *The*

Children's Hour, as it was finally titled, for a March, 1962 release. Swink's editing included a jumpcut that was to scandalize Andrew Sarris when he reviewed *The Collector.*[4] *The Children's Hour* opened, *with* a Production Code seal, March 14 at New York's Astor and Trans-Lux Fifty-second Street theaters. The reviews were crushing.

Bosley Crowther led off saying in his opening paragraph that "it is hard to believe that Lillian Hellman's famous stage play, *The Children's Hour,* could have aged into such a cultural antique in the course of three decades as it looks in the new film version . . . but here it is, fidgeting and fuming, like some dotty old doll in bombazine with her mouth sagging open in shocked amazement at the batedly whispered hint that a couple of female schoolteachers could be attached to each other by an 'unnatural love.' "[5] Crowther found the film simply incredible. "The hint is intruded with such astonishment and it is made to seem such a shattering thing (even without evidence to support it) that it becomes socially absurd. It is incredible that educated people living in an urban American community today would react as violently and cruelly to a questionable innuendo as they are made to do in this film. And that is not the only incredible thing in it. More incredible is its assumption of human credulity. It asks us to believe the parents of all twenty pupils in a private school for girls would yank them out in a matter of hours on the slanderously spread advice of the grandmother of one of the pupils that two young teachers in the school were 'unnatural.' " *Time* said the film was directed at the assumption "the perceptive level of the audience is that of a roomful of producers' relatives" while admitting that Shirley MacLaine "all forlorn, gives the best performance of her career."[6] *Newsweek* said: "few things are so frustrating as the movie that takes a purposeful whack at a serious theme and just doesn't quite connect head-on,"[7] and *The New Yorker*'s Brendan Gill said Wyler "carries on" as if he had only just learned about lesbianism and was feeling distinctly let down by human nature. "Grown men and women whisper fearful home truths that we in the audience aren't allowed to hear, eyes roll, bodies totter and I wound up every bit as angry at Mr. Wyler as I was at the nasty little brat."[8] The new *Playboy* magazine also chimed in, saying the source material had been "heavily diluted."[9]

Was the source material worth the effort? Pauline Kael wondered. Treating the film as "a note" at the end of her review of *A View from the Bridge*, she called *The Children's Hour* "such a portentous lugubrious dirge (that seems to be part of the funeral of Hollywood moviemaking) that I developed a rather perverse sympathy for the rich old lady villainess—I thought the schoolteachers treated her abominably. Where I come from if somebody, particularly an older person, says, 'I've been wrong, I'm sorry, what can I do to make amends?' you take the hand they hold out to you. I've never understood Lillian Hellmanland, where rich people are never forgiven for their errors. But then, has Miss Hellman ever recognized hers? I can't help thinking she wouldn't waste any sympathy on sexual deviation among the rich. Aren't we supposed to feel sorry for these girls because they're so hardworking, and because, after all, they don't *do* anything—the lesbianism is all in the mind (I always thought this was why lesbians needed sympathy—that there isn't much they *can* do). There has been some commiseration with Wyler about the studio hacking out the center of the film; that's a bit like complaining that a corpse has had a vital organ removed. Who cares? I'm not sure the material of *The Children's Hour* would work even if you camped it up and played it for laughs; I don't know what else you could do with it." [10]

The reviews hurt. They implied a loss of touch with the *zeitgeist*, with the feedback that was the life and breath of movies. *Time*'s swipe at the perception level being that of a roomful of producers' relatives was painfully accurate. Wyler, Mirisch, UA *et al* had thought themselves very brave.

What hurt most was that Lillian Hellman hated the picture. "She put her finger on what was wrong," Wyler remembered. "I had been too faithful to the original and made no attempt to modernize and bring it up to date. I had made no effort to change it in the light of the past thirty years. She said that if she had done the screenplay, she would have changed a lot of things that I, because I had so much respect for her as an author and because I still remembered what I had *not* been able to do in the old picture, had stuck to."

The Mirisch brothers shucked off the failure. "Sometimes you hit, sometimes you miss," they yawned. Their *West Side Story*, directed by Robert Wise and Jerome Robbins, was a smash hit and millions were pouring in. But Wyler wondered. Was Hollywood mired in its own insolent insularity, as feisty little film magazines contended? Was the Production Code they had so carefully tiptoed around *that* archaic? Was what they called bold and direct simply routine, if not ridiculous? Highly individualistic movies were what everybody wanted all of a sudden.

Most of his colleagues at Directors' Guild meetings derided the "young cinema," but Wyler was among those wondering whether the writing was not on the wall. The failure of *The Children's Hour* forced him to take stock. Was he one of a "dozen men of great talent continuing to turn out pictures with the easy assurance of an earlier age" in an industry letting itself slide into uneasy middle age, as Penelope Houston observed in 1963, when the devaluation of Hollywood reached "alarming proportions." Or could the "new cinema" be overpowered by sheer weight, dazzle, "production values," and knowhow?

The French example was disconcerting, infuriating, and beguiling. Like his fellow filmmakers, he had caught *Breathless, Les 400 Coups, Les Cousins* and read the raves Jean-Luc Godard, François Truffaut, and Claude Chabrol garnered. He had been compelled to think again about his own terms of reference. Movies used to be impersonal because of constraints—he was the first to remember his clammy Goldwyn beginnings. Now, they were personal because of indulgence. *Breathless* and *The 400 Blows* were inflated B pictures and Alain Resnais' *L'Année dernière à Marienbad* committed the ultimate sin of being a bore. To the punctilious perfectionist in him, the broken rules were offensive. Raoul Coutard shot straight in the sun in Jacques Demy's *Lola* and the "new cinema" was guilty of being exhibitionist, full of dandyish conceits and self-display.

Yet, there was something unsettlingly sympathetic in the New Wave. Behind the extravagant language and perverse adulation of Hollywood veterans was an undeniable passion for the cinema. An industry must somehow blend creative idealism with hard-eyed pragmatism, but it *was* refreshing to meet *cinéphiles* who didn't talk box-office grosses and gee-whiz projections like the unending stream of Hollywood talent peddlers and average producers with average reactions to average success who constantly knocked on his door. By definition the movies *were* hermaphrodite—half art and half lucre—but here were gifted, hungry, and crazy people who wanted less to make a dollar than to make a splash. The big words of devotion to culture were, of course, easily sprung—"quality of existence," "catching the art fever," "mass elite" were the new catch phrases—but moviegoers were becoming fickle and unpredictable and the new films seemed to be finding fresh, young, and well-educated audiences.

A diversion from introspection came from the Union of Cinema Workers of the U.S.S.R. Willy accepted the invitation and, from the moment he and Talli reached Moscow, was given the warmest of welcomes.

"I have never been received as well anywhere as we were there," he recalled. "We visited everywhere, the studios, of course, where they showed us some of their new films. They gave us the best treatment, a secretary-interpreter, a chauffeur, and a car. They gave parties in my honor, speeches, a trip to Leningrad, where we met Grigori Kozintsev, who was just starting his *Hamlet* and with whom we have stayed in contact. In Moscow, it was such directors as Mark Donskoi, Sergei Bondarchuk, who was starting *War and Peace,* Mikhail Kalatosov, Grigori Chukrai, Joseph Heifitz, and Sergei Youtkevich."

On their own, the Wylers toured Tbilisi, Yerevan, and Sochi, from where they took a Black Sea cruise. In Odessa they walked the steps of Eisenstein's *Potemkin* and Willy got a manicure that had his fingers bleeding.

"The people in the movie industry had seen all my pictures, and they were particularly crazy about *The Little Foxes* and *The Best Years of Our Lives,* although none of these had been shown in public. A film that was shown, and everybody in the Soviet Union had seen, was *Roman Holiday.* Whenever we got into a restuarant or a hotel, our interpreter would say something to the waitress or the desk clerk and their faces would light up. 'Aaaah,' they'd exclaim. What the interpreter was saying was that I was the director of *Roman Holiday.*

During their London stopover on the way home, a young man called up saying he was preparing a book on the silent American cinema and asked for a brief interview. Wyler agreed and when Kevin Brownlow arrived, he asked about Fred Niblo's *Ben-Hur* and the silent western days for his book.[11] He wondered if his hosts would be interested in seeing Willy's very first two-reeler. Talli had never seen *Crook Buster* and Willy didn't even know a print was still in existence. Ten minutes later, Brownlow had set up a 16mm projector and, on the wall of the Claridge's hotel room, Jack Mower suddenly rode hellbent for leather down a pristine Laurel Canyon.

When the Wylers returned home, the buzz was the *Cleopatra* caper and Darryl Zanuck's takeover of Twentieth Century-Fox, which was soon to make Willy a member of the company's board of directors.

When Richard Burton had been in Paris in June to film his scenes in *The Longest Day,* he had told Zanuck some of what was going on in Rome and suggested that the producer (and major Fox stockholder) drop in on Joseph Mankiewicz's set in Rome. The filming ended on July 24 and budget estimates showed the picture had cost a staggering $44 million. *Cleopatra* was an inexcusable blunder and many Fox executives considered Zanuck as Spyros Skouras' obvious replacement ("Darryl himself helped to crucify me," Skouras whimpered) which DFZ became after a stormy board meeting on July 25.

Zanuck's first order of business was closing down the studio, laying off two thousand employees, and expanding the board to fifteen by adding himself, his attorney, Arnold Grant, and Willy Wyler.

"I only attended two board meetings," Wyler recalled. "Three people had been on the phone from New York to get me to join —Zanuck, Skouras, and the attorney, Louis Nizer. They said that what was needed was a filmmaker, somebody who knew production, and I certainly agreed with that. I remember voting in favor of spending $2 million that Zanuck said he needed to finish *Cleopatra.*"

Wyler didn't find his fellow board members, all financiers and Wall Street attorneys, particularly interesting nor his counsel avidly sought and as soon as it was evident his resignation wouldn't embarrass anyone, he quit.

Leaving his son Richard unofficially in charge of the closed studio, Zanuck flew to his home base in Paris to supervise the last preparation for the launching of *The Longest Day** and to plow through the scripts owned by Fox. He immediately postponed *Take Her, She's Mine* and canceled *Promise at Dawn* and *Ulys-*

---

* Andrew Marton, Ken Annakin, and Bernard Wicki were the credited directors of *The Longest Day,* with Elmo Williams, Gerd Oswald, and Zanuck himself directing interior indoor scenes.

ses. He liked *The Enemy Within,* based on Robert Kennedy's book about James Hoffa, approved it, then held it up for fear of trouble from the powerful labor leader. In September, *The Longest Day* opened in Paris and, for a day, Zanuck owned the city. With Georges Cravennes and Fred Hift in charge of the ballyhoo, the premiere started with an amplified Edith Piaf singing "La Marseillaise" from atop the Eiffel Tower, followed by an extravagant display of fireworks and crack regiments from each of the Allied powers of World War II parading down to the Champs Elysées theater, where Charles de Gaulle and his entire cabinet attended the premiere. In New York, political, military, and Hollywood celebrities attended the opening, sending off *The Longest Day* to a profitable year-long run. With *The Longest Day* out of the way, Zanuck bent over the one lingering problem, *Cleopatra* (he and Mankiewicz fought publicly and privately over the cutting of the picture), and gave the go-ahead on *The Sound of Music,* with Ernest Lehman as writer and William Wyler as director.

"Again, I was intrigued about something I had never done before—a musical," Wyler recalled. "I was a fine person to do a musical, hard of hearing, but I was told not to worry about the music. When Darryl first called me from New York and said, 'What about doing *The Sound of Music?*' I said, 'Musicals are not my line.' He asked me to come to New York anyway and have a look at it. I did. I talked with him about it and took another couple of weeks to think about it. Lehman kept after me and I finally said yes. This was not the kind of thing I really wanted. I said, 'Okay, I'll do it,' because it was a new form, though I didn't like the story."

The tale of the Trapp family had been filmed by Wolfgang Liebener (with Ruth Leuwerick as the novice and Hans Holt as Herr Trapp) in 1956 by Gloria Films, Berlin. *Die Trapp Familie* had been produced by an old friend, Wolfgang Reinhardt, the son of Max Reinhardt. Willy had known Wolfgang during his Hollywood exile, where, together with John Huston, he had been the coscripter of William Dieterle's Bette Davis starrer *Juarez.* Wolfgang's brother Gottfried had been among the guests on Summit Drive for the *Le Diable au corps* screening the day Ernest Lubitsch died and Willy had been with Wolfgang when, for the first time, he had visited his father's old theater in East Berlin.

Max Reinhardt had died in exile in 1943 but the old doorman was still there and burst out in tears when he recognized the son. In what felt like a surreal replay of a Wolfgang Reinhardt–John Huston 1930s script, the doorman had taken them through the old theater, showing them Hitler's favorite box and Max Reinhardt's old office.

Wolfgang felt the Trapp story was failsafe. It had everything—nuns (a gutsy Saint Teresa novice), children (seven of them ranging from six to sixteen), family drama (daddy as a stiff-necked Austrian widower), and, since the milk of human kindness had to be cut with a little sting, Nazis. Shooting it on location would give it storybook Salzburg and Alpine vistas to melt in with Richard Rodgers' music.

Wyler cast Julie Andrews. "I had seen her play *My Fair Lady* in New York and was very impressed. She was working on *Mary Poppins*. I went over to the studio and Walt Disney showed me some rushes and introduced me to her on the set."

Before pushing off for Salzburg, Wyler and Lehman met the Baroness von Trapp, the owner of a Vermont ski lodge, who came down to New York to meet them. A woman in her seventies, she showed up at the St. Regis Hotel in a dirndl costume. When Wyler asked her why, unlike most Austrian aristocrats of 1936, her late husband had not liked Hitler, she said, "He was so vulgar." When he asked if she had ever met the Führer, she remembered she and her husband had seen him once. "In a beer hall, in Munich. He was with these fellows. All so noisy."

Afterward, Lehman told Wyler to forget this meeting with their real-life heroine—Julie Andrews had now signed to play her—and writer and producer-director flew to Austria to begin scouting locations and to meet with the burgomeister of Salzburg.

Speaking in German, Willy couldn't resist reminding his honor of the recent past when nine out of ten Austrians had received Hitler with open arms. He told the mayor, "We have a scene of the 1936 Anschluss in the picture and we want to stage this out in the open, with Germans marching, swastikas everywhere, and the whole population out cheering and throwing flowers. You know, the way it really happened," he added pointedly.

"Yes," the mayor sighed.

"I don't want to make any trouble," Wyler continued. "Maybe

some people won't like this. Do you think I'll have any problems?"

"No, I don't think so," his honor replied with a tired smile. "We survived that, we'll survive this, too."

Lehman kept telling Wyler that Nazism was not what *The Sound of Music* was about. Wyler agreed. "I knew it wasn't really a political thing. I had a tendency to want to make it, if not an anti-Nazi movie, at least say a few things. It was true that Nazism was not what the musical was about; I knew it would be a success, although not *that* big."

As he and Lehman scouted Tyrolean locations and argued about the Austrian people's real sentiment in 1936, Columbia Pictures' studio head, Mike J. Frankovich, sent Wyler a script that made him drop everything else. The script had been written by two young expatriate North Americans and was an adaptation of the first novel of an exciting new British writer. "I had to make a choice. I knew I wouldn't get the money from *The Collector* I would make on *The Sound of Music,* but this story fascinated me. *Sound of Music* didn't, and I asked to be let out."

In December, Twentieth Century-Fox announced the codirector of *West Side Story,* Robert Wise, had been signed to direct *The Sound of Music.*

Much later, Wise wrote to Wyler, saying he didn't know why he had given up *The Sound of Music* but that he considered himself lucky to have inherited it.

Wyler was already in London setting up the production of *The Collector.* Talli joined him and together they heard the news of President John F. Kennedy's assassination in Dallas. When they returned home a week later, they found a letter from the White House. "The President requests the pleasure of the company of Mr. Wyler at luncheon on Tuesday, December 10, 1963, at one o'clock." The letter was postmarked November 21, the day before the murder.

PART SIX

The Later Films

34

"When she was home from her boarding-school, I used to see her almost every day sometimes, because their house was right opposite the Town Hall Annexe. She and her younger sister used to go in and out a lot, often with young men, which, of course, I didn't like. When I had a free moment from the files and ledgers, I stood by the window and used to look down over the road over the frosting and sometimes, I'd see her. In the evening, I marked it in my observation diary, at first with X, and then, when I knew her name, with M. I saw her several times outside, too. I stood right behind her once in a queue at the public library down Crossfield Street. She didn't look once at me, but I watched the back of her head and her hair in a long pigtail. It was very pale, silky, like Burnet cocoons. All in one pigtail coming down almost to her waist, sometimes in front, sometimes at the back. Sometimes, she wore it up. Only once, before she came to be my guest here, did I have the privilege to see her with it loose, and it took my breath away, it was so beautiful, like a mermaid."

In the opening paragraph, John Fowles introduces the forebodings for evil and the meticulous compulsion of the neurotically repressed young clerk, Freddie Clegg, who "collects" the girl of his dreams like a butterfly so she may be tamed into loving him. The subject was ideally suited for a film and the two-member cast ideally suited for Wyler. Here was an eerie contest of wits and glands. Here, his way with actors, his high-polish craftsmanship could come into its own. Here, he could carve performances out of soft soap, or, as Charlton Heston had put it, "build a tower of toothpicks atop a milk bottle." An added challenge was the fact that *The Collector* was a one-situation drama, repeating again and again the emotional yoyo effect of the girl's escape efforts and her captor's squashing all hopes.

Wyler disposed of the introductions in twenty silent minutes: Freddie Clegg, a butterfly collector by avocation, is painfully in love with Miranda, an art student, who doesn't know he exists, a girl who is superior socially and intellectually to him, a girl who is warm, happy, snooty, and healthy. When he wins an enormous sum at the football pools, he buys a lonely country house, fixes up the cellar with everything he imagines she needs, including books and clothes in her size, then kidnaps her, overpowering her with chloroform, as he does butterflies. The film's opening is both restrained and forceful. Freddie cruises about London in his pickup van, following his victim. Miranda disappears into an underground station. He drives off. We pick him up parked along a curb. There, in the side mirror, walking along in all innocence and beauty, is the girl.

Stanley Mann and John Kohn were the authors of the screenplay Mike Frankovich had sent to Wyler. Mann was the Canadian scenarist of *The Mouse That Roared* and *Women of Straw* and had just finished *A High Wind in Jamaica*. Kohn was a former television producer, now associated with Jud Kinberg, another New Yorker expatriate in London, who had been with John Houseman on Playhouse 90. Kohn and Kinberg had read Fowles's novel in manuscript and had taken it to Frankovich. Twenty-four hours later, they had his okay to purchase *The Collector*. Next, the two young producers decided Terence Stamp should play Freddie. Stamp had been the golden-haired *Billy Budd* on film and the working-class womanizer *Alfie* on the stage, and he was far from convinced that his next should be *The Collector*. Kohn and Kinberg kept after him. They didn't want someone who looked like Bela Lugosi, they told everybody. Freddie would be more frightening if he looked gentle and innocent.

Except for *Ben-Hur*, Wyler had been his own producer for years. When negotiations started, Frankovich wondered how to solve the delicate situation of three producers. "They bought the story and got the script together," Willy said, "let them produce; it's okay with me as long as I have the last word."

Frankovich agreed. Kohn and Kinberg stayed on as the producers on Wyler's terms.

Kohn and Kinberg had in mind to shoot *The Collector* entirely in its natural habitat, but Wyler made it "a runaway in reverse"—not out of compassion for Hollywood unions, but, as he told *Variety,* for his own comfort.[1] Six months at home was distinctly more appealing than six months in a London hotel. All exteriors, however, were to be shot in and around London.

During the first scouting trip to London, Wyler liked the work of British art director John Stoll and brought him back to Hollywood to build the interiors.

Production started April 13, 1964 at Columbia's Gower Street studios with Robert Surtees on camera (Robert Krasker replaced him in Britain because of British union rules) and Bob Swink was back in the cutting room. Stamp put Wyler to the test the first few days by walking through a retake. Wyler fixed him with an icy stare, said, "Of course, we will have to shoot that again," and Stamp settled down to deliver his best. "He was very good," Wyler recalled. "His was the more interesting part. She's a completely healthy normal girl, whereas he's abnormal—gentle one moment and violent the next."

Samantha Eggar was another story. Wyler had been smitten by her lustrous auburn hair, her green eyes, and fresh beauty (in a stunning switch, Wyler and Surtees photographed her face in all its freckled splendor while Stamp's face was given a gauzier treatment). Her experience totaled drama school, repertory Shakespeare, and small parts in four movies, including *Psyche 59.* Her first reading was disappointing and it looked as if she would be dropped, perhaps in favor of Natalie Wood. "For a few days I thought of making things easy for myself," Wyler told *Time.*[2] Instead, he decided to exert all his wiles on the twenty-five-year-old actress.

Samantha was not allowed to leave the set during the day. On Sundays, she was obliged to rehearse from late morning to late at night. To coach her, Wyler called in Kathleen Freeman and the character actress not only forced Samantha to struggle with the role, but hyped it up further with horror stories about a paranoid schizophrenic relative until Samantha was thoroughly psyched. The turning point came when she watched Stamp sing a merry-mad cockney song and, as she watched, a tear came slowly down her cheek. "That was what we both needed," Freeman told *Time.* "She knew she was at last involved with the part."

Wyler tyrannized Samantha in scenes where she was to look frightened, told her when to smile, when to frown, when to inhale and when to exhale. "He's the hardest man I've ever worked with," she told the few newsmen allowed to visit the restricted set. "I guess I was supposed to feel trapped, and I did. I lost ten pounds."

Her cheeks hollowed and her shadows darkened. In the film's most excruciating moment, the confused and frightened Miranda strips and offers herself to her jailer. At last able to make love to her, Freddie proves to be impotent. Shocked and appalled, he rejects her violently. For Miss Eggar, it was the very embarrassment that gave veracity to her fumbling, desperate, and virginal attempts to seduce her captor—which was precisely what Wyler was after. "We went as far as we could with the nudity," he said later, "sort of tasteful, early nudity."

The bathtub scene was shot and reshot for five hours and it took several days to get a scene revealing Freddie's defensive mechanism. Here, he engages Miranda in a discussion of J. D. Salinger's *Catcher in the Rye.* Desperate, she tries to point out its virtues, but Freddie's lower-middle-class morality has been affronted by the book's "dirty" situations and "dirty" words.

Fowles was brought over and, to the press, the London college professor confided he planned to give up teaching and to concentrate on writing. Samantha told newsmen she saw the film and Fowles's book as something more than suspense and that her character showed the indomitable will to survive in a healthy human being. "Miranda comes into this situation as a young woman who has always been protected in her home and in her schools," she told *New York Times*'s Murray Schumach, one of the few newsmen allowed to visit the set. "Her adolescent approach and good family background make her trusting. In this cellar, where she is held captive, she matures." [3]

In his interviews, Stamp said he knew everything it was possible to know about his character and that he was trying to relate Freddie to other people's problems. "He has a boy's dream," Stamp told Schumach. "I had those dreams when I was fourteen or fifteen. He doesn't really believe he is doing anything wrong. What really saves his character is that he believes the girl will really fall in love with him." Wyler also claimed he remembered a compelling fascination for a girl he had not dared approach when he was fifteen. "Almost every young man has met a girl whom he'd like to kidnap and just keep her locked up . . . own her," he told the *Los Angeles Examiner*. "Ordinarily, nobody does anything about it. This man does. I think this picture is going to enable me to portray two characters whom I have never seen on the screen before." [4]

On a sunny Saturday morning in May, Willy took time out to give away his eldest daughter in marriage. Twenty-four-year-old Cathy was married to Robert Sind in a ceremony held in the garden on Summit Drive and the newlyweds established residence in New York.

After forty-two days of interiors on Gower Street, *The Collector* moved to England. Freddie's house had been difficult to find and Wyler and Stoll had scoured outer London suburbs before finding an isolated Victorian villa in Kent. The summer of 1964 Talli remembered as all sunshine in the British isles, but each day Willy, Kohn, and Kinberg feared the next would bring with it pouring rain, which would ruin sequences already shot in sunny weather and push the budget over the $2-million mark. The threat of rain made Wyler push his crew beyond union rules, calling lunch at two o'clock in the afternoon. "When I was setting up shots after one o'clock, I could see them go into a huddle," he recalled. "I had been warned about the 'I'm all-right, Jack' mentality. Any time they wanted they could pull the switch, but they never did. They'd say, 'Okay, gov'nor' and go on working."

A feature of British filmmaking habits he wished Hollywood would adopt was the staff tea boy, who not only served tea but came around every hour with little sandwiches, sausages, ice cream, and sweets. "For very little expense, you have a thing that's very good for the morale of crew and cast."

At the end of the London filming, Melanie—like Cathy and Judy before her—went to Switzerland for a year to learn French.

There was a good deal of talk of softening the ending and making Miranda escape death in the cellar, but Wyler stuck to Fowles's tragic and perverse finale, in which impulse became vice. If she was rescued, Wyler reasoned, *The Collector* would be just another melodrama. The people who would complain about her tragic death would protest even louder if she were plucked from

---

tragedy in the last reel. *Newsweek* was to find that forgoing retribution was what made *The Collector* "one of those rare, fortunate accidents—an American film of seriousness, integrity and real merit." [5]

Wyler agreed with Columbia that there was no reason to get *The Collector* out in a hurry, that a Christmas booking to qualify for Academy consideration might even hurt this different and starless film. Cannes had been kind to *Friendly Persuasion,* why not try the top film festival?

If handled properly, it was felt all around, *The Collector* would be put over handily by word-of-mouth, that increasingly important phenomenon, even if it meant a slower payoff. "Sometimes, the distribution of a film is faster than its word-of-mouth gets around," Wyler told *Variety.* "There are millions of people who would have enjoyed dozens of films they never got a chance to see." Wyler and Swink took their time cutting *The Collector* and Maurice Jarre—just signed to write the music for David Lean's *Dr. Zhivago*—scored it.

The Collector opened June 2, 1965 at the Coronet and Paris theaters in New York. It was a critical triumph, and Wyler flew to Cannes with the film.

Although Bosley Crowther professed himself a little shocked by the "weirdo" hero and found Stamp mystifying in the beginning but turning in psychic circles toward the end, the veteran critic said, "Wyler turned in a tempting and frequently startling, bewitching film" [6] Judith Crist termed it a "very high-class horror film" and Stamp an extraordinary actor. "He defies conclusion; is it mad to kidnap and imprison a young woman for one's own purpose? 'There'd be a blooming lot more of this if more people had the time and money,' is his retort. . . . Are we up against a madman—or is it the voice of the mob, the know-nothing out to destroy what he does not understand? The Picasso reproduction is ripped, the book torn to shreds with a fury and suddenly, we see that Stamp has injected a pathos into the fury, and almost against our will, the heart is touched, just as Miranda's is. And we join her in the desperate hope against hope that this is not total madness, that somewhere behind those too-blue eyes there is a vulnerability, the spark of sanity remaining." [7]

"A lot of nonsense has been written in supposedly serious film histories about what is cinema and what is not, and a prejudice persists in favor of the great outdoors as against the presumably 'stagy' indoors," Andrew Sarris wrote. "Yet, I can't think of anything more exciting and more cinematic than locking up a boy and a girl in an old house and an intriguing situation. Just as the human voice is the most sublime musical instrument, the human face and body are the most sublime visual subjects, and one shot of Samantha Eggar's elongated leg turning on a water faucet is worth every shot of every antelope that ever roamed." Sarris defended the film against British charges that a modest, low-budget project had been blown up to a million-dollar extravaganza. "For the most part, I'm glad Wyler won out. I'm a little sick of modest, low-budget, offbeat projects and I don't think it's very wise to inflict unattractive people on audiences for long periods of time. People just stay away from the theater. The point is that I am glad this project went a bit Hollywood." [8]

Stanley Kauffmann found the film superior to Fowles's novel. Wyler had directed "with such skillful concentration on interplay that we are never conscious that this is a film sustained by two actors. Wyler takes every moment for what it is, as it comes along, and makes the most of it; it is only retrospectively that we see it is a bravura accomplishment." [9]

Cannes 1965 was the year when Sean Connery's tattoo marks were called the only appealing thing in sight. *The Collector* was in competition with such entries as Roman Polanski's *Repulsion* and Masaki Kobayashi's *Kwaidan,* but also Kevin Brownlow's *It Happened Here* (Kevin had no vintage two-reelers to show on hotel-room walls this time) and Richard Lester's *The Knack*. Wyler gave interviews right and left saying he didn't like the French title *L'Obsédé* because it revealed the film's key idea before there was time to establish it on the screen. He also revealed he would make a third film with Audrey Hepburn, called *Venus Rising*. For a change, Talli wasn't along, but Melanie, approaching her fifteenth birthday, had finished her year in Switzerland and joined her father on the Croisette.

Perhaps not unsurprisingly, *The Collector*—the only film allowing any point to be made of acting—won the major acting trophies (no Cannes jury had ever given both best actor and actress award to performers in a same film). Calling *L'Obsédé* one of Wyler's best films, *Cahiers du Cinéma*'s Jacques Bontemps said the moments which seemed the most inspired may also be the most calculated and deliberate. Nevertheless, "they are also the instances when the two actors give the best of themselves (and that isn't little) and give the film a series of resonances that Wyler couldn't totally have planned. A great actor (Stamp) here gives us his logbook of an exploration of inner limits we so often refuse to consider (it will be necessary to get back to the profound similarities and differences of several recent movies dealing with madness). What we are shown here—and it's fitting the form is a two-character play—is perhaps the substance at the bottom of all love, or, at least, it is its metaphor that here reaches poetic dimension." [10]

In the end, Wyler was happy. *The Collector* had given him more satisfaction (and a lot less money) than *The Sound of Music*. He never regretted the switch.

ABOVE, with Mother on the set of *The Best Years*

BELOW, bar sequence in *The Best Years of Our Lives*—Dana Andrews in phone booth and, in foreground, Hoagy Carmichael, Harold Russell, and Fredric March

TOP, with Robert Sherwood and Samuel Goldwyn behind *The Best Years of Our Lives* trophies

MIDDLE, Willy and Talli visiting Laurence Olivier on *Hamlet* set

BELOW, directing Montgomery Clift and Olivia de Havilland in *The Heiress*

LEFT, with Laurence Olivier and Vivien Leigh on *Carrie* set

MIDDLE, in the princess chair on *Roman Holiday* set, between Cathy and Judy Wyler

BOTTOM, directing Audrey Hepburn and Gregory Peck in *Roman Holiday* on the Spanish Steps

TOP, behind *Desperate Hours* cast and setside visitors: Humphrey Bogart, Carol and Penelope Reed, Talli, and Fredric March

MIDDLE, in the driver's seat on *The Big Country* set. In foreground, Charlton Heston, Carroll Baker, Jean Simmons, and Gregory Peck

LEFT, "Not the first ass I've directed"—daughter Melanie on *The Big Country* set

TOP, directing Dorothy McGuire and Gary Cooper in *Friendly Persuasion*

MIDDLE, Stephen Boyd and Charlton Heston in *Ben-Hur*

LEFT, on *Ben-Hur* set with Charlton Heston

ABOVE LEFT, between Melanie and David, on *Ben-Hur* set

ABOVE RIGHT, on *Ben-Hur* set

BELOW, with James Garner, Shirley MacLaine, and Audrey Hepburn on *The Children's Hour* set

ABOVE, directing Samantha Eggar and Terence Stamp in *The Collector*

LEFT, with Barbra Streisand on *Funny Girl* set

ABOVE, with Lillian Hellman, in 1969

BELOW, with Lola Falana on *The Liberation of L. B. Jones* set

35

Pushed by harsh economic realities rather than universal conscience, the Hollywood of the mid-1960s was going international and taking up residence in new media guru Marshall McLuhan's global village. While, ironically, the new radical cinema was puritanically nationalistic, the "big movies" flew, at best, flags of convenience (was *Dr. Zhivago* Russian as its origins, Spanish and Finnish as its locations, British as its director and cast, or American as its money?).

Shooting *The Bible,* John Huston was sharing—unequally— Rome's Cinecitta with Joseph Mankiewicz, making *Anyone for Venice?* In Mexico, Howard Hawks was finishing *Eldorado* and Richard Brooks beginning *The Professionals.* In Tokyo, Charles Walters was shooting *Walk, Don't Run* with Cary Grant and Samantha Eggar, a new mother, and, since *The Collector,* a new star. David Lean and Ken Annakin were dividing Spain between *Dr. Zhivago* and *The Battle of the Bulge,* Robert Wise was filming *The Sand Pebbles* in Taiwan, George Roy Hill was grinding out *Hawaii* in—Hawaii, while Blake Edwards was shooting *The Great Race* around the world. The fever was catching. In Almeria in southern Spain, Sergio Leone was cannibalizing tradition with his successful "spaghetti westerns." François Truffaut was set to make *Fahrenheit 451* in English even though he didn't speak the language, and there were rumors that Michelangelo Antonioni was preparing a film about "swinging London."

Wyler had been one of the first Directors' Guild members to

break out of the studios and make *Roman Holiday* in its natural habitat. Since then, he had made *Ben-Hur* in Rome and part of *The Collector* in London. Why not make *Venus Rising* in Paris? Unlike most of his globe-trotting confreres who had made movies on the banks of the Seine, he spoke the language.

The story was awfully derivative—*Charade, Topkapi, Love in the Afternoon, Gigi, Sabrina,* and *Roman Holiday* immediately came to mind—but the central conceit was funny: Like his father and grandfather before him, Bonnet had always made a very nice thing out of selling masterpieces alleged to be from the family "collection," but, in reality, bogus items he manufactured in his attic. That the old fraud's daughter would want him to go straight and would fall in love with a society detective bent on exposing the hereditary gift was the stuff cream puffs were made of.

The tradition was, perhaps, more Viennese than Parisian, but *Venus Rising* was actually American, a short story by George Bradshaw.[1] Before Wyler was back from Cannes, Darryl Zanuck proposed it to him, with Fred Kohlmar as the producer and production starting immediately.

Kohlmar was a former assistant to Samuel Goldwyn who had worked with Zanuck since DFZ's takeover of Fox and was the producer of pictures directed by John Ford, George Cukor, Joshua Logan, and Richard Quine. He had had Harry Kurnitz write the *Venus Rising* script and the legendary wit and collaborator of such items as Billy Wilder's *Witness for the Prosecution* and Hawks's *Hatari!* had turned out a screenplay that "yielded a twitter a minute."

Wyler moved his office to the Fox lot and immediately set to work. *Venus Rising*—the title had to be changed, he decided—was a film in which the props were almost as important as the cast and he had visions of scores of magnificent fakes. That meant engaging, if at all possible, Alexander Trauner.

Trauner was a short and friendly art director who never went anywhere without his pet dachshund, lived in Paris, and came to Hollywood now and then to create marvelous sets, such as Wilder's Old Bailey courtroom for *Witness for the Prosecution* and the fabulous Rue Casanova for *Irma la Douce.* Trauner, it turned out, was available.

Once in Paris, Wyler told Trauner *Venus Rising* had too much action to shoot in a real museum and that they would have to build a set. They agreed reproductions wouldn't photograph well.

"Don't worry," the little Hungarian said.

"Are you going to rent real masterpieces?" Wyler asked, adding that the insurance on the real stuff would be prohibitive.

"Don't worry."

Trauner built the museum set on the studio Boulogne stage and one day called Wyler to show him.

"And there they were, fabulous Renoirs, Picassos, Degas, all the impressionists, Rembrandts, Tintorettos, da Vincis, El Grecos— all fakes, of course," Willy recalled. " 'How did you get these?' I asked."

The paintings were not exact copies. Where Renoir had three nudes, the fake Renoir would have two and the canvas be of a different size. A Trauner Cézanne was called *Portrait of Madame Nemours,* a Goya was titled *Pilgrimage to San Isidro* (a Californian's in-joke on the U.S.–Mexican border crossing point at Tijuana). The sculptures included a full-sized Maillol, two Giacomettis, and the film's marble star—a twenty-nine-inch replica of Cellini's *Venus Rising,* which the plotline had Mlle Nicole Bonnet and detective Simon Demott steal from the museum in the dead of night.

By guaranteeing them absolute anonymity and plenty of money, Trauner had recruited several young artists. Traditionalists faked moderns and the moderns gleefully painted copies of classic masters.

When Talli joined him, Willy sublet a small townhouse on Rue Weber, a short, quiet street near the Bois de Boulogne. The house came complete with a servant couple. The husband was the cook and the memory of his gourmet cuisine remained with the Wylers for years. Traveling fellow-directors came to dinner and George Stevens, in turn, rented the house when he made *The Only Game in Town* in Paris in 1968.

Wyler liked the French working schedule. Shooting from noon to 7:30 without any break—there was always time to grab a sandwich and a cup of coffee between setups—was the most civilized way to make movies. "Such hours are for the consideration of the artists, not for the convenience of grips and stagehands," he said. "In Hollywood, some actors have to get up by five in order to get

---

381

to the studio and through wardrobe and makeup for a scene at nine. I find it hard to watch a love scene at 9 A.M., much less play one."

Peter O'Toole was cast as Simon Demott and July 25 set for shooting start. All exteriors had to be shot in August when Paris was empty of Parisians and Préfecture de Police permission for street filming was a little easier to obtain. Besides Audrey Hepburn and O'Toole, Hugh Griffith was cast as third-generation art forger, Bonnet. George C. Scott was given the role of David Leland, the wealthy American collector who yearns to whisk both Audrey and the nude Cellini back to his Stateside lair. The remainder of the cast was French—Fernand Gravey, Marcel Dalio, Jacques Marin and Moustache. The crew was also half and half, with Charles Lang on camera and Bob Swink this time both editor and second-unit director. Paul Feyder, the son of Jacques Feyder, whom Wyler had once known and admired (he had seen *La Kermesse héroique* more than twice), was first assistant and François Moreuil was the personal assistant to the director. Miss Hepburn was dressed by Givenchy, bejeweled by Cartier, and coiffed by Grazia de Rossi.

Scott had been called a couple of weeks before he was needed and had been given time off, on salary and expenses, to sit out the waiting period in New York. When called, he flew back to Paris. Although he wasn't needed, the assistant director had him on call for an evening rehearsal of an office scene in which his character sat in on a conversation between Audrey Hepburn and another actor.

"Tomorrow at 12 o'clock we start shooting," Wyler told Scott as everybody left for the night.

The next day at noon, Audrey and the other actors in the office scene were on the set, but not George C. Scott. At 1 o'clock, Paul Feyder called the actor's hotel apartment and was told by a man servant that Scott could not be disturbed. When the assistant asked if Scott was sick, the man said yes and a doctor was dispatched to the apartment. At 2:30, the doctor came back saying he had been thrown out of Scott's bedroom. At 3, Wyler began working on another scene. At 5, Scott walked on the set.

Wyler was in his dressing room.

"Hello Willy," Scott grinned cheerfully.

"Hello George," Wyler began slowly. "I expected you earlier."

Before either of them could continue, Feyder stuck his head in, announcing the company was ready for the next setup.

"Excuse me, George," Wyler said, getting up. "Please wait for me."

The scene was complicated and took Wyler through to the 7:30 "wrap." When he returned to his dressing room, Scott was gone. Then and there, Wyler fired him.

The next day, Audrey tried to intercede and still later telegrams arrived from Darryl and Richard Zanuck asking Wyler to reconsider. "No hard feelings, but I just don't need that," Wyler answered, pointing out that neither part nor actor were important enough to warrant the hassles that might occur once Scott had been established in the film. "I think he was a bit surprised," Wyler said years later. "In any case, it was no reflection on his ability and it surely had no effect on his career."

Scott's replacement was Eli Wallach.

Opposite O'Toole's wide-eyed emoting, Audrey played her fawnlike charm, looking amazed, standing slightly knock-kneed, walking with her tiny tiptoe teeter. A wry, giddy scene has them discover love in a broom closet and Wyler has them play the sequence in a sexy whisper.

Director and cast enjoyed making fun of the art world and the Trauner collection held the publicity spotlight, although not always to Fox's liking. Fakery and thievery in the screenplay spilled over. Authentic thieves made away with several objects d'art, including two *col de cygne* vases. One Saturday morning, five masked men tied up the studio concierge, cracked the safe, and escaped with the following week's French payroll of $20,000.

On Monday, when the cast prepared to continue the shooting of the Great Museum Robbery sequence, the set swarmed with authentic detectives, mingling with uniformed Keystone Kops and extras disguised as *flics*. As in the film—newly entitled *How to Steal a Million Dollars and Live Happily Ever After*—the heist remained unsolved.

There were other oddities. When *Le Figaro* reporters found Jean-Pierre Schecroun, a noted art forger, living in an apartment overlooking the studio, the newspaper jumped to the conclusion that he had made Trauner's art collection. Schecroun had just finished a five-year prison term for doing a few Picassos and Mirós. Not only was he clean, he had successfully broken into a new form—pop art. Trauner wouldn't say whether his countryman, Elmyr de Hory, the art forger who was to be eulogized in a biography by Clifford Irving,* had contributed to the collection. By now, the Parisian press called it the Kléber-La Fayette collection —a reference to the Etoile area telephone prefix and the La Fayette department store.

The eventual fate of the Kléber-La Fayette masterpieces began to become the butt of jokes and to lead to not so funny enquiries. Zanuck and the Fox publicity men decided to roll with the punch and, in its November 12 issue, *Life* could announce that Zanuck had decided to print a catalogue and hold a Paris vernissage, a "full-fledged art exhibition with cocktails and chatter.

"Afterwards, the works will be sent to the U.S.—which lets art treasures enter free of tariff but, unaccountably, puts a tax on fakes, thus impeding the fine craft of fakery." *Life* noted. The exhibition was held at New York's Parke-Bernet Galleries.

Trauner said he felt the whole thing might be of interest to art students. To people with a too vivid imagination, he said, the canvas and materials used were, of course, modern. To expose the great Boulogne fraud, all anyone had to do was to turn the pictures over and see the brand new canvas they were painted on.

In November, the Cinémathèque française organized an *Hommage à William Wyler* with Willy attending the first showing of *The Little Foxes.* Henri Langlois composed the program notes. The emigrant from Mulhouse, he wrote, "is the man who, toward the end of the 1930s, created a new style. It is fitting to associate with Wyler the turning point which—by error of judgment now corrected by the passage of time—postwar critics attributed to *Citizen Kane,* when, in fact, [Orson] Welles, in this film, was still groping and being influenced by Wyler. This style is the exact opposite of a kind of filmmaking still haunted by the versatility and impressionism of the silent era, a silent cinema which considered fluidity and imprecision the height of perfection. Yet Wyler excelled here, too. Isn't *Dodsworth,* together with certain King Vidor films, one of the most perfect successes? Nothing could have forewarned the 1936 admirers of *Dodsworth* and *These Three* that Wyler was soon to question everything by turning filmmaking into an equation, as if it were all a question of proportions, geometric forms and perspectives. . . .

* Clifford Irving, *Fake!*, McGraw-Hill, New York, 1970.

"Whatever the charm of *These Three* and the keen perception and moving simplicity of the psychological analysis of *Dodsworth,* Wyler's personality will remain closely linked with a compounded, expert, and forceful art form which gave the 1940s' U.S. cinema its tone and influenced numerous filmmakers on four other continents. Because it is completely dominated by the art of acting, this form, like the old German cinema, associates static stir and a feel for volume with the controlled dynamics of a chiseled, yet invisible, expressionism.

"After making American cinema part of himself, Wyler's strength lies in having gone all the way in analyzing the most delicate and impressionistic of human feelings and to have put his art and his direction-of-actors science at the service of a new concept. This concept was to allow him to go beyond naturalism and, without betraying truth or simplicity in acting, give performances the intense strength which the masters of the German silent cinema had reached, but without resorting to their artifices [*déformations*] and their symbolism." [2]

How to Steal a Million—as the film was finally called—was completed December 3 and edited during the winter. Released in July, 1966, its reception was lukewarm. Its reviews were mild as was its success. Wyler, himself, was only mildly satisfied with the film.

"You're not remotely expected to go away believing that bearded Hugh Griffith could ever, for one moment, be the superlative art counterfeiter he is gleefully made to appear, or that he (or his crafty grandfather) could have faked a statuette of Venus so true to form that it is exhibited in a Paris museum as one of Benvenuto Cellini's greater works," Bosley Crowther wrote in his last review of a Wyler film (he was to retire in 1968). "Nor are you expected to credit the wholly theatrical conceit that his daughter, a luscious Audrey Hepburn, could be so morally disturbed and concerned about the fakery being discovered that she secretly and pleadingly persuades a handsome 'society burglar,' whom Peter O'Toole lightly plays, to join her in a desperate maneuver to steal the statuette from the museum. The whole thing is clearly preposterous—as preposterous as the complicated scheme Mr. O'Toole works out for the burglary, or the twist in which he turns out to be a sleuth who has been commissioned to uncover Mr. Griffith's wily game, or the gaily eccentric wardrobe of Givenchy costumes that Miss Hepburn wears. Never mind. It may all be deception—a piece of fictitious trickery as crafty as those phony Van Gogh paintings or the glistening Cellini statuette. It is still a delightful lot of flummery while it is going on, especially the major, central business of burglarizing the museum." [3] *Time* said the film's glossy tone brushed out any forward momentum. "In a film that cries for wild hilarity and a heady spirit of adventure, everything that is going to happen happens according to long-established rules of the game, from the first skittish encounter to the last eager kiss," [4] while *Newsweek* wondered whether Audrey wasn't trading too heavily on her "usual selection of charm."

Two months after the release of *How to Steal a Million,* Wyler became a grandfather. Cathy gave birth to a boy whom they named Billy. It seemed only yesterday to Talli and Willy, that he had made *Wuthering Heights* and they had named their own first baby after the heroine in the Emily Brontë story.

36

On his sixty-fifth birthday, Willy started his first musical. What made him accept it was the chance to do yet another type of film and the chance to launch an exciting new star's big-screen career. The combination was felicitous, building a tower of toothpicks in a new dimension on top of a multisplendored pop bottle. A creature in a leopard-skin coat seen from the rear, Barbra Streisand slides into the first frame of *Funny Girl*. In a slightly overhead angle shot, the camera follows her to a mirror, where Barbra–Fanny greets her own reflection with a sardonic, "Hi, gorgeous."

The plunge into movies by the twenty-five-year-old superstar was surrounded by appropriately extravagant statistics. For the *Funny Girl* role, which she had created on Broadway and carried through two healthy seasons plus a London West End run, Columbia Pictures paid her the fattest fee ever paid for any debut. The budget for her next, *Hello, Dolly* for Fox, came to $20 million. In the past eighteen months, she had knocked off four million-seller record albums, enchanted seventy million TV viewers, and lured one hundred thirty thousand New Yorkers into Central Park for a concert.

"At the beginning, I guess, before we started the picture, we had the usual differences most people have," she said afterward. "At that point, I think I knew more about *Funny Girl* than Mr. Wyler. I had played it a thousand times and had read all the revisions of all the scripts—for the movies and the play. But once we started . . . well, it couldn't have been a more creative relation. I don't know what people are used to . . . well, it's just the fact that people want to make trouble. But, I mean, when two people discuss things. We tried different things and experimented and so forth. It was stimulating and fun and good things came out. And, I guess, bad things, too. But, I mean, it's the only way to work."

The Broadway *Funny Girl* Barbra Streisand knew so well was actually a "dry run" for the film. The story of Fanny Brice was the property, in more senses than one, of Ray Stark, a former literary agent who had married Frances, the only child of Fanny Brice and gambler Nicky Arnstein. Stark had handled such writers as J. P. Marquand and Ben Hecht before joining Famous Artists Agency, where he had represented Marilyn Monroe, Kirk Douglas, and Richard Burton. In 1957, he had formed, with Eliot Hyman, Seven Arts Productions, serving as vice-president until 1966 when he had broken out on his own. He had just produced Huston's *Reflections in a Golden Eye,* starring Marlon Brando and Elizabeth Taylor, when *Funny Girl* got under way.

Stark had had the idea of doing a biopic about his mother-in-law since her death in 1951. Brooklyn-born Fannie Borach was an obscure Jewish comedienne appearing in a burlesque show called *The College Girl* when fate struck. In the show, she sang "Sadie Salome," a ballad composed for her by Irving Berlin. The year was 1910. Florenz Ziegfeld saw and heard her in *The College Girl* and, at $75 a week, signed her to sing "Lovey Joe" in his *Follies* revue. The rest was legend.

Various writers had tried their hand on her hypnotic life, including Hecht ("You write it a little fancy, kid, but you've got some of it straight," she told him) and Isobel Lennart had come up with *My Man,* a sanitized (Stark would call it "affectionate") biography of Fanny Brice.

"Books are the most personal form, plays open up more, and films are worlds unto themselves," Stark wrote in a newspaper article retracing the genesis of *Funny Girl.* "It seemed wise to open it halfway as a trial before going the whole way with a film and also to be able to view a 'dry run' for a film." [1] To own everything about his late mother-in-law, Stark bought the plates from a publisher of a biography he didn't like, signed the still-living Arnstein into silence, and purchased from studios previous screenplays and treatments commissioned from Hecht and Henry and Phoebe Ephrons. Carol Burnett and Anne Bancroft were first choices for the stage version. "If Anne had done it, the form would have been more play-with-musical than musical," Stark wrote. "Then a friend of my wife's saw Barbra Streisand's photograph in the *New York Times Magazine* section in her Miss Marmelstein outfit from *I Can Get It for You Wholesale.*" [2]

After music and lyrics by Jule Styne and Bob Merrill, lengthy rehearsals and Boston tryouts, *Funny Girl* became one of the ten longest-running Broadway musicals and, in 1966, Stark asked Wyler to see Barbra Streisand in the London production. Other directors were also approached, including Sidney Lumet, who backed out, as the euphemism goes, "because of artistic differences" with Stark. In early 1967, Columbia nearly dumped the "filmusical" also.

Herbert Ross, a lanky former dancer and choreographer, had directed Barbra in *I Can Get It for You Wholesale* and, together with Miss Lennart and production designer Gene Callahan, had been on the project for almost a year when Wyler joined. Mike Frankovich, now head of Columbia production, insisted on a director who could "handle" superstar Streisand. When Columbia agreed to a number of specifics, Wyler signed on.

The most important of Wyler's demands was that Ross be given complete authority over the choreography. Another was a cutoff date. Wyler had a commitment at Fox to do *Patton,* which he wanted to get underway in Spain in 1968. "It probably will turn out like many times in the past, finishing upon one and starting preparations on another," he told *Variety* [3] before flying off with Stark to meet Barbra in New York.

Wyler felt moviegoers were far more demanding than Broadway audiences. Stage audiences accepted stage conventions; they never moved in on the scenic spectacle (except when they looked through their opera glasses), whereas filmgoers expected to be carried through hedges of chorus girls and soar above choreographed color dynamics in an orgy of stereophonics.

The story was not what attracted him. He found it another piece of glitzy and mechanical showbiz iconography. But, there was Barbra and her nervy incandescence.

"Going into a song in real life is most unrealistic," he told *Variety,* "but the far-reaching talents of Miss Streisand, who injects tremendous emotion into a lyric, will sustain the believability of the Fanny Brice story in her early days."

It was *Wuthering Heights* in a new dimension—how to tone down grandiloquence without, at the same time, rubbing out magnetism and glow. Whereas Larry had been the stage actor supreme, Barbra's specialty was to destroy the distance between herself and her boisterous persona. By making parochial Jewishness her personal trademark, she seemed less typically Jewish—and more modern—than Sylvia Sidney, Judy Holliday, or Fanny Brice, who had restrained their mannerisms and intonations and, sometimes, had seemed to carry their Jewishness like a cross. Theirs had been an era of less ethnic tolerance. Barbra's appeal was nonethnic in the sense that Jewishness was now in and hip.

"What captivated me was, of course, Barbra, and my principal concern was to present her under the best possible conditions as a new star and a new personality. She was terribly eager, like Bette Davis used to be, to do different and new things. She wanted everything to be the very best. The same as I do."

Fanny Brice's rise from the pushcart-laden Lower East Side to Ziegfeld stardom and a baronial Long Island estate was achieved with broad strokes. The durable Styne-Merrill songs, from the original score, were to be given fuller range in the cinematic sweep—"People," "You Are Woman, I Am Man," "Don't Rain on My Parade," "I'm the Greatest Star." New tunes by Styne and Merrill included "Roller Skate Rag," as background for a funny rollerskating routine, a parody on the Swan ballet, and a title song. Also added were "Second-Hand Rose," by James Hanley and Grant Clarke, "I'd Rather Be Blue," by Fred Fisher and Billy Rose and, as a poignant finale, Maurice Yvain's "My Man."

Mayor John Lindsay tried to get Columbia to shoot *Funny Girl* in New York but Manhattan locals of the International Alliance of Theatrical and Stage Employees (IATSE) refused to match California labor contract offers and the film was shot at Columbia's Gower Street lot. With Omar Sharif as Arnstein and costarring Kay Medford, Anne Francis, and Walter Pidgeon as Florenz Ziegfeld, *Funny Girl* went before the cameras in July—a few days before the outbreak of the Israeli-Egyptian Six Day War.

The war sent jitters through Hollywood's Jewish community. Of all pictures in production, *Funny Girl* had as costar the cinema's only internationally known Egyptian actor. Emotions against Sharif ran high. Some wanted him replaced for fear of a pro-Israeli backlash against him and, subsequently, *Funny Girl.*

Others found photos of Sharif in an Egyptian uniform. Still others wanted to get a statement from him condemning Egypt and together with Abe Lastfogel, Sharif's agent, Wyler stepped in and called such demands "ridiculous."

"People lost their heads," Wyler recalled. "There was a story in one column that said, 'Omar Kisses Barbra—Egypt Angry,' to which Barbra said, 'Egypt angry! You should hear what my Aunt Sarah said!' Because he was an Egyptian, what were we supposed to do—fire him, or hang him?"

The anti-Sharif hysteria died down with Israel's victory. The photo of Sharif in uniform turned out to be from a film he had made in Cairo, playing an airline pilot.

Barbra had clashes with Stark. When Wyler saw how her husband, Elliott Gould, handled her after she emerged from these confrontations, he thought of himself and Margaret Sullavan. "Elliott handled these things a lot better than I did," he remembered. "He came in and sort of straightened things out. He was very good at that. Still, they broke up. Those situations—right out of *Funny Girl* also since Arnstein couldn't handle Fanny Brice's fame either—are very hard to cope with."

The showbiz drama of destructive love between winner-wife and loser-husband was, by definition, a tribute to the woman, but Wyler gave Sharif–Arnstein one brilliant scene.

Funny Girl was almost all Streisand's, and Wyler got along very well with his leading lady, sometimes jokingly turning his bad ear to her constant explanations. "She fusses over things, she's terribly concerned about how she looks, with the photography, the camera, the makeup, the wardrobe, the way she moves, reads a line. She'd tell the cameraman that one of the lights was out—way up on the scaffold. If the light that was supposed to be on her was out, *she* saw it. She's not easy, but she's difficult in the best sense of the word—the same way I'm difficult."

"I don't just expect obedience. I don't like an actor or actress who says, 'Okay, boss, what do you want me to do?' I say to them, 'What do *you* want to do? You've read the script and you know what's in it so *you* show *me*. Show me what you want to do.' I've got an idea, but maybe they've got a better one and I want to see it. Then together we may be able to find a better one still. The actor has to put himself in another person's skin and think like somebody he isn't. I can help and guide but he has to do it finally.

I can't do it for him. I can guide his thinking—because if he *thinks* correctly, thinks like the character he is playing, there is very little he can do wrong. Making films is also a very complex, highly technical business. Barbra responded to direction very well."

Barbra told it a little differently. "I feel we had a great sort of chemical relationship. Willy can't, um, dissect a scene for you. I mean, he would go, 'Oomph, a little more oomph,' and I'd say, 'Okay, I know what you mean.' And I would give it a little more oomph. A lot of people are not like that, but I couldn't have wanted a better relationship. He let me see the rushes with him, and I'm supposedly the first actress who's seen them. He knows I'm not destructive. I'm very objective about my work."

Wyler would take her to dinner sometimes, but instead of an evening of relaxation she would bring the script along and go over the following day's scenes, telling him what had happened in that particular scene of the stage version during road showings in Philadelphia and Buffalo and ten other cities.

Life's John Hallowell saw them at work during her Swan Queen parody number. "Ross was explaining the number—loud so Wyler could hear—and Barbra began dancing. There was a lot of laughter, even applause, although Wyler didn't say anything. Perhaps he couldn't hear," Hallowell wrote. "Streisand came over to him and started explaining what she was doing. Her hands were going everywhere, like an Italian woman explaining a traffic accident to a cop. Here, I was doing this, there, I was doing that —wanting things to be all right with this man, wanting his approval very much. To hell with all the others who say they love me, she seemed to be saying. Wyler will determine my first picture.

"Sunk down in his chair, the director didn't seem to hear. Streisand started explaining again. All of a sudden, Wyler held up one hand: 'Just tone it down.' They looked at one another. Everyone waited for her to explode and say the hell with your love, who needs it? Streisand nodded and walked back out onto the cold rehearsal floor. This time when she did the number, it was so funny, she cracked herself up."

Make Barbra play convincingly, keep the reins on her enthusiasm.

In May, Willy again took a Saturday off to give away his second daughter in a ceremony in the garden on Summit Drive. Judy married Wylie Sheldon, a young lawyer in San Francisco.

At the cast party at the end of filming, Wyler presented Barbra Streisand with two gifts—a director's megaphone in mock recognition of her devotion to every aspect of filmmaking including directing, and a telescoping baton.

"She pays the keenest attention to the orchestration and the playback. She has a very sharp ear", Willy said with a touch of jealousy.

"He wants me to go on scoring," Barbra answered, presenting him with an eighteenth-century gold watch, inscribed "To make up for lost time."

The $8.8-million roadshow world premiered September 19, 1968 at Broadway's Criterion Theater. Reviewers hammered at the obvious—Streisand's engrossing, compelling, and poignant talent and the thin, musically inadequate and average cornball story. Renata Adler, whose days as the *New York Times*'s film critic were already numbered, tore into *Funny Girl* mercilessly, calling it an "elaborate, painstaking launching pad, with important talents of Hollywood, from the director, William Wyler, on down, treating Barbra rather fondly, improbably, and even patronizingly as though they were firing off a gilded broccoli." [4] *Life*'s reviewer couldn't help comparing *Funny Girl* with that other musical about a superstar of the past, *Star!*, saying it was the contrast that counted—"*Funny Girl* succeeds, *Star!* does not."

"*Funny Girl* is so much better than I thought it would be that I am almost tempted to recommend it," Andrew Sarris wrote. "But a few words of warning may be in order at the outset. Musicals have never been everyone's cup of tea, but the Broadway bonanzas of recent years have become a veritable anathema to a new generation of intellectuals. I am certainly not defending the brainwashing procedures by which an overpriced hit show continues to sell out (literally and figuratively) long after Zero Mostel has been replaced by Eddie Bracken. Nor is it merely crotchety nostalgia to suggest that the Broadway musical stage has gained in vulgarity what it has lost in vitality over the past two decades. A minor writhe-rock frolic like *Hair* seems ten years ahead of its time because it is only two or three years behind while the rest of Broadway is twenty years behind. . . . in all fairness to Miss Streisand, she might have fallen flat on her face after all the

393

building and she didn't. Practically every song number elicits spontaneous applause from the paying customers, and even this certified Barbraphobe found himself stirred on occasion by La Streisand's talent and energy." [5]

Pauline Kael was more generous. "Barbra Streisand arrives on the screen when the movies are in desperate need of her," she began. "The time is perfect. There's hardly a star in American movies today, and if we've got so used to the absence of stars that we no longer think about it much, we've also lost one of the great pleasures of moviegoing: watching incandescent people up there, more intense and dazzling than people we ordinarily encounter in life, and far more charming than the extraordinary people we encounter, because the ones on the screen are objects of pure contemplation—like athletes all wound up in the stress of competition—and we don't have to undergo the frenzy or the risk of being involved with them. In life, fantastically gifted people who are driven can be too much to handle; they can be a pain. In plays, in opera, they're divine, and on the screen, where they can be seen in their perfection, and where we're even safer from them, they're *more* divine.

"Let's dispose, at once, of the ugly-duckling myth. It has been commonly said that the musical *Funny Girl* was a comfort to people because it carried the message that you do not need to be pretty to succeed. That is nonsense; the 'message' of Barbra Streisand in *Funny Girl* is that talent is beauty. And this isn't some comforting message for plain people; it's what show business is all about. . . ." [6]

37

While everybody went to see "what show busine
Talli and Willy made a first trip to Israel in
Six Day War had stirred his dormant Jewish co
he was more than curious about the Hebrew stat

"We had a marvelous time," he recalled. "Gen
mander of the Air Force, got us a military plai
around—the Mitla Pass, Sinai, The Golan Heigl
ruins of hundreds of Egyptian tanks and trucks in
flew right up to the Suez Canal full of floating and

The Israeli Minstry of Culture film division ask
a documentary, "the kind I'd made for the Air F
Belle, Thunderbolt."

He declined. "You may take only six days to wi
takes longer than that to make a picture," he smi

Strife and bitterness not only separated the bar
Canal, it also divided Americans. The summer o
the height of protest over a war that had become a
a Great Society coming apart. Serious problems see
themselves in scenes of gaudy theatricality—"c
abounded, between black and white, radical and cc
dean, child and parent. And, all too often, the sta
with blood. Why? Were Americans naturally a "vi
as it was now fashionable to suggest, a nation of shc
ild exaggerations, quick with both fads and fists?
Civil rights were largely won, but civil realities w

atter. Wholesale reform, through Congress or the courts, threat-
ned to become a thing of the past, and the black man's struggle a
iecemeal affair. The We Shall Overcome of 1963 was giving way
o the clenched fist. The country seemed to be undergoing a sort
f voluntary resegregation as blacks withdrew into their own so-
iety, their own visceral organizations, their own college curricu-
ums, in part to avoid the smothering embrace of liberal white
goodwill." Violence, it seemed, was what race and war had in
ommon.

While *In the Heat of the Night* proved that race was by no
neans taboo on the screen, Vietnam had prompted only silence.

The outbreak of World War I when Griffith was at work on
Birth of a Nation, had the cinema rally around the flag. In 1914,
he film industry had been as naïve politically as it had been
primitive technologically, but it had recorded that war from the
oint of view of United States pacifism and neutrality through
militancy and final disillusionment with the old world. As Hitler
ad marched into Poland, mighty Hollywood had swung behind
e Allied cause and, beginning with *The Best Years of Our
ives,* it had even asked searing postwar questions. The Korean
nflict had brought the run-of-the-barrel *Hell Squad* and *War
ero* B-movies. Except for John Wayne's hawkish *The Green
erets* for Universal, Hollywood was sitting this one out.

George S. Patton—the most aggressive and flamboyant commander ever to wear an American uniform—was an odd screen
hero in 1968. He had been a superpatriot, a warlord, a samurai, a
millionaire soldier whose career read like a fever chart, a man of
flinty courage, big hurts, and a scathing tongue. Producer Frank
McCarthy, who had known Patton during World War II, had
first proposed the project to Fox in 1951. Now, Darryl Zanuck felt
a big picture about the oversized figure could repeat the box-
office success of *The Longest Day.* Only this time, they would do
better—enlarge the scope and the background and avoid "cameo"
performances of known actors that had driven the cost of *Th
Longest Day* to intolerable levels.

Cost factors aside, there was only one country where *Pc
could be made—Spain. Only the Spanish army had the nec
World War II hardware in working condition. Only Spai
provide landscapes and architectural variety sufficiently
to simulate locations in Tunisia, Italy, France, and

The Battle of the Bulge would be staged in the Segovia highlands west of Madrid, while the African and Sicilian campaigns, including the El Guettar battle that employed two thousand extras, were to shoot in Almeria. The Basque region around Pamplona would double for France of 1944. Amphibious operations of the 1943 Sicily landing would be filmed at some NATO base or in California, while the inimitable English village of Knutsford, near Manchester, where Patton had had 1944 headquarters, would be filmed in—Knutsford.

McCarthy's wall-sized production chart included seventy-one locations on three continents—in North Africa, Spain, England, and the United States; the armor added up to fifty-four tanks; the *Patton* air force to four Heinkels, four Messerschmidts, and ten Allied warplanes. Production headquarters would be the Samuel Bronson studios in Madrid, the tentative budget a shade over $10 million, and production starting date scheduled for late 1968 to shoot the Ardennes offensive during the snowy season in the Segovia highlands.

Wyler had to admit that *Patton* was, physically, too big for him. He had had ulcer flare-ups on the last two films, and the one time he and Talli had visited Madrid the food had not agreed with him. *Patton* would be a very physical picture. There would be the biting snows of the High Sierras and the heat of Almeria and the Moroccan locations. He would have to stage tremendous tank battles. Scott was not yet cast, but was obviously the best choice. After *How to Steal a Million* how could they possibly work together? And living in Spain for eight months? It all spelled nightmare to Talli and she urged Willy to give up this project. So he asked Richard Zanuck to be relieved.

In the fall of 1968, Franklin J. Schaffner replaced Wyler as the *Patton* director and lost fourteen pounds during the eight months in Spain. Both he and McCarthy had a rough time with their violently individual leading man and Wyler considered he made a great contribution to the picture by bowing out.

Instead of the story of the magnificent anachronism, Wyler got to make an unforgiving film about racism—*The Liberation of L. B. Jones.*

"I had always wanted to do something on the racial issue," Wyler said later. "The question had been touched, very delicately, in *The Little Foxes,* and when Ronald Lubin brought me

Jesse Hill Ford's novel, it seemed a good story, very powerful, very blunt, in a way a harsh and shocking story. When the author came to us and I asked him, 'Aren't you putting it on a little thick?' he answered, 'Not at all, it is all based on facts.' "

Jesse Hill Ford's 1965 novel had been bought by independent producer Lubin and screenwriter Stirling Silliphant, the movie and TV writer. "It is, I'm sorry to say, a subject which has big studios more than slightly wary," Silliphant said in 1966. "It deals as you may know, with the very rich Negro of the title, who is cuckolded by a white man and who, as a man cherishing his dignity, demands that his white lawyer get him a divorce—an action that uncovers a barrel of civil rights fish in a Southern town that is enough to scare a senator or a studio chief."

Together, Ford and Silliphant had written the script, and when Lubin couldn't get anywhere with the project, the trio had thought of writing and producing a stage version, mainly to show that *The Liberation of Lord Byron Jones* wouldn't cause a riot. Meanwhile, Silliphant wrote a film exploring the same territory —*In the Heat of the Night,* for Norman Jewison. This runaway success, with Sidney Poitier as an urbane black detective and Rod Steiger as a seedy Southern police chief, was an added source of frustration for Lubin, Silliphant, and Ford (the latter now back in his native Tennessee). What the trio obviously needed was a big-name director. On August 7, 1968, Wyler signed an exclusive five-picture contract with Columbia, and the next day *The Hollywood Reporter* announced the first film would be *The Liberation of Lord Byron Jones*—a title later shortened to *The Liberation of L. B. Jones* lest any customers be misled into expecting a costume historical drama, possibly involving a poet. The second picture would be *Quarante Carats,* the May-December love comedy by Pierre Barillet and Jean-Pierre Gredy, which David Merrick had produced on Broadway as *40 Carats.*

In February 1969, Wyler went to Tennessee to scout locations and to meet Ford in his home town of Humboldt, eighty miles northeast of Memphis. Driving out of Memphis, he suddenly spotted an airplane in a park, did a double-take and made a u-turn to have a second look. There was his B-17—the Memphis Belle which the city had bought from the Air Force and made into a monument.

Tennessee *was* another world, flat cotton country with acreage set aside for raising strawberries or feeding Black Angus and Hereford cattle. Driving up to Humboldt, he first saw the old quarry ponds where they used to cut rocks for buildings, then the swamp where cypresses rose from dark stained waters. South of town were the Indian mounds known as the Mountains of Gilead, which had been the title of Ford's first novel. On the city limits were the cemetries—one for white folks and one for blacks.

Ford lived with his wife and four children outside town. The forty-year-old author was "a blood and bones Southerner for generations back" who, as a Fulbright scholar in Norway, had become fascinated by what he called the "wonderment at the greatest nation in the world being a biracial society." What had made him write *The Liberation of Lord Byron Jones*—based, at least loosely, on a course of events that had taken place a decade earlier in Humboldt—was the realization that what he had always taken for granted and thought commonplace was actually exotic to mainstream America.

The story was unsparing. Before the events have taken their last Aristotelian turns there are two ghastly murders, black by white and white by black. There are beatings, sex by extortion, and a total and willful perversion of the law by the law. There is no punishment and no death-bed remorse. Both murderers go unpunished and the inference is that nothing has changed or will change. The driving force of the plot is simply that Lord Byron Jones discards his inferiority complex and sues for divorce—a maneuver designed to expose the sinners and, incidentally, "nigger law" and the hypocrisy of the state of Tennessee. His "liberation" is his murder.

Could they shoot the exteriors in Humboldt? It all felt like a replay of Salzburg as Wyler went to city hall and about town weighing civic and public opinion. The Hollywood cast and crew would obviously be mixed and he would tolerate no attempts, overt or covert, to have black actors live in one hotel and the mainly white crew lodged in another. A new Holiday Inn outside town proved to be the solution. The whole company would stay there.

Back on the Coast, he and Lubin cast the picture. Roscoe Lee Browne, fresh from *The Comedians* with Richard Burton and Elizabeth Taylor, was chosen to play the title role. This native of

Woodbury, New Jersey, who had abandoned teaching to make his acting debut with the New York Shakespeare Festival, had the subtlety and complexity Wyler wanted. To play his selfish and sassy wife whose affair triggers the racial crisis, twenty-five-year-old Lola Falana was chosen. It was her American screen debut, following a couple of bit parts in Italian quickies and the role of Sammy Davis, Jr.'s girlfriend in the Broadway production of *Golden Boy.* With top billing, Lee J. Cobb signed on as Oman Hedgepath, the town lawyer aware that racism is ugly but knowing better than to rock the boat. Yaphet Kotto, who later replaced James Earl Jones in Broadway's long-running *The Great White Hope,* was cast as Sonny Boy Mosby, the local black kid coming home to settle old scores. Anthony Zerbe, who had made his screen debut in *Cool Hand Luke,* was cast as Mrs. Jones's policeman lover, a portrayal of arrogant power and odd pathos, while Arch Johnson was given the role of the older cornfritter cop, a more hateful man because he is incapable of detecting the faintest trace of evil in himself. Lee Majors and Barbara Hershey were given thin, token parts as Hedgepath's liberal nephew and his young wife.

In May, cast and crew arrived in Humboldt, fictionalized as Somerton. Russ Saunders, a former all-star football player who knew Southern mentality toward outside film crews, was production manager (as he had been on *Bonnie and Clyde*). Robert Surtees was on camera, Robert Swink was editor and second-unit director. Spending over $250,000 in Humboldt and environs, the company filmed in half a dozen small towns—Humboldt, Trenton, Gibson, and Brownsville, and all eighty-odd members of cast and crew stayed at the Holiday Inn.

No incidents marred the filming and former college professor Browne came up with the only memorable crack of the shooting.

"How come you don't talk like other colored folk?" he was asked in town one day.

"Because," he said, arching an eyebrow, "when I was young, we had a white maid."

Author Ford was in on the filming as production consultant and Wyler put him in a scene with Dub Taylor, who played the mayor. Swink's second-unit shooting included the opening and closing scenes with the train and Sonny Boy's killing of cop Johnson in a threshing machine.

"Bob Swink has always come back with better than I expected, something of his own added to the scene," Wyler remembered. "I've sent him out to do scenes I wouldn't give to any second-unit director, scenes with principals, not just action."

Once the location filming was finished, *The Liberation of L. B. Jones* took over five soundstages on Gower Street. The junkyard of Jones's murder filled one stage, complete with the hulls of sixty wrecked cars, and Jones's funeral parlor with casket display and embalming room took up another. Filming was completed July 11.

Wyler and Swink cut the picture during the fall with Elmer Bernstein supplying the music. Bernstein felt music should be used sparingly. "I don't think you should have any music here," he told Wyler during one screening room session. "I think the scene plays well. I can't improve it." Novel music in Willy's ear.

The first cut was ready in November and false rumors began circulating that Columbia was nervous about the film and that Wyler was locked in a struggle with the studio brass over demands that he soften certain passages. In early December, *L. B. Jones* was previewed in Encino, an upper middle-class white Los Angeles suburb. The most provocative response was the walkout of an adult couple. On the way out, the husband muttered, "If you want to start a riot this is the way to do it," a comment that on December 8 Dorothy Manners' syndicated column blew up to an actual riot with members of the audience running "up and down the aisles, yelling and beating on seats."

Whether he thought it was his civic duty or so he could whip up publicity, Lubin later announced he had received personal telephone threats and that Columbia Pictures had received bomb threats. Questioned by reporters, he admitted the threats might be coming from crackpots, but crackpots, he said, were more dangerous than rational critics.[1] A month after the opening, Kotto got into the act and told the trade papers the picture might trigger antiwhite violence in black communities.[2] Wyler never received threats, but abusive letters, calling him a "nigger lover" and asking him how he dared to make such a picture, were sent to him.

After a New York preview marked by a fist fight between a white patron and a black youth, *The Liberation of L. B. Jones* opened to mixed reviews. At best, it was called a brutal, credible, powerful, deeply disturbing, and depressed film. "What the picture is about, of course, is not simply the events themselves, but what they say about the environment in which they arise; most centrally the on-going immutable and settled presumption of white superiority and black inferiority," Charles Champlin wrote. "But there is also the paralyzing presumption of the impossibility of change, even by men of goodwill or men with glimmerings of remorse, sympathy or understanding. . . . Given the power of film, the question becomes not whether a film this strong meets the test of believability, but what the consequences may be of releasing it in a volatile and tumultuous time. The producers are now being careful to make very clear that the story in fact has its origins in fact, on the grounds, presumably, that to have invented and filmed such a story could be called unconscionable at this time.

"The concern may be well taken. But it is sad to think so. The real test is credibility. There are true stories we can't believe and fictions we can believe because they square with the realities we have experienced. The events of *Liberation* meet the test of credibility, including the evidence of the double standards of sexual conduct as they affect race." [3]

As Wyler had asked Ford when they first met, most critics wondered whether the film didn't lay it on a little thick.

"*The Liberation of L. B. Jones,* which purports to be a contemporary story of racial injustice and death in a small Southern city, offends our sensibilities because its own sensibilities are fixed ten, or fifteen, years in the past," *Newsweek* wrote. "With such volatile dramatic material as this, a movie that's out of date seems maddeningly out of touch." [4]

Outdated or ahead of his time? Andrew Sarris was more prophetic when he underlined the newness of *The Liberation of L. B. Jones,* saying it might be the first American movie, either black or white, to dramatize the matter-of-fact exploitation of black women by white sexsupremacists. "Certainly it is the first American movie to countenance and even condone bloody revenge by the black against his white oppressor," Sarris wrote in *Show,* bemusedly wondering how Wyler could "slither off a slice of Stage Delicatessen salami like *Funny Girl* to the black bread of racial agitprop."

Less than a year after *The Liberation of L. B. Jones,* the black wave broke. As the new, eminently commercial movies by blacks about the black experience—usually featuring black avengers instead of black victims—reached their peak in 1972, someone at Columbia told Wyler the only thing wrong with *L. B. Jones* was that its director wasn't black. Wyler, however, analyzed the reasons for the box-office failure with less self-indulgence. With himself and with Jesse Hill Ford, he had debated the idea of a less depressing ending. Black Panthers, for example, could arrive on the train in the fadeout, suggesting that change was around the corner and that the town would get what it deserved. But that, he felt, would take the audience off the hook. "Perhaps it was a mistake, commercially, not to do it, but I wanted the audience to go out with a sense of guilt, of embarrassment at knowing what was going on and perhaps a feeling that they should do something about it." But that didn't work either. Because mostly black audiences came to see the film and got a sense of satisfaction while white audiences stayed away *en masse.*"

What happened to Ford after the film formed a harrowing and deadly comment on *The Liberation of L. B. Jones.* Returning to Humboldt from the premiere and launch ballyhoo, Ford was greeted by a sullen town. Even some of the town's blacks resented the picture because they were portrayed as being easily defeated and the author's teenage son found himself involved in a couple of ugly scraps. When the boy didn't return home one night, Ford anxiously watched the long private road leading to his house. As he peered out of the window, he saw a car come up the road, stop and turn off headlights and engine.

Calling the police, Ford grabbed a rifle and went out. Sneaking up to the car, he shouted, "I've called the police, come on out!" The figure behind the wheel started the motor and gunned the car forward. Ford took one shot at the fleeing car. The bullet went through the back window and killed the driver instantly. The dead man turned out to be a black Marine, home on leave before going to Vietnam. With him was a girl and, in the back of the car, a sleeping baby. They had been petting.

The Humboldt establishment, angry at being portrayed in book and film as bigots, saw an occasion to prove to the world that contrary to Jesse Hill Ford fiction, a white man cannot kill a black man and get away with it. Ford was charged with first degree murder.

403

The road to trial was long and arduous. Feeling Ford's unfortunate bullet was fired with more stupidity than murderous intent, Wyler phoned from Hollywood and offered to be a character witness, telling the writer that the attorney he needed now was a real-life Oman Hedgepath, the clever and bigoted lawyer Lee J. Cobb played in the film. "I've got him," Ford answered. Before the case went to trial, however, Ford's old Tennessee criminal lawyer died. Two younger attorneys finally defended the writer.

At the trial, Ford was acquitted.

38

Wyler approached his half century in films with persistent inquisitiveness, detached compassion, and a leap toward that other total cinema—home movies in Super 8. He also neared the fiftieth anniversary of *Crook Buster* with tickling indications that *his* cinema was about to come in from the cold.

As films marched toward the mid-1970s, the thrusts and themes pointed toward a Wylerian renaissance—a reemergence of style and sheen, professionalism and perfection. The hottest young filmmakers were not Dionysian rebels but Hollywood intellectuals who suddenly weren't measuring themselves against current obsessions, but against past excellence. When the 1971 New York Film Festival lionized him for *The Last Picture Show,* Peter Bogdanovich said all the great movies had already been made.

The Wylerian cinema was unfashionable during the Aquarian age when the message was fracturing spontaneity, borderline amateurism, and the exaltation of the self. Intense, visionary trading on an amplified "now" was—cinematically and emotionally—the antithesis of artistic mastery and perfection, even if progression in the arts seemed to be a perpetual swing between forethought and intoxication. Imperceptibly, it seemed, the pendulum was moving back toward perfection.

But, as Stuart Hampshire said in a warning against a too intense view of literature—and Wyler would agree in regard to films—"when works of the imagination are fingered and tested for directly evident social and moral relevance, we get disastrous dismissals and misunderstandings."

Creativity was always simpler and more complex in movies than in other consumer arts. The medium was hardly out of the penny arcades before entrepreneurs discovered the motherlode that was to be mined in restaging famous plays and famous novels, making most of history's screenfare re-creation and the director an interpretative rather than a creative animal. Since movies were such porous mixtures of intentions and accidents, cinematic authorship was in structure and performance and in transposing preexisting materials to the complex codes and channels of film emotions. Film creativity was nearly always *au second degré,* narrative experiments, going beyond the subject, architectural volumes created with a certain arrangement and a sense of "rhythm."

And here, Wyler could lean back and let aesthetics catch up with him again.

From the beginning, he had probed the deeper maze of modern sensibility. From the two-reelers on Uncle Carl's back lot, where he had wanted "to make them a little different," he sought the answers in his own craft. By the high thirties when his awareness of himself as a creative person became established, he explored new territories and, before he was forty, had invented a new dramatic trigonometry that reverberated through film aesthetics for the next two decades. His directing not only created new visual patterns and heightened dramatic honesty, it allowed him to analyze the most delicate and impressionistic of human feelings. His direction, which allowed the acting to shine with maximum force and clarity, was centered on the actor. Doing a film for him, as Charlton Heston said, was "like getting the works in a Turkish bath." Besides coming out smelling like roses, some of the victims of his painstaking devotion to perfection decorated their mantelpieces with Oscars—Bette Davis and Walter Brennan, and Audrey Hepburn, Olivia de Havilland, Greer Garson, Teresa Wright, Fay Bainter, Barbra Streisand, Fredric March, Burl Ives, Hugh Griffith, Heston, and that agonizing amputee Harold Russell, who tested the liberal conscience in *The Best Years of Our Lives.* After the crucible of war, which gave his work edge, purity, and directness, he was the consummate director who could take any material to any degree of dramatic voltage. In 1948, André Bazin could sum him up as an artist who knew that to simplify was to clarify, a filmmaker with humility toward both material and audience who, with maximum transparency, could reduce the distance between screen and mind and, while stripping away emotional overloads and superfluous motion and refraction, could create one of the most personal styles.

The times, however, turned Nietzschean—the charm of imperfection had creators beguiled more with what they hinted at than with what they achieved—and evolution was increasingly measured *against* Wylerian reason and skill (now called gloss). In the sixties, film appeal was in texture and tone, in slight narratives, vacuous responses, shifting energies, and a sense of complicity with youth, which now openly displayed its strength, allure, and power. The tell-it-like-it-is credo had filmmakers trying not to pander or to con, but honesty was confined only to content. Form was typed to amplified hyperbole. Everything was glare, shiny surfaces, volume, and metaphor.

The shift brought amateurism into fashion. Of necessity, everybody suddenly was a "Renaissance man." With the technical advances—faster film stocks, faster lenses—that made the proletarization of the medium possible, came an easier style of directing. As a matter of course, the "available light" school of photography made Tolandian deep-focus *mise en scène* an impossibility. Simple camera setups, rack focusing, elimination of master shots became the rule during the 1960s when audiences were increasingly conditioned by television and, for a while at least, by psychedelic "mixed media" bombast. The aim of direction was more to surprise than to clarify, to overwhelm than to elucidate. To let stories seem to tell themselves, without conspicuous camera movements to draw attention to the director's shaping intelligence, seemed too simple. Yet the quality of intelligence was always the unifying force of filmmaking.

The shift in public sensibilities, perception, and awareness brought inflation, zap, and intuitive minds to the movies. With chilling ruthlessness, it also shortened careers, not only those of elder statesmen, but those of yesterday's gurus and superstars (Jean-Luc Godard bedeviled by the siren calls of revolutionary self-hatred, didn't make it into the seventies) and it seemed unlikely that any talent could ever endure a Wyler's fifty years in film and be around in the 2020s.

Wyler did lean back.

A month after the release of *The Liberation of L. B. Jones,* sister-in-law Cathy O'Donnell had died of cancer at the age of forty-five. The Robert Wylers had been childless, and the deeply shaken widower continued to live alone in his home on Wetherly Drive, above Sunset Boulevard. On the morning of January 17, 1971, Willy had been on the phone asking his brother to come out to the beach house and spend the day with them. Robert had said he might come in the afternoon, and that evening a doctor called to tell them Robert was dead, felled by a second and massive heart attack.

"Cathy's death had been terrible—cancer that went on and on —and that was what really killed my brother," Willy felt. His funeral arrangements included an insertion in the newspapers in Mulhouse. When Willy and Talli were in France that summer, Mulhouse was included on their list of stops, and Willy personally went around to thank people who had sent condolences.

The summer also brought happier occasions. In June, the Wylers became grandparents a second time when Cathy and Robert Sind had a girl, Amy.

Later in 1971, Talli and Willy went around the world, taking in the sights of India, Thailand, Nepal, and (because they were friends of *Horsemen* author Joseph Kessel) Afghanistan, which they found fascinating. They also attended the Cannes festival that year, where Willy, René Clair, Ingmar Bergman, Federico Fellini, and Luis Bunuel were given special trophies as the most-honored directors of the festival's first twenty-five years. A year later, he dropped the Columbia project *40 Carats,* asked the studio to be released from the three remaining films of the contract and passionately resumed the travels. The antipodes were visited in 1973—Alaska, southernmost Argentina, Antarctica, and the jungles of the Amazon River.

The scripts kept coming. He was looking for a new project, although not too hard, and he often took a script along in the suitcase to while away a rainy hotel evening. Too much of it was déjà vu.

"Making a picture is just too goddamn much work. I mean aside from the intellectual demands, it's hard physical work, getting up early in the morning, working all day and many nights, getting up in the middle of the night to make notes about yesterday's rushes that you must remember to get right in tomorrow's shooting. It's a twenty-four-hour job and during filming there is no family life, I don't see friends, I don't go out. It takes a helluva lot out of me. I did it for over forty years. Now, unless something really excites me . . ."

In the meantime, the free form of home movies had his enthusiasm. A camera buff since the days when he found photographs easier than letterwriting to tell those back home what the new world was like, he shot documentaries in 8mm of Tierra del Fuego tribes and Gobi Desert camel trains. He was even a menace to fellow tourists. More than one Instamatic-toting admirer of exotica has had a graying man with a furtive cigarette come up and suggest that exchanging places with the wife would mean also getting the Taj Mahal in the picture.

Renouncing the cigarette was the hardest withdrawal. A smoker since his teens, he suffered bronchitis and dire warnings from doctors had him playing games with Talli and with himself. Relapses occurred at the sight of an ash tray.

When the Wylers weren't on the road—by 1973, South Sea islands and Australia were the only unvisited landmasses—they shuttled between Summit Drive and the beach house in Malibu. The house on Summit Drive was too big now—in 1973, Melanie was a history major at the University of California at Berkeley and David was attending the University of Puget Sound in Tacoma, Washington—but, as Talli joked, "only Mary Pickford has been here longer than we have, now." The social calendar included friends, screenings, and gatherings such as a directors' luncheon at George Cukor's for Luis Bunuel—"a defiant smoker, he"—during the Spanish filmmaker's Hollywood visit in 1972. The patriarchal John Ford had defied rain and illness to come, George Stevens came up from Marina del Rey. In the living room, Alfred Hitchcock and Robert Wise discussed the shocking prices of French vintages.

Over the cracked crab, Billy Wilder said, "I think we should make it perfectly clear to Mr. Bunuel that we eat like this every day and discuss ideas about the ceenayma."

"Excellent," said Bunuel, with a look of enchanted disbelief.

". . . and four servants always," Wilder added.

Cukor remembered when he and Bunuel were both under contract at MGM but the exiled Spaniard was given nothing to do.

"I heard there was some sort of blacklist," Cukor began.

"*Lista negra*," Rafael Bunuel translated for his father.

"But it was not then for politics," said Don Luis, "it was because I was a rebel, very independent."

"I went to Irving Thalberg," Cukor continued, "and told him it was disgraceful that a great talent like Mr. Bunuel should be on any blacklist. Thalberg said, 'Why, there isn't any blacklist and I'll see he's taken off it!'"

Ford had to leave early, with a gruff embrace for the guest of honor, and to Willy, "It's your turn to do *The Three Godfathers.*"

When affectionate evenings were held on Summit Drive, Willy saw his guests to the bricked driveway and when everybody was off took Alex, his black Labrador Retriever, for a walk in the garden and along the road.

He would probably see Bunuel next year at Cannes, or Cukor and Wise at a Directors' Guild meeting, or Hitchcock at another retrospective. Tributes were, perhaps, a way of life also. If the tragedy in Dallas had made him miss the luncheon with John F. Kennedy in 1963, President and Mrs. Johnson honored him together with others, at The White House two years later. Spontaneous homage, however, was what meant most like Laurence Olivier on the Dick Cavett Show remembering who had opened his eyes to cinema back on the set of *Wuthering Heights*. Or a note his daughter Melanie brought home from Moscow from the poet Yevgeny Yevtushhenko, ending in a fractured Russian-English with, "Thank you for your existence."

NOTES

CHAPTER ONE

1. "Zugewandter Ort." Historical notes based on André Brandt and Raymond Oberle, in *Mulhouse vous accueille,* Syndicat d'initiative, Mulhouse, 1969, and *Mulhouse en 1870,* Bulletin trimestrial No. 4, Société industrielle de Mulhouse, 1970.

CHAPTER FOUR

1. In *New York World,* 1923 quoted by Andrew F. Rolle, *California, A History,* Thomas Y. Crowell, New York, 1969.

2. In *The American Mercury,* quoted by Kevin Brownlow, *The Parade's Gone By,* Alfred A. Knopf, New York, 1968.

3. Arthur Knight, *The Liveliest Art,* Macmillan, New York, 1957.

CHAPTER FIVE

1. Ben Hecht, *A Child of the Century,* Simon and Schuster, New York, 1950.

2. Josef von Sternberg, *Fun In a Chinese Laundry,* Macmillan, New York, 1965.

3. *Daily Review,* March 13, 1927.

4. *Ibid.,* May 18, 1927.

5. *Variety,* September 18, 1927.

6. *Variety,* March 7, 1928.

7. *Chicago Herald,* August 19, 1927.

8. Uncle Carl's haberdashery parable notwithstanding, *Shooting Straight* was cut to a two-reeler. Universal renewed its copyright to the title and story in 1924, which may explain erroneous legends to the fact that Ford made *Shooting Straight* twice. Per Calum, *John Ford, en dokumentation,* Det danske Filmmuseum, Copenhagen, 1968.

CHAPTER SIX

1. Frank Capra, *The Name above the Title,* Macmillan, New York, 1971.

2. *Los Angeles Express,* November 20, 1928.

3. *Today's Cinema,* March 29, 1928.

4. *L'Hebdo,* November 14, 1928.

5. Joseph Franklin Poland, James Gruen, John B. Clymer, Rob Wagner, Earl Snell, and Samuel M. Pike, per *American Film Institute Catalog,* R. R. Bowker, New York and London, 1971. Clymer alone received screen credit.

6. *New York Times,* August 8, 1929.

CHAPTER SEVEN

1. Peter B. Kyne, *The Three Godfathers,* Cosmopolitan Book Co., New York, 1913.

2. *New York Times,* December 28, 1929.

3. *Variety,* January 1, 1930.

4. *New York Post,* February 15, 1930.

5. *Cinémonde,* February 15, 1930.

6. *Variety,* August 27, 1930.

7. *New York Times,* August 23, 1930.

8. *Variety,* March 25, 1931.

9. John Drinkwater, *The Life and Adventures of Carl Laemmle,* G. P. Putnam's Sons, New York and London, 1931.

CHAPTER EIGHT

1. *Variety,* January 12, 1932.

2. *Boston Herald,* December 14, 1931. F. W. (Friedrich-Wilhelm) Murnau died in 1931, a year after completing *Tabu,* codirected by Robert Flaherty.

3. Bob Thomas, *Thalberg, Life and Legend,* Doubleday, Garden City, N.Y., 1969.

4. *New York Times,* July 30, 1932.

CHAPTER NINE

1. Elmer Rice, *Minority Report, An Autobiography,* Simon and Schuster, New York, 1963.

2. Ben Hecht, *A Child of the Century,* op. cit.

3. Gene Fowler, *Good Night, Sweet Prince, The Life and Times of John Barrymore,* Viking Press, New York, 1944.

4. *The New Yorker,* December 11, 1933.

5. *New York Herald Tribune,* December 8, 1933.

6. *New York Times,* December 8, 1933.

7. *Cue* magazine, August 8, 1953.

8. *Cinema,* Volume 3, No. 5, Summer 1967.

9. Pauline Kael, *Kiss Kiss Bang Bang,* Little, Brown, Boston, 1968.

CHAPTER TEN

1. Edna Ferber (1887–1968) published *"Glamour,"* together with seven other short stories, under the title of the longest of them, *They Brought Their Women,* Doubleday, New York, 1933.

2. *Variety,* May 15, 1934.

CHAPTER ELEVEN

1. *Variety*, November 14, 1933.
2. *New York Telegraph*, February 2, 1935.
3. *New York American*, February 1, 1935.
4. *New York Herald Tribune*, February 1, 1935.
5. *New York Daily Mirror*, February 1, 1935.
6. *New York Times*, February 1, 1935.
7. *Buffalo, (N.Y.) Times*, February 15, 1935.
8. *Washington News*, February 14, 1935.

CHAPTER TWELVE

1. King Vidor, *A Tree Is a Tree*, Harcourt, Brace, New York, 1952.
2. *New York Times*, November 28, 1935.

CHAPTER THIRTEEN

1. Sam Goldwyn, *Behind the Screen*, George H. Doran Co., New York, 1923.
2. Tom Milne, *Mamoulian*, Thames and Hudson, London, 1969.
3. Aaron Latham, *Crazy Sundays, F. Scott Fitzgerald in Hollywood*, Viking Press, New York, 1971.
4. Quoted in John Keats, *You Might As Well Live, The Life and Times of Dorothy Parker*, Simon and Schuster, New York, 1970.
5. Mark Schorer, *Sinclair Lewis, An American Life*, McGraw-Hill, New York, 1961.
6. Lillian Hellman, *An Unfinished Woman*, Little, Brown, Boston, 1969.

CHAPTER FOURTEEN

1. *Sight and Sound*, Vol. 5, No. 18, Summer 1936.
2. *New York Times*, March 19, 1936.
3. Quoted in Karel Reisz (ed.), *William Wyler, An Index*, British Film Institute, London, 1958.
4. Charles Higham, *Hollywood Cameramen*, Indiana University Press, Bloomington and London, 1970.
5. Lester Koenig, "Gregg Toland, Film-Maker," in *The Screen Writer*, December 1947.
6. Charles Higham, *Hollywood Cameramen*, op. cit.
7. *New York World-Telegram*, March 1, 1936.
8. *New York Times*, March 3, 1936.
9. *New York Herald Tribune*, March 29, 1936.
10. *New York World-Telegram*, March 19, 1936.
11. *Boston Herald*, March 29, 1936.
12. *Boston Traveler*, March 28, 1936.
13. *The Spectator*, May 1, 1936.
14. *The New Statesman*, March 1, 1936.
15. *The Sunday Express*, April 24, 1936.
16. *The Daily Mail*, May 4, 1936.

CHAPTER FIFTEEN

1. Richard Griffith, *Samuel Goldwyn, The Producer and His Films*, Museum of Modern Art Library, New York, 1956.

2. Mark Schorer, *Sinclair Lewis, An American Life,* op. cit.

3. Ibid.

4. *New York Times,* February 26, 1934.

5. Mary Astor, *My Story, An Autobiography,* Doubleday, Garden City, N.Y., 1959.

6. Howard Teichman, *George S. Kaufman, An Intimate Portrait,* Atheneum, New York, 1972.

7. *The New Yorker,* October 3, 1936.

8. *New York Post,* September 24, 1936.

9. *New York Times,* September 24, 1936.

10. *New York Times,* November 12, 1936.

11. Edna Ferber, *A Peculiar Treasure,* Doubleday, Garden City, N. Y., 1938.

CHAPTER SIXTEEN

1. John Baxter, *Hollywood in the Thirties,* Paperback Library, New York, 1970.

2. *New York Post,* August 31, 1937.

3. *New York Times,* August 25, 1937.

4. In *Night and Day,* November 25, 1937.

5. Georges Sadoul, *Histoire du Cinéma mondial,* Flammarion, Paris, 1949.

6. Bette Davis, *The Lonely Life,* G. P. Putnam's Sons, New York, 1962.

7. In *Cinema,* Vol. 3, No. 5, 1967.

8. Pauline Kael, *Kiss Kiss Bang Bang,* op. cit.

9. In *William Wyler, An Index,* op. cit.

10. Bette Davis, *The Lonely Life,* op. cit.

CHAPTER SEVENTEEN

1. *Variety,* June 16, 1937.

2. *New York Times,* July 26, 1939.

3. *Variety,* July 7, 1939.

4. Bob Thomas, *Selznick,* Doubleday, Garden City, N. Y., 1970.

CHAPTER EIGHTEEN

1. In *Woman's Home Companion,* December 1950.

CHAPTER NINETEEN

1. E. Weir, *Contemporary Reviews of the First Brontë Novels,* Brontë Society Transactions, London, 1947; Winifred Gerin, *Emily Brontë,* Clarendon Press, Oxford, 1971.

2. Quoted in *Time* review of *Wuthering Heights,* April 17, 1939.

3. *New York Herald Tribune,* Paris, July 12, 1938.

4. Felix Barker, *The Oliviers,* J. B. Lippincott, New York, 1953.

5. David Niven, *The Moon's a Balloon*, G. P. Putnam's Sons, New York, 1972.

6. *New York Times*, April 16, 1939.

7. *The Observer*, April 3, 1939.

8. *The Times*, April 26, 1939.

9. *Variety*, July 11, 1971.

10. *Los Angeles Times*, August 17, 1971.

CHAPTER TWENTY

1. James D. Horan and Paul Sann, *Pictorial History of the Wild West*, Crown Publishers, New York, 1954.

2. *The Hollywood Reporter*, January 6, 1940.

3. George Fenin and William K. Everson, *The Western*, Orion Press, New York, 1962.

4. *New York Times*, October 25, 1940.

5. *Newsweek*, September 30, 1940.

CHAPTER TWENTY-ONE

1. *New York Times*, November 23, 1940.

2. Bette Davis, *The Lonely Life*, op. cit.

3. André Bazin, *Qu'est-ce que le cinéma*, Vol. 2, Editions du cerf, Paris, 1959.

4. Bette Davis, *The Lonely Life*, op. cit.

5. *Time*, September 1, 1941.

6. In *Sequence*, New Year 1951; Karel Reisz, *The Later Films of William Wyler*.

CHAPTER TWENTY-TWO

1. *Time*, June 29, 1942.

2. In an interview with Christian Viviani, *Positif*, Paris, September 1972.

3. Lillian Hellman, *An Unfinished Woman*, op. cit.

4. *New York Times*, June 5, 1942.

5. *New York Herald Tribune*, June 7, 1942.

6. *Look*, August 11, 1942.

7. *Life*, June 8, 1942.

CHAPTER TWENTY-THREE

1. Frank Capra, *The Name above the Title*, op. cit.

CHAPTER TWENTY-FOUR

1. Arch Whitehouse, *The Years of the War Birds*, Doubleday, Garden City, N. Y., 1960.

2. *New York Times*, April 14, 1944.

3. Arthur Knight, *The Liveliest Art*, op. cit.

CHAPTER TWENTY-SIX

1. William Wyler, "No Magic Wand," in *The Screen Writer*, February 1947.

---

2. Lester Koenig, "Gregg Toland, Film-Maker," in *The Screen Writer*, December 1947.

3. *New York Times*, November 22, 1946.

4. *The Nation*, December 7 and December 14, 1946.

CHAPTER TWENTY-SEVEN

1. Capra, in *The Name above the Title*, op. cit.

2. *Los Angeles Examiner*, November 15, 1947.

3. Charles Higham, *Hollywood at Sunset*, Saturday Review Press, New York, 1972.

CHAPTER TWENTY-EIGHT

1. Frank Capra, *The Name above the Title*, op. cit.

2. *San Francisco Chronicle*, November 12, 1949.

3. *New York Times*, October 7, 1949.

4. *Ibid.*, October 16, 1949.

5. *New York Herald Tribune*, October 2, 1949.

6. Arthur Knight, *The Liveliest Art*, op. cit.

CHAPTER TWENTY-NINE

1. *Variety*, May 24, 1950.

2. W. A. Swanberg, *Dreiser*, Charles Scribner's Sons, New York, 1965.

3. Charles Higham, *Hollywood Cameramen*, op. cit.

4. *New York Times*, November 7, 1951.

5. *Newsweek*, November 11, 1951.

6. *Time*, October 29, 1951.

7. *New York Times*, November 4, 1951.

8. *New York Times*, July 17, 1952.

CHAPTER THIRTY

1. *Time*, September 7, 1953.

2. *New York Times*, October 6, 1955.

CHAPTER THIRTY-ONE

1. Jessamyn West, *To See the Dream*, Harcourt, Brace, New York, 1956.

2. *New York Times*, November 2, 1956.

3. *The New Yorker*, November 5, 1956.

4. *Time*, November 10, 1956.

5. In *Cahiers du Cinéma*, December 1955.

6. In interview with *Picture Show and Film Pictorial*, London, November 30, 1957.

7. *New York Times*, October 2, 1958.

8. *Newsweek*, September 8, 1958.

9. *Time*, September 8, 1958.

10. *The Times*, January 8, 1959.

11. *Films and Filming*, February 1959.

12. In *The Observer*, January 11, 1959. Miss Lejeune was obviously thinking of Andrew Wyeth's painting of a crippled girl.

CHAPTER THIRTY-TWO

1. Extracts from Heston's diary were published in *Cinema*, Vol. 2. No. 2, 1964.
2. In *American Cinematographer*, February 1960.
3. *Variety*, January 12, 1959.
4. In *Action*, Directors' Guild of America bimonthly, January–February 1967.
5. *Wall Street Journal*, May 18, 1959.
6. *Variety*, November 20, 1959.
7. *New York Times*, November 19, 1959.
8. *Variety*, April 20, 1966.
9. *Cinema*, Vol. 3, No. 5, 1967.

CHAPTER THIRTY-THREE

1. Shirley MacLaine, *Don't Fall Off the Mountain*, W. W. Norton, New York, 1970.
2. *New York Times*, June 25, 1961.
3. *Newsweek*, March 12, 1962.
4. *Village Voice*, June 24, 1965.
5. *New York Times*, March 15, 1962.
6. *Time*, February 9, 1962.
7. *Newsweek*, March 12, 1962.
8. *The New Yorker*, March 17, 1962.
9. *Playboy*, April 1962.
10. Pauline Kael, *I Lost It at the Movies*, Little, Brown, Boston, 1965.
11. Kevin Brownlow, *The Parade's Gone By*, op. cit.

CHAPTER THIRTY-FOUR

1. *Variety*, June 3, 1964.
2. *Time*, June 18, 1965.
3. *New York Times*, June 7, 1964.
4. *Los Angeles Examiner*, May 31, 1964.
5. *Newsweek*, June 21, 1965.
6. *New York Times*, June 18, 1965.
7. *New York Herald Tribune*, June 27, 1965.
8. *Village Voice*, June 24, 1965.
9. *The New Republic*, June 19, 1965.
10. *Cahiers du Cinéma*, No. 171, October 1965.

CHAPTER THIRTY-FIVE

1. Published in a collection of short stories by George Bradshaw, *Practice to Deceive*, Harcourt Brace, New York, 1962.
2. Henri Langlois, La Cinémathèque française, Musée du Cinéma présente *Hommage à William Wyler*, November 1966.
3. *New York Times*, July 15, 1966.
4. *Time*, July 25, 1966.

CHAPTER THIRTY-SIX

1. *Los Angeles Herald-Examiner,* October 6, 1968.
2. *Variety,* March 31, 1967.
3. Ibid.
4. *New York Times,* September 20, 1968.
5. *Village Voice,* October 10, 1968.
6. *The New Yorker,* September 28, 1968.

CHAPTER THIRTY-SEVEN

1. Ibid., March 10, 1970.
2. *The Hollywood Reporter,* April 24, 1970.
3. *Los Angeles Times,* March 15, 1970.
4. *Newsweek,* March 30, 1970.

AWARDS—WILLIAM WYLER

Academy of Motion Picture Arts and Sciences Awards:
IRVING G. THALBERG MEMORIAL AWARD—1966—for consistent high quality of production achievement.
MRS. MINIVER—1942—for direction and for best picture.
THE BEST YEARS OF OUR LIVES—1946—for direction and best picture.
BEN-HUR—1959—for direction and best picture.

> Only John Ford has received more Academy Awards for directing (1935 *The Informer*, 1940 *The Grapes of Wrath*, 1941 *How Green Was My Valley*, 1952 *The Quiet Man*) than Wyler and Frank Capra (1934 *It Happened One Night*, 1936 *Mr. Deeds Goes to Washington*, and 1938 *You Can't Take It with You*).

Nominations for Academy Awards:
For directing:
DODSWORTH—1936
WUTHERING HEIGHTS—1939
THE LETTER—1940
THE LITTLE FOXES—1941
MRS. MINIVER—1942
THE BEST YEARS OF OUR LIVES—1946
THE HEIRESS—1949
DETECTIVE STORY—1951
ROMAN HOLIDAY—1953
FRIENDLY PERSUASION—1956
BEN-HUR—1959
THE COLLECTOR—1965
For producing:
THE HEIRESS
ROMAN HOLIDAY

FRIENDLY PERSUASION
New York Film Critics Award:
  WUTHERING HEIGHTS—1939
  THE BEST YEARS OF OUR LIVES—1946
  BEN-HUR—1959
Directors Guild Awards:
  D. W. GRIFFITH AWARD—for distinguished achievement in motion picture direction—1966.
  BEN-HUR—for the most outstanding directorial achievement—1959.
Directors' Guild Nominations for
Directorial Achievement:
  ROMAN HOLIDAY—1953
  FRIENDLY PERSUASION—1956
  THE BIG COUNTRY—1958
  BEN-HUR—1959
  THE CHILDREN'S HOUR—1961
  FUNNY GIRL—1968
Foreign Awards:
  The British Film Academy Award—for the best film from any source shown in the United Kingdom:
    THE BEST YEARS OF OUR LIVES—1947
    BEN-HUR—1959
  French Victoire Awards:
    MRS. MINIVER—1946
    ROMAN HOLIDAY—1955
    BEN-HUR—1961
Special Trophy to most honored directors of Cannes Film Festival's first twenty-five years, Cannes, 1971.
  Golden Palm—Cannes Film Festival—*FRIENDLY PERSUASION*—1957
  David Di Donatello Award—for *BEN-HUR*—1960–61
Japanese Awards:
  New Kyushu Press Fan Prize—Satsumayaki Vessel—1951—for best director and consistently fine film productions over a number of years.
  Mask pledged to God of Kasuga—from governor of Tokyo for *THE BEST YEARS OF OUR LIVES*—the best American picture released in 1948.
  Eigasekaisha Award for *DETECTIVE STORY*—1953.
  Mirika Kai (Movie Critics' Club) Award for *DETECTIVE STORY*—best produced foreign motion picture released in Japan in 1953.
  Kinema Jumpo Award—for best picture—*THE BIG COUNTRY*—1958.
  Kinema Jumpo Award—for best direction—*THE BIG COUNTRY*—1958.
  Tokyo Motion Picture Fans Association—for best director—*THE BIG COUNTRY*.

Tenth Fukuoka Prefectural Best Movie Awards Festival—best direction award presented by Fuku-Nichi Newspaper Enterprises for *BEN-HUR*.

Association of Film Journalists of Finland Award for *THE HEIRESS*—1949–50.

Association of Film Journalists of Finland Award for *THE COLLECTOR*—1965.

Finnish Film Magazine *Elokuva-Aitta* Diploma for *ROMAN HOLIDAY*—1954.

Finnish Film Magazine *Elokuva-Aitta* Certificate for *BEN-HUR*, Best Foreign picture for 1961.

Finnish Journalists—Diploma—*THE COLLECTOR*—1965.

Belgium Award—FILM REFERENDUM—for *BEN-HUR*—1961.

Incontri internazionali del cinema, Sorrento, September 1970.

Spanish Movie Magazine *Triunfo* Award for *DETECTIVE STORY*—1952–53.

Spanish Diploma of Honor for *THE HEIRESS*—1949–50.

Vichy Referendum—Celestin du Cinéma Award for *ROMAN HOLIDAY*—1954.

Ici-Paris (French weekly) Special Award for *ROMAN HOLIDAY*.

Award Decret—Ceskoslovenskeho Film Festival—*BEST YEARS OF OUR LIVES*—1948.

Academy of Motion Picture Arts and Sciences of Argentina—*DETECTIVE STORY*—1953.

Pusan Daily News Film Award—1958—for Best Foreign Director—*BEST YEARS OF OUR LIVES*.

U.S. Awards:

Federation of Motion Picture Councils Award of Exceptional Merit for *FRIENDLY PERSUASION*.

Federation of Motion Picture Councils Annual Award for *BEN-HUR*—best drama of 1959.

One World Award for Motion Pictures—1950—"for the quality of his work as a director, the way he has handled one world themes in the motion picture medium, and for his support of one world causes."

Hollywood Foreign Press Association Award for Best Direction—*BEN-HUR*—1959.

Hollywood Foreign Press Association Nomination for Best Direction:

> *BEN-HUR*—1959
> *THE CHILDREN'S HOUR*—1961
> *THE COLLECTOR*—1965
> *FUNNY GIRL*—1968

The Greater Los Angeles Press Club—for distinguished contribution to the art of the motion picture, climaxed by production of *BEN-HUR*.

Decorations:

U.S. Legion of Merit—citation for distinct contribution to the efforts of the Army Air Force by an objective portrayal of its aims, functions, and successes in global warfare through the medium of the motion picture—the widely distributed picture *MEMPHIS BELLE* was conceived, directed, and produced by Colonel Wyler. The success which has attended the showing of this film has brought great benefit to the Army Air Force and reflects credit upon the courage, craftmanship, and devotion to duty displayed by this officer in this difficult assignment. He was charged with producing and directing a second motion picture depicting the activities of fighter-bomber groups in the Mediterranean Theater of Operations. Colonel Wyler's work will live on as an accurate historical portrayal of Army Air Forces' efforts to effect victory in World War II.

Air Medal—citation for meritorious achievement while serving as observer on five separate bombardment missions over enemy-occupied Continental Europe. The courage and skill displayed by Major Wyler on each of these missions reflect the highest credit upon himself and the Armed Forces of the United States.

Presidential citation to 91st Bombardment Group—1947.

AMVETS Certificate of Merit for outstanding service to the organization and to the welfare of our nation—1949.

The American Legion—commendation for interest in the problems of the physically handicapped veteran and his impression on the American people through his motion picture direction of the unending obligation to those who sacrificed their physical welfare.

French Legion of Honor—1945.

Italian "Star of Solidarity"—1954.

Italian "Al Merito della Repubblica italiana"—1961.

FILMOGRAPHY

Silent Films:
Two-reelers

Between 1925 and 1927, Universal produced 135 two-reel westerns of the Mustang series. William Wyler made 21 of them. In order of the Motion Picture Booking Guide release date, they included:

CROOK BUSTER
Universal, Mustang, released Dec. 26, 1925.
Story and scenario: Leigh Jacobson.
Cast: Jack Mower

THE GUNLESS BAD MAN
Universal, Mustang, released March 13, 1926.
Story: John Hall.
Cast: Jack Mower

RIDIN' FOR LOVE
Universal, Mustang, released April 17, 1926.
Story: William Wyler. Scenario: Joseph Murray.
Cast: Jack Mower

FIRE BARRIER
Universal, Mustang, released June 12, 1926.
Story: C. D. Lenington. Scenario: William Lester.
Cast: Jack Mower

DON'T SHOOT
Universal, Mustang, released August 26, 1926.
Story and scenario: William Lester.
Cast: Jack Mower, Fay Wray

THE PINNACLE RIDER
Universal, Mustang, released October 30, 1926.
Story and continuity: William Lester.
Cast: Jack Mower

MARTIN OF THE MOUNTED
Universal, Mustang, released December 11, 1926.
Story and continuity: George Plympton.
Cast: Edmond Cobb

TWO FISTER	Universal, Mustang, released January 8, 1927. Story and continuity: George Plympton. Cast: Edmond Cobb
KELCY GETS HIS MAN	Universal, Mustang, released February 19, 1927. Story and scenario: William Lester. Cast: Edmond Cobb
TENDERFOOT COURAGE	Universal, Mustang, released February 26, 1927. Story: F. V. Lautzenhiser. Cast: Fred Gilman
THE SILENT PARTNER	Universal, Mustang, released March 19, 1927. Story: Basil Dickey. Scenario: George Morgan. Cast: Edmond Cobb

(The third time this title was used in a silent film. In 1917, it was a five-reeler directed by Marshall Neilan for Jesse L. Lasky productions and in 1923 a six-reeler directed by Charles Maigne for Paramount.)

GALLOPING JUSTICE	Universal, Mustang, released April 9, 1927. Story and scenario: George Plympton
THE HAUNTED HOME- STEAD	Universal, Mustang, released April 16, 1927. Story: L. V. Jefferson. Cast: Fred Gilman, Violet La Plante
THE LONE STAR	Universal, Mustang, released May 7, 1927. Story and scenario: William Lester. Cast: Fred Gilman
THE ORE RIDERS	Universal, Mustang, released May 21, 1927. Story and scenario: William Lester. Cast: Fred Gilman
THE HOME TRAIL	Universal, Mustang, released June 4, 1927. Story: Rhea Michell. Cast: Fred Gilman
GUN JUSTICE	Universal, Mustang, released July 2, 1927. Story and scenario: William Lester. Cast: Fred Gilman
PHANTOM OUTLAW	Universal, Mustang, released July 16, 1927. Story and scenario: William Lester. Cast: Fred Gilman
SQUARE SHOOTER	Universal, Mustang, released August 13, 1927. Story: Kenneth Langley. Cast: Fred Gilman

THE HORSE *TRADER*	Universal, Mustang, released August 20, 1927. Story: Brandt Riley. Cast: Fred Gilman

(Shelved for slightly over a year after completion; figures in 1926 production lineup.)

DAZE IN *THE WEST*	Universal, Mustang, copyrighted Library of Congress, Catalog of Entries, Motion Pictures, August 16, 1927. Story: Billy Engle. Scenario: William Lester. Cast: Vin Moore

Five-reel westerns

While directing two-reelers of the Mustang series, Wyler also directed six of Universal's Blue Streak five-reel westerns. A total of 53 films were produced in this series between 1925 and 1927.

LAZY *LIGHTNING*	Universal, released December 12, 1926. Length: 4,572 feet. Story: Harrison Jacobs. Cinematography: Eddie Linden. Cast: Arthur Acord, Fay Wray, Bobby Gordon, Vin Moore, Arthur Morrison, George French

STOLEN *RANCH*	Universal, released December 26, 1926. Length: 4,587 feet. Story: Robert F. Hill. Screenplay: George H. Plympton. Cinematography: Al Jones. Cast: Fred Humes, Louise Lorraine, William Norton Baily, Ralph McCullough, Nita Cavalier, Edward Cecil, Howard Truesdell, Slim Whittaker, Jack Kirk

BLAZING *DAYS*	Universal, released March 27, 1927. Length: 4,639 feet. Story: Florence Ryerson. Screenplay: George H. Plympton and R. Hill. Cinematography: Al Jones. Art director: David S. Garber. Cast: Fred Humes, Edna Gregory, Churchill Ross, Bruce Gordon, Eva Thatcher, Bernard Suegel, Dick L'Estrange

HARD FISTS	Universal, released April 24, 1927. Length: 4,387 feet. Screenplay: William Lester and George H. Plympton from Charles A. Logue, *The Grappler.* Cinematography: Edwin Linden. Art director: David Garber. Cast: Art Acord, Louise Lorraine, Lee Holmes, Albert J. Smith

THE BORDER *CAVALIER*	Universal, released September 18, 1927. Length: 4,427 feet. Screenplay: Basil Dickey. Titles: Gardner Bradford. Cinematography: Al Jones. Art director: David Garber. Cast: Fred Humes, Joyce Compton, C. E. "Captain" Anderson, Gilbert "Peewee" Holmes, "Smilin' " Benny Corbett, Dick L'Estrange, Scott Mattraw, Boris Bullock

STRAIGHT *SHOOTIN'*	Universal, released October 16, 1927. Length: 4,205 feet. Screenplay: William Lester. Titles: Gardner Bradford.

Cinematography: Milton Bridenbecker. Art direction: David Garber.

Cast: Ted Wells, Garry O'Dell, Lillian Gilmore, Joe Bennett, Al Ferguson, Wilbur Mack, Buck Connor

DESERT
DUST

Universal, released December 18, 1927. Length: 4,349 feet. Screenplay: William Lester. Titles: Gardner Bradford. Cinematography: Milton Bridenbecker. Art director: David Garber.

Cast: Ted Wells, Lotus Thompson, Bruce Gordon, Dick L'Estrange, Jimmy Phillips, Charles "Slim" Cole, George Ovey

THUNDER
RIDERS

Universal, released April 8, 1928. Length: 4,363 feet. Screenplay: Basil Dickey and Carl Krusada. Titles: Gardner Bradford. Cinematography: Milton Bridenbecker. Editor: Harry Marker. Art Director: David Garber.

Cast: Ted Wells, Charlotte Stevens, William A. Steele, Gilbert "Peewee" Holmes, Dick L'Estrange, Bill Dyer, Leo White, Julia Griffith, Bob Burns

ANYBODY
HERE SEEN
KELLY?

Universal, released September 9, 1928. Length: 6,243 feet. Producer: Robert Wyler. Screenplay: John Clymer. Titles: Walter Anthony and Albert De Mond. Story: Leigh Jason. Cinematography: Charles Stumar. Editor: George McGuire.

Cast: Tom Moore (*Pat Kelly*), Bessie Love (*Jeanette Lavelle*), Tom O'Brien (*Buck Jones*), Kate Price (*Mrs. O'Grady*), Alfred Allen (*Sergeant Malloy*), William Benge (*Butler*), Rose Gore (*French mother*)

THE
SHAKEDOWN

Universal, released March 10, 1929 with "talking sequences." Length: 6,613 feet. Story and screenplay: Charles Logue and Clarence J. Marks. Title and dialogue: Albert De Mond. Cinematography: Charles Stumar and Jerome Ash. Editor: Lloyd Nosler and Richard Cahor. Music: S. Joseph Chariavsky. Recording engineer: Roy Hunter.

Cast: James Murray (*Dave Roberts*), Barbara Kent (*Marjorie*), George Kotsonaros (*Battling Roff*), Wheeler Oakman (*Manager*), Jack Hanlon (*Clem*), Harry Gribbon (*Dugan*)

THE LOVE
TRAP

Universal, released July 19, 1929 (78 minutes). Silent with last 2 reels "talking." Screenplay: John B. Clymer and Clarence J. Marks after story by E. J. Montague. Titles: Albert De Mond. Dialogue: Clarence Thompson. Editor: Maurice Pivar. Cinematography: Gilbert Warrenton.

Cast: Laura La Plante (*Evelyn Todd*), Neil Hamilton

(*Paul Harrington*), Robert Ellis (*Guy Emery*), Jocelyn
Lee (*Bunny*), Norman Trevor (*Judge Harrington*), Cla-
rissa Selwynne (*Mrs. Harrington*), Rita La Roy (*Iris Harrington*)

All Sound:

HELL'S HEROES	Universal, released January 5, 1930 (65 minutes). Based on the novel *The Three Godfathers,* by Peter Kyne. Screenplay and dialogue: Tom Reed. Cinematography: George Robinson. Editor: Harry Marker.

Cast: Charles Bickford (*Bob Sangster*), Raymond Hatton
(*Wild Bill Kearny*), Fred Kohler (*Barbwire Gibbons*),
Fritzi Ridgeway (*Mother*), Maris Alba (*Girl*)

THE STORM Universal, released New York, August 22, 1930. Based on
the play *Men without Skirts* by Langdon McCormick.
Screenplay: Wells Root and Charles Logue. Dialogue:
Wells Root. Cinematography: Alvin Wyckoff.

Cast: Lupe Velez (*Manette*), William Boyd (*Burr*), Paul
Cavanaugh (*Dave*), Ernest Adams, Tom London, Nick
Thompson

A HOUSE DIVIDED Universal, released December 5, 1931 (70 minutes). Assistant producer: Paul Kohner. Based on a story by Olive
Edens, "Heart and Hand." Screenplay: John B. Clymer
and Dale Van Every. Dialogue: John Huston. Cinematography: Charles Stumar. Editor: Ted Kent.

Cast: Walter Huston (*Seth Law*), Kent Douglass (*Matt
Law*), Helen Chandler (*Ruth Evans*), Vivian Oakland
(*Bess*), Frank Hagney (*Mann*), Mary Foy (*Mary*)

TOM BROWN OF CULVER Universal, released June 1932 (70 minutes). Based on a
story by George Green and Dale Van Every. Screenplay:
Tom Buckingham. Cinematography: Charles Stumar.

Cast: Tom Brown (*Tom Brown*), H. B. Warner (*Dr.
Brown*), Slim Summerville (*Slim*), Richard Cromwell
(*Bob Randolph*), Ben Alexander (*Ralph*), Sidney Toler
(*Major Wharton*), Russel Hopten (*Doctor*), Andy Devine
(*Call boy*), Willard Robertson (*Captain White*), Norman
Philips, Jr. (*Carruthers*), Tyrone Power, Jr. (*John*)

HER FIRST MATE Universal, released in 1933 (66 minutes). Adaptation from
the stage play *Salt Water,* by Dan Jarrett, Frank Craven,
and John Golden. Screenplay: Earl Snell, H. M. Walker,
and Clarence Marks. Cinematography: George Robinson.
Supervisor: Henry Henigson. Sound engineer: Gilbert
Kurland.

Cast: Slim Summerville (*John Horner*), Zasu Pitts (*Mary
Horner*), Una Merkel (*Hattie Horner*), Warren Hymer

(*Percy*), Berton Churchill (*Davis*), George Marion (*Sam*), Henry Armetta (*Socrates*)

COUNSELLOR
AT LAW
Universal, released December 25, 1933 (78 minutes). Adapted from the play by Elmer Rice. Screenplay: Elmer Rice. Cinematography: Norbert Brodine. Producer: Henry Henigson. Editor: Daniel Mandell. Sound: Gilbert Kurland.

Cast: John Barrymore (*George Simon*), Bebe Daniels (*Regina Gordon*), Doris Kenyon (*Cora Simon*), Onslow Stevens (*John P. Tedesco*), Isabel Jewell (*Bessie Green*), Melvyn Douglas (*Roy Darwin*), Thelma Todd (*Lillian LaRue*), Mayo Methot (*Zedorah Chapman*), Richard Quine (*Richard*), Marvin Kline (*Herbert Howard Weinberg*), Conway Washburn (*Arthur Sandler*), John Qualen (*Breitstein*), Bobby Gordon (*Henry Susskind*), John Hamond Dailey (*McFadden*), Malka Kornstein (*Sarah Becker*), Angela Jacobs (*Goldie Rindskopf*), Clara Langsner (*Lena Simon*), T. H. Manning (*Peter J. Malone*), Elmer Brown (*Francis Clark Baird*), Barbara Perry (*Dorothy*), Victor Adams (*David Simon*), Frederic Burton (*Crayfield*), Vincent Sherman (*Harry Becker*)

GLAMOUR
Universal, released April 1934 (74 minutes). Based on a short story by Edna Ferber. Adaptation: Doris Anderson. Continuity: Gladys Unger. Cinematography: George Robinson. Editor: Ted Kent.

Cast: Paul Lukas (*Victor Banki*), Constance Cummings (*Linda Fayne*), Philip Reed (*Lorenzo Valenti*), Joseph Cawthorne (*Ibsen*), Doris Lloyd (*Nana*), Lyman Williams (*Forsyth*), David Dickinson (*Stevie*), Peggy Campbell (*Amy*), Olaf Hytten (*Dobbs*), Alice Lake (*Secretary*), Lita Chevret (*Grassie*), Phil Reed (*Jimmy*), Luis Albernie (*Monsieur Paul*), Yola D'Avril (*Renee*), Grace Hale (*Miss Lang*), Wilson Benge (*Pritchard*), Louise Beavers (*Millie*), Jessie McAllister (*Landlady*)

THE GOOD
FAIRY
Universal, released February, 1935. Based on a play by Ferenc Molnar. Adapted for the screen by Preston Sturges. Cinematography: Norbert Brodine. Producer: Henry Henigson.

Cast: Margaret Sullavan (*Luisa Ginglebusher*), Herbert Marshall (*Dr. Max Sporum*), Frank Morgan (*Konrad*), Reginald Owen (*Detlaff*), Alan Hale (*Schlapkohl*), Beulah Bondi (*Dr. Schultz*), Cesar Romero (*Joe*), Eric Blore (*Dr. Metz*), Al Bridges (*Doorman*), George Davis (*Chauffeur*), Hugh O'Connell (*Gas collector*), June Clayworth (*Actress*)

428

THE GAY
DECEPTION
Twentieth Century-Fox, released September, 1935 (79 minutes). Based on a screenplay by Stephen Avery and Don Hartman. Additional dialogue by Arthur Richman. Cinematography: Joseph Valentine. Produced by Jesse L. Lasky.

Cast: Francis Lederer (*Sandro*), Frances Dee (*Mirabel*), Benita Hume (*Miss Channing*), Alan Mowbray (*Lord Clewe*), Akim Tamiroff (*Spellek*), Lennox Pawle (*Consul General*), Adele St. Maur (*Lucille*), Ferdinand Gottschalk (*Mr. Squires*), Richard Carle (*Mr. Spitzer*), Lenita Lane (*Peg DeForrest*), Barbara Fritchie (*Joan Dennison*), Paul Hurst (*Bell captain*), Robert Greig (*Adolph*), Luis Alberni (*Ernest*), Lionel Stander (*Gettel*)

THESE
THREE
Distributed by United Artists, released April 10, 1936 (90 minutes). Production: Goldwyn. Producer: Samuel Goldwyn. Assistant director: Walter Mayo. Screenplay: Lillian Hellman (based on her play *The Children's Hour*). Editor: Daniel Mandell. Cinematography: Gregg Toland. Music: Alfred Newman.

Cast: Miriam Hopkins (*Martha Dobie*), Merle Oberon (*Karen Wright*), Joel McCrea (*Dr. Joseph Cardin*), Catherine Doucet (*Mrs. Mortar*), Alma Kruger (*Mrs. Tilford*), Bonita Granville (*Mary Tilford*), Marcia Mae Jones (*Rosalie*), Carmencita Johnson (*Evelyn*), Margaret Hamilton (*Agatha*), Marie Louise Cooper (*Helen Burton*), Walter Brennan (*Taxi driver*)

DODSWORTH
Released by United Artists, released September 18, 1936 (90 minutes). Assistant director: Merritt Hulburd. Screenplay: Sidney Howard (based on his own play and the novel by Sinclair Lewis). Cinematography: Rudolph Maté. Editor: Daniel Mandell. Music: Alfred Newman.
Cast: Walter Huston (*Samuel Dodsworth*), Ruth Chatterton (*Fran Dodsworth*), Paul Lukas (*Arnold Iselin*), Mary Astor (*Edith Cortright*), David Niven (*Major Clyde Lockert*), Maria Ouspenskaya (*Baroness von Obersdorf*), Gregory Gaye (*Kurt von Obersdorf*), Odette Myrtil (*Renee de Penable*), Kathryn Marlowe (*Emily McKee*), John Payne (*Harry McKee*), Spring Byington (*Matey Pearson*), Harlan Briggs (*Tubby Pearson*), Beatrice Maude (*Marymaid*)

COME AND
GET IT
Released by United Artists, previewed at Warners, Hollywood October 26, 1936 (105 minutes). Directed by William Wyler and Howard Hawks. A Samuel Goldwyn production. Based on a novel by Edna Ferber. Screenplay: Jules Furthman and Jane Murfin. Associate producer:

Merritt Hulburd. Cinematography: Gregg Toland and
Rudolph Maté. Special effects: Ray Binger and Paul
Eagler. Music: Alfred Newman. Editor: Edward Curtiss.
Assistant director: Walter Mayo.

Cast: Edward Arnold (*Barney Glasgow*), Joel McCrea
(*Richard Glasgow*), Frances Farmer (*Lotta Morgan and
Lotta Bostrom*), Walter Brennan (*Swan Bostrom*), An-
drea Leeds (*Evvie Glasgow*), Frank Shields (*Tony*)
Schwerke), Mady Christians (*Karie*), Mary Nash (*Emma
Louise Glasgow*), Clem Bevans (*Gunnar Gallagher*),
Edwin Maxwell (*Sid Le Maire*), Cecil Cunningham
(*Josie*), Harry Bradley (*Gubbing*), Rollo Lloyd (*Stew-
ard*), Charles Helton (*Hewitt*), Philip Cooper (*Choir
boy*), Al K. Hall (*Goodnow*)

DEAD END Released by United Artists, released August 27, 1937 (93
minutes). Production and producer: Samuel Goldwyn.
Associate producer: Merritt Hulburd. Screenplay: Lillian
Hellman (based on the play by Sidney Kingsley). Assis-
tant director: Eddie Bernoudy. Cinematography: Gregg
Toland. Editor: Daniel Mandell. Music: Alfred Newman.

Cast: Sylvia Sidney (*Drina*), Joel McCrea (*Dave*), Hum-
phrey Bogart (*Babyface Martin*), Wendy Barrie (*Kate*),
Claire Trevor (*Francey*), Allen Jenkins (*Hunk*), Marjorie
Main (*Mrs. Martin*), Billy Halop (*Tommy*), Huntz Hall
(*Dippy*), Bobby Jordan (*Angel*), Leo Gorcey (*Spit*), Ga-
briel Dell (*T.B.*), Bernard Punsly (*Milty*), Charles Peck
(*Philip*), Minor Watson (*Mr. Griswald*), Ward Bond
(*Doorman*), Charles Helton (*Whitey*), James Burke
(*Mulligan*), Elisabeth Risdon (*Mrs. Connell*), Esther
Dale (*Mrs. Fenner*), Marcelle Corday (*Governess*)

JEZEBEL Production: Warner Brothers, released March 26, 1938 (103
minutes). Producer: William Wyler. Executive producer:
Hal B. Wallis. Associate producer: Henry Blanke. Assis-
tant director: Bob Ross. Screenplay: Clements Ripley,
Abem Finkel, and John Huston (based on the play by
Owen Davis). Cinematography: Ernest Haller. Editor:
Warren Low. Music: Max Steiner. Art direction: Robert
Hass. Costumes: Orry-Kelly.

Cast: Bette Davis (*Julie*), Henry Fonda (*Preston Dillard*),
George Brent (*Buck Cantrell*), Margaret Lindsay (*Amy*),
Donald Crisp (*Dr. Livingstone*), Fay Bainter (*Aunt
Belle*), Richard Cromwell (*Ted*), Henry O'Neill (*Gen-
eral Bogardus*), Spring Byington (*Mrs. Kendrick*), John
Litel (*Jean La Cour*), Gordon Oliver (*Dick Allen*), Janet
Shaw (*Molly Allen*), Theresa Harris (*Zette*), Margaret
Early (*Stephanie Kendrick*), Irving Pichel (*Huger*), Eddie

Anderson (*Gros Bat*), Lou Payton (*Uncle Cato*), George
Renevant (*De Lautrur*)

WUTHERING
HEIGHTS

Distributed by United Artists, released April 13, 1939 (103
minutes). Production: Goldwyn. Producer: Samuel Gold-
wyn. Assistant director: Walter Mayo. Screenplay: Ben
Hecht and Charles MacArthur (based on the novel by
Emily Brontë). Cinematography: Gregg Toland. Editor:
Daniel Mandell. Music: Alfred Newman. Art direction:
James Basevi. Costumes: Omar Kiam. Special character
makeup: Blagoe Stephanoff. Technical adviser: Peter
Shaw.

Cast: Merle Oberon (*Cathy*), Laurence Olivier (*Heathcliff*),
David Niven (*Edgar*), Flora Robson (*Ellen Dean*), Don-
ald Crisp (*Dr. Kenneth*), Geraldine Fitzgerald (*Isabella*),
Hugh Williams (*Hindley*), Leo G. Carroll (*Joseph*),
Cecil Humphreys (*Judge Linton*), Miles Mander (*Lock-
wood*), Romaine Callender (*Robert*), Cecil Kellaway
(*Earnshaw*), Rex Downing (*Heathcliff as a child*), Sarita
Wooton (*Cathy as a child*), Douglas Scott (*Hindley as a
child*), Mme. Alice Ehlers (*Harpsichordist*)

THE
WESTERNER

Distributed by United Artists, released September 20, 1940
(100 minutes). Production: Goldwyn. Producer: Samuel
Goldwyn. Screenplay: Jo Swerling and Niven Busch
(based on a story by Stuart N. Lake). Cinematography:
Gregg Toland. Editor: Daniel Mandell. Music: Dimitri
Tiomkin. Special effects: Archie Stout and Paul Eagler.

Cast: Gary Cooper (*Cole Harden*), Walter Brennan (*Judge
Roy Bean*), Fred Stone (*Caliphet Mathews*), Doris Dav-
enport (*Jane-Ellen Mathews*), Forrest Tucker (*Wade
Harper*), Lilian Bond (*Lily Langtry*), Paul Hurst
(*Chickenfoot*), Chill Wills (*Southeast*), Charles Halton
(*Mort Borrow*), Tom Tyler (*King Evans*), Dana Andrews
(*Bart Cobble*), Roger Gray (*Homesteader*), Trevor Bur-
dette (*Shad Wilkins*)

THE LETTER

Warner Brothers, released November 24, 1940 (95 min-
utes). Production: Warner Brothers. Producers: Jack L.
Warner and Hal B. Wallis. Associate producer: Robert
Lord. Screenplay: Howard Koch (based on the play by
W. Somerset Maugham). Cinematography: Tony Gaudio.
Editor: George Amy. Music: Max Steiner. Musical direc-
tion: Leo F. Forbstein. Costumes: Orry-Kelly. Art direc-
tion: Carl Jules Weyl.

Cast: Bette Davis (*Leslie Crosbie*), Herbert Marshall (*Robert Crosbie*), James Stephenson (*Howard Joyce*), Frieda
Inescort (*Dorothy Joyce*), Gale Sondergaard (*Mrs. Ham-*

mond), Bruce Lister (*John Withers*), Elizabeth Earl
(*Adele Ainsworth*), Cecil Kellaway (*Prescott*), Sen Yung
(*Ong Chi Seng*), Doris Lloyd (*Mrs. Cooper*), Willie Fung
(*Chung Hi*), Tetsu Komai (*Headboy*)

THE LITTLE
FOXES

Distributed RKO-Radio Pictures, released August 29, 1941
(116 minutes). Production: Goldwyn. Producer: Samuel
Goldwyn. Screenplay: Lillian Hellman (based on her
own play). Additional scenes and dialogue: Dorothy Par-
ker, Arthur Kober, and Alan Campbell. Cinematogra-
phy: Gregg Toland. Editor: Daniel Mandell. Music:
Meredith Willson. Costumes: Orry-Kelly. Art direction:
Stephen Goosson.
Cast: Bette Davis (*Regina Giddens*), Herbert Marshall
(*Horace Giddens*), Teresa Wright (*Alexandra Giddens*),
Richard Carlson (*David Hewitt*), Patricia Collinge
(*Birdie Hubbard*), Dan Duryea (*Leo Hubbard*), Charles
Dingle (*Ben Hubbard*), Carl Benton Reid (*Oscar Hub-
bard*), Jessie Grayson (*Addie*), John Marriott (*Cal*), Rus-
sell Hicks (*William Marshall*), Lucien Littlefield (*Man-
ders*), Virginia Brissac (*Mrs. Hewitt*), Terry Nibert
(*Julia,* Alan Bridge (*Hotel manager*), Charles R. Moore
(*Simon*)

MRS.
MINIVER

Metro-Goldwyn-Mayer, released May 1942 (134 minutes).
Produced by Sidney Franklin. Screenplay: Arthur Wim-
peris, George Froeschel, James Hilton, and Claudine
West (based on the book by Jan Struther). Cinematogra-
phy: Joseph Ruttenberg, Editor: Harold F. Kress. Music:
Herbert Stothart. Song "Midsummer's Day" by Gene
Lockhart. Art direction: Cedric Gibbons.
Cast: Greer Garson (*Mrs. Miniver*), Walter Pidgeon (*Clem
Miniver*), Teresa Wright (*Carol Beldon*), Dame May
Whitty (*Lady Beldon*), Reginald Owen (*Foley*), Henry
Travers (*Mr. Ballard*), Richard Ney (*Vin Miniver*),
Henry Wilcoxon (*Vicar*), Christopher Severn (*Toby Min-
iver*), Brenda Forbes (*Gladys*), Clara Sandars (*Judy Min-
iver*), Marie De Becker (*Ada*), Helmut Dantine (*German
flier*), John Abbott (*Fred*), Connie Leon (*Simpson*), Rhys
Williams (*Horace*)

MEMPHIS
BELLE

Distribution: Paramount. Released April 15, 1944 (41 minutes). Production: War Activities Committee. Producer:
William Wyler. Script: William Wyler. Cinematography:
Major William C. Clothier and Lieut. Harold Tannenbaum. Additional photography: William Wyler. Editor
Sgt. Lynn Harrison. Music: Gail Kubik. Narration: Lester Koenig

THUNDER-BOLT	Released July 26, 1947, by Monogram through arrangements with Carl Krueger Productions and the USAAF. Produced under the command of Lieut. General Ira C. Eaker. Script: Lester Koenig. Editor: William Wyler, assisted by John Sturges. Music: Gail Kubik. Introduced by James Stewart. Narrated by Eugene Kern and Lloyd Bridges
THE BEST YEARS OF OUR LIVES	Distributed by RKO Radio, released November 22, 1946 (172 minutes). Production: Goldwyn. Producer: Samuel Goldwyn. Screenplay: Robert E. Sherwood (based on the novel in verse *Glory for Me* by MacKinlay Kantor). Cinematography: Gregg Toland. Editor: Daniel Mandell. Music: Hugo Friedhofer. Art directors: George Jenkins and Perry Ferguson. Production assistant: Lester Koenig. Cast: Myrna Loy (*Milly Stephenson*), Fredric March (*Al Stephenson*), Dana Andrews (*Fred Derry*), Teresa Wright (*Peggy Stephenson*), Virginia Mayo (*Marie Derry*), Cathy O'Donnell (*Wilma Cameron*), Hoagy Carmichael (*Butch Engel*), Harold Russell (*Homer Parrish*), Gladys George (*Hortense Derry*), Roman Bohnen (*Pat Derry*), Ray Collins (*Mr. Milton*), Steve Cochran (*Cliff*), Minna Gombell (*Mrs. Parrish*), Walter Baldwin (*Mr. Parrish*), Dorothy Adams (*Mrs. Cameron*), Don Beddoe (*Mr. Cameron*), Erskine Sanford (*Bullard*), Marlene Ames (*Luella Parrish*), Michael Hall (*Rob Stephenson*)
THE HEIRESS	Paramount, released October 1949 (115 minutes). Production: Paramount. Producer: William Wyler. Associate producers: Lester Koenig and Robert Wyler. Assistant director: C. C. Coleman, Jr. Screenplay: Ruth and Augustus Goetz (based on their own dramatization of Henry James's *Washington Square*). Cinematography: Leo Tover. Editor: William Hornbeck. Music: Aaron Copland. Art direction: John Meehan and Harry Horner. Cast: Olivia de Havilland (*Catherine Sloper*), Ralph Richardson (*Dr. Austin Sloper*), Montgomery Clift (*Morris Townsend*), Miriam Hopkins (*Lavinia Penniman*), Vanessa Brown (*Maria*), Mona Freeman (*Marian Almond*), Ray Collins (*Jefferson Almond*), Betty Linley (*Mrs. Montgomery*), Selena Royle (*Elizabeth Almond*), Paul Lees (*Arthur Townsend*), Harry Antrim (*Mr. Abeel*), Russ Conway (*Quintus*), David Thursby (*Geier*)
DETECTIVE STORY	Paramount, released in November 1951 (103 minutes). Production: Paramount. Producer: William Wyler. Screenplay: Philip Yordan and Robert Wyler (based on

the play by Sidney Kingsley). Cinematography: Lee Garmes. Editor: Robert Swink. Art directors: Hal Pereira and Earl Hedrick.

Cast: Kirk Douglas (*Detective James McLeod*), Eleanor Parker (*Mary McLeod*), William Bendix (*Lou Brody*), Lee Grant (*Shoplifter*), Bert Freed (*Dakis*), Frank Faylen (*Gallagher*), William Philips (*Callahan*), Grandon Rhodes (*O'Brien*), Luis van Rooten (*Feinson*), Cathy O'Donnell (*Susan Carmichael*), Horace McMahon (*Lt. Monaghan*), Warner Anderson (*Endicott Sims*), George Macready (*Schneider*), Craig Hill (*Arthur Kindred*), Joseph Wiseman (*Charles Gennini*), Michael Strong (*Lewis Abbott*), Gerald Mohr (*Jacopetti*)

CARRIE   Paramount, released July 1952 (118 minutes). Producer: William Wyler. Associate producer: Lester Koenig. Screenplay: Ruth and Augustus Goetz (based on the novel *Sister Carrie* by Theordore Dreiser). Cinematography: Victor Milner. Editor: Robert Swink.

Cast: Laurence Olivier (*George Hurstwood*), Jennifer Jones (*Carrie Meeber*), Miriam Hopkins (*Julie Hurstwood*), Eddie Albert (*Charles Drouet*), Basil Ruysdael (*Mr. Fitzgerald*), Ray Teal (*Allan*), Barry Kelley (*Slawson*), Sara Berner (*Mrs. Oransky*), William Reynolds (*George Hurstwood, Jr.*), Mary Murphy (*Jessica Hurstwood*), Harry Hayden (*O'Brien*), Charles Halton (*Factory foreman*), Walter Baldwin (*Carrie's father*), Dorothy Adams (*Carrie's mother*), Jacqueline de Wit (*Carrie's sister*), Harlan Briggs (*Joe Brant*), Donald Kerr (*Slawson's bartender*), Lester Sharpe (*Mr. Blum*), Don Beddoe (*Mr. Goodman*), John Alvin (*Stage manager*)

ROMAN   Paramount, released August 1953 (119 minutes). Produc-
HOLIDAY   tion: Paramount. Producer: William Wyler. Screenplay: Ian McLellan Hunter and John Dighton (based on a story by Ian McLellan Hunter). Cinematography: Frank (Franz) Planer and Henri Alekan. Editor: Robert Swink. Art direction: Hal Pereira and Walter Tyler. Music: Georges Auric.

Cast: Gregory Peck (*Joe Bradley*), Audrey Hepburn (*Princess Anne*), Eddie Albert (*Iring Radovich*), Hartley Power (*Mr. Hennessy*), Harcourt Williams (*Ambassador*) Margaret Rawlings (*Countess Vereberg*), Tullio Carminati (*General Provno*), Paolo Carlini (*Mario Delani*), Claudio Ermelli (*Giovanni*), Paola Borboni (*Charwoman*), Alfredo Rizzo (*Taxicab driver*), Laura Solari (*Hennessy's secretary*), Gorella Gori (*Shoe seller*), Heinz Hindrich (*Dr. Bonnachoven*), John Horne (*Master of ceremonies*), Count Andrea Eszterhazy, Col. Ugo Ballerini, Ugo De Pascale, and Bruno Baschiere (*Embassy aides*)

THE DESPERATE HOURS	Paramount, released October 5, 1955 (112 minutes). Producer: William Wyler. Associate producer: Robert Wyler. Screenplay: Joseph Hayes (based on his novel and play). Cinematography: Lee Garmes. Editor: Robert Swink. Art directors: Hal Pereira and Joseph MacMillan Johnson. Music: Gail Kubik. Sound: Hugo Grenzbach and Winston Leverett.

Cast: Humphrey Bogart (*Glenn Griffin*), Fredric March (*Dan Hilliard*), Arthur Kennedy (*Jesse Bard*), Martha Scott (*Eleanor Hilliard*), Dewey Martin (*Hal Griffin*), Gig Young (*Chuck*), Mary Murphy (*Cindy Hilliard*), Richard Eyer (*Ralphie Hilliard*), Robert Middleton (*Kobish*), Bert Kreed (*Winston*), Alan Reed (*Detective*), Ray Collins (*Masters*), Whit Bissell (*Carson*), Ray Teal (*Fredericks*)

FRIENDLY PERSUASION	Allied Artists, released November 25, 1956 (139 minutes). Producer: William Wyler. Associate producer: Robert Wyler. Production assistant: Stuart Miller. Second unit director: Thomas Carr. Screenplay: Michael Wilson (based on the novel by Jessamyn West). Cinematography: Ellsworth Fredericks. Editors: Robert Swink, E. A. Biery, and R. A. Belcher. Music: Dmitri Tiomkin.

Cast: Gary Cooper (*Jess Birdwell*), Dorothy McGuire (*Elisa Birdwell*), Marjorie Main (*Widow Hudspeth*), Anthony Perkins (*Josh Birdwell*), Richard Eyer (*Little Jess*), Robert Middleton (*Sam Jordan*), Phyllis Love (*Mattie Birdwell*), Mark Richman (*Gard Jordan*), Walter Catlett (*Professor Quigley*), Richard Hale (*Purdy*), Joel Fluellen (*Enoch*), Theodore Newton (*Army major*), John Smith (*Caleb*), Mary Carr (*Quaker woman*), Edna Skinner, Marjorie Durant, and Frances Farwell (*Widow Hudspeth's daughters*), Russell Simpson, Charles Halton and Everett Glass (*Elders*)

THE BIG COUNTRY	United Artists, released October 1, 1958 (166 minutes). Produced by William Wyler and Gregory Peck. Screenplay: James R. Webb, Sy Bartlett, and Robert Wilder. Adaptation: Jessamyn West and Robert Wyler (based on a novel by Donald Hamilton). Cinematography: Franz F. Planer. Supervising editor: Robert Swink. Edited by Robert Belcher and John Faure. Music: Jerome Moross. Costumes: Emile Santiago and Yvonne Wood.

Cast: Gregory Peck (*James McKay*), Jean Simmons (*Julie*

Maragon), Carroll Baker (*Patricia Terrill*), Charlton Heston (*Steve Leech*), Burl Ives (*Rufus Hannassey*), Carles Bickford (*Major Henry Terrill*), Alfonso Bedoya (*Ramon*), Chuck Connors (*Buck Hannassey*), Chuck Hayward (*Rafe*), Buff Brady (*Dude*), Jim Burk (*Cracker*), Dorothy Adams (*Hannassey woman*)

BEN-HUR   Metro-Goldwyn-Mayer, released November 18, 1959 (212 minutes). Producer: Sam Zimbalist. Screenplay: Karl Tunberg (based on the novel by Lew Wallace). Cinematography: Robert L. Surtees. Music: Miklos Rozsa. Additional photography: Harold E. Wellman, A.S.C., and Pietro Portalupi. Art direction: William A. Horning, Edward Carfagno. Set decorations: Hugh Hunt. Special effects: A. Arnold Gillespie, Lee LeBlanc, and Robert R. Hoag. Color consultant—settings: Charles K. Hagedon. Editors: Ralph E. Winters and John D. Dunning. Second unit directors: Andrew Marton, Yakima Canutt, and Mario Soldati. Assistant directors: Gus Agosti and Alberto Cardone. Makeup: Charles Parker. Unit production manager: Edward Woehler. Recording supervisor: Franklin Milton. Sound recordists: Sash Fisher and William Steinkamp. Costumes: Elizabeth Haffenden. Color consultant—costumes: Joan Bridge. Hair styles: Gabriella Borzelli.

Cast: Charlton Heston (*Judah Ben-Hur*), Jack Hawkins (*Quintus Arrius*), Stephen Boyd (*Messala*), Haya Harareet (*Esther*), Hugh Griffith (*Sheik Ilderim*), Martha Scott (*Miriam*), Sam Jaffe (*Simonides*), Cathy O'Donnell (*Tirzah*), Finlay Currie (*Balthasar*), Frank Thring (*Pontius Pilate*), Terence Longdon (*Drusus*), André Morell (*Sextus*), Marina Berti (*Flavia*), George Relph (*Emperor Tiberius*), Adi Berber (*Malluch*), Stella Vitelleschi (*Amrah*), Jose Greci (*Mary*), Laurence Payne (*Joseph*), John Horsley (*Spintho*), Richard Coleman (*Metellus*), Duncan Lamont (*Marius*), Ralph Truman (*aide to Tiberius*), Richard Hale (*Gaspar*), Reginald Lal Singh (*Melchior*), David Davies (*Quaestor*), Dervis Ward (*Jailer*), Claude Heater (*The Christ*), Mino Doro (*Gratus*)

THE   [British title: *The Loudest Whisper*] United Artists—
CHILDREN'S   Mirisch, released March 1962 (109 minutes). Pro-
HOUR   ducer: William Wyler. Associate producer: Robert Wyler. Screenplay: John Michael Hayes (based on Lillian Hellman's stage play of the same name). Cinematography: Franz F. Planer. Editor: Robert Swink. Art

direction: Fernando Carrere. Music: Alex North. Sound: Fred Lau. Assistant director: Robert E. Relyea.

Cast: Audrey Hepburn (*Karen Wright*), Shirley MacLaine (*Martha Dobie*), James Garner (*Dr. Joe Cardin*), Miriam Hopkins (*Mrs. Lily Mortar*), Fay Bainter (*Mrs. Amelia Tilford*), Karen Balkin (*Mary Tilford*), Veronica Cartwright (*Rosalie*)

THE
COLLECTOR

Columbia, released June 1965 (119 minutes). Producers: Jud Kinberg and John Kohn. Screenplay: Stanley Mann and John Kohn (based on the novel by John Fowles). Cinematography: Robert Surtees in Hollywood and Robert Krasker in England. Music: Maurice Jarre. Art director: John Stoll. Editor and second unit director: Robert Swink.

Cast: Terence Stamp (*Freddie Clegg*), Samantha Eggar (*Miranda Grey*), Mona Washbourne (*Aunt Annie*), Maurice Dallimore (*Neighbor*)

HOW TO
STEAL A
MILLION

Twentieth Century-Fox, released July 1966 (127 minutes). Producer: Fred Kohlmar. Screenplay: Harry Kurnitz (based on a story by George Bradshaw). Cinematography: Charles Lang. Editor and second unit director: Robert Swink. Assistant director: Paul Feyder. Music: Johnny Williams. Production designed by Alexander Trauner. Unit production manager: William Kaplan. Sound: Joseph de Bretagne and David Dockendorf. Production assistant: François Moreuil. Orchestration: James Herbert. Makeup: Alberto de Rossi and Frederick Williamson. Hair styles: Alexandre. Hairdresser: Grazia de Rossi. Miss Hepburn's clothes: Givenchy. Miss Hepburn's jewelry: Cartier, Paris.

Cast: Audrey Hepburn (*Nicole*), Peter O'Toole (*Simon Demott*), Eli Wallach (*David Leland*), Hugh Griffith (*Bonnet*), Charles Boyer (*De Solnay*), Fernand Gravey (*Grammont*), Marcel Dalio (*Senor Paravideo*), Jacques Marin (*Chief guard*), Moustache (*Guard*), Roger Treville (*Auctioneer*), Eddie Malin (*Insurance clerk*), Bert Bertram (*Marcel*)

FUNNY GIRL

Columbia Pictures and Rastar Production, released September 19, 1968 (151 minutes). Producer: Ray Stark. Screenplay: Isobel Lennart (based on the musical play and book by Isobel Lennart). Cinematography: Harry Stradling. Musical numbers directed by Herbert Ross. Music: Jule Styne. Lyrics: Bob Merrill. Music supervised and conducted by Walter Scharf. Editor: Robert Swink. Unit manager: Paul Helmick. Sets: William Liernan. Assistant directors: Jack Roe and Ray Gosnell. Properties: Richard M. Rubin. Script supervisor: Marshall Schlom. Costumes: Irene Sharaff. Additional songs: Maurice Yvain, Albert Willemetz, Jacques Charles, and Channing Pollock; James F. Hanley and Grant Clarke; Fred Fisher and Billy Rose.

Cast: Barbra Streisand (*Fanny Brice*), Omar Sharif (*Nick Arnstein*), Kay Medford (*Rose Brice*), Anne Francis (*Georgia James*), Walter Pidgeon (*Florenz Ziegfeld*), Lee Grant (*Eddie Ryan*), Mae Questel (*Mrs. Strakosh*), Gerald Mohr (*Branca*), Frank Faylen (*Keeney*), Mittie Lawrence (*Emma*), Gertrude Flynn (*Mrs. O'Malley*), Penny Santon (*Mrs. Meeker*), John Harmon (*Company manager*)

THE LIBERATION OF L. B. JONES

Columbia, released March 1970 (102 minutes). Producer: A Ronald Lubin. Screenplay: Stirling Silliphant and Jesse Hill Ford (based on the novel by Jesse Hill Ford). Cinematography: Robert Surtees. Editor: Robert Swink. Production manager: Russ Saunders. Assistant director: Tony Ray. Art director: Kenneth Reid.

Cast: Lee J. Cobb (*Oman Hedgepath*), Roscoe Lee Browne (*Lord Byron Jones*), Anthony Zerbe (*Willie Joe Worth*), Lee Majors (*Steve Mundine*), Lola Falana (*Emma Jones*), Barbara Hershey (*Nella Mundine*), Yaphet Kotto (*Sonny Boy Mosby*), Zara Cully (*Mama Lavorn*), Arch Johnson (*Stanley Bumpas*), Fayard Nicholas (*Benny*), Brenda Sykes (*Jelly*), Joe Attles (*Henry*), Eve McVeagh (*Miss Griggs*), Sonora McKellar (*Ponsella*), Chill Wills (*Mr. Ike*), Lauren Jones (*Erleen*), Dud Taylor (*Mayor*), Larry D. Mann (*Grocer*), Ray Teal (*Police chief*), Robert Van Meter (*Blind man*), Jack Ginnage (*Driver*), John S. Jackson (*Suspect*)

BIBLIOGRAPHY

Astor, Mary, *A Life on Film*, Dell Publishing, New York, 1967. *My Story, An Autobiography*, Doubleday, Garden City, New York, 1959.

Barker, Felix, *The Oliviers*, J. B. Lippincott, New York, 1953.

Baxter, John, *Hollywood in the Thirties*, Paperback Library, New York, 1970.

Bazin, André, *Qu'est-ce que le cinéma*, Editions du cerf, Paris, 1959.

Bluestone, George, *Novels into Films*, Johns Hopkins Press, Baltimore, 1957.

Brandt, André, and Oberle, Raymond, *Mulhouse vous accueille*, Syndicat d'initiative, Mulhouse, 1969.

Brownlow, Kevin, *The Parade's Gone By*, Alfred A. Knopf, New York, 1968.

Calum, Per, *John Ford, en dokumentation*, Det danske Filmmuseum, Copenhagen, 1968.

Capra, Frank, *The Name above the Title*, Macmillan, New York, 1971.

Crowther, Bosley, *Hollywood Rajah, The Life and Times of Louis B. Mayer*, Holt, Rinehart & Winston, New York, 1960.

Davis, Bette, *The Lonely Life*, G. P. Putnam's Sons, New York, 1962.

DeMille, Cecil B. *Autobiography*, Prentice-Hall, Englewood Cliffs, New Jersey, 1959.

Drinkwater, John, *The Life and Adventures of Carl Laemmle*, G. P. Putnam's Sons, New York and London, 1931.

Fenin, George, and Everson, William K. *The Western*, Orion Press, New York, 1962.

Ferber, Edna, *A Peculiar Treasure*, Doubleday, Garden City, New York, 1938.

Fowler, Gene, *Good Night, Sweet Prince, The Life and Times of John Barrymore*, Viking Press, New York, 1944.

Fraenkel, Heinrich, *Unsterblicher Film*, Kindler Verlag, Munich.

Gerin, Winifred, *Emily Brontë*, Clarendon Press, Oxford, 1971.

Goldwyn, Sam, *Behind the Screen*, George H. Doran Co., New York, 1923.

439

Griffith, Richard, *Samuel Goldwyn, The Producer and His Films,* Museum of Modern Art Library, New York, 1956.

Hanson, Curtis Lee, "William Wyler," in *Cinema* magazine, Vol. 3, No. 5, 1967.

Hecht, Ben, *A Child of the Century,* Simon and Schuster, New York, 1950.

Hellman, Lillian, *An Unfinished Woman,* Little, Brown, Boston, 1969.

Higham, Charles, *Hollywood Cameramen,* Indiana University Press, Bloomington and London, 1970.

————, *Hollywood at Sunset,* Saturday Review Press, New York, 1972.

Horan, James D., and Sann, Paul, *Pictorial History of the Wild West,* Crown Publishers, New York, 1954.

Kael, Pauline, *I Lost It at the Movies,* Little, Brown, Boston, 1967.

————, *Kiss Kiss Bang Bang,* Little, Brown, Boston, 1968.

Keats, John, *You Might As Well Live, The Life and Times of Dorothy Parker,* Simon and Schuster, New York, 1970.

Knight, Arthur, *The Liveliest Art,* Macmillan, New York, 1957.

Latham, Aaron. *Crazy Sundays, F. Scott Fitzgerald in Hollywood,* Viking Press, New York, 1971.

MacLaine, Shirley, *Don't Fall Off the Mountain,* W. W. Norton, New York, 1970.

Milne, Tom, *Mamoulian,* Thames and Hudson, Cinema One Series, London, 1969.

Niven, David, *The Moon's a Balloon,* G. P. Putnam's Sons, New York, 1972.

Reisz, Karel (ed.), *William Wyler, An Index,* British Film Institute, London, 1958.

————, *The Later Films of William Wyler,* Sequence, 1951.

Rice, Elmer, *Minority Report, An Autobiography,* Simon and Schuster, New York, 1963.

Rolle, Andrew F. *California, A History,* Thomas Y. Crowell, New York, 1969.

Ruddy, Jonah, and Hill, Jonathan, *Bogey, The Man, The Actor, The Legend,* Tower Books, New York, 1965.

Sadoul, Georges, *Histoire du Cinéma mondial,* Flammarion, Paris, 1949.

Schorer, Marc, *Sinclair Lewis, An American Life,* McGraw-Hill, New York, 1961.

Sternberg, Joseph von, *Fun in a Chinese Laundry,* Macmillan, New York, 1965.

Swanberg, W. A. *Dreiser,* Charles Scribner's Sons, New York, 1965.

Teichman, Howard, *George S. Kaufman, An Intimate Portrait,* Atheneum, New York, 1972.

Thomas, Bob, *Thalberg, Life and Legend,* Doubleday, Garden City, New York, 1969.

———— *Selznick,* Doubleday, Garden City, New York, 1970.

Vidor, King, *A Tree is a Tree,* Harcourt Brace, New York, 1952.

Weír, E. *Contemporary Reviews of the First Brontë Novels,* Brontë Society Transactions, London, 1947.

West, Jessamyn, *To See the Dream*, Harcourt, Brace, New York, 1956.
Whitehouse, Arch, *The Years of the War Birds*, Doubleday, Garden City, New York, 1960.
Zierold, Norman, *The Moguls*, Coward-McCann, New York, 1969.

INDEX